INDIGENOUS MEN AND MASCULINITIES

INDIGENOUS
MEN AND
MASCULINITIES

Legacies, Identities, Regeneration

Edited by
Robert Alexander Innes and Kim Anderson

UMP
University of Manitoba Press

University of Manitoba Press
Winnipeg, Manitoba
Canada R3T 2M5
uofmpress.ca

19 18 17 16 15   1 2 3 4 5

Cover photo by Thosh Collins
Cover design: Marvin Harder
Interior design: Karen Armstrong Graphic Design

Library and Archives Canada Cataloguing in Publication

Indigenous men and masculinities : legacies, identities, regeneration/
Kim Anderson, and Robert Alexander Innes, editors.

Includes bibliographical references.
Issued in print and electronic formats.
ISBN 978-0-88755-790-3 (pbk.)
ISBN 978-0-88755-479-7 (pdf)
ISBN 978-0-88755-477-3 (epub)
ISBN 978-0-88755-227-4 (bound)

1. Native men—Canada—Social conditions. 2. Native men—Canada—
Psychology. 3. Native peoples—Kinship—Canada. 4. Masculinity—Social
aspects—Canada. I. Anderson, Kim, 1964–, editor II. Innes, Robert
Alexander, editor

E98.M44I53 2015   305.38'897071   C2015-903456-6
                                                C2015-903457-4

The University of Manitoba Press gratefully acknowledges the financial support
for its publication program provided by the Government of Canada through the Canada
Book Fund, the Canada Council for the Arts, the Manitoba Department
of Culture, Heritage, Tourism, the Manitoba Arts Council,
and the Manitoba Book Publishing Tax Credit.

Contents

III. Living Indigenous Masculinities and Indigenous Manhood

IV. Conversations

List of Tables

List of Illustrations

INDIGENOUS MEN AND MASCULINITIES

Who's Walking with Our Brothers?

Robert Alexander Innes and Kim Anderson

In June 2012, Métis artist Christi Belcourt put out a call for moccasin tops, known as "vamps," as part of a project to honour the missing and murdered Indigenous women in Canada. The organizers had hoped to receive 600 vamps, but instead received over 1,800. The vamps were put together to form an art installation called *Walking With Our Sisters* that will end up travelling across Canada to nearly thirty locations by 2020. This initiative follows the work of other activists; for example, the Native Women's Association of Canada (NWAC) first reported the issue of missing and murdered Indigenous women in their 2008 report *Voices of Our Sisters In Spirit*, and NWAC has undertaken a very successful awareness campaign through its annual Sisters in Spirit Vigils held in many communities across Canada.[1] The *Voices of Our Sisters In Spirit*, Sisters In Spirit Vigils, and the *Walking With Our Sisters* installation have brought national attention to the Indigenous women who have gone missing or who have been murdered in Canada.

As these campaigns demonstrate, substantial attention has been focused on the struggles of Indigenous women, and rightfully so, considering their social and economic conditions. In comparison, however, there is a lack of theoretical and applied scholarly work about Indigenous men and masculinities. This reflects the fact that there is little activism or political will to address Indigenous men's issues, and as a result there are very few policies or social programs designed for Indigenous men, including those who are trans-identified, as well as women who identify with Indigenous masculinities.

There is, however, an emerging field of Indigenous masculinities studies, and this allows those of us involved to investigate an area that has been largely ignored.

In many ways, the conditions of Indigenous men, though distinct, are similar to those of Indigenous women, but these conditions have not really been acknowledged beyond news reports of their criminal behaviour. Indigenous men also face the same sort of race and gender biases as do other men of colour, and this leads to a host of social issues for them and their communities. In Canada, for example, and in comparison to non-Indigenous Canadians, Indigenous men have shorter life spans,[2] are less likely to graduate from high school,[3] are more likely to be incarcerated,[4] and are murdered at a higher rate. With the lack of political will and public awareness of Indigenous men and masculinities, we might well ask: Who is walking with our brothers?

Indigenous men and those who identify with Indigenous masculinities, as this book shows, are faced with distinct gender and racial biases that cause many to struggle. This book of essays explores and seeks to deepen our understanding of the ways in which Indigenous men and those who assert an Indigenous male identity perform their masculine identities, why and how they perform them, and the consequences to them and others because of their attachment to those identities. As the authors in this volume clearly show, the performance of Indigenous masculinities has been profoundly impacted by colonization and the imposition of a white supremacist heteronormative patriarchy that has left a lasting and negative legacy for Indigenous women, children, Elders, men, and their communities as a whole. At the same time, this book details the regeneration of positive masculinities currently taking place in many communities that will assist in the restoration of balanced and harmonious relationships.

One step toward achieving healthy Indigenous masculinities and communities includes reaching an understanding of how race and gender bias intersect to disadvantage Indigenous men, and how this disadvantaged position has had negative ramifications for Indigenous communities. In a January 2014 piece for *Al Jazeera* online, UCLA law professor Khaled Beydoun provides a discussion of the intersection of race and gender bias experienced by men of colour in the United States that is applicable to Indigenous men in Canada and their experiences.[5] Beydoun links the negative treatment heaped on men of colour not only to racial discrimination but also to gendered discrimination. However, since these acts of discrimination are against men (of colour), most people fail to see them being tied to gender. As Beydoun points out:

> Gender discrimination is overwhelmingly discussed and ex-
> amined within a vacuum, divorced from the racial realities that
> broaden its practical relevance. As a result, gender discrimina-
> tion—in both lay and academic circles—is largely understood as
> animus endured by women, and most frequently, white women....
>
> Discrimination endured by men of colour is framed within liberal
> circles as racial or ethnic animus, but seldom—if ever—examined
> from a conjoined gender lens. The distinct tropes associated with
> black and brown masculinity, however, attract a distinct brand of
> *gendered racism* reserved for men of colour. Indeed, being both
> minority and male in the US today invites a brand of gendered
> stigma that is under-discussed in media and academic circles, and
> marginalised by a narrow conception of gender discrimination.[6]

It is important to note that Beydoun's discussion of the experience of
gender bias and men of colour does not downplay, ignore, or trump women's
experiences. As he states, "The prevalence of patriarchy, violence toward
women, and the feminisation of poverty, among other structural obstacles
uniquely faced by women in the US and elsewhere, cannot be overstated."[7]
For Beydoun, then, acknowledging the particular kind of gender bias men
of colour endure expands our understanding of how gender discrimination
works with racial discrimination to oppress, and his position encourages us to
think about how to include gender analysis when examining the lived experiences of men of colour. As he concludes, "The pervasive forms of gendered
bias and violence that are specifically reserved for men of colour, in the streets
of the US, within its halls of power, and its public and private institutions,
must be figured into prevailing conceptions of gender discrimination."[8]

A comparison of the murder statistics of Indigenous men and women in
Canada compiled by Statistics Canada, researchers, and the Royal Canadian
Mounted Police (RCMP) provides insight into the degree to which the con-
ditions of Indigenous men are not fully acknowledged—or even understood.
As these data point to the level of race and gender bias Indigenous men
face, we think they are valuable in setting the context for the articles in this
book. We offer some of this material as an introduction into our work with
Indigenous men and masculinities. As with the Sisters In Spirit Vigils and
Walking With Our Sisters installation, unpacking the way violence plays out
in Indigenous men's lives is a good way to begin engaging a broader practice
of gender-based analysis in the service of decolonization.

Recognizing the Challenges

Though the statistics for missing and murdered Indigenous women and men over the last two decades have not been entirely reliable, recent data are starting to shed more light on the level of violence they experience. For example, in 2006 Statistics Canada reported that between 1997 and 2004 there were 141 Indigenous women and 329 Indigenous men murdered (See Table 0.1).

Table 0.1. *Number of Indigenous victims of homicide in Canada, by sex and accused-victim relationship, 1997-2004.*

Relationship to the victim	Female number	Female percent	Male number	Male percent	Total number	Total percent
Spouse [i]	38	27	33	10	71	15
Parent [ii]	12	9	14	4	26	6
Other Family [iii]	12	9	61	19	73	16
Other intimate Family [iv]	15	11	4	1	19	4
Acquaintance [v]	49	35	174	53	223	47
Stranger	15	11	43	13	58	12
Total	141	100	329	100	470	100

Source: Statistics Canada, Canadian Centre for Justice Statistics, Homicide Survey; Statistics Canada *Measuring Violence Against Women: Statistical Trends*, catalogue number 85-570-XWE200601 (includes North America Indian, Inuit, and Métis).

i. *Includes married, common-law, separated, divorce, and (ex) same-sex spouses*

ii. *Includes biological or legally adoptive parents, step-parents, and foster parents*

iii. *Includes children, siblings, and all other family members related through blood, marriage, adoption, or foster care*

iv. *Includes current or former boyfriends/girlfriends and extra-marital lovers*

v. *Includes friends, neighbours, business relationships, causal acquaintances, etc.*

Table 0.1 shows that there are more Indigenous men murdered than women in four of the six categories. Of importance is the number of Indigenous people murdered by people they know, many of whom are family members. Also, according to Statistics Canada, between 1997 and 2000, Indigenous men were victims of homicide nearly two and a half times more than Indigenous women, almost seven times more than white men, and over fifteen times more than white women. Further to this, in Canada, Indigenous men were charged with homicide over four times more than Indigenous women, almost nine times more than non-Indigenous men, and nearly ninety times more than white women. Typically, Indigenous men are compared to white men and Indigenous women with white women. A comparison between

Indigenous men and non-Indigenous women shows the high level of violence Indigenous men face compared to the level of violence encountered by white women. This is significant, as the perception by many is that white women face a higher risk for violence.[9]

Figures from the RMCP show, further, that in the province of Saskatchewan, between 1940 and 2015, thirty-eight Indigenous men as compared to eighteen Indigenous women went missing. These figures have to be used with caution, however, as information for doing a full analysis is lacking. For example, there is no indication of whether these figures include urban jurisdictions or whether a person comes off the list of missing if found. Interestingly, in that same period, forty-six white men and fourteen white women went missing. Although at first glance it appears non-Indigenous men are at a higher risk of going missing, when you take into consideration the provincial Indigenous population, Indigenous men and women are at much greater risk of going missing than are white men. White women are numerically the largest group in the province and are by far the least likely to go missing.[10]

Significantly, NWAC argues that the number of murdered and missing Indigenous women is much higher than the number recorded by the RCMP and Statistics Canada. NWAC reports that over 600 Indigenous women have gone missing or have been murdered, with over 340 being murdered between the 1960s and the mid-2000s.[11] This figure is higher than the Statistics Canada-recorded figure for the number of murdered Indigenous men, though the StatsCan figure only reflects a seven-year period. NWAC's definition is slightly broader than that used by police agencies. For their *Voices of Our Sisters In Spirit* report, NWAC defined murder as referring to "the deaths result-ing from homicide or negligence." NWAC also tracked cases of "suspicious deaths." "Suspicious deaths" refer to "incidents that police have declared as natural or accidental but that the family or community members regard as suspicious."[12] NWAC's report effectively showed how the definition of murder used by police agencies does not adequately address the violent realities of Indigenous women. Broadening the definition of murder to include deaths by negligence and suspicious deaths underlines the extent of violence faced by Indigenous women in Canada.

NWAC's lobbying efforts to raise the issue of missing and murdered women has led to new research and to the revelations of even higher numbers of missing and murdered women. For example, Maryanne Pearce, a doctoral student at the University of Ottawa, found that 824 Indigenous women have been missing or murdered from at least the 1950s.[13] In reaching her figure,

Pearce scanned thousands of documents, such as newspapers articles, websites, public police files, and missing person posters. The news of her findings received national news coverage. However, as a private citizen, Pearce did not have the authority to access the extensive police records or the capacity to collate those records even if she had been able to access them.

In May 2014, the RCMP released a report in which they compiled all the known police records from across Canada relating to missing and murdered Indigenous women.[14] According to this new report, the RCMP determined that there were 1,181 missing and murdered Indigenous women in Canada. Of this number, 1,017 women were murder victims. This figure is significant not only because the number of murdered Indigenous women is much higher than had ever been officially recognized but also because these numbers were recorded between 1980 and 2012, unlike the NWAC numbers, which recorded figures from the 1960s, and Pearce's numbers, which were recorded from the 1950s. Clearly, if the RCMP had gone as far back as the 1950s, the numbers would be much higher. To demonstrate the level of violence Indigenous women face compared to non-Indigenous women, in the province of Saskatchewan, Indigenous women make up less than 7 percent of the provincial population, yet they accounted for 153 out of the 269 (or 55 percent) of the total number of women murdered.[15]

Though actual numbers are much higher than the census numbers discussed above, there is some consistency with the RCMP numbers. For example, both the census and the RCMP note that the overwhelming majority of victims knew their killers. According to the census, nearly 90 percent of the female victims knew their killers and, in the RCMP reports, 95 percent of the female victims knew their killers. It is unclear from both figures whether the perpetrators were Indigenous or not. However, we can assume that Indigenous men were engaged in some of this violence.

NWAC's challenge to the accuracy of the official figures for Indigenous women, combined with the most recent numbers released by the RCMP, also suggests that any official figures for Indigenous men are incorrect. In fact, in May 2014, *Vice News* reported that an independent researcher had gathered a list of missing and murdered Indigenous men in Canada dating from the 1960s.[16] Over a nine-month period, Jennifer Mt. Pleasant searched various on-line and news sources and uncovered over 600 names of Indigenous men. It should be noted that Mt. Pleasant's figure is higher than the original number of missing and murdered Indigenous women released by NWAC. Like Pearce, Mt. Pleasant did not have access to the police records and therefore the number can be assumed to be incomplete.

The violence in the lives of Indigenous men has thus received some attention from researchers and the press. Within three months after the *Vice News* article appeared, another news article was published in the *Toronto Star,* revealing that Indigenous men in Canada are murdered at a much higher rate than Indigenous women.[17] The reporter notes that Indigenous women are more likely to suffer from physical crimes, such as spousal abuse, than are Indigenous men. Nonetheless, he goes on to point out that Indigenous men are murdered at a higher rate, stating:

> Between 1980 and 2012, 14 per cent of female murder victims with a known ethnicity were aboriginal, far exceeding their 4 per cent share of the female population, according to Statistics Canada.
>
> But 17 per cent of male murder victims were also aboriginal during that time. In total, nearly 2,500 aboriginal people were murdered in the past three decades: 1,750 male, 745 female and one person of unknown gender.[18]

In addition, the reporter notes that in the province of Manitoba, "more aboriginal people have been murdered in the past three decades than non-aboriginal, though the province is just about one-sixth native. Seventy-one per cent of those nearly 500 aboriginal homicide victims were men."[19] That the StatsCan figures for murdered Indigenous women are lower than those found in the RCMP report implies that the number of murdered Indigenous men may be even higher yet.

These statistics on violence can inform a larger discussion about Indigenous men's lives in Canada, pointing out that Indigenous men have a high risk of adopting negative lifestyles that lead to violence, addictions, and incarceration, and that these challenges can be linked to race and gender bias.[20] Interestingly, according to the census figures above, 86 percent of the murdered Indigenous men knew their killers. Though there are no official records to indicate who the killers are of Indigenous men, if we consider the possibility that many of the killers could have been Indigenous men and if we factor in the possibility that a number of the strangers who murdered Indigenous men could also have been Indigenous, we need to consider the implications of Indigenous men as killers of Indigenous men. A significant outcome of these biases is that Indigenous men are more often viewed as victimizers, not as victims; as protectors rather than those who need protection; or as supporters, but not ones who need support. We see this as resulting from the hegemonic masculinity that is perpetuated through white supremacist patriarchy and conveyed by education, news, and entertainment institutions. The hegemonic nature of these perceptions leads them to become normalized and perpetuated through everyday interactions. These perceptions are so pervasive, it is next to impossible for Indigenous men not to be exposed to them. As a result of the colonization of their lands, minds, and bodies, many Indigenous men not only come to accept these perceptions but also come to internalize them.

The racialized and gendered perceptions of Indigenous peoples globally are used, in part, as justification for both the access to Indigenous lands and resources and the subordination of Indigenous peoples by white men and, to a lesser extent but in significant ways, by white women in support of white male power structures. The negative perceptions white people have of Indigenous men help to explain white people's fear of them. Fear of men of colour on the part of whites is equally prevalent. As Beydoun points out, the hegemonic nature of the fear of *"minority masculinities"* is rooted in Western society and acts as a counterpoint to the preferred hegemonic white hetero-patriarchal masculinity:

> The black and brown bodies of men of colour incite an overwhelming fear for onlookers, whether politicians, policemen, or television viewers, who interpret their *minority masculinity* as threatening and deviant. Terrorists instead of American citizens, gang-members not undergraduates, and dreadlocked thugs instead of Stanford graduates—is the confined view of black and brown men that still prevails today. This in part, must be attributed to the confined discourse and definition of gender discrimination.[21]

The historical narrative that still holds true today is that white women are in constant danger of succumbing to violence at the hands of Indigenous men (and other men of colour), even though in reality they are the least likely to experience violence. However, white women are attuned to the perceived dangers Indigenous men pose to them. For example, white female university students in Saskatchewan have told us that they heard an initiate must rape a white girl to get into a Native gang. This says much about how they, as well as white men, might respond to the perceived threat posed by young Indigenous men in general. As the conveyors of the hegemonic masculinity, many white men feel duty bound to not only protect their "property" and therefore their claim to the land but also to protect themselves, and especially, white women from Indigenous men. Indigenous men are considered violent and dangerous; this is highlighted by the number of shooting deaths of unarmed Indigenous men by police officers, with relative impunity and with little outcry from the public.[22]

The ways in which hegemonic masculinity has acted to subordinate Indigenous men encourages them to similarly assert power and control by subordinating Indigenous women and women of colour, as well as white women (where circumstances allow), other Indigenous men who are considered physically and intellectually weak, and those who do not express a heteronormative identity. The ideals of the current hegemonic masculinity are what all men must strive to achieve and uphold in order to be recipients of male privilege to its fullest extent. As a result, many Indigenous men abide by these ideals, even though doing so contributes to their own subordination as a group. As non-whites, Indigenous men's privilege is ultimately subordinated by white male privilege, so they are then confined to achieve their privilege through the oppression of those who are perceived from a hegemonic masculine perspective as being weaker and more vulnerable than they are.

The current hegemonic masculinity, then, has affected Indigenous men and their communities in complex ways. Nonetheless, many Indigenous men across the globe have begun to question and challenge how their current identities serve to reinforce the colonial legacy of subordination. They are making strides to regenerate positive ways of expressing the diverse range of Indigenous masculinities that reflect their contemporary realities. They are seeking out identities based on Indigenous understandings and that can contribute to the decolonization of Indigenous peoples. An important step in this process is acknowledging that Indigenous men do benefit from male privilege, as well as recognizing and acknowledging that, at the same time, many experience a level of victimization, violence, and subordination based on their race and gender that is similar, though manifested in different ways, to that of Indigenous women, and that the oppression suffered by both is tied to the colonization and acquisition of Indigenous lands.

Giving Voice to the Legacies, Identities, and Acts of Regeneration

In June 2012, we (Innes and Anderson) organized a day of panels on Indigenous masculinities for the Native American and Indigenous Studies Association (NAISA) annual meeting, which took place in Uncasville, Connecticut, that year. We had a panel on "Identities" and another on "Queer Indigenous Masculinities," and then hosted a roundtable of interested scholars, activists, and community workers. The interest and turnout were tremendous, and the dialogue was very rich, demonstrating that there is a broad and international scope of approaches to and interests in Indigenous masculinities. At the end of the roundtable we announced that we would like to meet with anyone who wished to contribute an article to a book on Indigenous masculinities. We had no physical location to meet, so we decided to meet in the hallway on the eleventh floor of the conference hotel. Amid the comings and goings of hotel guests and staff, fifteen to twenty people showed up, supplemented by people we had met at supper or on a bus during a conference tour. We enthusiastically discussed the possibility of this book, and many of the authors in this volume were at the initial "hallway" meeting. People talked about how the time was right to start to focus on issues facing Indigenous men and those who assert male identities in order for our communities to overcome many of the social calamities we face. We believe that the enthusiasm of those participants at the NAISA panels and at the "eleventh-floor" discussions, of those who have worked with us on our Bidwewidam Indigenous Masculinities project (see final chapter in this book), and of those who have committed to this volume reflects the growing number of Indigenous men who are committed to achieving mino-bimaadiziwin, a vision of the Anishinaabek that signifies "the good life."[23]

The experiences of Indigenous men and those who identify with Indigenous masculinities are varied and complex and no one book can possibly reflect all those lived experiences. Nonetheless, the essays that came together for this book represent a cross section of disciplinary approaches and reflect the range of topics found within the growing field of Indigenous masculinities studies. The authors come from a variety of academic and non-academic backgrounds, including literature, history, sport, sociology, women's studies, and Indigenous studies. Our intention is to introduce the field of Indigenous masculinities through multiple lenses, approaches, voices, and genres. We have arranged the book into four sections with four articles in each section, reflecting this diversity.

The first section, "Theoretical Considerations," addresses the lack of theoretical work on Indigenous masculinities and sets forth ways we can interrogate our understanding of these constructions. First, Bob Antone outlines how he came to a Haudenosaunee Indigenous knowledge understanding of masculinities. This grounds the book in one Indigenous standpoint, as Antone frames his work from within the cosmology of his people, the Oneida. Scott Morgensen then traces the roots of colonial masculinity to argue that the heteropatriarchal environments that we now suffer were created by Europeans as part of the colonization process. He offers hope, emphasizing that, since this manifestation of heteropatriarchy was created, it is not necessarily a permanent or natural human condition and therefore can be altered or ended. Leah Sneider then shows how Indigenous feminism and masculinities studies can further our understanding of how the colonial concepts of race and gender have undermined the notion of complementarity among genders. Sneider's chapter makes connections between this loss of gender complementarity and weakened Indigenous sovereignty. The final chapter in this section, by Brendan Hokowhitu, teases out the complex ways Indigenous masculinities and sexuality have been essentialized into colonial binaries, internalized by Indigenous men and manifested in a heterosexual Indigenous patriarchy reinforced by notions of tradition and authenticity.

The four chapters in section two explore Indigenous masculinities through "Representations in Art and Literature," the name of the section. In the first chapter in this section, Kimberly Minor unpacks how Mandan leader Mató-Tópe's self-portraits act to sabotage colonial images of the noble savage conveyed through popular nineeenth-century artists George Catlin and Karl Bodmer. Minor argues that Mató-Tópe's images allow for a closer representation of early Indigenous masculinities, offering an entry point into the discussion of how Indigenous men might represent themselves. Erin Sutherland's chapter follows with an example of this in a contemporary context. She analyzes the works of contemporary artists Terrance Houle and Adrian Stimson to show how performance art pieces can challenge hegemonic masculinities and provide positive alternatives as acts of decolonization. We then turn to the notion that masculinities are not always tied to men or men's bodies with Lisa Tatonetti's chapter. Tatonetti builds upon Judith Halberstam's influential work *Female Masculinity* to explore the way in which fictional female characters with masculine behaviours manifest in Indigenous literature. She looks at Louise Erdrich's character Celestine James in *The Beet Queen* to argue that affective power, or female masculinity, is a "radically resistant" identity position. This position challenges heteromasculinity, drawing on notions of gender found within queer studies by detailing how Indigenous female masculinity has been and in many cases still is an accepted aspect of many Indigenous societies. Her chapter is a reminder that gender within most Indigenous societies was not tied to an individual's biological makeup and that a masculine identity is not confined to males. The last chapter in this section, by Niigaanwewidam James Sinclair, provides a literary expression of many of the subjects found in this book. Sinclair addresses violence and its related challenges, and he also gives expression to the sacredness of fatherhood and Indigenous men's relationship to the power of women, as represented through traditional knowledge and story.

The chapters in the next section, "Living Indigenous Masculinities and Indigenous Manhood," present studies of Indigenous masculinities in the context of sports, gangs, prisons, and identity reclamation. In the first chapter of this section, Phillip Borell uses Hokowhitu's idea of colonial genealogy and applies the theory of coloniality to look at the decision of Māori rugby player James Tamou to play for the Australian national team. Borell shows how this decision caused a national controversy, while also offering an opportunity to investigate the intersection of sport, Indigenous masculinities, nationalism, and colonization. Robert Henry's chapter on Indigenous street gangs follows the groundbreaking work of R.W. Connell and James Messerschmidt's "Hegemonic Masculinity: Rethinking the Concept."[24] Henry examines Indigenous masculinities at the global, regional, and local levels to show that Indigenous male bodies are constructed as threats to colonial order and therefore are relegated to the lawless margins. In the next chapter, Allison Piché presents a case that arts-based prison programs offer an alternative to the toxic masculinities found in the state-operated corrections systems many Indigenous men find themselves in. Together, Henry's and Piché's chapters offer a glimpse into how to challenge both the real and imagined ecologies of violence that Indigenous men face, and which were addressed earlier in this introduction. The final chapter in this section is by Lloyd Lee, which begins with the Diné principle of Sa'ah Naagháí Bik'eh Hózhóón. Lee offers this as a framework on how to live well and with beauty and happiness, which can be a guiding force to Diné women and men as they work to undo many of the effects of colonization.

In the final section of the book, "Conversations," we present the voices of Indigenous men directly, with discussions on what it means to be male and to assert masculine identities. We begin with Ty Tengan's conversations with Vietnam War veterans Thomas Ka'auwai Kaulukukui, Jr. and William Kahalepuna Richards, Jr. on the subject of Hawaiian warriorhood and Kū, their deity of "male generative force and productivity."[25] In the next chapter, Sam McKegney guides us through a conversation between Indigenous authors Gregory Scofield, Richard Van Camp, Warren Cariou, and Daniel Heath Justice—a poet and three novelists. This conversation took place in Niigaanwewidam James Sinclair's Native studies class at the University of Manitoba in the winter of 2013, and relates understandings and issues of masculinities from Indigenous men who create male characters for their works. Sasha Sky's chapter then follows with a transcribed conversation of six members of the "Crazy Indians" Brotherhood. This organization is comprised of former gang members who continue to work in the manner of gangs, but instead promote healthy, crime-free and drug-free lifestyles. This chapter offers an example of men who have chosen to provide service rather than fear to the community. As transcribed conversations, the first three chapters in this section thus offer the reader an opportunity to engage in their own analysis of Indigenous men's discussions. In the final chapter, Kim Anderson, John Swift, and Robert Alexander Innes offer Indigenous voices and draw analysis out of a number of focus groups they conducted during their three-year (2011–14) Bidwewidam Indigenous Masculinities research project. These voices demonstrate how many of the themes in our research project intersect with themes in this book, giving shape to the emerging field of Indigenous masculinities.

As a collection, *Indigenous Men and Masculinities: Legacies, Identities, Regeneration* reminds us that Indigenous men and those who identify with Indigenous masculinities can and do exemplify "mino-bimaadiziwin," the good life. Though there are many caught in cycles of dysfunction, there are many others seeking ways to obtain "the good life," more still who want to, and plenty of role models who have always been living in a good way. The journey away from the negative impacts of colonization and the imposition of the white supremacist heteropatriarchal masculine identities is long and arduous, but it is a journey that will ultimately strengthen Indigenous nations. As with Indigenous women, Indigenous men will need support as they embark on that passage. The authors in this volume recognize the challenges Indigenous men must deal with and have chosen to research, write, and talk about those challenges as a means of walking with our brothers as they decolonize and move forward.

Notes

1   Native Women's Association of Canada, *Voices of Our Sisters In Spirit: A Report to Families and Communities* (Ohsweken, ON; Saint-Lazare, PQ: Gibson Library Connections, 2008).
2   Statistics Canada Demography Division, 2001.
3   Statistics Canada, 2011.
4   Canada, Office of the Correctional Investigator, *Aboriginal Inmates* (Ottawa: Government of Canada, Corrections Research Branch of the Department of Public Safety, 2008).
5   Khaled Beydoun, "More Than Thugs: The Case of Richard Sherman and Other Men of Colour," *Al Jazeera Online*, 29 January 2014, http://www.aljazeera.com/indepth/opinion/2014/01/more-than-thugsthe-case-richar-2014125134532950282.html.

6   Ibid., par. 4.

7   Ibid., par. 9.

8   Ibid., par. 9.

9   To put this into context, according to the RCMP, between 1980 and 2012, there were 5,439 non-Aboriginal women murdered in Canada (they do not specify how many of this women were not white).

10   Saskatchewan Association of Chiefs of Police webpage, http://www.sacp-ca/missing/index (accessed 20 July 2015).

11   Native Women's Association of Canada, *Voices of Our Sisters In Spirit: A Report to Families and Communities*, 2nd ed. (Ottawa: NWAC, March 2009), 88, http://www.nwac.ca/sites/default/files/download/admin/NWAC_VoicesofOurSistersInSpiritII_March2009FINAL.pdf.

12   Ibid., 5.

13   Maryanne Pearce, "An Awkward Silence: Missing and Murdered Vulnerable Women and the Canadian Justice System" (LLD diss., University of Ottawa, 2013).

14   Canada, "Missing and Murdered Aboriginal Women: A National Operation Overview" (Ottawa: Royal Canadian Mounted Police, 2014).

15   In comparison to the 1,017 Indigenous women who were murdered, the report noted that 5,439 non-Indigenous women were murdered in the same time period. In other words, 16% of all women who have been murdered nationally were Indigenous women even though they make up about 2% of the national population. See Canada, "Missing and Murdered Aboriginal Women…," 9. This is not to suggest that violence towards white women is insignificant, but it does highlight the fact that Indigenous women and men are murdered at a higher proportion to their population and yet the level of fear and concern for the safety of white women is not matched with the actual level of violence faced by Indigenous women and men.

16   Martha Troian, "An Independent Database Has Found Canada Lost Over 600 Missing and Murdered Aboriginal Men," *Vice News Online*, 20 May 2014, http://www.vice.com/en_ca/read/an-independent-database-has-concluded-canada-has-lost-over-600-missing-or-murdered-aboriginal-men.

17   Eric Andrew-Gee, "Aboriginal Men Murdered at Higher Rate than Aboriginal Women: The Death of 15-Year-Old Tina Fontaine Casts Spotlight on Homicide Epidemic Ravaging Indigenous Communities for Decades," *thestar.com*, 22 August 2014, http://www.thestar.com/news/gta/2014/08/22/aboriginal_men_murdered_at_higher_rate_than_aboriginal_women.html.

18   Ibid., para. 4 and 5. See also Sherene H. Razack, "'It Happened More Than Once': Freezing Deaths in Saskatchewan," *Canadian Journal of Women and the Law* 26, no. 1 (2014): 51–80.

19   Andrew-Gee, "Aboriginal Men Murdered at Higher Rate than Aboriginal Women," para. 14.

20   It should be noted that, as authors in this book point out, the social and economic conditions of Indigenous peoples worldwide are similar to those in Canada.

21   Beydoun, "More Than Thugs," para. 18, emphasis in original.

22   For example, see Canadian Press, "Alberta RCMP Shoot, Kill Man After Road Stop Altercation," *National Post Online*, 4 August 2013, http://news.nationalpost.com/2013/08/04/alberta-rcmp-shoot-kill-man-after-road-stop-altercation/.

23   Gross states that the Aninshinaabe understanding of the "good life" is encapsulated in bimaadiziwin and defines it as "having a long and healthy life, and was the life

goal of the Anishinaabe... bimaadiziwin served as an underlying theme of most religious structures." Lawrence Gross, "Bimaadiziwin, or the 'Good Life,' as a Unifying Concept of Anishinaabe Religion," *American Indian Culture and Research Journal* 26, no. 1 (2002): 15–16.

24 R.W. Connell and J.W. Messerschmidt, "Hegemonic Masculinity: Rethinking the Concept," *Gender and Society* 19, no. 6 (2005): 829–59.

25 See Tengan, "'The Face of Kū,'" 231 (in this volume).

I. THEORETICAL CONSIDERATIONS

CHAPTER 1

Reconstructing Indigenous Masculine Thought

Bob Antone

This is a story of a search for Indigenous knowledge that constructs masculinity within a reflective process; an examining of my personal journey to dismantle the Westernized male acculturation influencing the contemporary construct of being a Haudenosaunee man.

This homecoming is a journey of sourcing original thought. For this reason, I open this chapter by introducing core elements of Haudenosaunee knowledge/original thought, as represented in Figure 1.1. This figure references the Haudenosaunee Creation story, the Ceremonies, the Great Law, and the Gaiwiio. These cultural sources form the Ukwehu:we (literally, Real Human Being or Iroquois) masculine mindset.

As Indigenous people, our reality began long before 1492, and so we begin by seeking understanding of our Creation stories. One cannot be Indigenous or contemplate Indigenous masculinities without the original knowledge of Creation informing and supporting one's spirit and thought. Haudenosaunee knowledge is permeated with a theological world view rooted in a pragmatic spirituality of dream, storytelling, relationship, morality, dependency, thankfulness, and operating with a Good Mind.

Ceremony is another significant component toward centring our identity through Haudenosaunee knowledge. Today, culture is acted out in ceremonies in the longhouse[1] and continues to be the foundation of who we are as Haudenosaunee. The many ceremonies are celebrations of life, Haudenosaunee attachment to the traditional foods, and enacting the

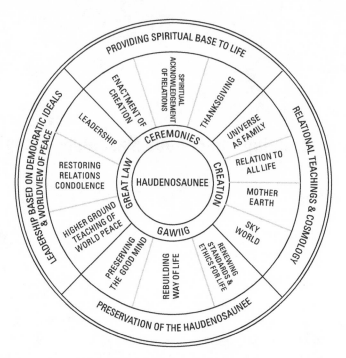

Figure 1.1. *Haudenosaunee Knowledge.*

creation of Mother Earth. Learning ceremony places the Ukwehu:we in a different spiritual place than Western constructs of spirituality.

The Great Law of Peace is the third source of Haudenosaunee knowledge that came to the people through a messenger we call the Peacemaker. The importance of the Great Law is its contribution to Haudenosaunee identity and spiritual purpose. The message came to the Ukwehu:we over a thousand years ago and has been the defining teachings of being the Haudenosaunee. When the teachings originally came to the people, it was during a time when violence was rampant among them. The teachings of peace, power, and the Good Mind address the issue of violence within the community.

A fourth foundation of our knowledge dates back to 1799, when our people received a message from a Seneca visionary named Handsome Lake. Through the power of dream, visions came to this reluctant soul, an ordinary man who had lost most of what he loved to the invading forces. By 1799, the force of the colonization had turned our communities into oppressive, violent, addicted environments, which were the products of war, colonization, genocide, and the cruelty of the oppressors. Handsome Lake addressed the state of our nations by sharing his vision of a need to stay away from the *"mind* changers" of the white man, which included their alcohol, laws, Bible, diseases, and music. The message was to keep the four sacred ceremonies going, follow the teachings of the Good Mind, ensure the raising of chiefs and clan mothers, and adjust the way one lived to keep life simple and meaningful. The Gaiwiio, Handsome Lake's message, set in motion a process for the decolonization of Haudenosaunee communities. For the last 214 years, this effort has grown among us.

Handsome Lake advocated for the continuance of the Great Law, the original teachings of non-violence. The Western illusion of discovery and dominance of other cultures is in direct conflict with the traditional constructs of peace and non-violence. The other significant cultural difference is the all-encompassing matrifocal or women-centred foundation of Haudenosaunee culture rooted in the constructs of Mother Earth, Grandmother Moon, Three Sisters' foods, and clan mothers who select the leadership and identity based on who your mother is. As Ukwehu:we men, our psyche has to accept those teachings if we are going to decolonize.

Recently, I spoke at the Great Law Recital held in my community, Oneida Settlement. The presentation labelled the experiences of our ancestors and our own life experiences as colonization, and our recovery as decolonization. We were naming our reality; a thought process that originates in the depth of our collective Haudenosaunee mind. This chapter documents my journey from my time as a young man to that Great Law Recital of 2013, as a facilitator of decolonization work and as a Haudenosaunee man unravelling and shedding the colonial cloak of Western masculinity through the application of the knowledge represented in Figure 1.1.

Historical Background

Understanding how history contributes to masculine identity is vital to uncovering the decolonized Indigenous man, and so I also offer my history by way of introduction. My history is about a homeland in upstate New York, the relocation to southern Ontario of 391 Oneidas, and the creation of a new community in Southwold, Ontario, which we call Oneida Settlement. In 1844, four years after the migration, the British government reported that "there were...6 frame and 48 log homes with 4 wigwams...and a total of 335 acres under cultivation."[2] The people busied themselves with re-establishing a community.

In March of 1850, the Oneidas sent a delegation to the Six Nations at Grand River to request that the chiefs come and condole and raise new chiefs to form a new Oneida Settlement government. The British Indian agent Clench attended the meeting at Grand River and observed "the ancient ceremony of burying the hatchet between the Six Nations and the Oneidas who had shed each other's blood at the instigation of the British and American Governments."[3] The act of reconciliation is a natural Haudenosaunee process; it is not one bound in sympathy but in finding KaɁnikohli:yo, a communal Good Mind shared in the equal and joyful presence of one another. The Good Mind is one of the founding principles of the Great Law and the traditional customs that continue to inform the roles of men and women and the relationships between them.

Oneida people remained attached to their homelands 150 years after a migration that did not sever their ties to the United States. The Oneida went on with rebuilding their nation, exiled in the Beaver Hunting Grounds.[4] The community was thus governed by the Chiefs' Council until the Canadian colonial imposition of the Indian Act Band Council system in 1934. For ninety-six years, the community enjoyed the exclusive extension of the traditional form of government from their homelands. Traditional forms of government continued to inform the men on how leadership, respect, communal relations, peace, and the Good Mind principle structured and organized the community. The Chiefs' Council continues holding regular meetings today.

In spite of our ability to hold onto the Chiefs' Council, by the late 1960s, the elders, chiefs, and clan mothers publicly announced the dire situation of cultural loss. Young Oneidas acknowledged the call and returned to the longhouse to help with the recovery. It was this call that caught my attention, and I returned home to help. In 1969, I was around when a group of Oneidas from Wisconsin began their cultural recovery process. A relationship grew between the Wisconsin and Ontario Oneida communities, both spiritual and personal in nature, commencing a new chapter in the Oneida cultural recovery.

The Oneida Chiefs' Council, with the assistance of younger men, began to travel regularly to every Grand Council at Onondaga and the Six Nations meeting at Grand River, picking up the responsibilities of leadership and carrying the voice of the Oneida Nation Council. The young men, like me at the time, accompanied the chiefs to learn.

The 1970s was a very volatile time in Indian Country, providing Indigenous men with opportunities to organize, demonstrate, voice their anger, and refuse to be shackled by the settler governments. Groups of Oneida men and women travelled to the various events from Wounded Knee, South

Dakota; Washington, DC; Ottawa, Ontario; and First Nations communities across Canada and the U.S. to demonstrate, participate, and learn about the struggle of all Indigenous peoples.

In 1982, a condolence ceremonial known as the Raising of Chiefs and Clan Mothers was held in the Oneida Settlement, advancing the construction of an original government. To increase the connection with our relatives in Wisconsin, Faith Keepers were selected and appointed with the sanction of the central fire of the Oneida Nation at Southwold. Faith Keepers, chiefs, and clan mothers travelled to Wisconsin to officiate over the ceremonial proceeding at a mid-winter ceremony. More men were taking on long-forgotten responsibilities.

The significance of this work was acknowledged with the placing of an official "fire" at the longhouse in Wisconsin in 2004, the first in the twenty-first century. This was a culmination of forty-four years of cultural revitalization work by many Oneidas from different communities with the assistance of the Haudenosaunee, the longhouses of the other nations. Language programs are now offered in all three communities despite differences in other areas, such as land claims and politics. Oneidas continue to journey between communities, building relationships and learning together. These efforts create new roles for men as teachers while renewing their ancient roles as orators.

The Iroquoian linguist and ethnographer J.N.B. Hewitt explored our culture and religion through the language, identifying "Kalenna" as the "mystic potency"[5] or "spiritual bundle"[6] that each person is born with. All Iroquois have an innate spiritualism, cultivated for generations, increasing the desire for their own identity. The soul or spirit of the Ukwehu:we man is charged with a duty inherently attached to Haudenosaunee teachings. Perhaps as a result of this spirit, the forces of assimilation and acculturation pressuring Oneidas to change and be white, Christian, tax paying, landless, uncultured, marginalized, second-class citizens, and followers of the band council system did not prevail. The power of the Kalenna (spiritual bundle), Ka?nikohli:yo (the Good Mind), and the flexibility of the culture and teachings absorbed the cultural shock and helped us to resist.

Among the Oneida communities, the Oneida Settlement[7] maintains the cultural practices more successfully. We are a more closed, isolated society, which has helped us to resist the assimilation efforts of the settler society. Even though most Euro-American and Canadian writers/researchers predicted that the culture would end, our recent history has proven that their ethnocentric view was wrong. Yet political, social, and cultural experiences of the last thirty-five to forty years demonstrate that Ukwehu:we men in general need to continue to work to retain and regain the mental, emotional, and spiritual space for the following principles:

- Oneida women are the critical identity holders of the nation.

- The women continue to pass on the inner desire to be Oneida and to be a part of something larger, the Haudenosaunee.

- Proximity to the rest of the Haudenosaunee is a critical factor in the sharing of culture.

- Marriage between communities and nations helps to maintain the Haudenosaunee identity.

- The relationship between Six Nations of the Grand River and the Oneida Settlement increases the viability of the traditional forms of belief through ceremonial, constitutional, governmental, and traditional clan roles.

- The ceremonial system of reconciliation settles disputes and historic disagreements to rejoin the original order of peace, friendship, and the Good Mind.

This is a part of my history that I have been deeply involved in for over forty years. It is this history that informs my spiritual and political masculine thought.

Putting Knowledge into Practice: Initiating Men's Healing

My adult life began with the realization that our culture was under threat, as the Elders feared that no one wanted to learn. My life direction has taken me on a path involved in community organizing and social service work, seeking ways to restrengthen culture and wellness, ways to combat racism, and ways to secure sovereignty and self-determination. As the son of a father who was sentenced to ten years in a residential school, I realized early on that I carry the scars of multi-generational genocidal Canadian programs and I sought a greater understanding of the role of men in Indigenous society. I could see that the heart and spirit of men had fallen victim to colonialism and internalized oppression. I wanted to explore what Indigenous men needed to challenge the internalized oppressive behaviours of men.

During the same time that Indigenous political activism was happening, Indian Country was witnessing the birth of a new home for the cultures in the healing continuum that had emerged. This movement was led by women, inspiring us to ask the questions, Where were the men? What was preventing them from accessing this phenomenon of healing?

Part of the answer could be found in the historical record, which showed how colonialism continues to influence the path of Indigenous men. The role of men as protectors and providers for their clan families was dismantled by the invading colonial masculinity. The invaders were primarily European testosterone-driven egomaniacs in search of wealth or souls. The more contact our Nations had with them, the more disoriented the men became. We came to know settler men as the Axe People. In the Oneida language, they are referred to as those who make axes or as "the ones who cut down the trees." As the forest disappeared in the wake of the settlers, our ancestors witnessed the rape of Mother Earth, the evidence of cultural difference.

Within this context of cultural disorientation and colonialism, men struggled to find their place. During the Oka Crisis of 1990 at Kanesatake, the Haudenosaunee experienced the culmination of the oppressive force of Canada and Quebec playing itself out.[8] We witnessed the rise of the warrior construct as an image of resistance and freedom for Indigenous peoples. The Oka Crisis or Mohawk Crisis allowed First Nations men who witnessed the oppression to release their pent-up political and spiritual anger and frustrations.

After 1990, my friends and I began to travel to British Columbia to participate in retreats involving vision and fasting ceremonies held in the mountains. It was during one of these trips that a vision came to me in the sweat lodge. I opened my eyes to see the image more clearly, and this is what I saw:

I could see the men standing on a mountain, a thousand or more high on the mountain, facing each other in a circle, and at the core, the sound of the truth could be heard from afar, ripped from their souls through the memories of a collective painful scar, releasing them from the past to accept the world today, accepting a reality of their own, not feeling they had to pay for something orchestrated by the colonial destroyers' rampant diseases, warfare, rape, residential schools, and evil land takers needing to seek forgiveness from the women and children who felt the pain of the lost men on the path of self-destruction. From the gathering on the mountain, they made their journey in succession down a long, winding path, entering the community hall, forming a huge circle of a thousand men or more. Each man stood and told his story; filling the room with regret, he would collapse in tears and weeping, asking to be released from the pain and to be free again as an Onkwehonwe man. The colours glistened in the vision, showing the strength of the spirit of the Anishnawbe man. Then the vision was gone, and I was back in the lodge.

My immediate thought was that men need to get involved in healing. They needed to expose their stories to the world and face the demons left behind by the settlers and colonial manipulators. For several years, I carried that dream with me, wondering how this could be done. In my community organizing and development work, I began to encourage men I met or knew to get involved.

I noticed over the years that what men seemed to struggle with was their anger. I was no different. The ongoing anger that one experiences is the single most powerful disruption in families today. Male anger is destroying Indigenous families and societies. Most men hide their anger and at times use it against their families. As men, we need to face this reality and come to terms with what it is.

At the same time, this is not just about angry men; it is about having to survive generations of oppression. The invaders' intentional effort to damage and destroy Indigenous families and cultures is well documented. The anger becomes more than a normal feeling; it has long roots traced through time, beginning with the first death among our people from the diseases, the invasion, and the murder of families by the colonial armies, the distribution of alcohol to gain signatures on fake treaties, the loss of home and homelands, having to escape and find a safe place to live and rebuild a culture. After these experiences, the settlers followed, demanding that our children be sent to schools to rid them of their language, culture, and family ties. They continue to steal our lands, extracting all the natural resources, raping our Mother Earth again and again.

As we enter the twenty-first century, Indigenous men need to find the peace within to be creative in our efforts to rebuild and recover from the destructive force of "Western civilization," a barbaric force of limited humanity, a society of war mongers.

I remember an Indigenous man once telling me it is okay to be angry at injustice but not to let anger create injustice toward one's own people. The challenge is to re-establish the role that Indigenous men in First Nations' societies play through a multi-faceted purpose that includes personal wellness, strengthening strong families, and sovereign First Nations that build revitalization movements politically, socially, and culturally—a program that ripples out to Indigenous communities, finding and helping Indigenous men discover, recover, and build their own Indigenous capacities.

Developing Men's Programming

As I began to work with other Indigenous men in the healing movement, I found it challenging to find materials suitable to Indigenous men. I examined a number of books and organizations devoted to the renewal of men's role in society that began to circulate in the 1980s and 1990s. Men generally were feeling trapped in the masculinity of American society: a gun-toting, John Wayne mentality. Much of the work we reviewed did not discourage this individualistic way of thinking. We were looking for materials that spoke to the virtues of Indigenous values or, at the very least, culturally neutral ones.

What was currently available for Indigenous men to study was limited. Three resources were selected for their usefulness in working with Indigenous men. The first was Kivel's 1998 publication *Men's Work*, which was relevant because it was the result of his work at the Oakland Men's Project, where he helped men confront and change violent behaviour. One of the things he pointed out is that men are trained by society to be soldiers, and that "male violence is a force which keeps systems of exploitation and violence in place."[9] Kivel noted, "The past cannot totally explain why men commit violence. The present is not simply the result of all past experiences and training.... Not every boy who was beaten grows up to beat his children, wife, or partner. Men decide to commit acts of violence. Men decide whether to take responsibility for those acts or to avoid responsibility."[10] The book offered a curriculum of twenty-two exercises for each topic, including becoming a father; cultural, racial, and class background; male spirituality; and getting help from others. The second resource we found relevant was *Power and Control: Tactics of Men Who Batter*.[11] This 1984 multi-media curriculum addressed the issues of family violence and men's power and control behaviours. The third resource was Fanning and McKay's 1993 *Being a Man*, which was helpful in curriculum development with its focus on "gendergraphs"; nurturing fathering; the importance of introspection; and clarifying and expressing feelings.[12] The external information developed by Western non-native programs helped us understand the impact on changing violent traits and the process for dealing with related masculinity issues. Most of the material was helpful in understanding colonialism and limited in assisting with Indigenous approaches. Finally, the Aboriginal Healing Foundation published a handbook in 2005 that addressed some of the questions faced by Indigenous men.[13]

I worked with other Indigenous men to begin to incorporate some of this material into the healing program we were designing. Addressing violence was central to our work.

Table 1.1. *Violence in Indigenous communities.*

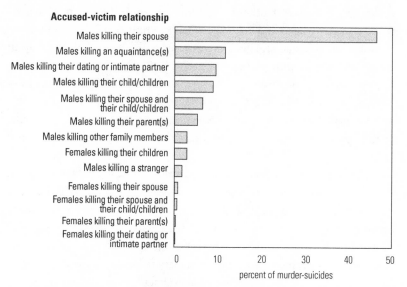

Accused-victim relationship

Note: Excludes incidents where the sex and/or age of victim was unknown and where the relationship between the victim and the accused was unknown.

In 2011, Statistics Canada published a report in which it stated, "As in previous years, the majority of victims of family violence were females. They represented 80% of spousal victims, 63% of parents victimized, 58% of extended family members victimized, 57% of child victims and 57% of sibling victims."[14] The 2011 statistics reflected similar stats from 1998, the time I began to work as the executive director of the Kiikeewanniikaan Healing Lodge, a holistic healing centre located in the Munsee Delaware Nation. By 2000 we had seen enough women who had experienced verbal, sexual, and physical abuse that we knew the statistics were true. It was time to bring the vision into reality and develop a healing program just for men, and to teach men the skills they needed to work with other men.

Through the collaboration of the First Nations Technical Institute (FNTI) and St. Lawrence College, we developed a diploma program in social services. With the assistance of Dr. Jim Dumont, Ojibwa Elder/teacher and traditional chief of the Eastern Door of the Midewiwin, I built a curriculum. We had worked together for a number of years, and this gave us the opportunity to continue our collaborative approach in cultural revitalization. We designed a program specifically for Anishnawbe/Ukwehu:we[15] men who wanted to make a healthy difference in their families and communities.

One of the original reasons for the program was to find a way to combat family violence. The curriculum asked participants to consider why all the violence was occurring when we come from cultures that have fundamental beliefs in kindness, peace, caring, and sharing. It exposed the fact that violence is an aftereffect of assimilation and colonization, caused by post-traumatic stress disorder (PTSD); and it facilitated the decolonization of masculinity through the original cultural teachings by putting cultural knowledge back in Indigenous homes to stop family violence.

A universal principle among Anishnawbe/Ukwehu:we men who are immersed in their cultures is the role of fire, symbolically and in life. Fire is representative of the spirit of the human being. In both Haudenosaunee and Anishinaabe cultures, man is considered responsible for care taking of fire. With those thoughts in mind, we developed a program, entitled Tending the Fire. This was a two-year program designed to reclaim Anishnawbe/ Ukwehonwe teachings, to learn about self, and to learn strategies to help other men, families, and communities tend and fix the fires so they would burn pure. During the program, the learner attended thirteen required weekly sessions of forty hours of training each, receiving in total 520 hours of onsite training. In addition, an optional ten days (100 hours) were offered for those who wished to practise their skills of helping in a residential program.

Culture-based or traditional teachings formed the foundation of Tending the Fire. This program was also designed to be a discovery path, asking, "What has caused Indigenous men to be afraid of their own cultures and teachings?" The original teachings are essential ingredients in the rebuilding and recovery of self-esteem and the empowerment of Indigenous men.

Working with Men's Fire

Originally, the idea of a men's program had come in a vision in a lodge, seeing men healing, discovering, seeking, and sharing with the people their renewal as Indigenous men. In working on men's programming, we had to ask what was missing from our lives as men in the twenty-first century. The very essence of being an Indigenous man had been stolen and lost over the years of survival, and had been replaced with messages of *"Be like us and you will be accepted and a part of white society."* Canada has spent millions of dollars designing and implementing programs to erase the Indigenous out of the man, to "kill the Indian and save the man."[16]

In Haudenosaunee original teachings, man as a human being was given a distinct place within the universal family. The original teachings speak of human beings completely dependent on all the other life forms to survive.

The human is the least significant in the total sacred cycle of life. The human is a part of the food chain as a consumer of other life forms. Not one other living being depends on the human being. As a result, the human being is a predator, dependent and needing the bodies of other living beings to survive. Originally, Indigenous men understood this, and cultures evolved that practised and understood the role of the human being within the greater family of life forces as outlined in the original teachings in Figure 1.1.

Five hundred years of contact riddled with atrocities has left behind a society of Indigenous men lacking true joyful identities, their authentic humanness erased by generations and countless acts of violence against them. These experiences have left behind *beings* who have survived through small acts of control and power, who have become household oppressors. They mimic the oppressors they hate, as if this is the only way to be a man. At those moments when one of them strikes another human being, they are making a choice. In domestic violence, rage is not blind or blameless; it is masculine rage making a decision.

The original sacred role of Indigenous men was reset to a path of self-destruction, and men are now trying to forget 521 years of invasion and genocide. The masculine role is interwoven within all life forces by a spiritual reciprocal connection understood within Indigenous cultures. Indigenous men are part of the human family who must find their place and make their own space for their thoughts and actions in contemporary reality. Indigenous masculinity is coming into its place, still defined by the Indigenous cultures. The family circle becomes more complete with the inclusion of the male spirit.

As a way of tapping into that spirit, we designed our curriculum around fire teachings from both Anishnawbe and Haudenosaunee cultures that speak directly to the role of the masculine energy of these societies. We engaged participants in activities that connected them to flint, fire, and the Grandfathers by teaching them how to make fire and construct bows; to do self-examinations with genograms and life lines; to expose and release anger; to establish personal ceremony to care for their manhood; to learn about women's teachings; and to practise reaching out to other men.

Our work began with teachings about the first Grandfather, Grandfather Rock, as it is so affectionately known among Indigenous peoples. It is the rock that carries the spark of life; Grandfather Rock has been given the responsibility to be the carrier of fire. The Anishnawbe understood this and called upon Grandfather whenever they needed fire. With that fire derives the continuation of life, symbolized and experienced in the fire itself. The fire is the source of warmth, the energy for cooking food, the light in the darkness, the energy used to work with wood to fashion homes, protection, and to create a safe, secure environment.

For the Haudenosaunee, the fire is the symbol of spirit of self, family, clan, and nation. The fire embodies all that is gifted from the higher power—the Great Spirit. Each person is given a fire to care for. When two people join together, they work to care for each other's fire and build a fire together, a family fire that is connected to the clan fire and, in turn, inseparable from the Nation fire.

Our other Grandfather—Eldest Brother (the sun)—is connected in the same way. Fire gives the gift of warmth to man. That warmth is about being connected to their relatives. Flint is the source of all the spiritual energy of the Eldest Brother—the sun. The flint then becomes a storage place for the energy that gives life. When the flint is struck and the spark jumps to the birch medicine (birch bark) and slowly becomes fire, we see the birth of spirit. This medicine is the gift of the birch tree. It is what the birch uses to heal itself, drawing from Mother Earth the healing power to cover an injury. As the birch tree heals, it leaves behind an enlarged growth. This hardened medicine of the birch tree becomes the partner to the spark of the flint. The two work to cause fire. With fire comes the thought and experience of spark-touching medicine from Mother Earth to create energy, the essence of spirit.

The power of flint within a flint point is Grandfather Rock fashioned with the power to take life. It is made to take life for a reason, and that reason is to give life. The arrowhead has the power to take life and to provide nourishment to the human beings who depend on the hunter in an explosive and dynamic expression of the energy in flint.

The hunter's bow is made from a tree relative that gives up life to enable the bow maker to fashion a tool to take life. Here we see the energy of the arrow and bow working together to aid human beings in their desire to survive and make life. The bow provides the trajectory power to the arrow, carrying the power to take life. Seeking a victim, it makes its kill, sending the spirit of the victim, an animal relative, to the spirit world. Oyuʔkwaʔuwé (sacred tobacco) is offered before and after a kill. This ensures that the power of the bow and arrow is never misunderstood or misused by the hunter. It is a constant reminder to the hunter that he carries the gift of the power to take life, joined with the ability to give life's nourishment to a family, clan, or village. The act of taking life cannot be exercised without knowing about and without acknowledgement of giving and sharing the nourishment.

The making of a tool that has this power is done with love and care. Fashioning a bow from a tree makes one look for the strength of the tree, seeing the lines of aging, choosing somewhere between the outside and the centre of the tree. It is in the thick layer where a year of strength is stored. Everything else around this layer is removed to reveal the instrument of trajectory power, a power collected and strung and released through the arrow and the flint point transforming into the power to take life.

The hunter is "the Seeker of his relatives" or "the one who looks for the fire in his relatives," as the hunter is described or thought of in two Native languages, Ukwehunwehnéha and Anishnaabemowin. The act of being a provider carries with it the responsibility for releasing that energy of *extinguishing life*. The food that is gained becomes a spirit food of nourishment, feeding the hunter's family fire.

We taught our program participants that over generations of this act, Indigenous men were cared for by being carefully cleansed by the medicines of smudge and song before and after the hunt. The returning hunter was received by family and community, making sure that the power of the ability to take life within the hunter was cared for with cleansing that brought the hunter back to balance. The power to take life is the spirit of the hunter, gathering emotional and physical energy, skill, and knowledge folded into the single act of drawing the string back and flinging the arrow to its destiny, taking the life of another life form. Reciprocity, respect, spiritualism, ceremony, and bravery are values that band together to form a caring male spirit. Ceremonially, cultures knew that it was necessary as a special consideration always to tend the masculine energy within our families. It is this one simple act, a cleansing ceremony to bring balance back to the male spirit, that has disappeared in our communities.

The male spirit had been conditioned for generations to be tended, but the invasion hampered the practice of this simple act of bringing balance back to the male spirit. Some of the more traditional hunters kept the practice alive, and during Tending the Fire program, we discovered the importance of the tradition. Indigenous men need this on a daily basis to fashion a caring personality that is always in balance. Every Ukwehu:we/Anishnawbe man has been given a part to play in the cycle of this gift—taking and giving life. This cycle is filled with the taking and giving of energy that leads to the one hard act of taking life—being a provider. Without the teachings, many hunters fulfilling their obligations become burdened with negative feelings of remorse or guilt. When these men do not or are not able to take their place within this cycle, their energy is trapped in an acculturate cycle of anomie. In

Figure 1.2. *The Good Mind.*

this acculturated cycle, pent-up energy turns into anger, leading to random acts of violence committed against women and children. Uneducated and uncultured power and control behaviours cause pure acts of aggression.

All human emotions are energy that can be acted upon or used to cause positive or negative encounters with the world. When the conscience is not schooled appropriately, the emotional energy causes random acts of violence. Most of us have spent some of our formative years learning about what we can get away with. The emotional energy that men exercise before some measure of conscience guides the use of the masculine energy is often unpredictable.

Without the teachings and care of the energy, the Indigenous conscience can falter and fail to react in the full expression of taking and giving life as a meaningful spiritual relationship with all life forms. The inadequacy of the conscience causes the energies to be misguided. Then, experiences of alcohol abuse, family violence, racism, and childhood traumas makes man vulnerable to the building of internalized energy that leads to anger. Forgotten cultural teachings further stimulate the release of negative masculine energy only to extinguish the fires of his loved ones, perpetrating family violence.

Those Indigenous men can find themselves a long way from their original roles and responsibilities. These teachings have limited bearing on their lives. Ultimately, the spirit of the Indigenous man is not cared for ceremonially or spiritually. In the Tending the Fire program, we proposed that the right to hunt and to take life is not cared for within the Indigenous man. In a more contemporary context hunting becomes the metaphor of man's engagement in difference lifestyles. The growth of the realization of these simple teachings helped to gain ground concerning family violence. The energy can be treated, and the balance of the male energy can be helped. The men who have attended Tending the Fire continue to seek knowledge of Indigenous masculinity through experiential learning. The cultured conscience of a man gives those emotions a set of parameters to function within, with a sense of morality, the principles we live by, building character that is balanced in accepting and understanding the power of their fire.

Conclusion

As a Haudenosaunee man, I have experienced the collective wisdom of the past generations; listened to and absorbed the narratives; gained political knowledge by being involved in resistance and advocacy; performed personal self-examination and healing; learned from my mistakes; and allowed the culture to guide my thoughts.

Much of our rich culture is still available to us. One of the major concerns is whether it will be available for the next seven generations. One way to make sure is to infuse our lives with the teachings and act out the essence of the culture in our everyday experiences. As Haudenosaunee men, we must begin to seize the teachings and have them form our behaviour. Figure 1.3 provides eight key words informing our minds to direct our behaviour, creating family, community, and society as Haudenosaunee. Affirmation and integration into Haudenosaunee identity are critical to the long-term positive development of men who have not had the opportunity to examine their culture or their families' lives. The self-examination course of action would be a decolonization process to achieve a cultural-based whole person. This is why, during the helping process, individuals need to come to terms with their own life path as a critical part of the long-term process of transformation.

We need to be Ka?nikohli:yo, not just in the longhouse but all day long, every day, throughout our lifetimes. The masculine energy of our communities has a greater responsibility to self-examine and rebuild a real sense of manhood that works with women to create a world free of violence. The journey to understanding decolonization in the context of masculinity requires letting go of power and control behaviours, the source of violence. The original teachings

of Indigenous cultures fashion men to be liberated, thoughtful in delibera-
tions, matrifocal, and self-determining in ways that honour our inner fire
and responsibilities toward all of life through the teaching of Kaʔnikohli:yo.

Notes

1 Longhouse is a term used to reference traditional people among the Iroquois. It
  is the primary building used for ceremonial activities and clan and community
  meetings. Haudenosaunee means people who build longhouses.

2 Alex Frank Ricciardelli, "Factionalism at Oneida, An Iroquois Indian Community"
  (PhD diss., University of Pennsylvania, 1961).

3 J. Campisi, "Ethnic Identity and Boundary Maintenance in Three Oneida
  Communities" (PhD diss., State University of New York, 1974), 270.

4 The 1701 Fort Albany Treaty recorded the territory as the Beaver Hunting Grounds,
  a joint use area of several Indigenous Nations. This is also acknowledged in oral
  history as well as under the Dish With One Spoon Treaty.

5 J.N.B. Hewitt, "Orenda and a Definition of Religion," *American Anthropologist* 4,
  no. 1 (1902): 13.

6 H. Elijah (Faith Keeper Oneida Longhouse) in discussion with the author, 2008.

7 The term "settlement" is used by Oneidas because they purchased the territory from
  the British in 1838–40 and do not like using the colonial term "reserve."

8 The Oka Crisis was a confrontation when the City of Oka attempted to take burial
  grounds from the Mohawk people of Kanesatake to expand a golf course.

9 Paul Kivel, *Men's Work: How to Stop the Violence that Tears Our Lives Apart* (Center
  City, MN: Hazelden Publishing, 1998).

10 Ibid., 101.

11 Ellen Pence and Michael Paymar, *Power and Control: Tactics of Men Who Batter: An
  Educational Curriculum* (Duluth, MN: Minnesota Program Development, 1986).
  http://www.duluth-model.org/.

12 Patrick Fanning and Matthew McKay, *Being a Man: A Guide to the New Masculinity*
  (Oakland, CA: New Harbinger Publications, 1993).

13 W.J. Mussell, *Warrior-Caregivers: Understanding the Challenges and Healing of First
  Nations Men* (Ottawa: Aboriginal Healing Foundation, 2005).

14 Statistics Canada, *Family Violence in Canada: A Statistical Profile, 2011* (Ottawa:
  Statistics Canada, 2011), http://www.statcan.gc.ca/daily-quotidien/130625/dq130625b-
  eng.htm.

15 Anishnawbe are Ojibway, and Ukwehu:we are Iroquois, Oneida.

16 In 1875, Captain Richard Henry Pratt, 10th Cavalry Buffalo Soldiers, founder of the
  Carlisle School for Indian Students, used this statement as the motto for retraining
  Indian prisoners in Florida and later in the school. See http://www.buffalosoldier.
  net/CaptainRichardH.Pratt.htm.

CHAPTER 2

Cutting to the Roots of Colonial Masculinity

Scott L. Morgensen

Colonial masculinities arose to violently control and replace distinctive gender systems among Indigenous peoples. Tracing any form of colonial masculinity to its historical roots may create useful tools for Indigenous or non-Indigenous people who wish to interrupt or undo its power. My critique of colonial masculinity in this essay presents a white settler response to Indigenous people who are participating in the redefinition and resurgence of Indigenous governance.[1] Across differences in law, culture, or relationships to colonization, many Indigenous modes of governance recall gendered epistemologies that can interrupt the foundations of colonial governance, including colonial masculinity, as reviewed in this volume by Leah Sneider. In addition, Brendan Hokowhitu in this volume asks how colonial interests within European settler states have helped craft "traditional" Indigenous masculinities that "functioned strategically through complicity with and assimilation into forms of invader masculinity." Hokowhitu invites the formation of Indigenous movements that refuse to reproduce heteropatriarchal power. In response, I turn to the work of identifying and challenging colonial masculinity within the political, economic, social, and cultural contexts of white settler societies: for their gendered transformation, as Indigenous critics argue, will be necessary to their decolonization.

Indigenous theories of gender and colonial power—and, notably among them, Indigenous feminist and Two-Spirit critiques—present the dynamic intellectual and political models to which this essay responds. Indigenous writers have illustrated the myriad ways that colonization acts through gender and sexuality, and they explain heteropatriarchy as a colonial construct within Indigenous and white settler societies. In the Spanish "extermination of the *joyas*" and its commitment to "gendercide," recounted by Deborah Miranda; the French and British stereotyping of Indigenous women that facilitated conquest and sexual violence, as told by Kim Anderson, Winona Stevenson, and Janice Acoose; and settler state impositions of heteropatriarchal rule explained by Bonita Lawrence and Pamela Palmater: gender and sexuality appear not incidental but instrumental to the colonization of Indigenous peoples.[2] As Sneider recounts, such works also teach that where gender complementarity within Indigenous societies set a basis for "social balance and the responsibility and power to act," European invaders interpreted this as a threat and made transforming or eliminating Indigenous gender systems a central tenet of their colonial regimes.

This essay traces how colonial masculinity arose in the Americas from within relations between Europeans and Indigenous peoples, as both an answer to changing European gender and sexual regimes and as a means to establish white settler law. I consider the following questions: What gendered subjectivities—what ways of thinking and living as gendered persons—did Europeans bring to the Americas and to their colonial relationships with Indigenous peoples? How did those subjectivities vary across early modern or modern gender systems; and in each case, how did they enact colonial violence? How did gender change among European settlers once they had established methods for governing white settler societies? And how did all of these changes in gender and governance produce specific forms of colonial masculinity? While my questions focus on the subjects and social lives that Europeans brought to or invented in settler states, I interpret them all as relational: for all formed in relation to Indigenous peoples and their colonization, given that *colonial* subjectivities exist to dominate another. From this premise my account sustains two key points. First, for colonial masculinity to achieve dominance, it had to be *invented*: European modes of manhood arrived on Indigenous lands, changed as they participated in colonial violence, and became entrenched as methods of settler rule. As creations of conquest, forms of colonial masculinity are not natural, necessary, or permanent, any more than is colonization itself. Second, amid the myriad changes that took place in colonial societies, as the logics and methods of colonization shifted, colonial masculinity also changed. Given that colonial masculinity had to change to sustain its power, we might hope that further changes could bring it to its end. But even if we accept colonial masculinity's mutability, we must beware of this: for if its function is to change, then our criticisms of it may only cause it to take new forms and persist. For this reason, I write to support all efforts to bring colonial masculinity to its end: a dissolution already envisioned and underway in Indigenous people's struggles for decolonization.

My account applies two approaches to historical analysis that I hope may be useful to critical Indigenous studies of masculinity. First, by emphasizing colonialism as relational, I reframe histories of gender and sexuality in early modern and modern Europe in terms of their dependence on colonization in the Americas. As Ann Stoler argued when applying the work of Michel Foucault to European colonies of extraction, I suggest that even if a theory of European gender or sexuality ignores colonial history, it may still leave clues to how those formations were remade by colonial relationships to Indigenous peoples.[3] Second, I speculate regarding how a return to the colonial archive, led by Indigenous criticism, might generate new knowledge. Revisiting historical evidence can shift expectations, as Linda Tuhiwai Smith argues, from stabilizing colonial premises to sparking anti-colonial modes of interpretation and analysis.[4] In these respects, my historical claims are speculative in that they are interested in further study, just as they attempt to incisively answer insurgent indigenist criticism that challenges gendered and sexual power. Located as I am within forms of colonial masculinity, as their white settler cisgender inheritor—despite being their potential queer target, or a critic of their power—the power of colonial masculinity shapes my life and informs any insights I can imagine. From this place, and as a contributor to this volume, I write in the hope that my critical takes on colonial masculinity may prove useful to Indigenous people who are reimagining Indigenous masculinities.

Early Modern European Manhood and the Colonial Encounter

As Spanish and Portuguese and, later, French, British, and Dutch colonists arrived in the Americas, their early modern European understandings of gender were redeployed in colonial encounters with Indigenous peoples. Historical scholarship on this era remains open to many questions: Across various sites, how did early modern European gender systems encounter and respond to Indigenous societies? How did they continue to form during the sixteenth and seventeenth centuries in specific relationship to the colonization of Indigenous peoples? What gendered qualities informed the initial colonial regimes that Europeans established in relation to Indigenous peoples? And how did all of these processes help establish forms of colonial masculinity on these lands? By beginning my account in early modern cases, I emphasize that if colonial masculinity arises as early as initial colonization in the Americas, then it did not form on identical terms to its practice today. Historians trace significant changes within and across early modern and modern European gender systems, not least of these being the redefinition of gender after the eighteenth century by modern sciences of race and sexuality. This historical specificity reminds us to carefully consider to what degree we can interpret early modern Europeans or Indigenous peoples of those times through analytics of "race" or "sexuality." Colonial gender systems formed dynamically in the sixteenth and seventeenth centuries on distinct terms: some of which, I speculate, must inform the initial and persistent shapes taken by colonial masculinity in the Americas.

The gendered re-evaluation of colonial encounters can take inspiration from the interest of scholars of early modern Europe in the malleability of manhood. For instance, Alexandra Shepard examines how in sixteenth- and seventeenth-century England, manhood was determined to be reserved to some according to markers of status or age. Denial of socially affirmed manhood to young or working-class men led to their asserting what Shepard calls alternative logics of manhood. But the tenuousness of these alternatives in English society highlighted that the manhood Shepard calls hegemonic asserted its priority by tying its qualities to manhood as such, and scrutinizing others for failing to achieve its status.[5] In a distinct case, Edward Behrend-Martinez traces how in seventeenth-century Spain, legal and ecclesiastical inquiries into cases of divorce due to impotence reveal that "manhood was a restricted status," one determined to fail to apply not just to females but also to males who could not meet standards of manly comportment or livelihood.[6] My interest here is in the implication of early modern European forms of manhood being understood as matters of achievement, as scarce goods, or as insecure or perishable if debility or certain gendered actions resulted in being "unmanned." Was manhood known, or under what conditions might it have been known as containing a threatening capacity to be lost due to failures to cultivate, protect, or retain its power?[7] Such concerns also animate modern "hegemonic manhood": Raewyn Connell's term for the dominant gendered form animating European empire and global capital.[8] Yet, as I will discuss, Michel Foucault raised similar arguments with respect to a shift from early modern European interpretations of sexual practice. Sexual sciences in the eighteenth century began defining sexual perversion as the property of sexual minorities; but early modern accounts tended to frame a perversion like sodomy as (what Foucault called) a "temporary aberration," and thus as a threat to manhood, given that it could be practised by, or potentially discovered among, any men.[9] With all this in mind, I ask: How did Europeans bring to the Americas knowledges that manhood as such, or their manhood in particular, required achievement or remained open to failure? And how might this have informed how colonizers differentiated Europeans from Indigenous peoples?

Indigenous feminist and Two-Spirit critics demonstrate that Indigenous gender systems appeared to Europeans to be ambiguous or aberrant. Indigenous scholars show that when Europeans encountered the complementarity of Indigenous women's and men's authority and leadership, they perceived it as a barrier or threat to imposing heteropatriarchal rule via economic, political, or religious means, as Sneider reviews. In particular, Winona Stevenson and Kim Anderson highlight sexual agency as a site of conflict, once Indigenous women's autonomy over desire, partnership, and marriage became targets for European reeducation, or were reframed by colonizers around sexual stereotyping that facilitated exploitation and violence against Indigenous women.[10] For Deborah Miranda, the gendered logic of colonization is exposed when Europeans rejected Indigenous peoples' recognition of gender roles that exceeded European ideas of binary sex/gender. Referencing the Spanish invasion of California as well as colonization across the Americas, Miranda explains that Europeans violently established colonial rule on heteropatriarchal terms by practising "gendercide": the systematic targeting, punishment, and attempted elimination of traditional gender roles that Indigenous people recognized as "neither fully male nor fully female ... but a unique blend of characteristics resulting in a third or other gender."[11] Across the hemisphere, Europeans encountered many Indigenous societies in which sex and gender were known to be greater than two, sexual partnership between people of the same sex was recognized or acceptable, and no edict held that human nature barred such diversity. Certainly, across their diversity Indigenous societies defined gender in a wide variety of ways, and not all recalled distinctive roles like those Miranda invoked.[12] Nevertheless, at the time of contact with Europeans, Indigenous peoples of the Americas shared in not having instituted something then emerging in Europe: total religious or scientific judgment of all non-binary gender and same-sex sexuality as immoral and unnatural. These are among the differences that set up manhood as a site of conflict within European efforts to assert control over Indigenous peoples.

With inspiration by such works, how can we trace the importance of gendered violence against Indigenous men, or against people whom Europeans perceived to be men, as part of the establishment of colonial rule? How did colonizers direct gendered violence against gender diversity, same-sex sexuality, or any implication that Indigenous men had failed to achieve European standards for manhood? Miranda recounts that manhood became central to colonial violence when Indigenous gender or sexual diversity exceeded what Europeans deemed permissible. Reports of Spanish invasions highlight the targeting of individuals whom invaders read as male-bodied or intersex and as living in what they perceived as a feminine gender role. Undoubtedly, many persons described in these ways presented the traditional gender diversity of their nations: which many Indigenous LGBTQ and Two-Spirit people reclaim today as their contribution to the resurgence of Indigenous culture and governance.[13] In many such traditions, people who were recognized within genders other than "woman" or "man" were, and remain integral to, families, partnerships, and collective culture, religion, and governance. Their lives significantly informed Indigenous understandings of human potential and differences in ways that colonizers refused to comprehend. Following Miranda, we see that Spanish efforts to practise gendercide against persons whom they read as gender-variant men—or *joyas* ("jewels") in the colonizers' terms—attacked not only those individuals but also the communities that had accepted and embraced them. Colonial violence against individuals also sought to violently restructure Indigenous peoples as a whole, so that the shared values that had accepted gender or sexual diversity also would disappear.

The capacity of this violence to illuminate colonial perceptions of manhood is deepened by the term first used by the Spanish to frame it— "berdache"—which tells a specific story of European heteropatriarchal and imperial aspirations. Of French origin, "berdache" translates as "kept boy" or "boy slave"[14]: that is, as a subordinate male (young, or read as youthful) who is imagined to have been turned into a sexual slave by adult men, and as a result to have been psychically if not also physically feminized.[15] In this early modern French and Spanish usage, the term purportedly translated a word from Farsi, which in its own right appeared to be reporting to Europeans that Middle Eastern or Muslim societies were a source of this form of violent adult male coercion of young men into effeminizing sexual relations. I write skeptically here to indicate the colonial violence already embedded in this term: Orientalist European fantasies about debased and effeminizing Middle Eastern or Muslim manhood fit the political uses of gender in early modern Europe. Immediately after achieving the Reconquista of the Iberian Muslim caliphates, Spanish conquistadores met Indigenous Americans through this racialized, imperialist, and Orientalist narrative. Of course, projecting "berdache" onto either Muslims or "Indians" also deflected attention away from the proclivities that European men knew already might be present among themselves. In turn, because "berdache" invoked not just one person but an imagined male sexual economy, its colonial usage in the Americas actually projected sexual immorality onto Indigenous men collectively. In this way, colonizers deployed "berdache" or similar stories about gender or sexual transgression among Indigenous men to justify violating and assimilating Indigenous *peoples* under colonial patriarchal rule: attacks on Indigenous manhood that targeted gender diversity proved crucial to establishing colonial rule. Then, the colonial relationships that the new social order established also produced *colonists*, just as they refashioned Indigenous people: for as victorious rulers, European men were positioned relationally to Indigenous people as manly and moral patriarchs, while subordination framed Indigenous male leadership in an unmanly status that could be read as undeserving of self-government. The gendered story of "berdache" functioned by altering identity for all Indigenous people *and* for European invaders, while facilitating broad establishment of a colonial and patriarchal social order.

With these histories in mind, I am curious about the degree to which European observers of early colonial encounters were interested in the vulnerability of either Indigenous or European manhood to being unmanned. For instance, such relationships appear to be raised in an oft-cited passage from Peter Martyr's portrayal of Vasco Nuñez de Balboa's 1513 invasion of the isthmus of Panama. Historians of early modern accounts of colonial encounters, or of Martyr specifically, can address the contexts that formed this text, and Martyr's potential political, cultural, or gendered investments in its narration. I approach it here not as an eyewitness account (which it is not) but as evocative of situated interests in gendered colonial narration. Martyr portrays Balboa arriving at the house of the leader of an Indigenous community after a military victory, where Balboa reportedly found the Indigenous leader's brother and up to forty other men dressed in women's apparel or cohabiting in same-sex relationships. Martyr then writes a scene that resonates with the accounts Miranda examined: he portrays Balboa ordering the male leader and his associates to be eaten alive by dogs, while making Balboa's men and the remaining Indigenous community witness to this act. Jonathan Goldberg interprets this passage by arguing that the murderous act "retrospectively justifies" Balboa's earlier slaughters in battle against Indigenous armies, when Spanish soldiers killed Indians "as animals"; or to quote Martyr's text, "hewed … in pieces as the butchers doo fleshe." Based on these accounts, Goldberg argues, "post-facto, the body of the sodomite takes on an originary status, as the cause for what was done to the Indians in the first place."[16] The implication I draw from Goldberg is the indication that at least some early modern European observers of conquest foregrounded the punishment of gender and sexual transgression as "retrospective justification" for conquest. Did, or how did European men foreground the punishment of gender or sexuality among Indigenous men, and people whom they perceived to be men, as key to establishing a political, and conquerable difference between Indigenous peoples and those who sought to rule, or replace them?

Taken together, these histories indicate to me that if gender or sexual practices among Indigenous men appeared to invaders to be at odds with European morality, then Indigenous practices could be reframed as the acts of an unmanly and degraded leadership in need of conquest for the sake of nature, church, or civilization. Yet, read in context of European men's known capacity for, or indulgence in acts now associated with others, such violence may not only be intended to destroy perversion elsewhere, but also may (try to) prove that perversion was being overcome among or *within* themselves. To what degree might we read European conquest as self-interested: informed by European men's fears of a capacity within their own manhood for self-betrayal or loss? I mean my speculations here to inform emergent understanding of the interactions between Indigenous and early modern European gender systems that sparked colonial masculinity. Some possibilities I perceive, which historical scholars may investigate to affirm, deny, or complicate, are as follows. What began as European forms of manhood, albeit already imperial ones, shored up their tenuous integrity (open to being undone by unmanly acts) through deeply gendered and sexualized conquests and relational colonial rule. These forms of masculinity become conquering by projecting their own capacity to be degraded onto others. Here I highlighted how an Orientalist and imperial relationship to Islam may have informed how explorers who sought to trade with, or conquer their "East" encountered "Indians" instead. The subsequent invasions of Indigenous peoples in the Americas set new contexts for producing European masculinities, as now expressly colonial: existing on others' territories, while affirming their own morality as well as the immorality of those whom they ruled through intimately colonial relationships. Violence continued, because colonization itself is violence; but it also was elaborated, as modes of policing, reeducation, and assimilation became methods for colonizers to secure an integrity they still perceived to be under threat. Targeting indigeneity as an origin of an "immorality" colonizers knew resided, or originated in, themselves, "colonial masculinity" served to control Indigenous people through the moral education of subordinates, even as this educative activity served to prove that colonial morality was secure.

If a social order formed on these terms, it should be no surprise if it were to give its agents the power and licence to practise what it deemed "immoral" as violence against those whom it occupied. Indigenous feminist and Two-Spirit critiques show that gender and sexual violence are crucial to colonial power. Here I engage their claims by asking if colonial masculinity formed in this way because colonizing men were known to be vulnerable to losing the very power they then exerted. Did colonizing men know that immorality might cause them to fail to achieve or retain manhood: so that violent acts of colonial subordination combined with projecting immorality onto Indigenous peoples to jointly address gendered and colonial failures? Whatever these questions might elicit in the eras I have evoked, they resonate in a period when colonial masculinity shifted: towards the related, yet distinctly modern, modes of power that define recent generations and our lives today.

Modern Colonial Masculinity: Shifting Colonial, Racial, and Sexual Power

Gendered and colonial power changed together in the eighteenth and nineteenth centuries when modern modes of governance emerged in Europe and in its colonies worldwide. These changes have been interpreted in studies of the "intimacies of empire," to use Ann Stoler's term, which address how local governance of colonial relations was informed by and helped shape new racial and sexual sciences and modes of population control.[17] A concentration of such studies on European colonies of extraction, however, has led to relatively less theorization of the relationship of Indigenous peoples to racial and sexual power in settler societies. Revisiting works in Indigenous studies and related fields, I ask here how colonial masculinity became embedded within modern modes of colonial, racial, and sexual governance in settler societies, and how its patterns might be identified and challenged today.

Scholars of European governance have noted a historical shift illuminated by Michel Foucault, in which the "sovereign power" characterizing medieval and early modern rule was displaced, or augmented, by modern practices of "governmentality." Foucault opens *Discipline and Punish*, his history of the prison in Europe, by arguing that the sovereign's divinely ordained authority was emblematized in the spectacular act of public execution, which taught witnesses that they might meet the same fate if they came under suspicion of transgression.[18] He argues that this mode of power altered as sovereignty came to be reimagined during the Enlightenment as shared by male property-owning citizens of the modern nation-state. Foucault presents this context for the rise of governmentality: the scientific, bureaucratic management of persons as constituents of "populations." His exemplary case of this new power's emergence is the modern prison, which displaced the sovereign's dungeon with scientific modes of population control based on surveillance. As in Jeremy Bentham's "panopticon"—which arrayed prisoners around a central station for continual monitoring by prison guards—the subject of governmentality learned self-policing in a context where thought and behaviour were constantly surveilled. For Foucault, governmentality thus came to signify both governance of populations and governance of the self, with the self being reimagined as a generalized member of a population as well as a target of regulation.

Foucault also developed his history of modern European power through transformations in gender and sexuality. We learn that the social management of desire and sexual relations shifted once nineteenth-century European sciences theorized "sexuality" as a foundation of the biological and psychic self.[19] The modern concept of "sexuality" narrowed natural or unnatural desires from qualities that any body could express to being the property of distinctive "abnormal" or "normal" sexual populations. For instance, sexologists claimed to have identified an "invert" or "third sex," intermediary between two naturally opposed sexes: a status that shifted after the turn of the twentieth century to inform the new scientific categories "homosexual" and "transsexual."[20] Governmentality mobilized new sexual sciences to target abnormal sexual populations for institutional observation or containment—in hospitals, mental institutions, prisons—to be studied, controlled, or "cured." Under these new sexual regimes, if a person otherwise known to be a "normal" woman or man were thought to exhibit signs of gender or sexual difference from binary sex or sexuality, they could be assigned an abnormal status that called for special institutional intervention. By creating a variety of (what Foucault called) new "species" of "abnormal sexual types," these new forms of governmentality housed perversions within minoritized social groups. But they also surveilled all people for signs of gender or sexual ambiguity that could result in containment or coercive reeducation.

Scholars of colonialism also illustrate shifts from sovereign power to governmentality, and correlative changes in theories. By correcting the limits of European works that ignore Europe's imperial presence, these scholars ask how the power that such works trace arises in relations among colonizers and colonized.[21] For instance, Indigenous and non-Indigenous scholars of white settler colonialism in the Americas already present a lengthy record of the governmental management of Indigenous peoples in sexualized terms. Zeb Tortorici explains how Spanish authorities in seventeenth- and eighteenth-century New Spain began elaborating methods for investigating sexual immorality among Indigenous men, by tracing chains of relationship through families, towns, and regions.[22] While those who were targeted remained subject to public execution, a relative de-emphasis during this period of that dramatic violence was joined by increased efforts to record networks of immoral practitioners. This suggests that both Indigenous peoples and male sexual outlaws (represented here, crucially, by Indigenous men) were being defined as populations for present and future colonial management. But such procedures became especially apparent once white settler colonialism was institutionalized by modern racial and sexual regimes.

Modern colonial governmentality is exemplified by the rapid expansion of European settler colonies and states from the late eighteenth through the nineteenth centuries, when European settlers as new majorities placed Indigenous peoples under increasingly militarized, incarcerating, and other institutional forms of management. For instance, in the United States and Canada, military removal and the creation of "Indian territory," reservations, reserves, and agencies all set standards for the colonization of Indigenous people via institutional containment. By the time of the Dakota War of 1862, the U.S. military internship of hundreds of resistant Dakota under the sights of Fort Snelling instituted the state's first "concentration camp," and modelled the militarized reservations that would follow for Dakota removed to the west.[23] A key example of colonial population control appeared in policies to forcibly assimilate Indigenous peoples through the residential/boarding school systems in Canada, the United States, and Australia.[24] As incarcerating encampments (prisons) these schools were filled once Indigenous communities were contained on reservations/reserves and had their children removed, who in many instances died or were disappeared.[25] Yet framing these modes of occupation, imprisonment, and policing as "education" shows how governmentality attempted to teach Indigenous people to be "self-governed" subordinates of colonial rule. Given that these schools' education in Christian civilizationalism was primarily religious, moralistic teaching about gender and sexuality also became central to the subordinate racialized role schools forced Indigenous people to learn to play within settler societies. And this entire project of cultural genocide rested on implementing a colonial sex/gender binary. By segregating children into two separate sexes, kin ties among siblings and clan members of different genders were broken, while children who already lived or later might have lived in a gender other than the two that the colonizers affirmed had their distinctive identities denied or erased.

Two gendered groups were defined by colonizers and expected to conform to strongly contrasting behaviours, as part of preparing Indigenous people for subordinate cultural, political, and labour roles in settler societies.

Such institutional settings created contexts for redefining colonial masculinity as governmentality in nineteenth- and twentieth-century settler states. By interacting with Indigenous peoples through the racial and governmental logic of "population," white settlers sought at once to *externalize* racialized Indigenous populations from settler society and to *internalize* the cultural difference of indigeneity among white settlers. To take the first example, colonial masculinity proved crucial to externalizing Indigenous people from spaces redefined as proper to white settlers. The siting of Indigenous reserves on lands marginal to settler capitalism taught white settlers that other Indigenous territories were emptied and theirs to inhabit; and enforcements of racial and spatial separation framed Indigenous people who crossed into (white settler) "public" spaces as out-of-place.[26] In her account of the murder of Pamela George, Sherene Razack interrogates the spatialization of settler society by white male prerogative, forming zones defined by the exposure of Indigenous women to white male violence and zones that relationally insulate white men from accountability for their violence; a process Sarah Hunt challenges in response to the ongoing disappearance and murder of Indigenous women.[27] I understand these works to be showing how the spatial and governmental techniques of settler colonialism mobilize colonial masculinity to draw and police colonial borders, to regulate Indigenous people as populations, and to subject Indigenous peoples to violence by positioning them in settler societies as perpetually "out of place."

In Canada, the Indian Act exemplifies the role that colonial masculinity plays in institutionally containing Indigenous people as subordinates to settler rule. The Act creates a controllable racial population by breaking up Indigenous nations: in the creation of "bands," spatially isolated from their broader nations and prevented from coordinating national governance; and in the creation of a new racial caste of "Indians," to whom state-designated "Indian status" is assigned to contravene Indigenous modes of belonging and governance. Once "Indian bands" become the only groups that may hold collective title to land on reserves—albeit spatially marginal land, as noted—moving outside the terms of bands or status threatens to erase access to Indigenous identity or community. Gender crucially structured all these effects of the Act, as carefully explained by Bonita Lawrence, Pamela Palmater, and Martin Cannon.[28] By imposing patrilineality as its method to transfer status, the Act disregards Indigenous kin ties that are not patrilineal and links

Indigenous identity to a patriarchal authority defined and imposed by the state. The Act specifically denied Indigenous women's agency by rescinding status and access to reserve land to any woman or her descendants who married or raised a family with a person without status. Lawrence explains that as a result, across Canada, originally matrilineal and unrecognized mixed-blood Indigenous communities have arisen, primarily in urban spaces, while Indigenous men with status have been invested with a patriarchal authority that was invented by colonizers, that devolved from colonial masculinity, and that depends for its existence on colonial rule.[29]

Even as modern modes of racialization and spatial policing limited and transformed Indigenous societies, they also created arenas in which colonial masculinity could identify with its new governmental authority. Historians of residential and boarding schools explain that white settlers formed deeply gendered and colonial identifications with their roles as educators and modellers of a new order. When Cathleen Cahill explains the identities of agents of the U.S. Indian Service as "federal fathers and mothers," or when Margaret Jacobs portrays how women who took up such roles understood themselves to be "white mothers to a dark race," we see the labour of colonial education giving its regulators gendered and colonial senses of self.[30] Maternal and paternal roles masked colonialism's violence, even as the patriarchal culture that they taught forced Indigenous youth into roles defined by European gendered, racial, and capitalist expectations. Yet in light of vast and growing evidence that the schools' violent incarceration and cultural genocide facilitated rampant sexual violence against Indigenous children, these identities appear in a very critical light. Fictive kinship in colonial education took place in a culture that linked immorality to indigeneity and morality to settler civilization: but so long as white settlers projected the source of immorality away from themselves, the violence visited on Indigenous people appeared to be sourced among *them* rather than among its colonial perpetrators.

Colonial masculinity also transformed once racial and sexual sciences integrated imagined aspects of indigeneity into colonial masculinity. New sciences of racial evolution made sensible the notion that colonial subjects might, or should internalize indigeneity—or, more aptly, a "primitivity" Europeans imaginatively associated with Indigenous peoples. Scientists and their adherents invoked biology to rewrite stories of the supremacy of European "civilization" over "barbaric" or "primitive" peoples and to argue that Europeans ruled because they were more evolved.[31] Yet given that, in this logic, the civilized had passed through the greatest number and degree of evolutionary stages, theories of racial evolution considered the possibility that Europeans' barbaric or primitive ancestry remained an interior potential. This concern resonated with older religious or legal accounts of moral sexual practice, in which moral people were known to contain a capacity for immorality, and that men must control this capacity or risk becoming unmanned. But new evolutionary sciences racialized dangerous desires: so that for civilized people, the battle became one of aligning an inner capacity to "go primitive" with an external role of policing the very racial populations whom they cast as primitive today.

For instance, late nineteenth-century anglophone North American colonial masculinity adopted this quality in stories that civilized men would be strengthened by indulging in "primitive" practices. In the "recapitulation theory of play"—which Gail Bederman traces to G. Stanley Hall, and that echoed in groups like the Boy Scouts of America or the YMCA—class-privileged white men addressed their imagined enfeeblement by a life removed from the labour of subordinate classes and racialized groups by naturalizing their own political authority.[32] Racial evolutionists explained this situation by referring to the biological process of recapitulation, recently observed in embryo development that appeared to morph from earliest to most recent ancestors. Popular science redefined childhood similarly by suggesting that children relived stages of evolutionary development on their way to adulthood. Bederman marks this as one source of the idiom "boys will be boys": the idea that boys are inclined to act in "wild" ways before, as youths or men, using civilized techniques to control such inclinations. Yet this idiom is explicitly colonialist and racist, given that recapitulation theory only imagined white boys as biologically capable of developing *from* a primitive to a civilized state. Evolutionists framed Indigenous, black, and other racialized male youth, and even young men of the European working-classes as possessing a recalcitrant or permanent primitive nature. In this logic, if they did try to adapt to civilizational standards, they would fail on biological grounds. Yet as recapitulation theory justified racial and economic inequality, it also invited white ruling classes to civilize their youth by letting them pass through each developmental stage and, in so doing, gain the strength that was rightfully theirs at the pinnacle of human biological evolution. The Boy Scouts and YMCA, among other groups, encouraged class-privileged white boys to cultivate survival skills, athletics, and leadership based on domination at appropriate ages, or stages of growth. In frontiersman and "Indian impersonation" practices, and in the popularization of coaching working-class white youth and youth of colour in athletics, propertied white settler men virilized themselves by appearing to absorb aspects of masculine strength from men whom they dominated, while asserting a paternal role as mentor and ruler of civilization.

Thus, just as detours through primitivity extended colonial masculinity's power, they also justified making "savagery" into a resource for white settler men when defining their civilization. Colonial discourses sourced savagery to racialized and Indigenous peoples, but white settler men simultaneously defined, invoked, and performed this violence as expressing their own advancement. In a moment of colonial virilization, *their* "savage" violence, as white men defending civilization, could become a sign of having *achieved* civilization. White settlers could frame any violent response to their rule by racialized or Indigenous peoples as a sign of constitutive savagery and as cause for subordination or elimination. If, as I intimated earlier, sourcing colonial violence to its victims also characterized early modern colonial masculinity, then this appears to have elaborated within modern colonial masculinity by being invested with the veneer of scientific order and truth. Moral questions about colonizing men's negative capacity for violence could be framed under modern colonial conditions as positive expressions of civilizational nature asserting or defending itself.

Colonial masculinity's modern transformations in settler societies also were shaped by new theories of its "sexuality," which by the twentieth century finally received a popular name: *heterosexuality*. The histories of sexuality we receive from Foucault and Jonathan Katz indicate that nineteenth-century sexual sciences documented "abnormal" populations decades before they imagined "normal" sexuality as the property of a group.[33] As well, in reflection of their debt to racial science, sexologists documented "homosexuality" as a deeply racialized status: a perversion linked to primitivity, it was imagined as connected to colonized and racialized people, as well as to an early stage of sexual evolution that the civilized supposedly surpassed. Yet these associations also meant that sexologists perceived Indigenous and racialized people as an archive of abnormal sexualities rather than representatives of a modern "sexual population." Sexual abnormality was first and most consistently isolated as a condition among *white* people, for whom imagined racial advancement made their putative sexual primitivity stand out. Recapitulation theory also implied that (white) homosexuals degenerated into a primitive sexual state resembling racialized or Indigenous sexuality. Once whites asserted homosexuality as a basis for positive identity, they embraced these ties to Indigenous sexual culture as a resource in their defence—a story I tell elsewhere as one basis of queer whiteness and queer settler colonialism.[34]

By way of contrast, as Katz explains, after years of documenting sexual perversions, sexologists perceived heterosexuals as a curiosity: a minority of otherwise-normal people who based their relations not on morality or capital, but on a sexuality that led them to desire an opposite sex. For some such people, rewriting dominant identities as heterosexual promised a modern freedom from religious or economic strictures over partnership, by centring the notion of a natural sexual drive. This concept's popularity in European and white settler societies buttressed their investments in the gender binary, by tying normal manhood and womanhood to a natural, exclusive desire to partner with an opposite sex. Yet it came to be embraced by people already positioned as sexually normal; that is, as Julian Carter explains, heterosexuality was initially restricted to whiteness.[35] As Cathy Cohen explains, heterosexuality has functioned as a tool of racism by enforcing assimilation into cultures of whiteness—a process Mark Rifkin specifically traces through settler-colonial efforts to "straighten out" Indigenous peoples—even as its boundaries remain policed so that black, Indigenous, and other colonized peoples seem incapable of achieving it.[36] Such scholarship indicates that being linked to heterosexuality has seemed to be one of the only ways for racialized and Indigenous communities to gain protection from sexualized and racialized policing by the white settler state. Yet as Jennifer Denetdale and Roderick Ferguson argue, this strategy has not aided the survival of LGBTQ Indigenous people or people of colour who experience displacement from their communities and further exposure to colonial, racist, gendered, and sexual violence.[37] With respect to Indigenous peoples, just as heterosexuality helped white settlers enforce colonial masculinity and whiteness, its adoption by Indigenous communities served as a further tool of colonization by turning them into policing agents for a patriarchal and now *heteronormative* settler society. Modern notions of sexuality, and of heterosexuality in particular, appear to be crucial aids to European colonization.

These histories of heterosexuality elicit both distinctions, and connections among the early modern and modern gender systems that produced colonial masculinity. From their earliest encounters Europeans brought patriarchal social orders and a rejection of gender and sexual practices they deemed to be unnatural. But recent conceptualizations of heterosexuality—two fundamentally opposed sexes, oriented by a natural sexuality towards one another and nothing more—do not explain the specific ways that gender violence took place in earlier colonial eras. My reading of scholarship on early modern colonial relations suggests that, when examining Spanish conquests (for instance) we should never assume that Europeans defending sexual morality imagined themselves as set apart from or as immune to the immorality that they assigned to Indigenous peoples. Beliefs among colonizing men that their manhood could fail—including by falling into unnatural sex—may have informed the violences they inflicted on Indigenous people. Reimagining Indigenous peoples as fantastically perverse also permitted colonizers, through colonial violence, to prove a right to rule that otherwise might have appeared tenuous or embattled, on *gendered* as well as colonial terms. These potential readings would not appear if we imagined that heterosexuality and its constitutive aversion to same-sex desire always informed Europeans and their conquests. More recent discourses on sexuality shifted both the reasons why colonial patriarchal violence transpired and the methods used to assert it.

Given these histories, I can offer a set of speculative conclusions about the scope of colonial masculinity in the Americas (with potential resonances with other colonial relationships, notably the colonization of other Indigenous peoples). This mode of gender arises across a boundary between the civilized and the primitive, and it functions to police that boundary: by defining them as separate, and by dividing and remaking peoples and lands. Its patriarchy and misogyny are directed at women in its own society, as well as at all other women and beings elsewhere, who are collectively feminized: and all to make them common objects of conquest and domination. From these bases, colonial masculinity changed alongside changes in European governance of gender and of imperial and colonial power. Yet throughout, older ideas remained active and could synergize with newer ones to augment its power. While early modern colonial masculinity was enacted and narrated through acts of spectacular destruction—annihilating targets taught obedience to all who remained—in the form of modern governmentality, colonial masculinity spatially reorganized populations, and through policing worked to coercively assimilate Indigenous people into colonial relationships.

When asserting civilized rule over primitive difference, colonial masculinity became defined by a potential failure of its own morality: it was in danger of becoming what it despised in its "others." Colonial acts proved a capacity to conquer and rule, but rule proceeded through repeated violences to indicate that it never lost its capacity. Yet with time, official narratives rewrote the power of colonial masculinity as natural to it, even as it required performance of that power by policing a spatially reordered colonial society. Fear remained that it could regress into base qualities beyond which it should have evolved. But this same idea let it draw on those qualities in defence of civilizational rule, while naming the colonized as their source. Thus, a consistent aspect of colonial masculinity (and of colonial, imperial, and white-supremacist power more broadly) appears to have been a refusal to take responsibility for its own violence. Put differently, colonial masculinity sustains both colonial and heteropatriarchal power by presenting its victims as the cause and proper recipients of its own violations.

Yet exposure to change has not threatened colonial masculinity; change becomes part of its perpetuation. While we may think that by admitting its own malleability, colonial masculinity proves it is not unimpeachable truth—and there is something to that—I approach this more skeptically. I cited cases in which imagining colonial masculinity as open to change motivated and enhanced its acts of violence. Stories of failure were useful to reproducing it; belief in its ability to change fed its efforts to secure its rule. Indeed, the myriad changes that colonial masculinity accommodated now form a resource from which it may draw, to switch among older or newer, farther or nearer modes of gendered colonization when this proves useful. If we want to critique or undermine this form of power, we must do more than say "It changes!"; or, seemingly better, "It's insecure! Even it doesn't think it's in control!" However much they might prove true, neither interrupts the capacity of colonial masculinity to exert power. Yet we can intervene by distinguishing the various power-moves of colonial masculinity, tracing each to its source in space and time, and beginning to anticipate how colonial masculinity might switch among them to suit its needs, as we build a critique that cuts to its roots and envisions its end.

Conclusion

This collection shows that Indigenous people are decolonizing masculinity as part of the broader decolonization of Indigenous peoples and settler societies. How such work proceeds will be determined from within the diverse situations that Indigenous peoples face. In accord, I conclude by suggesting tools that might aid Indigenous and non-Indigenous people in discerning qualities of colonial masculinity. Thinking with the histories I examined, we can ask whether qualities of colonial masculinity are at work in instances such as:

- when masculinity, acting violently, frames its target as the source of its own violence;
- when masculinity acts violently to prove that it is untainted by that to which it is opposed;
- when masculinity focuses on annihilating what it perceives to be a threat;
- when masculinity targets a perceived threat for containment, surveillance, and policing;

- any association of masculinity with sexual violence;
- any institution, relationship, or story that incites or supports these acts.

Many historical and cultural contexts can explain these situations; but in a white-supremacist settler society, each also exists in some relationship to the power of colonial masculinity. The histories I recalled clearly demonstrate that in white settler societies, white people are trained to embody, adapt to, and defend colonial masculinity, just as this gendered power surrounds and constrains the lives of Indigenous and all racialized peoples. Tracing how colonial masculinity gets embedded in whiteness, and in white settler nationalism and imperialism, can offer anti-colonial and anti-heteropatriarchal tactics for challenging white supremacy and white settler and imperial rule. As Hokowhitu argues, colonial education or decisions for surviving racism and colonization may have led Indigenous or racialized people to conform to, adopt or transform colonial masculinity, even to the point of it animating anti-colonial nationalism. In this light, work for decolonization can benefit by identifying where colonial masculinity masquerades as or gets incorporated into Indigenous self-determination struggles. The heteropatriarchal Navajo nationalism challenged by Denetdale, the gendered legacies of Indian status recalled by Lawrence, and "the colonial politics of recognition" mapped by Glen Coulthard can join Hokowhitu's claims to mark the dangers of accepting as "traditional" Indigenous governance any form of male leadership that emulates colonial masculinity.[38] As I understand their work, these scholars challenge associations of Indigenous leadership with state affirmation of patriarchal rule and its role in creating division, containment, policing, or exile. In its place they recall or renew other modes of Indigenous governance that reject heteropatriarchal violence and that are open to leadership by people of all gender identities.

Following the contributions of Two-Spirit/LGBTQ Indigenous people, challenging colonial masculinity also may ask how any form of governance has invested in colonial discourse on sexuality. In the same eras that modern science redefined racial evolution, white supremacy, and Indigenous disappearance, scientists proposed sexuality as a fundamental quality of human life. Yet other stories existed before this category, "sexuality," appeared or became dominant; and they can be retold, or new ones can be invented that leave the boundary-policing power of sexuality behind. Denetdale and Hokowhitu affirm broader anti-racist critical theories of sexuality, by showing how efforts to privilege heterosexuality also trace the ascendancy of colonial masculinity within Indigenous politics. Challenging the role of sexuality discourses in colonial rule may lead to rethinking who can be imagined as providing powerful or honourable leadership. As well, Two-Spirit/LGBTQ Indigenous people for generations have challenged white settler colonialism within U.S. LGBTQ politics, and have acted to protect Indigenous communities amidst the HIV/AIDS pandemic. In such work, Two-Spirit activists announce their efforts to reconnect to their nations and traditions, and to join in a resurgence of Indigenous governance that will jettison colonial modes of gender and sexuality.[39] Given these commitments to the collective liberation of Indigenous peoples, I am not surprised as a scholar or activist when I encounter Two-Spirit activism seeking to decolonize embodiment and desire not only for LGBTQ persons but for all Indigenous people.[40] With such work in mind, if the recent, Western construct "sexuality" makes both heteropatriarchy and colonization appear to be natural, how might setting this logic aside help change stories about the body, desire, relationship, kinship, community responsibility, or governance: and not only for Indigenous people, but also for racialized non-Natives and white settlers living in settler societies?

By tracing how colonial masculinity inheres in the colonial reality of settler societies, my essay suggests that it will end once settler societies and, indeed, all forms of colonialism come to their end. Yet however difficult or unimaginable that change might seem, I do think that colonial masculinity can be brought to its own end, by understanding its emergence and its function as a form of governance. Certainly, challenging colonial masculinity may proceed by having white settlers or other non-Indigenous people join Indigenous people in unlearning colonial habits of mind, redefining identities, and transforming relationships. All of this can begin before any radical change in political, economic, or social modes of governance takes place. Yet even as I understand changing the self to be necessary groundwork for broader change, I argue in closing that, for white settlers, simply focusing on changing the self will not be a sufficient response. The histories that I recalled, and the leading contributions by Indigenous scholars, suggest that cutting to the roots of colonial masculinity requires challenging the structuring logic and practice of all colonial governance, wherever this takes place. To undo colonial masculinity, white settlers must follow Indigenous and racialized people whose movements are challenging the political realities of settler colonialism and all colonial governance by re/imagining and creating decolonized futures.

Notes

1   Taiaiake Alfred and Jeff Corntassel, "Being Indigenous: Resurgences against Contemporary Colonialism," *Government and Opposition* 40, no. 4 (2005): 597–614; Kino-nda-niimi Collective, *The Winter We Danced: Voices from the Past, the Future, and the Idle No More Movement* (Winnipeg: Arbeiter Ring Publishing, 2014).

2   Janice Acoose, *Iskwewak—kah' ki yaw ni wahkomakanak: Neither Indian Princesses nor Easy Squaws* (Toronto: Toronto Women's Press, 1995); Kim Anderson, *A Recognition of Being: Reconstructing Native Womanhood* (Toronto: Second Story Press, 2000); Bonita Lawrence, *"Real" Indians and Others: Mixed-Blood Urban Native People and Indigenous Nationhood* (Lincoln: University of Nebraska Press, 2004); Deborah Miranda, "Extermination of the *Joyas*: Gendercide in Spanish California," *GLQ: A Journal of Lesbian and Gay Studies* 16, nos. 1–2 (2010): 253–84; Pamela Palmater, *Beyond Blood: Rethinking Indigenous Identity* (Saskatoon: Purich Publishing, 2011); Winona Stevenson, "Colonialism and First Nations Women in Canada," in *Scratching the Surface: Canadian Anti-Racist Feminist Thought*, ed. Enakshi Dua and Angela Robinson (Toronto: Women's Press, 1999).

3   Ann Laura Stoler, *Race and the Education of Desire: Foucault's History of Sexuality and the Colonial Order of Things* (Durham, NC: Duke University Press, 1995).

4   Linda Tuhiwai Smith, *Decolonizing Methodologies: Research and Indigenous Peoples*, 2nd ed. (New York: Zed Books, 2012).

5   Alexandra Shepard, *Meanings of Manhood in Early Modern England* (Oxford: Oxford University Press, 2003).

6   Edward Behrend-Martinez, "Manhood and the Neutered Body in Early Modern Spain," *Journal of Social History* 38, no. 4 (2005): 1073.

7   My questions here open to the varied directions in studies of gender in early modern Europe and European colonial projects. See, for instance, Susan Broomhall and Jacqueline Van Gent, eds., *Governing Masculinities in the Early Modern Period: Regulating Selves and Others* (London: Ashgate Publishers, 2013); Joan Cadden, *Meanings of Sex Difference in the Middle Ages: Medicine, Science, and Culture* (Cambridge: Cambridge University Press, 1993); Carla Freccero, *Queer / Early / Modern* (Durham, NC: Duke University Press, 2006); Maria Elena Martinez, *Genealogical Fictions: Limpieza de Sangre, Religion, and Gender in Colonial Mexico* (Stanford, CA: Stanford University Press, 2008); Michael Stolberg, "The Anatomy of Sexual Difference in the Sixteenth and Early Seventeenth Centuries," *Isis* 94 (2003): 274–99.

8   R.W. Connell and James W. Messerschmidt, "Hegemonic Masculinity: Rethinking the Concept," *Gender and Society* 19, no. 6 (2005): 829–59.

9   Michel Foucault, *The History of Sexuality: An Introduction*, vol. 1 (New York: Vintage Books, 1978), 43.

10   Anderson, *A Recognition of Being*, 79, 92; Stevenson, "Colonialism and First Nations Women," 59–61.

11   Miranda, "Extermination of the *Joyas*," 259, 279n7.

12   Daniel Heath Justice, "Notes Towards a Theory of Anomaly," *GLQ* 16, no. 1–2 (2010): 207–42; James Thomas Stevens, "Poetry and Sexuality: Riding Twin Rails," *GLQ* 16, nos. 1–2 (2010): 183–89.

13   See, for example, Qwo-Li Driskill, Chris Finley, Brian Joseph Gilley, and Scott Lauria Morgensen, the introduction to *Queer Indigenous Studies: Critical Interventions in Theory, Politics, and Literature*, ed. Qwo-Li Driskill, Chris Finley, Brian Joseph Gilley, and Scott Lauria Morgensen (Tucson: University of Arizona

Press, 2011), 1–28; Wesley Thomas and Sue-Ellen Jacobs, "'...And We Are Still Here': From *Berdache* to Two-Spirit People," *American Indian Culture and Research Journal* 23, no. 2 (1999): 91–107.

14 Walter Williams, *The Spirit and the Flesh: Sexual Diversity in American Indian Culture*, 2nd ed. (Boston: Beacon Press, 1986).

15 Contrary to the work of Richard Trexler or Ramon Gutiérrez, there is scant evidence across the hemisphere that slavery ever *produced* the gender diversity recognized in Indigenous traditions, while there is ample evidence crossing diverse societies (such as the Navajo and Mapuche) that when genders other than "woman" or "man" were acknowledged, their origin rested in creation stories or in traditional governance, religion, and social life. In this light, "slavery" is more likely a European imaginary of how unmanliness or perversion might be produced. The utility of this imaginary can be traced to the origin of the term "berdache." Ramón Gutierrez, *When Jesus Came, the Corn Mothers Went Away: Marriage, Sexuality, and Power in New Mexico, 1500–1846* (Stanford, CA: Stanford University Press, 1991); Ann Marie Bacigalupo, *Shamans of the Foye Tree: Gender, Power, and Healing Among Chilean Mapuche* (Austin: University of Texas Press, 2000); Wesley Thomas, "Navajo Cultural Constructions of Gender and Sexuality," *Two-Spirit People: Native American Gender Identity, Sexuality, and Spirituality*, ed. S.-E. Jacobs, W. Thomas, and S. Lang (Chicago: University of Illinois Press, 1997), 156–73; Richard Trexler, *Sex and Conquest: Gendered Violence, Political Order, and the European Conquest of the Americas* (Ithaca, NY: Cornell University Press, 1995).

16 Jonathan Goldberg, "Sodomy in the New World: Anthropologies Old and New," *Fear of a Queer Planet: Queer Politics and Social Theory*, ed. Michael Warner (Minneapolis: University of Minnesota Press, 1993). 4, 6–7.

17 See, for example, Antoinette Burton, ed., *Gender, Sexuality and Colonial Modernities* (New York: Routledge, 1999); Ann Stoler, *Carnal Knowledge and Imperial Power: Race and the Intimate in Colonial Rule* (Berkeley: University of California Press, 2002); Ann Stoler, ed., *Haunted by Empire: Geographies of Intimacy in North American History* (Durham, NC: Duke University Press, 2006).

18 Michel Foucault, *Discipline and Punish: The Birth of the Prison* (New York: Vintage, 1977).

19 Foucault, *The History of Sexuality*.

20 See, for example, Hubert Kennedy, "Karl Heinrich Ulrichs: First Theorist of Homosexuality," in *Science and Homosexualities*, ed. V.A. Rosario (New York: Routledge, 1997); Harry Oosterhuis, *Stepchildren of Nature: Krafft-Ebing, Psychiatry, and the Making of Sexual Identity* (Chicago: University of Chicago Press, 2000); James Steakley, "Per Scientiam Ad Justitiam: Magnus Hirschfeld and the Sexual Politics of Innate Homosexuality," *Science and Homosexualities*, ed. V.A. Rosario, (New York: Routledge, 1997).

21 See, for example, Stoler, *Race and the Education of Desire*.

22 Zeb Tortorici, "'Heran Todos Putos': Sodomitical Subcultures and Disordered Desire in Early Colonial Mexico," *Ethnohistory* 54, no. 1 (2007): 35–68.

23 Angela Cavender Wilson, *In the Footsteps of Our Ancestors: The Dakota Commemorative Marches of the Twenty-first Century* (St. Paul, MN: Living Justice Press, 2006).

24 Brenda Child, *Boarding School Seasons: American Indian Families 1900–1940* (Lincoln: University of Nebraska Press, 2000); Celia Haig-Brown, *Resistance and Renewal: Surviving the Indian Residential School* (Toronto: Arsenal Pulp Press, 1988); Margaret Jacobs, *White Mother to a Dark Race: Settler Colonialism, Maternalism, and*

the Removal of Indigenous Children in the American West and Australia, 1880–1940 (Lincoln: University of Nebraska Press, 2009).

25 The Canadian Press, "At Least 3000 Died in Residential Schools, Research Shows." *CBC News* 18 February 2013, http://www.cbc.ca/news/canada/at-least-3-000-died-in-residential-schools-research-shows-1.1310894.

26 Renisa Mawani, *Colonial Proximities: Crossracial Encounters and Juridical Truths in British Columbia, 1871–1921* (Vancouver: UBC Press, 2010); Myra Rutherdale and Katie Pickles, eds., *Contact Zones: Aboriginal and Settler Women in Canada's Colonial Past* (Vancouver: UBC Press, 2011).

27 Sherene H. Razack, "Gendered Racial Violence and Spatialized Justice: The Murder of Pamela George," in *Race, Space and the Law: Unmapping a White Settler Society* (Toronto: Between the Lines Press, 2002), 121–56; Sarah Hunt, "Why Are We Hesitant to Name White Male Violence as a Root Cause of #MMIW?" *Rabble*, 5 September 2014, http://rabble.ca/news/2014/09/why-are-we-hesitant-to-name-white-male-violence-root-cause-mmiw.

28 Martin Cannon, "The Regulation of First Nations Sexuality," *Canadian Journal of Native Studies* 18, no. 1 (1998): 1–18; Lawrence, *"Real" Indians and Others*; Palmater, *Beyond Blood.*

29 See also Taiaiake Alfred, *Peace, Power, Righteousness: An Indigenous Manifesto* (New York: Oxford University Press, 1999).

30 Cathleen Cahill, *Federal Fathers and Mothers: A Social History of the United States Indian Service, 1869–1933* (Chapel Hill: University of North Carolina Press, 2011); Jacobs, *White Mother to a Dark Race.*

31 Gail Bederman, *Manliness and Civilization: A Cultural History of Gender and Race in the United States, 1880–1917* (Chicago: University of Chicago Press, 1994); Julian Carter, *The Heart of Whiteness: Normal Sexuality and Race in America, 1880–1940* (Durham, NC: Duke University Press, 2007).

32 Bederman, *Manliness and Civilization.* See also John Donald Gustav-Wrathall, *Take the Young Stranger by the Hand: Same-Sex Relations and the YMCA* (Chicago: University of Chicago Press, 1998); Roberta Park, "Biological Thought, Athletics and the Formation of 'Man of Character': 1830–1900," in *Manliness and Morality*, ed. J.A. Mangan and J. Walvin (Manchester: Manchester University Press, 1987), 7–34; Benjamin Rader, "The Recapitulation Theory of Play," in *Manliness and Morality*, ed. J.A. Mangan and J. Walvin (Manchester: Manchester University Press, 1987).

33 Jonathan Katz, *The Invention of Heterosexuality* (Boston: Beacon Press, 1995).

34 Scott Lauria Morgensen, *Spaces Between Us: Queer Settler Colonialism and Indigenous Decolonization* (Minneapolis: University of Minnesota Press, 2011).

35 Carter, *The Heart of Whiteness.*

36 Cathy Cohen, "Punks, Bulldaggers and Welfare Queens: The Radical Potential of Queer Politics?" *GLQ* 3, no. 4 (1997): 432–65; Mark Rifkin, *When Did Indians Become Straight?: Kinship, the History of Sexuality, and Native Sovereignty* (New York: Oxford University Press, 2010).

37 Jennifer Denetdale, "Securing Navajo National Boundaries: War, Patriotism, Tradition, and the Diné Marriage Act of 2005," *Wicazo-Sa Review* 24, no. 2 (2009): 131–48; Roderick Ferguson, "Of Our Normative Strivings: African American Studies and the Histories of Sexuality," *Social Text* 23, nos. 3–4 (2005): 84–5.

38 Glen Sean Coulthard, *Red Skin, White Masks: A Critique of the Colonial Politics of Recognition* (Minneapolis: University of Minnesota Press, 2014); Denetdale, "Securing Navajo National Boundaries"; Lawrence, *"Real" Indians and Others.*

See also Brendan Hokowhitu, "Producing Elite Indigenous Masculinities," *Settler Colonial Studies* 2, no. 2 (2012): 23–48.

39 See, for example, Qwo-Li Driskill, et al., introduction to *Queer Indigenous Studies*; Brian Joseph Gilley, *Becoming Two-Spirit: Gay Identity and Social Acceptance in Indian Country* (Lincoln: University of Nebraska Press, 2006); Morgensen, *Spaces between Us*; Thomas and Jacobs, "'...And We Are Still Here.'"

40 See, for example, the work of the Native Youth Sexual Health Network. http://www.nativeyouthsexualhealth.com/ (accessed 15 March 2015).

CHAPTER 3

Complementary Relationships:
A Review of Indigenous Gender Studies

Leah Sneider

In a recent interview between Sam McKegney and Mohawk scholar Taiaiake Alfred, Alfred explains how women were the primary targets of colonization in Iroquoian cultures because they were not only the landowners but also the co-decision makers. Like many Indigenous cultures, the Iroquois rely on a central tenet of social balance. In order to create the imbalance necessary for colonization, Eurowestern society first subjugated Indigenous women to patriarchal rule. When asked if a Eurowestern focus on women as cultural and communal leaders results in Indigenous men feeling emasculated, Alfred explains, "The men are not emasculated because the women tend to be strong and influential and key decision makers...and the power and the self-esteem and all of that comes from the action, and carrying [the decision] out. So there's a balance."[1] With this statement, Alfred hits on a key element to Indigenous gender studies: social balance that derives out of common Indigenous epistemologies. Central to such an understanding of social balance lies an ethic of complementarity between individuals and the community to which they belong, an ethic that is shared amongst many community-centred Indigenous cultures. Furthermore, Alfred distinguishes the importance of the responsibility to act as another aspect and power of complementarity *across* genders.[2] This chapter attempts to trace the conversation in Indigenous gender studies regarding complementarity—as social balance and the responsibility and power to act—as a means to understanding the ways in which Indigenous gender studies as scholarly and practical modes also depend on complementarity. I begin by explaining the relationship between gender and nation and defining complementarity before providing a brief historical outline of gender violence and a review of current scholarship in Indigenous gender studies. I end by emphasizing the importance of complementary relationships as both independent and interdependent within Indigenous gender studies.

Complementarity as a Nation-building Tool

As explored directly in Laura F. Klein and Lillian A. Ackerman's collection *Women and Power in Native North America*,[3] and more indirectly in various other scholars' work to be discussed below, complementarity is both a social as well as a theoretical principle and ethic central to Indigenous studies. Complementarity summarizes concepts of responsibility and relationship in the maintenance of social or communal balance and comprises the overarching ideology behind actions or performances reflecting responsible, reciprocal, and respectful relationships.

In discussing the social systems of traditional Mesoamerican Indigenous societies, Lisa Mary Souza defines complementarity as the "contribution of both male and female as necessary to create the whole, and, thus, accorded both men and women important relationships and responsibilities in the household and the community."[4] She notes that labour roles were not delineated as either "private" or "public," "whereby men exercised a role in the community and women were relegated to the home" and made subject to male dominance as in Eurowestern societies: "Rather, Mesoamerican households were loosely organized social units whose members were obligated to each other and the community through shared responsibility."[5] Betty Bell confirms that in Ojibwe societies, "the 'separate spheres' of men and women...are often experienced as situations and as complementary distributions of power that allow, as well, for gender variance."[6] Kim Anderson agrees that "the division between genders in Native traditions is more reflective of the need for balance, complementarity, and reciprocity."[7] In discussing the Chipewyan, Henry S. Sharp explains, "Women's lives are predicated on different principles than are men's, and each gender thinks in the corresponding terms in the creation of their lives. The gulf between women and men in thought and perception of the culture they share is so great that it is the sharing itself that unites them rather than the content of the culture they share."[8] Complementarity does not enforce strict binaries but, rather, recognizes specifically delineated gender-based communal responsibilities; as long as individuals contribute to the community, their sex in relation to or as classified by their gender is ultimately irrelevant. Sharp provides a key differentiation between sex and gender and corresponding social organization: "Gender is a cultural construct...the biology of sex is not binary. Since the biology of sex is not binary, the existence of binary cultural categories of gender in any particular culture is something that needs to be demonstrated [in anthropological or historical studies] rather than assumed. Gender in Chipewyan culture is a pervasive mode of classification, but it is not a universally applicable classification."[9] In other words, gender is based on the nature of relationships and particular actions that determine social roles within a particular cultural context; it is not essential or predetermined but constantly shifting. Sharp provides an example by pointing to the symbolic connection between women and dogs in traditional Chipewyan culture, showing their relationship and associated values and responsibilities to men, who were dependent upon both women and dogs. It follows that any statement that compared women to dogs, which to non-Chipewyans might appear as degrading, "only serves to emphasize the bond between women and men and to emphasize the dependency of men upon women [and thus] provides a basis for women to exercise power over men."[10] Of course, a contemporary analysis might reveal significant changes in the relationship between women, men, and dogs. However, this example helps to demonstrate gender complementarity as a social system within which the self is known and understood primarily in relation to another and within a specific historical and cultural context.

Finally, recognized as a gender-balancing system, complementarity provides the basis for understanding and representing an Indigenous ideology of the nation as a people. According to Scott Lyons, "A people is a group of human beings united together by history, language, culture, or some combination therein—a community joined in union for a common purpose: the survival and flourishing of the people itself."[11] Complementarity helps ensure a cohesive whole focused on survival and a flourishing community but depends also on self-determination.

Expanding outward from culturally defined gender roles, complementarity helps us to distinguish self-determination from nationalism. Self-determination depends on a complementary relationship between independence and interdependence in order to avoid the potential oppression or subordination of certain individuals or groups of people within a community. In her chapter in *Making Space for Indigenous Feminism*, Emma LaRocque explains that "self-determination must mean that all individuals have a basic right to a certain quality of life, free from the violence of colonialism, racism/sexism and poverty, as well as from the violence of other humans, even if these other humans are one's people, or even one's relations, or are themselves suffering from colonial conditions."[12] However, as understood in Indian Country, self-determination is distinctly different from nationalism, which focuses exclusively on independence rather than interdependence and relationship. As LaRocque further notes, "It is in moments of nationalisms that we are most vulnerable not only to essentialisms/fundamentalisms, but to the disempowerment of women,"[13] and, I would add, anybody perceived as "other." LaRocque classifies a move toward nationalism as exclusive, static, and driven by hierarchies, binaries, and power-based social structures and is, therefore, dangerous because it lacks complementarity as a primary principle. However, an Indigenous feminist understanding of self-determination in connection to *nation building* is more inclusive, fluid, and gender balanced as a process of continual negotiation and decolonization focused on the people as a whole. Decolonization is an attempt at reclaiming epistemologies and social structures based in complementarity; decolonization first requires sovereignty.

Both the word and concept of sovereignty continues to develop and change in Indigenous studies (and in sometimes contentious ways), but generally refers to a people's right to self-govern as an independent entity. To do so, the people must also decolonize and maintain self-determination, both of which depend on the will of the people to establish themselves as a nation in culturally appropriate ways and as demonstrated through the people's stories and histories. Indigenous studies scholarship has explored many ways in which sovereignty is acquired and expressed, but only recently has Indigenous gender studies, Indigenous feminism in particular, attempted to explore the relationship between gender and sovereignty and nation building more fully while also attending to the importance of complementarity in the process of decolonization.

Recent Indigenous feminist and literary scholars have given voice to Indigenous histories and to women's stories, in particular. Stories that document the damage done by the imposition of patriarchy can inform Indigenous communities as they strive to rebuild sovereign nations built on principles of complementarity and balance. For instance, Andrea Smith's account of Indigenous women's experience with gender violence reveals the varied forms and consequences related with sexual assault, forced sterilization, and other institutionalized forms of race-based gender violence.[14] Bell explains that "'the story' of Native women and their relation to power and authority is often told, or lived, between conflicting 'traditions': on the one hand, the precolonial or 'traditional' status of women; on the other, the postcolonial advance of patriarchy into tribal nations."[15] Restoring Indigenous women's identities and traditional roles as caregivers and storytellers thus requires them to decolonize themselves and combat racist and sexist ideologies in order to fully realize national self-determination and sovereignty. Indigenous women work to maintain complementary relationships between themselves individually, as a group, and to their particular nations by maintaining stories and history as a method for decolonization. To participate in the efforts to prevent loss, Indigenous men also have to tend to their cultural roles and social complementarity in the wake of the introduction and uptake of patriarchy, as will be further discussed below.

Beyond its role in social organization and nation building, complementarity also encompasses the responsibility of sharing cultural knowledge and ideologies both within and between societies and nations. Rauna Kuokkanen discusses "hospitality" as a form of complementarity. She writes, "Hospitality is a continuous never-ending process of negotiation—a productive crisis in which we work continuously toward a new way of thinking and ultimately a new relationship in which [a cultural or ethnic group is] compelled to recognize and accept its responsibility toward the other."[16] Complementarity is the rhetorical hospitality within and between cultures and nations and the knowledge necessary to advance critical thinking and action as a social venture. The focus of Indigenous feminism has generally remained on Indigenous women, but it relies upon stories and histories by and about Indigenous men as complementary participants in the history of colonialism and patriarchy. Indigenous feminism and Indigenous masculinity studies thus share both purpose and theoretical approach and are distinct in their intended primary focus (men *or* women) only. Indigenous men and women maintain hospitality by sharing their experiences and traditional and contemporary knowledge with each other. Through these shared stories and histories and under the larger umbrella of Indigenous gender studies, Indigenous feminism and Indigenous masculinity studies can sustain a complementary relationship in order to decolonize together. Such decolonization requires an understanding of ongoing colonial gender violence.

Gender and Gender Violence across Cultures

An examination of the physical embodiments, performances, and applications or uses of gender provides understanding of the main differences between Eurowestern and historical Indigenous constructions. Eurowestern ideologies seek to keep nature and human, man and woman separate and easily categorized, while most Indigenous ideologies seek to balance a more nuanced relationship or complementarity between genders that serves the changing needs of communities and society in general. Bell explains that, "even though gender is central to the organization of Indigenous nations as distinct social and cultural systems, it is often not closely related to power or biology.... There is, however, no universal or necessary correlation between male and female descent and gendered positions of power and authority. Nor are gender and sex defined, necessarily, as culturally equivalent categories."[17] In other words, most historical Indigenous societies did not recognize the concept of gender as central to systems based on inequitable power relationships.

Instead of strict gender binaries, historical Indigenous societies conceived of what Anderson comes to understand is a "recognition of being," an understanding of one's sense of selfhood. Based on a conversation with Elder Shawani Campbell Star, Anderson explains, "Native womanhood is not about simply playing certain roles, or adopting a pre-set identity; rather that it is an ongoing exercise that involves mental, physical, spiritual, and emotional elements of our being."[18] From this perspective, Indigenous identity has little to nothing to do with biological sex or associated roles based on systems of power but rather a holistic understanding of presence or being in the world, which is built into ceremonies where men, women, and Two-Spirit people partake in particular roles and activities as discussed further in Brendan Hokowhitu's chapter in this volume. Therefore, to apply a Eurowestern understanding of gender to historical Indigenous identities is itself problematic and causes cultural, ideological, and methodological conflict.[19] Yet, with the drastic changes in contemporary Indigenous societies, Indigenous gender studies is tasked with exploring how Eurowestern ideologies have negatively affected Indigenous understandings of gender roles and power.

Gender relations are also key to understanding and developing a national identity. However, since concepts of gender are directly related to social systems, they can be a primary site of cultural conflict, contestation, and violence.[20] In her exploration of gender violence, Sally Engle Merry explains, "the conditions which breed gender violence include racism and inequality, conquest, occupation, colonialism, warfare and civil conflict, economic disruptions and poverty."[21] She calls such violence structural because it is "usually concealed within the hegemony of ordinariness, hidden in the mundane details of everyday life" and therefore "invisible and normalized" by dominant society.[22] She explains that violence itself is a performance of gender. In Eurowestern cultures, the perpetrator of violence performs masculinity while the victim performs femininity, which is taken up in Scott Morgensen's chapter in this volume.

Colonial/patriarchal systems rely on a gender/sex distinction to create a hierarchy where men rule and maintain dominance over women and as a justification for the conquest of pre-determined "weaker" and thus feminine "others." In her article "American Studies without America: Native Feminisms and the Nation-State," Andrea Smith writes that colonists forcefully implanted patriarchy as a means of conquest and domination. She explains, "Patriarchy in turn rests on a binary gender system; hence, it is not a coincidence that colonizers also targeted Indigenous peoples who did not fit within this binary model."[23] Upon contact, Indians in U.S. literary and national discourse were aligned with women as the mysterious "other." As Gerardine Meaney writes, "A history of colonization is a history of feminization. Colonial powers identify their subject people as passive, in need of guidance, incapable of self-government, romantic, passionate, unruly, barbarous—all of those things for which the Irish and women have been traditionally praised and scorned."[24] Morgensen explains that colonial masculinity developed in relationship to Indigeneity and relied on feminizing Indigenous men and women collectively to maintain their own sense of sexual morality but also to justify conquest.[25] From a non-Indigenous perspective, Nira Yuval-Davis explains that, in colonial ideology, "feminization and disempowerment are being equated."[26] Imagining the "Indian" as a simulation of what America most feared or misunderstood justified Eurowestern settlers' need to conquer Natives and either "protect" them from themselves or exterminate them, or at least their "savage" ways, from "civilized" cultures, which were defined by Eurowestern settlers' own sense of superior morality.

Patriarchy paired with race-based imperialism and colonization resulted in drastic changes in how Indigenous men in particular were perceived and treated. In *Savagism and Civilization*, Roy Harvey Pearce writes that "American Indians were everywhere found to be, simply enough, men who were not men," where "men" indicated higher (white) male beings who reigned over culture and society.[27] In most Indigenous cultures, Indigenous men did not "reign" in this sense. In attempting to grasp and conquer such an unknown "other," American settlers constructed the Indian as "a symbol for all that over which civilization must triumph as they expand into the western frontier. The Indian who was important to Americans setting out to make their new society was not the person but the type, not the tribesman but the savage, not the individual but the symbol."[28] This mythological or simulated Indian becomes the symbol of everything that Eurowestern Americans strove to prevail over, particularly their own inherent weaknesses, in the creation of a national character.

After being stripped of their sovereign national identities during advanced colonization, Indigenous men and women were expected to forsake their previous roles in their communities and adhere to the Western gender binary. Indigenous men were forced to become farmers, which in many Indigenous cultures made them "something other than a man" and more akin to women.[29] They were also expected to make decisions for the sake of the community as individuals rather than as members of a tribal council, a particular clan, or the community at large. Although most Indigenous cultures were more open to gender differences, their social structures and gender roles drastically changed in compliance to a more limited cultural ideology. Jennifer Gillan explains the holistic effects or soul wound resulting from the period of allotment as a rejection of a communal way of life in favour of "an individual's accumulation of possessions and his subsequent increase in social status."[30] She writes, "What arose in place of communal values was a culture of compensation that promised fulfillment through pursuit of private property, particularly consumer goods."[31] Such drastic social changes led to considerable unrest and division within both individuals and tribal communities. Indigenous men in particular suffered because the promised sense of power acquired through assimilation was entirely illusory and therefore an ideological trap; although pressured to do so, Indigenous men could never ascend to the same heights or social position as Eurowestern men because of Eurowestern perceptions of racial and cultural differences.

In her text *Conquest: Sexual Violence and American Indian Genocide*, Andrea Smith reveals the patriarchal and colonial roots of sexual violence against Indigenous women. She posits that sexual violence against women was and still is a primary tool of genocide. Smith cites several forms of sexual and gender violence against women, including forced sterilization, rape, environmental racism, and boarding-school policies. She asserts that sexual and gender violence includes any strategy that seeks to "not only destroy peoples, but to destroy their sense of being a people."[32] However, Smith only touches on the strategies and effects of sexual and gender violence against Indigenous men. Indeed, a historical and literary record of sexual or gender violence on Indigenous men reveals an entirely different story, but one that is intertwined with Indigenous women's stories, as the rest of this volume will reveal. As partners, kin, and friends, Indigenous men and women share each act of violence and must together deal with the individual and collective repercussions. Therefore, in order to understand the effects of sexual and gender violence on Indigenous communities, all the threads of this much larger story must be traced. Focusing our attention on women alone or even placing them in the centre does not effectively address ideological issues informing gender structures as a whole; rather, doing so perpetuates hierarchical dominance and oppression. Instead, Indigenous feminism and Indigenous masculinity studies must maintain a complementary relationship to fully understand colonial impacts on Indigenous communities and work together to decolonize.

Gender violence against Indigenous men is most fully explored in Ty P. Kāwika Tengan's *Native Men Remade: Gender and Nation in Contemporary Hawai'i*, which presents detailed ethnographic work on Hawaiian Indigenous men responding to colonial gender violence. Tengan asserts, "We need to see gendered social actors as complexly situated, located, and positioned in multiple settings and historical contexts."[33] Indigenous men have suffered similar types of gender-related oppression as Indigenous women. Regarding Indigenous Hawaiian men, Tengan explains, they "in general have lost their place and role in society. Often they linked this to the loss of the old ways— the religious formations, political systems, cultural practices, and relationships to land that our ancestors knew. With the arrival of colonialism, Christianity, and modernization, all of these configurations of knowledge and power were radically transformed."[34] Indigenous men, like all women under the white male gaze, become subject to a projected patriarchal hegemonic authority that seeks to reinforce both a gender- and race-informed hierarchy that asserts white male dominance.[35]

Cultural conflict drastically and negatively affects Indigenous males who seek to befriend their Eurowestern brothers in that they often assimilate perceptions of masculinity as well as Indigeneity that are damaging not only to themselves but also to all of those in relationship with them. Patriarchal hegemony proves to be a formidable opponent, with the potential for deeply wounding Indigenous men and Indigenous societies as a whole. The varied forms of gender violence as a method of colonization/genocide begins on an ideological level and becomes a performance that results in social division and conflict as explored by Morgensen, Hokowhitu, and others in this volume and elsewhere, as discussed below. Paula Gunn Allen states that such ideological impositions of "white-think" or a "system of mental processes…works for the survival and expansion of white culture, [but] it also results in the spiritual and psychic murder of those who exist outside its protection."[36] The cyclical effects of such historical gender violence include substance abuse, violence, and criminal activity often advanced by negative scholarly and literary depictions or representations of Indigenous men that support colonial efforts.[37] Furthermore, Indigenous men in governing positions of power who have assimilated to colonial systems and their corresponding gender violence further such efforts through, as Tengan explains, "their patriarchal and misogynistic brand of activism and for their political collaborations in the power structures of the colonial state."[38] Navajo historian Jennifer Nez Denetdale offers an example of this in her article "Chairmen, Presidents, and Princesses: The Navajo Nation, Gender, and the Politics of Tradition." She questions Navajo leaders' understanding of tradition and governance, noting that they are overly influenced by colonial models that limit women's access and participation. Denetdale claims that Navajo men have assimilated colonial ideologies and then claim them to be traditional.[39] The work of Indigenous scholars such as Tengan, Denetdale, and Hokowhitu demonstrate how Indigenous men seemingly unknowingly perpetuate oppression of themselves and their people in their uptake of colonial masculinities.[40]

In his discussion of Indigenous masculinity, Sam McKegney focuses on the drastic effect that stereotypes have on Indigenous men's self-perceptions. He distinguishes three particularly harmful stereotypes that demonstrate the ongoing degeneration of the Indigenous male role: the noble savage, the bloodthirsty warrior, and the drunken absentee. He explains that Indigenous men appropriate these simulations because they "offer relief from often-untenable social conditions as well as a sense of masculine agency that colonization has rendered difficult for many Indigenous men to attain in other ways [but are] problematic because they seek power through dominance and violence."[41] In other words, these simulations become tools of settler colonialism as they influence Indigenous men to continue the colonization of their own tribes.

In order to reveal the effects of colonization on Indigenous men, traditional knowledge must be disentangled from colonial ideologies. Lisa Kahaleole Hall writes, "Because colonization relies on forced forgetting and erasure, the need to bring the past forward into our consciousness is ongoing. Reconstructing tradition and memory is a vital element of Indigenous survival, and there is nothing simple or one-dimensional about the process of reconstruction."[42] Tengan has also written about this process, stating:

> The remaking of the [indigenous] self and society proceeds through the reconnection with and retelling of [story, history]—legends, histories, personal stories, and narrative accounts of events. The [men's eating house, gathering place] does this by contesting the dominant narratives of neocolonialism, modernity, and global capitalism; remembering lahui (collectivity as a people/nation) through the commemoration and reliving of

> indigenous histories; carrying out ritual practices that (re)utilize,
> (re)consecrate, and (re)create sacred sites and spaces;...rewriting
> and reforming the body as site of personal and collective strength;
> and reforming subjectivities through the telling and hearing of
> life stories.[43]

Similarly, Anderson proposes a process toward self-definition in response to
colonization that involves four steps: "resisting negative definitions of being;
reclaiming Aboriginal tradition; constructing a positive identity by translat-
ing tradition into the contemporary context; and acting on that identity in a
way that nourishes the overall well-being of our communities."[44] She clarifies,
"What is distinctly Aboriginal is the way in which past, present and future are
understood to be inextricably connected."[45] These steps toward self-definition
and understanding of being are therefore useful not just for the individual,
male and female, but also for the community as a whole. McKegney confirms
that "healing cannot take place in isolation but rather must occur with the
context of restoring balance to the broader community."[46] In other words,
healing relies on complementary relationships between individuals, the
community, and culture(s).

This understanding of gender, cross-cultural conflict, and the corresponding soul wound provides a more complete understanding of this historical
conflict and better informs those difficulties that Indigenous communities
currently face. Adaptation to such dire changes drastically affected the tribe
on the cultural/social level and not always to the direct benefit of the individual or culture/society itself. However, Indigenous gender studies helps to
trace the gender conflict and consequences along with adaptations to change,
both failed and successful. It creates an awareness of the pattern of change,
sets precedents, and helps to determine how change and potential ideological traps are or can be handled and healed in the present and the future. The
passing down of stories and lessons is the best way to keep traditions alive
and also to offer wisdom that may prove useful when adapted for changing
situations. Therefore, Indigenous gender studies offers theoretical and social
principles that can be applied within Indigenous studies more generally and
for the mutual benefit of both individuals and communities.

Decolonization through Complementary Relationships

Indigenous gender studies offers an analytical method to decolonize ideological oppression with a focus on concepts of gender, race, and national identity.
As Hall writes, "Indigenous feminism grapples with the ways patriarchal

colonialism has been internalized within Indigenous communities as well as with analyzing the sexual and gendered nature of the process of colonization."[47] As conceived by Indigenous feminism, Indigenous women preserve social balance by helping to renew *both* male *and* female leadership roles in the community as a method of decolonization. Therefore, an Indigenous feminist approach isn't limited to constructions of gender but more specifically addresses the colonial ideologies that inform constructions of gender, race, class, nationality, physical ability, and sexuality. However, Indigenous feminism relies on Indigenous masculinity studies to determine Indigenous men's complementary contributions to personal and communal decolonization.

Like Indigenous feminism, Indigenous masculinity studies must explore how race and gender ideologies are intimately and equally connected to national identity. In her article "Race, Tribal Nation, and Gender: A Native Feminist Approach to Belonging," Renya K. Ramirez emphasizes that "race, tribal nation, and gender should be non-hierarchically linked as categories of analysis in order to understand the breadth of our oppression as well as the full potential of our liberation in the hope that one day we can belong as full members of our homes, communities, and tribal nations."[48] Race and gender ideologies and corresponding hierarchical dominance helped fuel and perpetuate the stripping of Indigenous national sovereignty in paternalistic U.S. policies that conceived of Indigenous nations as inferior and in need of protection. For instance, perceiving tribal societies as uncivilized and inferior, the reservation system intended to make tribes more "civilized" partly by stripping Indigenous men of their social roles as warriors and making them become farmers or otherwise earn an income as head of household within a nuclear family. As explored in this volume and elsewhere, Indigenous masculinity studies scholars might ask: What have been the long-term effects of colonial ideologies on Indigenous men and masculinities?[49]

Discussions of sexual and gender violence against Indigenous peoples need to include an analysis of how this has affected Native men, because they too have experienced gender oppression and violence as a result of colonization. Ramirez agrees that "both Indigenous women and men should develop a Native feminist consciousness based on the assumption that struggles for social autonomy will no longer include the denial of Native women's gendered concerns and rights."[50] However, Indigenous men's gendered concerns and rights have also changed over time, most specifically in their roles and relationships within and outside of the community. As mentioned above, Indigenous men have been forced into acquiescing to a foreign political and ideological system that gives them ultimate power as head of household and community leaders and thus perpetuates patriarchal dominance-based sexism and gender violence within their communities. Violence against Indigenous men originates in such force and is perpetuated by their compliant complicity with ongoing oppression of their communities. In response to such dangerous complicity with colonial ideologies, Anderson explains that, "when we begin to reclaim our ways, we must question how these traditions are framed, and whether they are empowering to us."[51] Indigenous feminism offers a critical consciousness toward settler colonialism and its harmful ideologies that might also be usefully applied in Indigenous masculinity studies.

A combined Indigenous feminism and Indigenous masculinity studies approach offers a critical lens through which we can assess contemporary practices to identify and heal Indigenous communities from colonial influences, even those disguised as "tradition." As Denetdale and Mishuana Goeman claim in their introduction to a special issue of *Wicazo Sa Review* dedicated to Indigenous feminisms, "The structures of our lives as Native women and men are shaped by racism, sexism, and discrimination. We strive to recover our former selves and push toward creating better future selves by reclaiming Native values, which have seen us through multiple traumas, including land disposition and the loss of our freedoms."[52] Rather than attempting to revive "traditions" that have been mostly lost through colonization and are, therefore, somewhat contentious in both definition and practice, Indigenous masculinity studies, like Indigenous feminism, could focus instead on a set of values that have held strong and continue to guide and define Indigenous cultures in the face of ongoing colonization and neo-colonization. As one of these values, complementarity seeks to balance individual, cultural, and social needs through responsible, respectful, and reciprocal relationships.

At the centre of Indigenous gender studies are the effects that settler colonialism has had on both individuals and communities as a whole and the need to recover and/or transform tribe or culture-specific gender ideologies, knowledge, and practices. That Indigenous masculinity studies is complementary to Indigenous feminism has gathered steam only somewhat recently. It is important to note that Indigenous masculinity studies, like Indigenous feminism, is not singular (and therefore anti-essentialist) but encompasses various cultural, historical, and individual perspectives regarding a particular social role. As early as 1993, literary scholars began exploring the colonial influence on Indigenous men as represented in literature with the publication of Timothy Sweet's article "Masculinity and Self-Performance in *The Life of Black Hawk*." Sweet responds to Paula Gunn Allen's assertion that women's roles need recovery by adding men's roles to the discussion, particularly the role and performance of the warrior.[53] But only in the past eight years have other scholars more fully taken up global Indigenous masculinities, including previously discussed scholars Tengan and McKegney. In addition, Hokowhitu offers ongoing analysis of Māori masculinity and the ways in which colonial ideologies and stereotypes have negatively affected contemporary Māori men. Thus, he understands Indigenous masculinity as a "historical construction."[54] In his article, he concludes, "It is through Māori men's own culture [and education] that they will find what it truly means to be a Māori man."[55] However, as Indigenous feminist scholars have pointed out, sometimes these cultural practices need to adapt to contemporary needs and challenges. Lloyd L. Lee's most recently published *Diné Masculinities: Conceptualizations and Reflections*[56] offers Diné perspectives on masculinities and agrees that contemporary adaptations of culture-specific roles are necessary for community and cultural sustainability.

Hokowhitu's most recent work, "Producing Elite Indigenous Masculinities," explores the means by which Indigenous masculinities are discursively constructed and reified as subjects within a Foucauldian sense of colonial biopower and thus inform postcolonial tribal hierarchies. He writes: "I would argue that the postcolonial complex, through a force-field of discursive strategies, produces forms of indigeneity complicit with its agenda, which indeed are produced by the mere fact that they are more recognisable to the postcolonial state and are very much 'inside' it and complicit with postcolonial liberalization."[57] Hokowhitu focuses on the geneology of Indigenous heteropatriarchal masculinity to uncover the means by which Indigenous women and alternative masculinities are undermined and disempowered in Māori culture. In response, he proposes that "notions of self-critique and responsibility underpin these new cultural spaces, together with a will to investigate what is being included and thus excluded under the name of 'indigeneity.'"[58] He tasks Indigenous masculinity studies with assisting Indigenous nations and individuals to come to a more broadly understood and liberating recognition of being and self-definition that is neither stagnant or disempowering in any way. Thus, like Anderson and other Indigenous feminist scholars, Hokowhitu emphasizes a need for complementarity even in methodological approaches that are based within "self-critical awareness" and useful to Indigenous societies as a whole.[59]

Because self-determination, nation building, and decolonization require such awareness and complementarity, it is important to include Two-Spirit theories in the conversation. This is necessary in order to effectively include all varying perspectives regarding gender and the corresponding colonial impacts. Indigenous gender studies would thus benefit by addressing Two-Spirit experiences and theories, which identify the varying forms of gender and sexuality specifically as well as the cultural understanding and practice of relationships more generally. Morgensen explains that Two-Spirit identities encompass cultural practices, "which through kinship, economics, social life, or religion linked all Native people in relationship."[60] Sylvia Maracle, a Mohawk Two Spirit and executive director of the Ontario Federation of Indigenous Friendship Centres (OFIFC), explains that Two-Spirited people's spiritual orientations and closer proximity to a higher power is based on their unique dual composition of water and fire elements, which makes them not only more balanced but also more connected to others in the community whose orientations are *either* water *or* fire (female or male).[61] Of particular importance is the emphasis on personal and communal balance inherent to complementary relationships.

Combining all Indigenous gender-based theories allows for the full realization of decolonization by destabilizing static or binary gender ideologies and practices. In his article "Doubleweaving Two-Spirit Critiques: Building Alliances between Native and Queer Studies," Qwo-Li Driskill defines decolonization as an "ongoing, radical resistance against colonialism that includes struggles for land redress, self-determination, healing historical trauma, cultural continuance, and reconciliation" rather than a process with a definitive end point.[62] Although the primary focus for these various approaches to gender might differ, the purpose and process remain the same: individual, communal, cultural, and societal decolonization through the development of critical consciousness and activism. The goal, therefore, is to engage a decolonial process/radical resistance that simultaneously sustains complementary relationships. Finally, such a complementary Indigenous gender studies approach embraces differences and various voices as valuable to this process, regardless of whether a set of contemporary identities are considered "traditional" or not.

This chapter has attempted to outline the conversation regarding Indigenous gender studies broadly in order to inform the chapters and studies that follow. Furthermore, this outline focuses on a particular principle or approach to not only understanding these studies but also to employing them through the creation and maintenance of complementary relationships within and between varying Indigenous gender studies.

Notes

1   Sam McKegney, interview with Taiaiake Alfred, "Indigenous Masculinity and Warriorism," 11 February 2011, http://taiaiake.posterous.com/81790039. Also included in Sam McKegney, *Masculindians: Conversations about Indigenous Manhood* (Winnipeg: University of Manitoba Press, 2014), 76–86.

2   Alfred's full statement here could be perceived as sexist in that it assigns the power of action to men only, at least in a historical sense. The key difference here is that the responsibility to act in contemporary times cannot be limited to just the men, although this may have been true at some point in history for these and other groups.

3   Laura F. Klein and Lillian A. Ackerman, eds., *Women and Power in Native North America* (Norman: University of Oklahoma Press, 1995).

4   Lisa Mary Souza, "Women and Crime in Colonial Oaxaca: Evidence of Complementary Gender Roles in Mixtec and Zapotec Societies," in *Indian Women of Early Mexico*, ed. Susan Schroeder, Stephanie Wood, and Robert Haskett (Norman: University of Oklahoma Press, 1997), 200–1.

5   Ibid., 201.

6   Betty Bell, "Gender in Native America," in *A Companion to American Indian History*, ed. Phillip J. Deloria and Neal Salisbury (Malden, MA: Blackwell, 2002), 308.

7   Kim Anderson, *A Recognition of Being: Reconstructing Native Womanhood* (Toronto: Sumach/Canadian Scholars' Press, 2000), 50.

8   Henry S. Sharp, "Women and Men among the Chipewyan," in *Women and Power in Native North America*, ed. Laura F. Klein and Lillian A. Ackerman (Norman: University of Oklahoma Press, 1995), 73.

9   Ibid., 69.

10 Ibid., 71.

11 Scott Lyons, "Rhetorical Sovereignty: What do American Indians Want from Writing?" *College Composition and Communication* 51, no. 3 (2000): 454.

12 Emma LaRocque, "Métis and Feminist: Ethical Reflections on Feminism, Human Rights and Decolonization," in *Making Space for Indigenous Feminism*, ed. Joyce Green (New York: Zed Books, 2007), 61–2. See also *Indigenous Women and Feminism: Politics, Activism, Culture*, ed. Cheryl Suzack, Shari M. Huhndorf, Jeanne Perreault, and Jean Barman (Vancouver: UBC Press, 2011).

13 LaRocque, "Métis and Feminist," 68.

14 Andrea Smith, *Conquest: Sexual Violence and American Indian Genocide* (Cambridge, MA: South End Press, 2005).

15 Bell, "Gender in Native America," 307.

16 Rauna Kuokkanen, "Toward a New Relation of Hospitality in the Academy," *American Indian Quarterly* 27, no. 1–2 (2003): 267.

17 Bell, "Gender in Native America," 308.

18 Anderson, *A Recognition of Being*, 9.

19 Peter Bayers, "William Apess's Manhood and Native Resistance in Jacksonian America," *MELUS* 31, no. 1 (2006): 123–46.

20 Nira Yuval-Davis, *Gender and Nation* (Thousand Oaks, CA: SAGE Publications, 1997), 39.

21 Sally Engle Merry, *Gender Violence: A Cultural Perspective* (Malden, MA: Wiley-Blackwell Publishers, 2009), 2.

22 Ibid., 5.

23 Andrea Smith, "American Studies without America: Native Feminisms and the Nation-State," *American Quarterly* 60, no. 2 (2008): 312.

24 Gerardine Meaney, *(Un)like Subjects: Women, Theory, Fiction* (New York: Routledge, 1993), 233.

25 See Morgensen's chapter in this volume.

26 Yuval-Davis, *Gender and Nation*, 53.

27 Roy Harvey Pearce, *Savagism and Civilization: A Study of the Indian and the American Mind* (Baltimore: Johns Hopkins University Press, 1971), 6.

28 Ibid., 73.

29 Theda Perdue, "Writing the Ethnohistory of Native Women," in *Rethinking American Indian History*, ed. Donald L. Fixico (Albuquerque: University of New Mexico Press, 1997), 74.

30 Jennifer Gillan, "The Hazards of Osage Fortunes: Gender and the Rhetoric of Compensation in Federal Policy and American Indian Fiction," *Arizona Quarterly* 54, no. 3 (1998): 2.

31 Ibid.

32 Smith, *Conquest*, 3.

33 Ty P. Kāwika Tengan, *Native Men Remade: Gender and Nation in Contemporary Hawai'i* (Durham, NC: Duke University Press, 2008), 15.

34 Ibid., 5–6.

35 Scott Morgensen's chapter in this volume offers an insightful historical understanding of what he terms "colonial masculinity" affecting Indigenous men and societies in general.

36 Paula Gunn Allen, "'Indians,' Solipsisms, and Archetypal Holocausts," in *Genocide of the Mind: New Native American Writing*, ed. MariJo Moore (New York: Nations Books, 2003), 307.

37 Tengan, *Native Men Remade*, 9, 10.

38 Ibid., 10.

39 Jennifer Nez Denetdale, "Chairmen, Presidents, and Princesses: The Navajo Nation, Gender, and the Politics of Tradition," *Wicazo Sa Review* 21, no. 1 (2006): 9–28.

40 See Brendan Hokowhitu, "Producing Elite Indigenous Masculinities," *settler colonial studies* 2, no. 2 (2012): 45.

41 Sam McKegney, "Warriors, Healers, Lovers, and Leaders: Colonial Impositions on Indigenous Male Roles and Responsibilities," in *Canadian Perspectives on Men and Masculinities: An Interdisciplinary Reader*, ed. Jason A. Laker (Toronto: Oxford University Press, 2011), 258.

42 Lisa Kahaleole Hall, "Strategies of Erasure: U.S. Colonialism and Native Hawaiian Feminism," *American Quarterly* 60, no. 2 (2008): 279.

43 Tengan, *Native Men Remade*, 14–15.

44 Anderson, *A Recognition of Being*, 15.

45 Ibid.

46 McKegney, "Warriors, Healers, Lovers, and Leaders," 261.

47 Hall, "Strategies of Erasure," 278.

48 Renya K. Ramirez, "Race, Tribal Nation, and Gender: A Native Feminist Approach to Belonging," *Meridians* 7, no. 2 (2007): 22.

49 See Kim Anderson, Robert Alexander Innes, and John Swift, "Indigenous Masculinities: Carrying the Bones of Our Ancestors," in *Canadian Men and Masculinities: Historical and Contemporary Perspectives*, ed. Christopher Greig and Wayne Martino (Toronto: Canadian Scholars' Press, 2012).

50 Ibid., 22.

51 Anderson, *A Recognition of Being*, 36.

52 Mishuana Goeman and Jennifer Denetdale, "Native Feminisms: Legacies, Interventions, and Indigenous Sovereignties," *Wicazo Sa Review* 24, no. 2 (2009): 9–10.

53 Timothy Sweet, "Masculinity and Self-Performance in the *Life of Black Hawk*," *American Literature* 65, no. 3 (1993): 475–99.

54 Brendan Hokowhitu, "Tackling Māori Masculinity: A Colonial Genealogy of Savagery and Sport," *The Contemporary Pacific* 16, no. 2 (2004): 264.

55 Ibid., 277.

56 Lloyd L. Lee, *Diné Masculinities: Conceptualizations and Reflections* (North Charleston, SC: Createspace Independent Publishing Platform, 2013).

57 Hokowhitu, "Producing Elite Indigenous Masculinities," 45.

58 Ibid.

59 Ibid., 44.

60 Scott Lauria Morgensen, "Unsettling Queer Politics: What Can Non-Natives Learn from Two-Spirit Organizing?" in *Queer Indigenous Studies: Critical Interventions in Theory, Politics, and Literature*, ed. Qwo-Li Driskill, Chris Finley, Brian Joseph Gilley, and Scott Lauria Morgensen (Phoenix: University of Arizona Press, 2011), 135.

61 This is a much-simplified version of my understanding based on a conversation at the 2012 NAISA conference. I express my deepest thanks to Sylvia for explaining this to me.

62 Qwo-Li Driskill, "Doubleweaving Two-Spirit Critiques: Building Alliances between Native and Queer Studies," *GLQ: A Journal of Lesbian and Gay Studies* 16, no. 1–2 (2010): 69.

CHAPTER 4

Taxonomies of Indigeneity: Indigenous Heterosexual Patriarchal Masculinity

Brendan Hokowhitu

According to Foucault, the "essential problem of classical thought lay in the relations between name and order: how to discover a nomenclature that would be a taxonomy."[1] In relation to our task here, how have Indigenous masculinities been coded to produce truth and meaning, especially in relation to sexuality? Or, in other words, what are Indigenous masculinities for, and do they function as strategies of both colonization and decolonization?

First, what do I mean when I say "masculinity"? It probably goes without saying that my view of masculinity is anti-essentialist and that masculinity cannot be treated ahistorically, aculturally, or apolitically. More importantly, fundamental to outlining my approach to the analysis of Indigenous masculinity is the Nietzschean-based question, Why is masculinity necessary? That is, what does Indigenous masculinity enable in the colonial context? Like Homi Bhabha, I am interested in shifting "the question of identity from the ontological and epistemological imperative—*What is identity?*—to face the ethical and political prerogative—*What are identities for?*—or even to present the pragmatist alternative—*What can identities do?*"[2]

Such a shift in inquiry intuitively directs us away from the belief in a true, deep, and essential masculine core. It leads us to separate masculinity and sexuality from men and to see them simply as qualities or sets of attributes applicable to men or women. Simone de Beauvoir's famous statement "One is not born, but rather becomes, a woman"[3] is equally applicable to understanding masculinity and masculine sexuality. De Beauvoir's question problematizes the relationship between biological sex and gender, suggesting that women are not born with a gender, gender is constructed, and, similarly, the biological sexual binary does not equate with heterosexuality. Implicit within this analysis, then, is the sense that masculinity and sexuality do not exist, other than through historically constructed performance.[4] When Ann Oakley wrote *Sex, Gender and Society*,[5] and Sandra Bem[6] carried out her famous studies of androgyny, the academic world—at least—seemed to acknowledge that sex does indeed have little, if anything, to do with gender and, therefore, masculinity is simply a set of culturally constructed qualities.

Formalized Indigenous masculine (and thus feminine) cultures authenticated via "traditional" practices (which this chapter goes on to interpret) problematize the now conventional theoretical position within gender studies that gender is constructed. Yet, far from being rooted in Western notions of biological determinism that de Beauvoir, Oakley, and Bem railed against, venerated perceptions of Indigenous gender are typically grounded in the immaterial, that is, spiritual concepts of gender. Such a conversation has only begun between gender studies and Indigenous studies. Indeed, the broader question of how formalized Indigenous cultures (and the power of such culture) interact with post-structuralism, for instance, is one in dire need of critical investigation.

For the time being, however, what might appear like a nihilistic approach in examining what Indigenous masculinities and sexuality look like from a post-structural perspective (a perspective that inherently confronts cultural formalism, whether that be underpinned by biological determinism or by esoteric determinism), it is not my intent to move beyond the facticity of the matter. Indeed, abstract apolitical futility is one of the inaccurate criticisms often levelled at post-structuralism, whereas a deeper understanding of Michel Foucault's work, for instance, demonstrates the significance of material reality to biopolitical production. The construction of masculinities through the discursive terrain of colonial masculinity produces very real men, who inhabit history, who embody and thus make real the discursive field, who bring to life the world of forms so to speak. Therefore, although approached discursively, it is how masculinity and sexuality combine to construct reality that is of most import. As Foucault outlines in relation to sexuality: "It appears rather as an especially dense transfer point for relations of power...sexuality is not the most intractable element in power relations, but rather one of those endowed with the greatest instrumentality: useful for the greatest number of manoeuvres and capable of serving as a point of support, as a lynchpin, for the most varied strategies."[7] And it is largely the instrumentality, the strategic intent, of masculinity and sexuality that I am most interested in with regard to the discursive formations of Indigenous subjectivities.

Before beginning the chapter proper, it should be pointed out that when referring to Indigenous masculinity and sexuality, these are not stable singular concepts; their iterations intercede to produce a matrix of various masculinities evoked, in part, by sexualities. Thus, when referring to masculinity and sexuality, I refer to these concepts as areas of study, with the inherent understanding that there are multiple masculinities and sexualities. This is important to outline because when reading this chapter there may be the tendency to conceive of "Indigenous masculinity" as if I am referring to a singular conglomeration of masculinity. Indeed, although not unproblematic, one way of thinking about masculinity is through iterations of the matrix of masculinity and sexuality. In this chapter, for instance, I am particularly interested in describing Indigenous heterosexual patriarchy as a trope, and as a way of critiquing the emergence of knowledge that serves to limit Indigenous ontologies and thought. Yet this does not mean I think that this is the only iteration of Indigenous masculinity; far from it.

The Rubric of Indigenous Masculinities

Of significance here is how the study of Indigenous masculinities can aid in the theoretical analysis of power. Many Indigenous theorists have unquestioningly defined "critical theory" as that which lifts the colonizer's veil of power. Here, the colonial social world is determined by a conflict for power, especially in relation to Marxian historical materialism and the Hegelian master/slave dialectic. The classic conception of Indigenous critical theory is premised on a search for pure origins prior to colonization that, with the passing of time, enables the moral high ground over the polluted moral nature of neo-colonial society. Within this material and moral conflict, Indigenous political subjectivities have gained righteousness. A tempting launching pad for moral derision, yet one ultimately doomed to position Indigenous people as choiceless victims. Of course, pointing out the moral corruption of colonization has been a necessary project, yet reifying pre-colonial purity through tradition devalues an Indigenous existentialism located in the present, while failing to tease out the extremely important tensions within and beyond the colonizer/colonized dialect; tensions and complexities that must be addressed if we are to reconcile the victim mentality that inhabits many of our so-called cultural traditions.

Indigenous masculinities and their associated cultural performances in particular can and should be treated as a largely untapped rubric for examining the propagation of power in the colonial context. Accordingly, Indigenous masculinity, in serving two essentialized binary masters (i.e., colonized/colonizer and men/women), creates a model for looking at power within the colonial context where the two essentialized notions associated with the dominance of colonized man over the Indigenous man, and man over woman, create the ambivalent figure of the Indigenous heterosexual patriarch. Both oppressor and oppressed.

I foreground this positioning here because one of the fresh insights Indigenous masculinity studies makes possible in the colonial context is an understanding of power beyond the dialectic of a single binary. Simply put, Indigenous masculinity allows us to clearly form an understanding of power as post-hegemonic, as productive; as both oppressor and oppressed. The dialectics between heteropatriarchal masculinity and feminism, and colonized/colonizer become complicated, as Indigenous masculinities are both imbibed with privilege and denied; both performing colonial heteropatriarchy and resisting it. Yet, somehow, through the productive nature of power, colonized Indigenous masculinities were delimited as a domain, were defined, were given the status of a describable object, so that today we understand a certain type of masculinity as truthfully and naturally representative of "traditional" Indigenous masculinity. And so I return to the key questions, What are Indigenous masculinities for and why in particular are traditional Indigenous masculinities necessary in the colonial complex? In terms of Indigenous masculine sexuality, such a positioning would also suggest that Indigenous sexuality has both been oppressed and come to oppress. The Indigenous heterosexual patriarch, for instance, cuts an ambivalent figure, both admired in his moments of mimicry, yet increasingly abhorred and held in contempt in moments where he fulfils hypermasculine stereotypes, such as the violent criminal.

What are Indigenous Masculinities for?

It must be prefaced that this chapter specifically relates to the context of Indigenous masculine sexuality in New Zealand, and so may or may not relate to other Indigenous contexts, yet I largely employ the nomenclature "Indigenous" not as a universal but rather to keep in step with the cadence of this collection. In keeping with a Nietzschean genealogical method, it is prudent to retrace the disciplinary function in the creation of post-contact Indigenous masculinities. As Paul Rabinow says, "The end of good government is the correct disposition of things—even when these things have to be invented so as to be well governed."[8] In this context, the postcolonial constructions of "traditional" Indigenous masculine cultures (e.g., as zealously patriarchal and heterosexual) were invented in part to mirror Victorian masculinity so that settler states could better intervene into, could better assimilate, and could better govern Indigenous communities. Part of such mimicry, in terms of sexuality, was alignment with the normative heteropatriarchy of the bourgeois family. Although completely underanalyzed in Indigenous studies, it is the normalization of the heteropatriarchal family and concomitant normalization of heterosexuality within Indigenous communities that has served to strongly code sexuality and ostracize other sexual ontologies.

Foucault asks, is it possible to lay down the rules that allowed for the appearance or erasure of discursive formations? Simply put, how do we now come to understand Indigenous masculinity and sexuality, and what are the genealogical paths that have led to these understandings? Given that, in the mind of the Enlightened European the colonial field was a void of knowing, which necessarily needed to be conceived of and given Western meaning. What conditions enabled the void to be transcended, what objects came to fill this field, how were Indigenous masculinities and sexualities constructed, produced and given status through the production of Indigenous subjectivities? How did Indigenous masculinities and sexualities manifest to be nameable and desirable?

A starting point for analyzing Indigenous masculinities is understanding invader masculinities. In the postcolonial East-Indian context, Ashis Nandy sees masculinities through a complex relationship between colonizer and colonized, one which dehumanizes and objectifies both.[9] Likewise, the facticity of the colonial complex compelled Indigenous masculinities to interweave with colonial beliefs about Indigenous men, in general, and with the patriarchy and heteronormativity of dominant forms of invader masculinity, in particular. Dominant invader masculinity was inherently tied to European humanism. As David Goldberg outlines: "The voices of Rousseau and Kant reverberate not just through the Enlightenment but across the moral domain of modernity. [Heterosexual], self-commanding reason, autonomous and egalitarian, but also legislative and rule-making, defines a large part of modernity's conception of the self."[10] The liberal humanist appeal to the individual is, more succinctly, an appeal to an idealized universal European masculinity, where European bourgeois heterosexual masculinity came to represent humanity: "This Man, rational, self-determined and, since

Descartes at least, the centre of his universe, serves as the privileged unmarked term against which all humans are measured."[11] Deviance from this world of European masculine forms—that is, feminine, non-European, and non-heterosexual—was central to the "othering" process of European colonization.

Dominant forms of European masculinity were focused on the rational achievement of mind over body. As Tim Edwards writes, this was to be achieved "whether through self-restraint or disciplines of power and strength."[12] Valorization of reason and rationality in the eighteenth-century Enlightenment is decisive to the formation of invader masculinities. In *Masculinities and Culture*, John Beynon points out, "Reason and feeling were separated and masculinity came to be associated with the objective, the practical, the scientific and the technological."[13] Undoubtedly, the colonial power complex established invader masculinity through its claim that the invading heterosexual male embodied the power of human reason and, thus, represented the interests and will of humanity. Ironically, European masculine authority and reason was depicted as dispassionate, disembodied, and, consequently, as an objective lens through which reality could be viewed.

Enlightenment philosophers committed to moral notions of equality and autonomy avoided inconsistency on the question of racialized subordination by denying the rational capacity of Indigenous peoples in the colonies, thus denying the very condition of their humanity.[14] Colonial discourses often aligned Indigenous masculinity with feminine traits. In comparison to an all-knowing and reasoned European masculinity, Indigenous masculinity, sexuality, and reason was described as passionate, determined by the senses, irrational, intuitive, provocative, and whimsical.[15] In relation to sexuality, Foucault argues that "repression ha[d] indeed been the fundamental link between power, knowledge, and sexuality since the classical age."[16] The mind/body duality when transferred to the colonizer/colonized dichotomy, tended to make the flesh into the root of all evil. The emblazoned piety of heterosexual European sexuality drew a line separating itself from the sun-kissed passion of Indigenous flesh.

However, as I argue here, while most commentators have outlined that the dominant forms of invader masculinities were held to be inversely related to the mind of Indigenous men, power's productive nature imposed a different set of rules. These rules challenged this dialectic so that aspects of invader masculinity were necessarily imbibed into the burgeoning post-contact Indigenous masculinity and so-called traditional masculine sexuality, which has since been allocated disciplinary and authoritative power through notions of tradition and authenticity. Put more plainly, as hybrid postcolonial cultural formations sprouted, Victorian heterosexual patriarchy (i.e., the *modus operandi dominari*) coalesced with Indigenous culture and, importantly, "tradition" to produce what might be referred to as a "dominant" form of Indigenous masculinity; the heterosexual patriarch.

Here it is important to draw attention to the idea of "dominant masculinity"; what Pierre Bourdieu refers to as "masculine domination" or "libido dominandi" and what Robert Connell refers to as "hegemonic masculinity." While limited, these analyses are important as a starting point to deconstructing dominant forms of Indigenous masculinities. Both, in their differently theorized ways, refer to an ideologically dominant masculinity discursively produced through practice and materialized/engendered in male bodies. Connell, using Antonio Gramsci's notion of "hegemony" via gender, for instance, describes the symbolic power associated with simply being a man: "Hegemonic masculinity can be defined as the configuration of gender practice which embodies the currently accepted answer to the problem of the legitimacy of patriarchy, which guarantees (or is taken to guarantee) the dominant position of men and the subordination of women...it is the successful claim to authority, more than direct violence, that is the mark of hegemony."[17] Here Connell, in using Gramscian thought, suggests that men claim authority simply because of their gender, but similarly, that women consent to this authority not because of force alone but more importantly because of gendered cultural symbolism; that is, the power constructed as culturally inherent and associated to being a man.

Hegemonic masculinity is possibly useful in thinking about postcolonial formations of Indigenous masculinity where, in certain "traditional" ceremonies, for instance, simply being a man enables authority and subordinates women within and/or excludes women from the so-called traditional activities. Indeed, on initial analysis, hegemonic masculinity rings true for certain Indigenous contexts. Yet hegemony theory first and foremost was designed to comprehend class subordination within a vertical model of power and, therefore, to my mind at least, it lacks the robustness to comprehend the biopolitical potential and horizontal nature of power within the postcolonial context. While the biopower of Indigenous masculinities enables, for example, the exclusion of Indigenous women from roles deemed "the realm of men" (including tribal leadership), it would be disingenuous to conceive of Indigenous masculine power vertically (i.e., as hegemony in relation to class was) where all Indigenous men hold symbolic power. Simply constructing Indigenous men, for instance, as the subordinators of Indigenous women fails to comprehend the construction of Indigeneity itself that (as is so evident with Indigenous masculinity) should be conceived of as both repressive and productive.

Thus, masculine domination is a discursive propagation, produced, internalized, and effected through male bodies, but it is not male domination per se. Put more positively, there is nothing biologically determined or culturally essentialist about masculine oppression, yet the men produced through ideologically dominant forms of masculinity are very real and have very real consequences for women and other men.

Indigenous Masculinity and Sexuality

As already stated, this chapter starts from the premise that what we call "traditional Indigenous masculinity" is in actuality a particular masculinity that has developed since colonization; in part, at least, mimicked on dominant forms of invader masculinity. I hasten to point out that I do not use "mimicry" as some throwaway term; rather, mimicry at gunpoint is a more apt coinage. Mimicry tends to be understood through a natural hierarchical dialectic, where an inferior culture mimics the superior culture; yet the facticity of the matter saw accommodation of an invading culture as increasingly the only way for Indigenous peoples to survive.

This is not to say, however, that Indigenous men unwittingly fell into heteropatriarchy and innocently enjoyed its benefits; there must be more responsibility than that. And it is this responsibility, through demystifying the genesis of post-contact Indigenous masculinities, that I am most interested in. To paraphrase Stuart Hall, Indigenous cultures have come to a point where we can no longer translate our collective identities through the innocent Indigenous subject.[18] Indigenous heteropatriarchal men have willingly enjoyed a dividend through association with dominant forms of colonizer subjectivities. Regardless of the atrocity of colonization, it is an inauthentic position to eternally point the moral finger at the ethical corruption of colonization for, in this instance, the contemporary heteronormative patriarchal face of many Indigenous cultures remains to subjugate women and alternative forms of Indigenous masculinity and sexuality.

Yet perhaps it is necessary to provide an essentialist imagining of the innocent pre-contact Indigenous masculine subject and sexualized subjectivity, as a point zero. Perhaps he/she was androgynous. Perhaps sexuality was free of the repressive and singular nature that has become traditionalized into the core of post-contact masculinity. Perhaps there was no compulsion to overcome the hesitation to speak about sex and sexuality in all its variety.[19] Perhaps the symposium on Indigenous sexuality from whence this chapter derives speaks to another time, when no such symposia were necessary. I imagine pre-colonial societies to be much like the seventeenth-century Europe that Foucault imagined: "Sexual practices had little need of secrecy; words were said without undue reticence, and things were done without too much concealment; one had a tolerant familiarity with the illicit....It was a time of direct gestures, shameless discourse, and open transgressions, when anatomies were shown and intermingled at will…it was a period when bodies 'made a display of themselves.'"[20]

As the story goes, colonization brought with it the productive and repressive nature of nineteenth-century bourgeois orthodoxy, stoicism, and clear gender divisions, determined by heterosexuality. Hegemonic British culture, in particular, was in a constant apprehensive state regarding the contamination of the masculine by the feminine. Hence, the production of private boys' schools, and the explicit inculcation of stoicism through sports such as cricket and rugby. In the New Zealand context, it is no coincidence that colonial authorities attempted to create a Māori gentry modelled on their British counterparts through the creation of Māori boys' private boarding schools where rugby in particular played a central role in producing a certain form of heterosexual masculinity, an "old-boy" masculinity, and, in particular, a burgeoning form of hybridized masculine leadership that would enable more effective assimilation as, once schooled, the subjectivity returned to provide leadership in communities in the rural margins.

In general, then, one of the symptoms of Indigenous masculinity's mimicry of invader masculinity was the divestment of the feminine out of the masculine. In a Lacanian sense, a masculine subject position was seen to be a rejection of the feminine subject in unconscious terms. The foundation of post-contact Indigenous masculinity, thus, was based upon what Indigenous masculinity was not. Such foundational insecurity has led to ritual displays of physical manliness and hypermasculinity, along with the traditionalization of heterosexuality, homophobia, and patriarchy. And here patriarchy is defined as including crude acts of aggression, but more importantly as "men's control of women's bodies and minds…deeply entrenched in rituals, routines and social practices."[21]

The Heteropatriarchal Indigenous Family

Key to the inculcation of heteropatriarchy within Indigenous masculinities was the reconfiguring of the relational social stratification to mirror the bourgeois European family with its focus on economic rationality and normativity. Jock Phillips has outlined what this looked like in New Zealand:

"Through much of the nineteenth century the family was accepted as an essentially patriarchal institution. By law, men controlled the property in any marriage and the family was seen as a functional economic unit under the leadership of the male."[22] Thus, some forms of Indigenous masculinity came to include "ownership" over land, women, and children, which also reflected the kind of hyperdomineering masculine sexuality that has subjugated the New Zealand sexscape.

One of the purposes of inculcating Indigenous cultures with heteropatriarchy was to produce men who would conceive of paternal responsibility as a natural way of being. Moreover, "as long as the nineteenth century patriarch provided for his family, he could regard himself a 'good father' and was, thereby, licensed to absent himself emotionally and, in the process, wreak huge damage on his family."[23] The governance of Indigenous men into patriarchal roles was ratified through the organization of European bourgeois domestic life; the ideology and practice of "separate spheres." So-called traditional Indigenous culture came to reflect gender-role separation where a domestic sphere of action was defined for women, whereas men (but not all men) controlled the finances and, importantly, the political and public spheres. In New Zealand, for example, even today as these pseudo-traditions are maintained, seldom if ever are women allowed to talk in the "traditional" public sphere. The assimilation of invader masculinity into Indigenous masculinity led to the public face of power at least to be exclusively male. Indigenous masculine leadership came to reflect modernity's masculinity. Similarly, Indigenous heterosexuality came to reflect such a sentiment where Indigenous women became the property of men and, thus, under these conditions were given very little say in the matter.

The mimicry of dominant invader sexuality by Indigenous men occurred in convergence with pre-colonial culture. Sexuality became carefully confined. Anatomies were no longer shown and they no longer intermingled at will; rather, they were moved into the confines of the home: "The conjugal family took custody of it and absorbed it into the serious function of reproduction."[24] Productive heterosexual patriarchy became the model, the norm—the post-contact tradition that reflected invader culture, yet also reproduced the focus of Indigenous cultures on genealogical lineage.

In the patriarchal Indigenous bedroom, pre-contact genealogical traditions (i.e., sexual partnering that was determined by producing offspring who held appropriate hereditary lines) merged with the demand for fertility by the utilitarian modern colonial and capitalist state. As Foucault questions in another context, "At a time when labour capacity was being systematically exploited, how could this capacity be allowed to dissipate itself in pleasurable pursuits, except in those—reduced to a minimum—that enabled it to reproduce itself?"[25] Under these conditions, the majority of sexual practices that were previously (i.e., pre-contact) barely worth mentioning due to their ordinary nature (or so my imaginings tell me) become repressed. Sexuality becomes singular in its hidden performance within the heterosexual parents' bedroom, while other forms of sexuality lie vanquished outside of "tradition": "Nothing that was not ordered in terms of generation or transfigured by it could expect sanction or protection. Nor did it merit a hearing. It would be driven out, denied, and reduced to silence. Not only did it not exist, it had no right to exist... repression operated as a sentence to disappear, but also as an injunction to silence, an affirmation of nonexistence, and, by implication, an admission that there was nothing to say about such things, nothing to see, and nothing to know."[26]

Such is the repressive and silencing nature of tradition and authenticity in Indigenous discourses. Or rather, the recourse to origins of sexuality has produced an invented tradition of heteropatriarchal sexuality that serves to de-authenticate other forms of sexuality.

Heterosexuality as a strategic object of the colonial complex was instilled into dominant forms of post-contact Indigenous masculinity; strategic, on the colonizer's part, in terms of reproducing upstanding heterosexual brown citizens, but also strategically repressive on behalf of a dominant Indigenous masculinity wilfully disciplining and excluding variant forms of sexuality that represented anti-conformity through tacit understandings of tradition and authenticity.

Tradition, Authenticity, and Neo-traditionalism

While there is nothing inherently malevolent with the representation of Indigenous culture through tradition, it is the fixated and arrested nature of so-called authentic Indigenous masculinities and sexualities that causes me to be most anxious. At this point, I'd like to draw upon one of Foucault's most significant questions which, from my perspective, Indigenous studies has not truly engaged with. How does the Indigenous subject become a subject? Typically, in the colonial context, power is very much seen as something that is performed *on* the Indigenous subject. Yet, as Foucault says, each society has its regime of truth, its "general politics" of truth: that is, the types of discourse that it accepts and makes function as true. In relation to a key underpinning of Foucault's work, then, I ask the question: How do dominant forms of

Indigenous masculinity and sexuality function to create the Indigenous subject and, consequently, in terms of necro-power, function to symbolically kill other forms of Indigenous subjectivity? How do Indigenous cultural truths enact a variety of operations on Indigenous bodies, thoughts, and conduct to enable self-understanding as an Indigenous subject? How have discursive formations within Indigenous cultures themselves functioned to discipline Indigenous subjectivities? Particularly, how do tactics of tradition and authenticity determine Indigenous self-definition, subjugation, and exclusion?

For Foucault, such self-discipline was typically mediated through an external authority figure. For Indigenous peoples, I believe such an external authority figure is animated through the discursive formation of Indigenous cultures as authentic and traditional. Foucault may ask Indigenous cultures, then, Who is speaking and who is authorized to speak? and thus what forms of Indigenous subjectivity are being subjugated?

Here, Foucault's line of questioning becomes important to how Indigenous studies could develop because it does not ask what is authentic, what is traditional, what in *origin* was true and real prior to the colonial invader, but rather why have authenticity and tradition come to play such a central role in how Indigenous cultures discipline subjectivities? The notion of tradition is especially dangerous when it is predicated on the concept of authenticity simply because it relies on the idea that a homogenous Māori culture, for example, ever existed and that this cultural monolith is knowable, predictable, and can be authenticated. In the New Zealand context, the recent spate of self-created "pseudo-identity scales" rating Māori identity would suggest the process of cultural self-discipline is well embedded. Typically, these scales rate one's Māori identity in relation to a number of key authenticity determinants such as fluency in the Māori language, visits to your marae or homelands, involvement in activities such as kapa haka, commitment to community groups, and so on. While I must highlight that none of these performances of culture are in any way oppressive in and of themselves, the idea that an Indigenous person must enact certain behavioural ideas to be considered authentically Indigenous *is* extremely repressive.

Clearly, then, tradition is a strategic object that serves to protect dominant forms of Indigenous masculinity and sexuality and, for the neo-colonial project, reifies a focus on the past, promoting nostalgia at the expense of an existential immediacy. This dialectic between reverence for the past and discontent in the present, as previously alluded to, remains in the binary where the purity of the pre-colonial past is lamented in the polluted present. The discursive formation of a pure and authoritative masculinity and sexuality serves to immobilize alterity. As a strategy of biopower, then, tradition has served to kill variant forms of Indigenous subjectivity. Alternative forms of masculinity and sexuality became anomalies, deviant, plastic, excluded from community, from ritual, from existence. As Judith Butler puts forth: "Gender is thus a construction that regularly conceals its genesis; the tacit collective agreement to perform, produce, and sustain discrete and polar genders as cultural fictions is obscured by the credibility of those productions—and the punishments that attend not agreeing to believe in them; the construction 'compels' our belief in its necessity and naturalness."[27] In kapa haka (Māori performing arts), for example, the traditional art as we know it today is undoubtedly a colonial construction. When kapa haka was revived in the 1920s, it came to resemble the colonial physical education practice of the time, in strict and uniform lines with a stringent gender division with females in the front and males in the back. Furthermore, androgynous components of pre-contact kapa haka were genderized. For example, the androgynous poi ball came under the domain of women because of its aesthetic nature, while virulent haka came to be dominated by men. Now consumed as traditional, the familial performance of kapa haka as a gendered construction, as Butler asserts, serves to conceal its genesis, while naturalizing gender representations as authentically Māori. Gender is thus a construction that regularly conceals its genesis; the tacit collective agreement to perform, produce, and sustain discrete and polar genders as cultural fictions is obscured by the credibility of those productions—and the punishments that attend not agreeing to believe in them; the construction "compels" our belief in its necessity and naturalness.[28]

Likewise, the heteronormativity of Indigenous sexuality through the idea of tradition and the search for origins, in producing the heteropatriarchal Indigenous elder who embodies an authenticated sexuality, serves to conceal the genesis of that sexuality, as produced, as a cultural fiction. For Indigenous peoples, the punishment of not acceding to such fictions is disbarment through de-authenticating tactics, which serve to drive such subjectivities from communities.

In the neo-colonial context, Indigenous nationalist movements have inadvertently served to reproduce disciplinary forms of Indigenous masculinity and sexuality. The project of "decolonization" focused the rocky ship through a cultural renaissance (that was necessarily incomplete) and the notion of liberation. The Indigenous liberation project sought to unveil colonial oppression, while "it remained the task of identity politics to emancipate, free or liberate a true, or more essential, individual or collective self."[29] Thus, the decolonial project often served to reassert a form of Indigenous masculinity especially that, in its cultural authenticity, reflected the collective will for liberation, when in reality it served to exclude alternative forms of masculinities and sexualities, and women from leadership roles. It is true that many Indigenous women have been at the forefront of the Indigenous liberation movement, yet it is also true that the radical voices of Indigenous women have often met resistance via the discursive formation of Indigenous structures, framed by Indigenous masculine power, located within the "traditional" tribal organizations. It is more often than not the voice of traditional structures that the neo-colonial media employs to subjugate the radical intent of alternative Indigenous voices; a classic divide-and-rule tactic.

What Can Indigenous Masculinities Do?

The formation of Indigenous nationalism was grounded in social relations that enabled narratives to be produced and later consumed. The production of these fictions was in no small way manufactured by heterosexual and patriarchal Indigenous men. To paraphrase Bhabha, it "is not what Indigenous sexuality *is*, but what Indigenous sexuality does, or what is done in its name, that is of political and cultural significance."[30] Here then, it is possible to imagine Indigenous sexualities that confound structural inequality and violate normalized definitions.

While I obviously find Foucault's analyses extremely useful for understanding how the discursive formation of Indigenous masculinities and sexuality function in the colonial complex, like Spivak I question the space post-structuralism leaves for a collective Indigenous voice when any construction of a collective is deemed essentialist.[31] For Indigenous people, our path must be one of post–post-structuralism for fear of destabilizing "the very identities, narratives and analytical tools that had charged a long history of popular anti-colonial struggles."[32] Thus, again like Spivak, I do envisage a strategic essentialism regarding Indigeneity. And, to a degree, Indigenous masculinity has functioned strategically through complicity with and assimilation into forms of invader masculinity so that Indigenous representation remained at the table. But at what cost? And what would strategic essentialism look like in terms of sexuality? Would we, as the story goes, reassert a history of Indigenous sexuality beyond the heteronormative myths we associate with chiefs and Indigenous princesses? Would our sacred maunga (mountains) have same-sex conjugal affairs?

Thus, I ask, is Indigenous masculinity and sexuality entirely historically contingent? Have Indigenous masculinities and sexuality only formed in the wake of colonization, complicit with invader subjectivities, yet resistant to colonization's ultimate goal: extermination? If the answers are yes, then the challenge Indigenous peoples face is to realize that the strategic function of traditionalized Indigenous masculinity and sexuality have now become an encumbrance, and that often we are left holding on to false traditions that only serve to exclude and limit Indigenous men to heteropatriarchal, hypermasculine, stoical, staunch, and violent discursive formations; often channelling them into destructive behaviours. The task of Indigenous masculinity studies is to embrace an existentialism that effects responsibility, and "that sense of choice and variety in self-definition that so many women have embraced as a means of personal and social liberation."[33] I hope Indigenous masculinity studies, through dismantling false notions, can help realize the assertion that in relation to their sexuality, Indigenous subjects "are much freer than they feel."[34]

Notes

1   Michel Foucault, *The Order of Things: An Archaeology of the Human Sciences* (New York: Routledge, 1972), 226.

2   Homi Bhabha, "Editor's Introduction: Minority Manoeuvres and Unsettled Negotiations," *Critical Inquiry* 23, no. 3 (1997): 434, cited in Simone Drichel, "The Time of Hybridity," *Philosophy & Social Criticism* 34, no. 6 (2008): 598.

3   Simone de Beauvoir, *The Second Sex* (Harmondsworth, UK: Penguin, 1984), 267.

4   Tim Edwards, *Cultures of Masculinity* (New York: Routledge, 2006), 109.

5   Ann Oakley, *Sex, Gender and Society* (London: Temple Smith, 1972).

6   Sandra Bem, "The Measurement of Psychological Androgyny," *Journal of Consulting and Clinical Psychology* 42 (1974): 155–62.

7   Michel Foucault, *The History of Sexuality: An Introduction*, vol. 1 (Camberwell, Australia: Penguin, 2008), 103.

8   Paul Rainbow, ed., *The Foucault Reader* (New York: Pantheon, 1984), 21.

9   Ashis Nandy, *The Intimate Enemy* (Oxford: Oxford University Press, 1983).

10 David Goldberg, *Racist Culture: Philosophy and the Politics of Meaning* (Oxford: Blackwell, 1993), 18.

11 Drichel, "The Time of Hybridity," 594.

12 Edwards, *Cultures of Masculinity*, 159.

13 John Beynon, *Masculinities and Culture* (Buckingham, UK: Open University Press, 2002), 59.

14 Goldberg, *Racist Culture*, 32.

15 Beynon, *Masculinities and Culture*.

16 Foucault, *The History of Sexuality*, 5.

17 Robert Connell, *Masculinities*, 2nd ed. (Berkley: University of California Press, 2005), 77.

18 Stuart Hall, "New Ethnicities," in *'Race', Culture and Difference*, ed. James Donald and Ali Rattansi (London: Sage, 1992), 252–9.

19 Foucault, *The History of Sexuality*, 24.

20 Ibid., 3.

21 Beynon, *Masculinities and Culture*, 85.

22 Jock Phillips, *A Man's Country? The Image of the Pakeha Male—A History* (Auckland, New Zealand: Penguin, 1987), 221.

23 Beynon, *Masculinities and Culture*, 129.

24 Foucault, *The History of Sexuality*, 3.

25 Ibid., 6.

26 Ibid., 4.

27 Judith Butler, *Gender Trouble: Feminism and the Subversion of Identity* (London: Routledge, 1990), 140.

28 Ibid.

29 Edwards, *Cultures of Masculinity*, 100–1.

30 Bhabha, "The Time of Hybridity," 598.

31 Gayatri Spivak, *In Other Worlds: Essays in Cultural Politics* (New York: Routledge, 2006).

32 Simon Featherstone, *Postcolonial Cultures* (Edinburgh: Edinburgh University Press, 2005), 18.

33 Laurence Goldstein, ed., *The Male Body: Features, Destinies, Exposures* (Ann Arbor: University of Michigan Press, 1994), viii.

34 Michel Foucault, "Truth, Power, Self: An Interview with Michel Foucault," in *Technologies of the Self: A Seminar with Michel Foucault*, ed. Martin Luther, Huck Gutman, and Patrick Hutton (Amherst: University of Massachusetts Press, 1988), 10.

II. REPRESENTATIONS IN ART AND LITERATURE

CHAPTER 5

Material of Masculinity: The 1832 and 1834 Portraits of Mató-Tópe, Mandan Chief

Kimberly Minor

Traditionally, Native American societies on the Great Plains explored their personal histories through the creation of shields, painted bison robes, warrior shirts, and drawings. These autobiographical designs, made almost exclusively by men, represented pictographic narratives that stood as visual shorthand for personal accomplishments, likened to one's résumé on a robe.[1] Most broadly, Native masculine identity drew from strong leadership ideals, war valour, and spiritual dedication, themes firmly anchored in the artwork itself. A warrior's societal position in the early nineteenth century came not simply from hunting, but through the performance of brave deeds and heroism in battle.[2] It was into this powerful warrior culture that Euro-Americans introduced their stereotyped idea of masculinity. More specifically, artists George Catlin and Karl Bodmer represented Native American men in a more stylized fashion; according to Euro-American cultural rules of masculinity discernible in their respective paintings *Máh-to-tóh-pa, Four Bears, Second Chief, in Full Dress* (1832) and *Mató-Tópe (Four Bears), Mandan Chief* (1834).

Catlin's and Bodmer's versions of Mató-Tópe suggest an unnatural evolution in Indigenous masculine identity as seen from a Euro-American perspective, unlike the two extant self-portraits by Mató-Tópe himself, in which he reutilized foreign tools, pen and paper, to define his masculinity in a more recognizable form.[3] As such, Mató-Tópe's self-portraits hold considerable potential to better document Native American masculine identity with a sophistication of communication absent from Bodmer's and Catlin's versions which are distinguished, rather, by the application of stereotypical preconceptions held by Americans and Europeans.

Mató-Tópe's drawings, fuelled by an interest in the new media available to him, frame singular achievements in his lifetime: his momentous clash with a Cheyenne male and the Mandan leader's commitment to ceremonial obligations. According to Prince Alexander Philipp Maximilian, a German anthropologist and Bodmer's patron, "Mató-Tópe stayed with us a long time and looked at [Bodmer's] drawings, which gave him much pleasure. Today he received several little things, like tin cups for colors, red pencils and gum elastic."[4] Maximilian's encouragement of Mató-Tópe's artistic inclination suggest the anthropologist's interest in assigning value to "artifacts"; the drawings served as a sample of Indigenous artistic aptitude among the many other material items received during his 1833 travels through the heartland of Indigenous territory. Furthermore, Mató-Tópe's modest style acts as a visual counterpoint to Euro-American traditions of creating images that reflect realism, and whose own civilizations seemed inexorably to be advancing. The idea of the primitive, writes Lucy Lippard, "suggests an early stage of 'development,' implying simplicity on the positive side and cruelty or barbarism on the negative side."[5]

Thus, the concept of the noble savage tinted the perspectives of Catlin and Bodmer as they painted their portraits of Mató-Tópe. The term "noble savage" developed in Europe out of characteristic Enlightenment ideas, such as the natural goodness of "man."[6] However, as contact continued between Europeans and Native Americans, the paradoxical nature of the concept became problematic—Natives personified natural innocence while simultaneously inhabiting a wild environment.[7] According to literary scholar Gail McGregor, "The primitive man was thought on the one hand to be freer, both physically and emotionally—less inhibited, less oppressed by the necessities of labor, less trammeled with constricting conventions; on the other hand, his simple austere lifestyle, devoid of luxury and sophistication, was supposed to inculcate both character and morality."[8] However, as European control lessened on American soil, the heartening idea of the noble savage shifted in its connotation to reflect more negative traits, such as reckless violence and boorish behaviour. Expressed collectively, these primitive qualities gave basis to the main framework upon which an implicit critique of Western advancement would be made: Native societies stood as a crude counterpoint to the so-called civilized structures of the West.

In the summer of 1832, Maximilian reported his impression of Native images as being nebulous: "I could not find, in all the towns of this country, a good characteristic representation of the Native Americans."[9] Bodmer's subsequent employment as a meticulous scientific illustrator provided Maximilian with a detailed visual resource for ethnographic study as he accompanied him to the United States from 1832 to 1834. Their combined observations culminated in the 1839 publication of *Reise in das innere Nord-America in den Jahren 1832 bis 1834* (Travels in the interior of North America 1832 to 1834), complete with Maximilian's abridged records of his journey and supplemented with Bodmer's eighty-one hand-painted aquatints of American wildlife and Native tribes.

Bodmer's specialized approach toward painting contrasted strongly with those of his contemporaries (such as Charles Bird King, Catlin, and even Alfred Jacob Miller), many of whom produced Native portraits that reinforced romantic imagery for commercial purposes.

Catlin viewed Native Americans as a rapidly disappearing race, and thereby hastened to record their portraits before their "inevitable" demise. Catlin's interest in Native Americans began during his tenure as a portrait artist in Philadelphia, where he first observed passing Native dignitaries on their way to Washington City to negotiate trade agreements. In 1832, over the course of less than ninety days, Catlin travelled 1,500 miles, and painted 135 paintings: sixty-six portraits, forty-four genre scenes, and twenty-five landscapes.[10] Catlin's emboldened sense of heroism fuelled his interest to paint as many portraits as possible, even at the risk of trading quantity for quality. Catlin stated, "I have flown to their rescue—not of their lives or of their race (for they are "doomed" and must perish) but to the rescue of their looks and their modes...yet, phoenix-like, they may rise from 'the stain of a painter's palette' and live again upon a canvas and stand forth for centuries yet to come, the living monuments of a noble race."[11] In contrast to Catlin, one can classify Bodmer's approach toward painting Native tribes as a keen attempt to amend scientific aesthetics on canvas. Defined first by its accuracy of detail, Maximilian praised the portrait of Mató-Tópe: "Mr. Bodmer painted the chief in his grandest dress. The vanity which is characteristic of the Indians induced this chief to stand stock still for several days, so that his portrait succeeded admirably."[12] In this context, Bodmer is seen to construct his paintings in a judicious and systematic manner, with precise attention to slight variances in skin tone, hair texture, and cephalic configuration.

The resultant images that Bodmer is able to develop and later denote on the page remain closely adherent to tribal individuality through the differentiation of clothing and facial paint. His astute paintings complement Maximilian's exhaustive written records that discuss Native culture with incisive detail. This apparent marriage of style reinforces the point around which the entire collection may be interpreted: as a careful study of Native environment in contrast to Catlin's effusive prose and portraits.

Mató-Tópe's own artistic endeavours became known through his bison hide paintings that frequently represented charging male figures with fluttering war bonnets, the imprint of horse stampedes, and the steady windfall of soaring arrows. Painted bison robes were produced in the Upper Missouri region and the greater Plains area from the late eighteenth century through the early twentieth century. The robes frequently document a series of conquests, and the events are conveyed by blocky figures of men in monochromatic colours shown in profile with rectangular bodies, stick-like legs and arms, and devoid of facial features. These pictographic figures cloaked the body in a record of one's historical deeds and formed an autobiographical narrative and cultural history of the tribe. Those who had played heroic roles in their own community earned the visible accolades that demonstrated their skillful battlefield tactics and individual acts of bravery.[13] Mató-Tópe's drawings form a natural extension of his bison robe paintings and their function to record lifetime achievements of a single individual.

Catlin's *Máh-to-tóh-pa, Four Bears, Second Chief, in Full Dress* (1832) and Bodmer's *Mató-Tópe (Four Bears), Mandan Chief* (1834) watercolour version, represent the Native warrior in three-quarter profile[14] (Figures 5.1 and 5.2). Mató-Tópe's stature fills the painting and dominates the composition. As an esteemed warrior and prominent tribal leader, Mató-Tópe's regalia befits his status: he wears a bison horn cap adorned with white weasel skins, a trailing war bonnet, quilled moccasins with attached wolf tails, and a feathered lance of scalps, presumably souvenirs of the slain.[15] His clothing invokes a salient reminder of previous injuries suffered in battle and the honour gained from defending his community.

Figure 5.1. Karl Bodmer (Swiss, 1809–1893), *Mató-Tópe (Four Bears), Mandan Chief,* 1834, watercolour on paper, Joslyn Art Museum, Omaha, Nebraska, Gift of the Enron Art Foundation, 1986.49.383.

Figure 5.2. George Catlin (American, 1796–1872), *Máh-to-tóh-pa, Four Bears, Second Chief, in Full Dress,* Smithsonian American Art Museum, Gift of Mrs. Joseph Harrison, Jr., 1985.66.128.

Mató-Tópe's lance in Bodmer's image projects tenuously to the right on a diagonal that succeeds in destabilizing his powerful and stationary pose. Its oblique position has an additional reconfiguring effect, in that it reduces his physical attachment to a weapon of threatening proportions, thereby diminishing his power. The intensity of Mató-Tópe's gaze helps steer our senses toward a closer engagement with the image, compelling the eye—in an almost obligatory fashion—to become conscious of the war scalps hoisted proudly on his lance. Yet, this is where we are concurrently placed at a distance, for the elusive shift of his gaze has the added effect of creating a remote sense of detachment. As viewers, therefore, moving through this pictorial landscape, we are left largely with an impression of a painting that lacks intimacy. In this way, a feeling of distance is created between the viewer and subject. No longer do we see Mató-Tópe simply as a person, but rather conceive of him as a specimen for Maximilian to examine, with the landscape acting purely as a reference to his "habitat."

Catlin's portrait presents Mató-Tópe's immense stature against an indistinct background which functions to create a more prominent feeling of enormity. This technique encourages the viewer to see Mató-Tópe as a mythic hero of enlarged proportions. Indeed, Catlin himself acknowledged not having "entirely represented everything in his portrait; having rejected such trappings and ornaments as interfered with the grace and simplicity of the figure."[16] The effect of rendering Mató-Tópe with few possessions places a greater emphasis on his virtuous character.[17] The faint brushstrokes that poorly estimate his clothing gain import only by the degree to which they help create a depth of focus that enhances his defined facial features and stately countenance.

In reflecting on Maximilian's expedition journals, contact is made with a similarly empowered version of Mató-Tópe: "The Mandan and the Manitaries [Hidatsa] are said to fight well, and there have been frequent acts of individual bravery. One of their most distinguished warriors is Mató-Tópe, who has killed more than five chiefs of other nations."[18] Catlin also commented further on Mató-Tópe's esteemed community status: "This extraordinary man, though second in office is undoubtedly the first and most popular man in the nation…he wears a robe on his back, with the history of his battles emblazoned on it; which would fill a book of themselves, if properly translated."[19]

A man's reputation, when severed from his status as a warrior, was also validated through specialization in other activities. Anthropologist Alfred Bowers recorded, "Some were leaders of buffalo hunts, fish-trappings, war expeditions, or various ceremonies, while others specialized as singers, painters, arrow makers, or storytellers."[20] Each role contributed to the prosperous function of the tribe, but only the idea of the male warrior gained any acclaim in the documentary records of Catlin and Maximilian as well as the portraits painted by Catlin and Bodmer.[21]

Equally important in moulding a man's character were the visible awards by which the society recognized military achievements. Bowers summarizes the public attention that included "a public parade with the victor mounted on a horse; the bestowal of a new name and the privilege of making a public display of giving away goods; the praises of relatives; and the right to wear emblems, symbolic of military accomplishments."[22] Scalping or disarming an enemy in hand-to-hand combat, stealing a horse from a nearby tribe, and leading a triumphant war party represented the process of counting coup.[23] Several scalps and other souvenirs of war (such as rifles and knives) served as physical proof of a warrior's bravery. These items would have been displayed publicly to decorate a shield or hoisted on a lance during a performance. The souvenirs earned through battle would qualify the warrior for entrance into merit-based societies, and allow for the gradual ascension in community leadership roles. Bowers recounts, "A great leader was a successful teacher who instructed his party in methods of 'striking the enemy' without loss to his own expedition."[24] The leader of the war party took great responsibility to ensure the safety of all his men during battle and upon their return home.

A myopic view of Mató-Tópe would render him merely as a war leader, a circumscribed perspective that underestimates the full extent of his responsibilities. In describing the social organization of the Mandan, Bowers details how two separate leaders were chosen by a council of sacred bundle owners to both govern and oversee the general welfare of the tribe.[25] The combination of military leadership and spiritual foresight lent a more unified front for the tribe. However, Bowers's dual classification does not accurately reflect Mandan leadership ethics. In actuality, the chosen chiefs were not confined exclusively to their prescribed roles—either as renowned war leader or spiritual guide—but rather, engaged in both religious rituals and military instruction simultaneously.

One particular coup represented on Mató-Tópe's untitled drawing shows him opposing a Cheyenne man in hand-to-hand combat (Figure 5.3).[26] Maximilian recorded in his journals how Mató-Tópe courageously brandished a battle ax, a stark detail that Catlin ignores in favour of noting how Mató-Tópe advanced toward the chief empty handed.[27] In a struggle for dominance, the Cheyenne struck Mató-Tópe's hand violently with a knife, and as the wound bled heavily, Mató-Tópe wrestled the knife from him. Catlin dramatically concludes, "He plunged it to his heart...and claimed in deadly silence the knife and scalp of the noble Cheyenne chief."[28]

Figure 5.3. Mató-Tópe (Native American, Mandan, c. 1795–1837), *Battle with a Cheyenne Chief,* 1834, watercolour on paper, Joslyn Art Museum, Omaha, Nebraska, Gift of the Enron Art Foundation, 1986.49.384.

Mató-Tópe's representation immediately engages the viewer in the scene of combat, as discarded rifles in the mid-ground lead to the central image of battle. In profile, Mató-Tópe covers his torso with red paint and wields an ax to prepare him against impending harm. The Cheyenne opponent, armed with a knife, lunges to disarm Mató-Tópe's weapon. The consequent hand laceration that Mató-Tópe endures bleeds uncontrollably onto the ground. This assault becomes the central focus of the drawing.

The prominent position of Mató-Tópe and the Cheyenne chief within a vacant space heightens the visceral aggression between the two men. The tangible absence of a landscape suggests an area of transcendence in which warfare is manifested as more than a physical display. The battlefield transforms from a physical site to one of spiritual action against ghostly or spiritual enemy powers.[29] Maiming the enemy represented a permanent conquest of not only physical power but of spiritual triumph as well.

In Mató-Tópe's personal account, he presents himself as a visually dominant individual through the explicit elaboration of his own dress. To a considerable extent, the fringed leggings, prominent coup markings, and extravagant war bonnet arouse ideas of greatness, and further inform the viewer that he outranks the Cheyenne chief. This drawing begins to establish Mató-Tópe as an active participant in the scene, but more importantly, goes on to challenge the provisional interpretations of Bodmer and Catlin, both of whom fail to address Mató-Tópe's multi-dimensional personhood.

Maximilian wrote, "Mató-Tópe brought me a drawing today he had done for me. It depicts him ~~characteristically~~ fighting with the Cheyenne chief."[30] Even though Maximilian strikes through the word "characteristically" in his journal entry, he still implies that fighting remains a sole occupation of Native men. Traits associated with warfare included ferocity, keen strategy abilities, and bravery in battle, but these qualities have been emphasized to such an extent as to fetishize the warrior so that these powers are commonly understood to be naturally *intrinsic*, rather than simply human traits valued for militaristic purposes.[31] Maximilian's word choice reflects a belief that Indigenous male individuals were driven by an innate need for battle and aggressive hostility. These misguided connotations continue the stereotype of a warrior and perpetuate a singular association between violence and physical altercation, rather than promoting the understanding that these intense actions were guided by a set of ceremonial knowledges that defined the art of warfare. Rituals and daily activities encouraged Indigenous men to strive towards physical and spiritual ideals as embodied by elders and supernatural entities represented in oral traditions. Physical events that occurred during a battle became a performance of reconciliation, an avenue to mitigate spiritual contact with the past, and a way to renew current familial connections.

The focus on warfare extends to Bodmer's and Catlin's portrayals of Mató-Tópe's clothing. In particular, the superficial attention and meticulous detail that Bodmer places on Mató-Tópe's regalia singularly presents him as an exotic species. According to Scott B. Vickers, portraying Indians as a type of exoticism transforms them into a moment of nostalgia, always receding into the past. This seems to be the basis for most primitivism and millenarianism, whose impossible fantasies lie either in an idealized past or a paradisiacal future.[32] The interest in showcasing unusual attire reinforces Mató-Tópe as an exotic "other," which makes it difficult to ascertain the full breadth of his multi-faceted personality. As Sally Robinson has noted, the visibility of "savage" male others—whose bodies are marked so that the white male can remain the paradoxical embodiment of the disembodied individual—offered evidence of a dangerous masculinity and enabled whites to practise modes of control.[33] Catlin's and Bodmer's one-dimensional portraits of Mató-Tópe render him static and motionless, as though frozen in time, which further

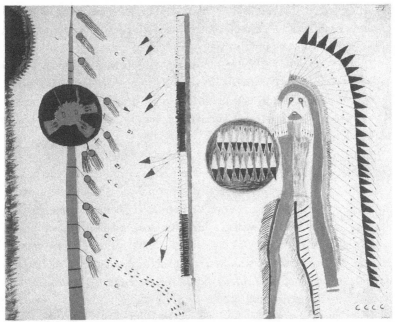

Figure 5.4. Mató-Tópe (Native American, Mandan, c. 1795–1837), *Mato-Tope: Self-portrait; Holding Feather-covered Shield, with Pair of Ceremonial Lances Thrust into Ground,* watercolour on paper, Joslyn Art Museum, Omaha, Nebraska, Gift of the Enron Art Foundation, 1986.49.318.

underscores the idea of him as an exotic species, stripped of personal agency and self-determination.

Intensely dehumanized, treated as nothing more than an object for study and typecasting, it is striking to see how strongly Mató-Tópe's drawings act as a medium through which he interprets his masculinity. This is seen best in an unidentified portrait collected by Maximilian, which shows a suggestive similarity of style to that of Mató-Tópe's previous drawing (Figure 5.4). A man in the right foreground, striped in war paint, faces the viewer, his body posed in an aggressive manner. The red lining of his war bonnet complements the red vertical stripe of paint snaking from his torso to his right foot. He hoists a feathered shield in his left hand, his right arm hidden by the trailing war bonnet. His facial features are indistinct—marked only by the use of red pigment outlining his eyes and mouth. A feathered lance bifurcates the composition and is balanced by a staff adorned with eleven scalps and a hanging drum. Scattered horse tracks run between the lance and a red staff signifying coups accomplished on horseback.

As described above, it is clear that Mató-Tópe does not define himself on the basis of Bodmer's external criteria nor by Catlin's romanticized ideal, but rather as a transient product of brave deeds and community involvement. The active combat with the Cheyenne chief reveals Mató-Tópe's enduring capacity to withstand pain, while the scalps from past defeated enemies and aggressive dance movements symbolize a protective defence of—and intense devotion to—his tribe. He dances not for his own benefit, but rather *for* that of the Mandan community at large.

Status as a warrior came not from physical and mental toughness alone, but was recognized more fully on the basis of one's familial dedication, cultural pride, and consensus of respect. In this vein, Native masculinity strongly favoured the merit of experience over the premium of hereditary lineage. Both drawings by Mató-Tópe reveal the prowess of his masculinity as established by a social organization in which courage and bold action garnered respect. A demonstrated involvement in war signalled the passage from adolescence into maturity, which, in turn, fostered greater gender separation, as few women participated in combat.

Many of these features share close associations with Euro-American traditions. Surely, Maximilian, having experienced an aristocratic upbringing as well as military experience, would have intuited similarities between his own sense of patriotic duty and the expectation of military service within the practices of Native American communities. Traditionally, military service, despite its sometimes deadly purposes, instilled in individuals the virtues necessary for self-government aimed at the common good—selflessness, courage, camaraderie, patriotism, and civic virtue.[34] The concept of European nobility beyond military participation for one's country included virtues such as bravery, selflessness, and a strict code of ethics—characteristics Maximilian closely observed of Mató-Tópe, and who he projected onto as one who demonstrated an unrelenting magnanimity toward his people.

The idea of kinship—relating to a group with a common interest (such as a tribe) outside of one's own immediate family—created a cultural tether for Mató-Tópe. Anthropologist Russell Thornton suggests how Native Americans interact with one another primarily as relatives—engaged in specific relationship roles as structured by the kinship system—at the same time that they interact in other social, political, economic, or religious roles.[35] The effects of Mató-Tópe's drawings sketch him as a hero contingent upon the collective support of his tribe, which is markedly distinct from the Western idea of individual valour. For example, the Peale Museum (which both Bodmer and Catlin visited) uplifted Revolutionary War heroes in bust portraits that concentrate on physiognomy rather than the individuals' actions. Yet Mató-Tópe's drawings place him directly in the action of war to promote his bravery rather than divorce himself from his achievements. Mató-Tópe's drawings represent the physical action of warfare against the Cheyenne chief as well as his communal involvement with his tribe. His untitled drawing where the lance divides the landscape represents an extension from the terrestrial to the celestial as Mató-Tópe mediates the intermediary space and protects his current community and also pays homage to his ancestors.

Intended as both autobiography and cultural representation, the collected paintings and drawings of Bodmer, Catlin, and Mató-Tópe occupy a middle ground of sorts, fluctuating between two ambitions: that of personal testament and cultural translation. In the former sense, Mató-Tópe's highly original work deals with acute topics ranging from personal masculinity, tribal dedication, and communal status. Despite their modest and elementary style, his drawings function most prominently in their ability to lend a genuine voice to his own culture, offering revelatory insight into Native American representation.

What Mató-Tópe considered to be his own personal narrative, however, was slowly restructured by the techniques of Bodmer and Catlin into a more homogenous identity. In accomplishing this end, it was necessary for both artists to translate Mató-Tópe through a systematic artistic process which provided distinct images that beguiled the Euro-American imagination. Though Bodmer and Catlin made an effort to provide a unique opportunity to explore various interpretations of Indigenous masculinity, the unintended consequence of their artistic styles not only perpetuates the idea of the noble savage but also submerges any viable record of Native history in fantasy. The status of this collection becomes most essential in terms of its capacity to elucidate early Indigenous masculinity, conceived firstly and most intimately by Mató-Tópe, but ultimately discredited by Bodmer and Catlin.

Notes

1   Hertha D. Wong, "Pictographs as Autobiography: Plains Indian Sketchbooks of the Late Nineteenth and Early Twentieth Centuries," *American Literary History* 1, no. 2 (1989): 295.

2   James D. Keyser, *Art of the Warriors: Rock Art of the American Plains* (Salt Lake City: University of Utah Press, 2004), 28.

3   Mató-Tópe has three painted bison robes attributed to him located at the following museums: Ethnological Museum Berlin, Bern Historical Museum, and Linden-Museum Stuttgart. I believe the combination of the painted bison robes and the drawings make him the most documented Native artist prior to the rise of ledger art in the 1870s.

4   Prince Alexander Philipp Maximilian, Stephen S. Witte, Marsha V. Gallagher, Dieter Karch, and Jack F. Becker, *North American Journals of Prince Maximilian of Wied September 1833–August 1834* (Norman: University of Oklahoma Press, 2012), 98.

5   Lucy Lippard, *Mixed Blessings: New Art in a Multicultural America* (New York: Pantheon Books, 1990), 24.

6   Gaile McGregor, *The Noble Savage in the New World Garden: Notes toward a Syntactics of Place* (Toronto: University of Toronto Press, 1988), 88. See also Helen Carr, *Inventing the American Primitive: Politics, Gender, and the Representation of Native American Literary Traditions, 1789–1936* (New York: New York University Press, 1996).

7   See also Robert F. Berkhofer, *The White Man's Indian: Images of the American Indian from Columbus to the Present* (New York: Vintage Books, 1978).

8   McGregor, *The Noble Savage in the New World Garden*, 12.

9   Ron Tyler, "Karl Bodmer and the American West," in *Karl Bodmer's North American Prints*, ed. Brandon K. Ruud (Lincoln: University of Nebraska Press, 2004), 4.

10 James Thomas Flexner, *That Wilder Image: The Painting of America's Native School from Thomas Cole to Winslow Homer* (Boston: Little, Brown, 1962), 83.

11 George Catlin, *Letters and Notes on the Manners, Customs, and the Condition of the North American Indians*, vol. 1 (1841; reprint, New York: Dover Publications, 1973), 35.

12 Maximilian, Witte, Gallagher, Karch, and Becker, *North American Journals of Prince Maximilian*, 240.

13 Raymond DeMallie, "Plains Indian Warfare," in *People of the Buffalo*, vol. 1, ed. Colin F. Taylor and Hugh A. Dempsey (Wyk auf Foehr, Germany: Tatanka Press, 2003), 72.

14 Both Catlin and Bodmer produced two paintings of Mató-Tópe, which show the rapport that the artists formed with the second chief in command, but for the scope of the essay I focus solely on the image of Mató-Tópe in his regalia.

15 The details that Bodmer records of Mató-Tópe's regalia have encouraged critics over the decades to consider Bodmer's drawing solely as an image of anthropological relevance. For example, William H. Goetzmann, Joseph C. Porter, and David C. Hunt, *The West as Romantic Horizon: Selections from the Collection of the InterNorth Art Foundation* (Omaha, NE: Center for Western Studies, Joslyn Art Museum, InterNorth Art Foundation, 1981), and William H. Goetzmann, "The Man Who Stopped to Paint America," in *Karl Bodmer's America*, ed. David C. Hunt et al. (Lincoln: Joslyn Art Museum & University of Nebraska Press, 1984), 15. The favour of descriptive language to label Mató-Tópe's regalia ignores Bodmer's stylistic decisions with the image.

16 George Catlin, *Illustrations of the Manners, Customs, and Condition of the North American Indians: In a Series of Letters and Notes Written During Eight Years of Travel and Adventure Among the Wildest and Most Remarkable Tribes Now Existing* (London: H.G. Bohn, 1848), 147.

17 Interpreted through a classical framework, Mató-Tópe's proud stance parallels the stance of Apollo Belvedere. See William H. Truettner, *Painting Indians and Building Empires in North America, 1710–1840* (Berkeley: University of California Press, 2010), 7–11, and Beth Tobin, *Picturing Imperial Power: Colonial Subjects in Eighteenth-Century British Painting* (Durham, NC: Duke University Press, 1999), 223.

18 Maximilian of Wied et al., *People of the First Man: Life Among the Plains Indians in their Final Days of Glory: The Firsthand Account of Prince Maximilian's Expedition up the Missouri River, 1833–1834* (New York: Dutton, 1976), 202.

19 Catlin, *Letters and Notes*, 92.

20 Alfred Bowers, *Hidatsa Social and Ceremonial Organization* (Lincoln: University of Nebraska Press, 1992), 91. The Mandan enjoyed a close relationship with the nearby Hidatsa and shared similar social constructions of military traditions and ceremonial rituals.

21 Women who assumed a warrior role or men who preferred a more domestic routine added a complex gender dynamic to the tribal community that Catlin and Maximilian exclude in favour of describing the heterosexual warrior. See Beatrice Medicine, "'Warrior Women': Sex Role Alternatives for Plains Indian Women," in *Learning to Be an Anthropologist and Remaining 'Native': Selected Writings*, ed. Beatrice Medicine and Sue-Ellen Jacobs (Urbana: University of Illinois Press, 2001), and Sabine Lang, *Men As Women, Women As Men: Changing Gender in Native American Cultures* (Austin: University of Texas Press, 1998).

22 Bowers, *Hidatsa*, 220.

23 John W. Loy and Graham L. Hesketh, "Competitive Play on the Plains: An Analysis of Games and Warfare among Native American Warrior Societies, 1800–1850," in *The Future of Play Theory: A Multidisciplinary Inquiry into the Contributions of Brian Sutton-Smith*, ed. Anthony Pellegrini (Albany: State of New York University Press, 1995), 87.

24 Alfred Bowers, *Mandan Social and Ceremonial Organization* (Chicago: University of Chicago Press, 1950), 66.

25 Bowers, *Mandan*, 33.

26 Both Catlin and Maximilian record the Cheyenne male as a chief of his nation.

27 Mató-Tópe represents this combat scene with the Cheyenne chief on the painted bison robes at the Bern Historical Museum and Linden-Museum Stuttgart.

28 Catlin, *Letters and Notes*, 154.

29 Susan Abram, "Real Men: Masculinity, Spirituality, and Community in Late Eighteenth Century Cherokee Warfare," in *New Men: Manliness in Early America*, ed. Thomas Foster (New York: New York University Press, 2011), 81.

30 Maximilian of Wied et al., *North American Journals*, 88.

31 Maureen Trudelle Schwarz, *Fighting Colonialism with Hegemonic Culture: Native American Appropriation of Indian Stereotypes* (Albany: State University of New York Press, 2013), 94.

32 Scott. B. Vickers, *Native American Identities: From Stereotypes to Archetype in Art and Literature* (Albuquerque: University of New Mexico Press, 1998), 42.

33 Sally Robinson, *Marked Men: White Masculinity in Crisis* (New York: Columbia University Press, 2000), 164.

34 R. Claire Snyder, *Citizen-Soldiers and Manly Warriors: Military Service and Gender in the Civic Republican Tradition* (Lanham, MD: Rowman & Littlefield Publishers, 1999), 8.

35 Russell Thornton, *Studying Native America: Problems and Prospects* (Madison: University of Wisconsin Press, 1998), 307.

CHAPTER 6

Indigenous Masculinities Explored through Performance Art in Kingston, Ontario

Erin Sutherland

In March 2012, I curated a performance series, "Terrance Houle and Adrian Stimson: Exploring Indigenous Masculinities," in Kingston, Ontario. One of the aims of the project was to produce a stage from which Indigenous artists could ignite conversations about models of Indigenous male identity. The resulting performance series involved two artists, Terrance Houle (Blood/ Ojibway) and Adrian Stimson (Siksika) and multiple performances, two of which I will explore in this chapter.

In the first performance, *Ipapá'kaawa*, Houle performatively engaged with his paternal lineage and Blackfoot ancestry by enacting a dream of his father's. Stimson's *Buffalo Boy's Born Again* followed Houle's performance, and explored the destructive force of colonialism, and specifically religion, on Indigenous identity.[1] The performance art of Houle and Stimson provides examples of performance that engaged with notions of identity as performed, as the artists questioned the construction of Indigenous masculinity, as well as the connection of "maleness" and representations of Indigenous men. Indigenous performance art questions hegemonic colonial ways of knowing and the recent work of Houle and Stimson demonstrates how Indigenous history, stereotypes, and colonialism can be reworked to create new and alternative understandings for Indigenous and non-Indigenous audiences alike. This chapter will explore the performances of Houle and Stimson in order to demonstrate the ways in which male performance artists create sites of interrogation where understandings of Indigenous masculinities are questioned and analyzed.

Performance Art

The practice of performance art reflects, magnifies, and at times distorts the viewer's beliefs, desires, and realities—all while seeming to act as a mirror. Thus, performance art allows Indigenous artists to do more than reflect colonialist beliefs held by their audiences. By promoting awareness of those beliefs, by mirroring them but from a new vantage point, the artist can perhaps provoke change in audiences' beliefs to better reflect more contemporary realities.

Stimson in particular has suggested that the artist can reflect society's beliefs back onto audience members and comment on the colonial project. He also explains that he performs, in part, because performance is part of his connection to his Blackfoot culture.[2] In this sense, his practice connects him to a traditional past while bringing those practices forward into a new time and space, demonstrating that Indigenous cultures are flexible and vital. Yet the aim is not merely to identify these histories, but to participate in the broader project of decolonization and reclaiming agency. Performance art not only can expose audience members to the colonial project, but it can also implicate them in this project and promote greater awareness.

Similarly, by using bell hooks's discussion of performance art as a means of intervening in dominant culture, Lynne Bell and performance artist Lori Blondeau (Cree/Salteau/Métis) write that Aboriginal performance art can lead the audience member to bear witness to difficult colonial histories.[3] Carla Taunton explains that performance art works as a tool of decolonization because it interrupts colonial narratives, intervenes in colonial spaces, and develops self-determination for both artist and audience.[4] For my purposes, as a curator I wanted to challenge the presumptions associated with what might be "natural"—or not—for Indigenous masculinities especially.

As I examine next, the performance art of Stimson and Houle invite reflection on Indigenous masculinities and the opportunity to reclaim identities that have been disrupted through colonization. The performances in Kingston demonstrate the ways in which performance allows artists to identify the influence of colonialism on Indigenous masculinities, as well as more contemporary, shifting concepts of masculine identities.

Terrance Houle, *Ipapá'kaawa*

Houle's performance, titled *Ipapá'kaawa*, which means "he dreamed" in Blackfoot, was in honour of his father, as it recreated his father's dream that was used in Houle's Blackfoot naming ceremony.

The performance space contained a platform, and directly beside the platform, in the corner, a mound of dirt. Behind the mound, twelve projections on the wall were created by the reflection of a single image in twelve rear-view mirrors.

Houle, dressed in jeans and a T-shirt, sat on a chair, took out his guitar, and played the song "Cody" by Mogwai.[5] His voice breaking at times, Houle's voice generated a sense of loneliness and melancholy that was enhanced by his isolated position on the dimly lit stage surrounded by the audience. At this moment in the performance, the projection on the wall changed to the image in a rear-view mirror of a car driving on a darkened highway; passing car lights and loneliness and sorrow seemed to fill the room.

The song lyrics and the image of the highway also referenced Houle's father. For instance, Mogwai's lyrics allude to Houle's father's Ojibway name, "Old Songs." Further, as Houle explains, the projections from the rear-view mirror of a car on a lonely highway were meant to evoke his father's experience of falling asleep while sitting in the passenger seat of a truck driving down a dark road. As he slept, his father received a dream in which he found himself laying naked in a pit that bison use for cleaning themselves and removing their molt. His father's dream was used during a naming ceremony in which Houle was given the name Iiniimahkiwah, meaning "Buffalo Herder."[6]

When the song ended, Houle began to slowly undress, removing all of his street clothes. After undressing, Houle used red lipstick to colour his face as well as the left side of his body. Covered in paint, he then donned the breechcloth that his mother made for him when he was ten years old, unapologetically letting his belly hang over the cloth.[7]

Kneeling down in the pile, Houle performatively enacted both his father's dream and the actions of a buffalo wallowing by digging and throwing soil and sand over his shoulder. On the wall behind him, the images changed to a herd of buffalo standing on the plains. Like the bison wallowing to remove their sloughed fur, Houle began to wash himself with the dirt, smearing the sand and soil over his face, arms, torso and back. Houle remained silent, his sadness and loneliness seemingly alleviated by the act of cleansing in the dirt.

Houle finished his performance by curling up on the bed of dirt to rest. As the performance came to an ambiguous conclusion, the images of the buffalo surrounded him and appeared to watch over him.

Adrian Stimson, *Buffalo Boy's Born Again*

Stimson began his performance as his performance alter ego, Shaman
Exterminator. Stimson describes the Shaman Exterminator as a figure who
contests appropriations and misrepresentations of Aboriginal cultures.[8] He
is hulking, and his presence is dark and foreboding. Dressed in more than
fifty pounds of buffalo hides and a hood of hide with buffalo horns, Shaman
Exterminator stumbled out into the gallery space, carrying a large wooden
cross and a bottle of red wine. On the wall at the front of the gallery, the
audience saw a moving image of Shaman Exterminator walking in the Black
Rock Desert. Stimson says that the scene was meant to refer to spaghetti
westerns—low budget, European-made western films—that perpetuated
the stereotype of Indigenous men as savage, unintelligent warriors.[9] Shaman
Exterminator started to stagger through the crowd, struggling under the
weight of the hides and the cross.

Dragging the heavy cross, his vision greatly obstructed by the buffalo
hide hood, Shaman Exterminator stumbled forward while, on the wall at
the front, historical images of Canada were projected. They included archival
photographs of residential school students and a photo of young Blackfoot
students on the front of a Christmas card, its caption reading "Suffer the
little children."[10]

At that moment, Shaman Exterminator dropped the cross. Three assistants took it onto a platform at the front of the gallery and drilled it into
the gallery wall. Buffalo Boy, dressed in red fishnet hose, sequined cowboy
hat, buffalo hide g-string and corset, and fringe vest then appeared from
under Shaman Exterminator's hides as the projection on the wall at the
front changed to archival footage of evangelical preachers. Stimson notes
that Buffalo Boy, Shaman Exterminator's alter ego, is "a trickster character.
He's campy, ridiculous and absurd, but he is also a storyteller who exposes
cultural and societal truths."[11]

Over Buffalo Boy's head, the preacher asked, "What is a born again
Christian supposed to be like? And how do you become born again?" The
projection then changed to that of a preacher ranting about the fires of hell,
immorality, and homosexuality. As these scenes played, Buffalo Boy, a figure
that transcends gender and sexuality and defies classification in Western
terms, was visibly affected by the hatred of the preachers. He stood in front
of the cross being prepared for his crucifixion and raised his arms, looking
to the sky. Bombarded by messages of hate and homophobia, Buffalo Boy
stood with his face to the sky as the preacher onscreen yelled, "God loves you
friend, but [homosexuality] is NOT NORMAL, and it will DROWN YOU!"

Video footage of people speaking in tongues then appeared on the wall at the front, and Buffalo Boy's hands started shaking, which morphed into a powwow dance, seemingly in a trance that protected him from the hatred on screen.

As Buffalo Boy "returned" to the space from his trance, he ascended the cross. The projection over the cross reads "Bufalus Pueri Rex Unus," which in Latin means "The One King Buffalo Boy." The three assistants tied him to the cross and he stood a foot off the platform. Then, for seven minutes, audience members were invited to have their photographs taken with Buffalo Boy on the cross. After seven minutes had elapsed, Buffalo Boy tore his hands from his bindings and stepped off the cross.

Analytical Review of the Performances

As the description of these performances suggests, both Houle and Stimson investigate Indigenous masculine identity formation at the intersection of race, gender, and sexuality. Through their interaction with the audience, the performances generated a space for alternative representations of Indigenous masculinities to historical and contemporary stereotypes. The artists used storytelling and personal narrative to translate an account of colonial history and its influence on their own identities, but also to show how their traditional (both historic and contemporary) connections have protected those identities. Secondly, both artists used their bodies as a—if not *the*—central medium for questioning stereotypical representations of Indigenous men.

Stimson attempts to talk back to the history of the "wild west" and the colonial project.[12] Most notably, we can see his connection to that history through the development of Buffalo Boy, a reference to Wild Bill Cody.[13] Yet we also see this through Stimson's use of archival photographs and discussions of the attempted genocide of Aboriginal peoples at the hands of colonists.

Connecting to the notion of talking back to history, Alanis Obomsawin suggests that colonial history has rendered Aboriginal peoples invisible through the destruction of Aboriginal histories.[14] Following this, Ty P. Kāwika Tengan writes that Indigenous men and concepts of masculinity have been erased by hegemonic imagery of Indigenous masculinity.[15] In reclaiming elements of Indigenous masculinities, men make visible the histories that have altered masculine identities and inform contemporary beliefs. Despite the historical attempt at erasure, Aboriginal storytellers "recuperate the collective stories and histories absent in the narratives of the dominant culture."[16] As a form of storytelling, Indigenous performance art excavates images that are marginalized, thereby making them visible. In visualizing marginalized narratives in the present, storytelling also provides a space in which to bring them into the present, allowing for conversations between the historical past, the present, and its participants, thereby communicating a reflexive encounter with the past.[17] Therefore, performance art, as a space of storytelling, visualizes marginalized images and histories, illuminating them for the audience member.[18]

Reflecting on his position as a storyteller, Stimson writes that, when he "appl[ies] [I]ndigenous knowledge through sharing stories," he is "resisting oppression, thereby transforming [himself] to become more than just a broken voice."[19] In Kingston, Houle and Stimson acted as storytellers, recounting historical narratives laced with both contemporary and ancestral connections, bringing them into the present, and elucidating them for the audience. The narratives, and the identities to which they are connected, are given voice and unearthed. As for the artists' investigation of Indigenous masculinities, the performances specifically make visible models of masculinities that have been made invisible through the colonial project and explore how the process of erasure occurred. Through the embodiment of their narratives the artists question representations of Indigenous male identity as informed by colonial narratives—identities that traditional knowledges both challenge and protect.

In Stimson's *Buffalo Boy's Born Again*, the artist brings to light the connection between Canadian governmental policies of assimilation, residential schools, and forced religious conversion, while also making visible the influence of those events on Aboriginal children, communities, and traditional ways of understanding gender and sexuality. The Shaman Exterminator first reveals himself as an obvious signifier of Christianity, Christ with the cross. In this moment, Stimson creates a connection between himself and Christianity, at the same time destabilizing and evoking the Passion through the Shaman Exterminator's inversion of Christ. Of note is Shaman Exterminator's bottle of wine, which he swigs intermittently as he struggles with the cross. Stimson said of the wine that it serves as a double signifier, both of the blood of Christ, used in Christian traditions, as well as the stereotype of the "drunken Indian."[20] During his tour of the gallery, archival photographs of children at residential schools foregrounded by thunderous choral music work to link the history of forced conversion to residential schools, and subsequently to the issues of substance abuse that result from cultural disjunctions. These connections unearth the histories of residential schools and their lasting impact, viewed in part by the issues of substance abuse that plague many Aboriginal communities today.

Stimson draws further attention to the fact that residential schools intentionally created a divide between generations and privileged the assimilation of Aboriginal boys to Western concepts of masculinity, further disconnecting them from Indigenous models of maleness.[21] This is in keeping with R.W. Connell's assertion that Indigenous gender orders were disrupted while colonial notions of masculinity were made available for consumption by Indigenous men.[22] As Scott Morgensen writes in this anthology, colonial masculinities were invented and altered to support conquest of Indigenous nations. As targets of conquest, Indigenous peoples were framed within colonial projections of gender in order to justify acts of colonial violence. The colonization of gender involved both the undermining of Indigenous gender orders as well as the imposition of colonial understandings of gender and sexuality, as a way to produce colonial patriarchy and systems of dominance. In this connection, residential schools disrupted the transmission of traditional gender orders by tearing children from their families, and replaced Indigenous understandings of gender hierarchies. Stimson's piece unearths those histories of disruption and enforcement of European gender orders and connects them to contemporary circumstances; by his embodiment we see how those histories affect Indigenous identity. Buffalo Boy's movement among images of children, thunderous choral music, the struggle with the heavy cross, and the wine all create very tangible connections between Indigenous identities and the history that is defined through the performance.

Stimson also demonstrates the impact of assimilation to Western values, and specifically heteropatriarchy, on models of Indigenous masculinity that include Two-Spirit traditions. As Michael Flood and his co-authors explain, models of queer masculinities are marginalized from Western concepts of "normal" masculinity through discursive operations similar to those producing racialized masculinities, in that both form constitutive "outsides" to white heteronormative masculinities.[23] While oppressions of race, gender, and sexuality are not equivalent, they are produced through similar processes of differencing that compose intersectional identities. As constructions of Native men produce the borders of normative masculinity, homosexuality "negates masculinity" and is understood as "lacking" masculinity, constituting what is "not" masculine.[24] Despite what is construed as inherent negativity in these positions, Indigenous identities that are, for instance, LGBTQ2 (Lesbian, Gay, Bisexual, Transgender, Queer/Questioning, and Two-Spirit), have their own positivities within the category of Indigenous masculinity. Through his practice, Stimson explores understandings of LGBTQ2 identities as examples of aspects of Indigenous masculinity by voicing his own experience as a Two-Spirit man.[25] In this way, he explores how these multi-faceted identities are not negations, but in fact positive and complex constructions that, in some cases, can be understood as Indigenous masculinities. In addition, Buffalo Boy, as a gender-bending trickster character, often "queers" the space, inserting his sexualized being and attempting to normalize the notion of Two-Spiritedness.[26] Through his discussion of both his struggles and his successes, the artist and the performer both bear witness to the silencing of Indigenous understandings of sexuality and gender and bring them forward into the present through the experience of the audience.

Understanding of Stimson's use of homophobic rants by preachers compounds the history of cultural assimilation, demonstrating the ways in which race, gender, and sexuality were and still are defined by the colonial project, disallowing and erasing alternatives. Buffalo Boy, as a Two-Spirit figure, is crucified for existing outside the norms permitted by colonialism, which we understand from the imagery of assimilation. The powers of religion against his identity are demonstrated in the preacher's pronouncements of homosexuality as abnormal and as "wicked." Linking to the residential school history presented earlier, Stimson demonstrates the way in which children were forced to understand masculinity as heteropatriarchal and Indigeneity and homosexuality or Two-Spirit identity as immoral and outside of the boundaries of "normal."

Stimson presents a model of Indigenous masculinity that includes Two-Spirit or queer identities, and therefore also exists outside the expected stereotype of the Aboriginal male, but he also shows how those models were disavowed. He uses historical references to translate the history of assimilation of Aboriginal communities to Western concepts of sex and gender, and the way it was enforced through hatred, violence, religion, and condemnation. Stimson identifies a model of Indigenous masculinity and, through its visualization, we understand that it has been erased by histories of colonial violence. The artist not only translates a larger history of the colonial project but also his own history, through the identification of his own struggle as someone who identifies as Two-Spirit.

Stimson's story, however, is not purely one of suffering. The artist also translates the protective element of his history through his use of paint (his painted face) and his powwow dance. In addition, through the process of rebirth, as he is resurrected, Stimson uses the words of the preachers to demonstrate his resiliency and the resiliency of Indigenous peoples. The resurrection perhaps explores the reconnection of Indigenous peoples with traditional understandings of gender and sexuality which, although Stimson has struggled with, he has also worked to recover. Though his dance, paint, and connection to his people, all embodiments of tradition, Buffalo Boy recovers from the crucifixion to rise again. The rebirth is perhaps the most important aspect of Stimson's piece as it symbolizes the re-membering of Indigenous understandings of sexuality and gender, despite the attempted destruction of those beliefs.

The embodiment of Indigenous knowledge, as presented in the use of dance, paint, and even buffalo hides, demonstrates how men are drawing from and reinforcing the strength of traditions to redefine Indigenous masculinities. In his book about Hawaiian masculinities and the effort of Hawaiian men to create empowered Indigenous identities, Tengan explores how life history narratives and storytelling allow for reconnection and remembering.[27] He identifies the way in which Hawaiian men have made use of storytelling and connections to traditions through other embodied practices to "work to negotiate the contradictions of defining self and nation."[28] As seen through, in part, the use of dance and paint, both Stimson and Houle made broad use of their own personal life narratives and their Blackfoot and Ojibway traditions in their work.

In both artists' performances, these contemporary traditions are employed to connote protection and safety, thereby evoking a resiliency of traditional forms as well as the empowerment of Indigenous masculinities through connections with traditions. For instance, Houle uses paint to protect himself from Western influence, even once he has tried to strip it away by removing his clothing. In the same way, Stimson uses Buffalo Boy's makeup like war paint, embodying the tradition of painting as protection and ceremony.[29] In addition to the paint, Stimson protects himself from the onslaught of hatred by entering a trance. His trance consists of shaking and powwow dancing, which he says demonstrates the resiliency of Aboriginal cultures.[30] In this moment, Buffalo Boy protects himself from the bombardment of religion and hate-filled homophobic speech utterances by connecting with his own cultural traditions. Stimson therefore demonstrates the use of culture to protect, as he survives the crucifixion to rise again, but also the resiliency of Aboriginal cultures, which continue and shift and do not remain static.

In connection with his own history, Houle's *Ipapá'kaawa* is an example of a life history narrative, in which he performs his deep-rooted connection to his family, ancestors, and culture. In *Ipapá'kaawa*, the artist performatively attempts to disconnect himself from the Western world and instead connects to his family history and traditions. Before entering his father's dream, however, Houle explores the struggle, as an Aboriginal man, to come to terms with colonialism and its influence on his identity. He shows himself as lonely and enveloped in sadness. In order to enter the dream, Houle strips away his Western clothing, which signifies the trappings of Western culture. Putting on his loincloth, he explores the potential to return to a contemporary experience of his culture, as he is comforted by the loincloth and its connection to his past.[31] In this moment, there is a connection to Tengan's Hale Mua, whose teaching includes a return to the malo, a traditional Hawaiian clothing for men. Tengan writes that, for many men, in stripping away their Western clothing, they struggle with bodily inhibitions and historical ignorance that are a result of the disconnection from the rituals of wearing the malo. The malo, which was originally a sign of masculinity, became commoditized in imagery of Hawaiian cultures viewed by outsiders.[32] In learning to wear the malo, the Hale Mua are returning to, and reclaiming, this signifier of masculinity. In the same way, Houle wears the loincloth to reappropriate a signifier, too. While the loincloth itself works as a tangible example of reappropriation, by stripping away his contemporary clothing and choosing to put on his loincloth, he takes back control over his body as an image of Indigenous masculine identity.

Furthermore, by scrubbing himself with dirt, Houle appears to wash away the influence of colonialism, attempting to fully engage with the dream, and perhaps merge with the herd of buffalo that encircle and protect him. Houle connects with the buffalo literally by his Blackfoot name, "Buffalo Herder." This name, a name that identifies him as a man who feeds his people, evokes another model of Indigenous masculinity. Houle tells the story of his name and, through the telling of the story, brings forward both a tradition and his identification with his responsibility as an Indigenous man that was gifted with the name.

A second theme that connects the performances is the artists' use of their bodies to engage with stereotypes of the hypermasculine noble savage or the violent and/or drunken Indian. In particular, their bodies act as sites of resistance, resignifying and reappropriating beliefs about Indigenous identity.[33] Both artists explore what a Native man "should" look like and invert those stereotypes—showing them *as* stereotypes. Richard Hill writes that Houle makes us aware of how our expectations of visible "Indianness" are somehow "antithetical to ordinary contemporary experience."[34] He also writes that Houle's humorous portrayals of himself in stereotypical "Indian garb" not only make us aware of the romanticism but also reveal the dangers of perpetuating those stereotypes as "truth."[35] In *Ipapá'kaawa*, we see that in a more sombre and serious way, Houle continues in his use of his body to make visible ideas about the expectations of "Indianness" and how those expectations influence his own identity. For instance, while the loincloth could be viewed as comforting, it is so tight that it causes his belly to sag over it and makes the viewer aware of his body's disjunction with stereotypical images of athletic Native bodies seen in conventional Hollywood westerns. Second, Houle's attempts to wash away colonial culture suggest another resistance to the stereotype of the noble savage. Here, he explores the disconnection between the expectations of Native male bodies and the lived reality of his own body.

Houle says that his work looks to share the taboos of the body with his audience and that his body is the most important element of his work because, in silence and gesture, he uses it to tell a story.[36] By disarming the audience, Houle reclaims his Indigenous masculine identity and body as unique, not so bound by the audience's expectations of tacit stereotypes.[37] In sharing his story through his body, he is demonstrating the way in which the body, as a carrier of signs and social constructions, can be used to evoke questioning to disrupt meta-narratives.[38]

Performance, as an embodied practice, is a way to transmit and store knowledge alternative to Western ways of understanding.[39] Stimson and Houle engaged with the audience to transmit such alternative social knowledge about Indigenous identities, insight that is and was discordant with colonial narratives of distortion and erasure. Such a process depends on audience members' participation, as they are the receivers of the artist's message. Aboriginal performance is powerful in that it challenges both Indigenous and non-Indigenous audiences to confront their beliefs about "Indianness."[40] Non-Indigenous viewers are asked to question representations of Indigenous peoples as constructions, and often overtly limited ones. While the artist cannot control what audience members take away from their performances, both artists have said that their work seeks to provoke audience questioning and encourage Indigenous and non-Indigenous viewers to mingle and connect.[41] Houle explicitly tries to build a bridge of understanding between non-Aboriginal and Aboriginal peoples by creating a space in which they can engage in discussions of Indigeneity together, perhaps forming connections through understandings of his investigations.[42]

In the performances presented during the series, the audience played a major role in the discussions of identity formation. For example, Houle's nudity in *Ipapá'kaawa* made many audience members uncomfortable. In that discomfort there is an awareness of "humanness in tandem with cultural identity."[43] The nudity in Houle's performance elicited a response from the audience members, who witnessed both his presence and their own reservations. Houle said that the nudity in the work is supposed to elicit reactions from audience members, to provoke them to question their own taboos, and to humanize him as an expressly Aboriginal male body.[44]

Stimson's performance also provoked reactions. For instance, his forced displacement of the audience as he moved around the gallery space worked to make the audience member an active participant. About his presence, Stimson said his work attempts to disrupt the space to claim it for himself.[45] In doing so he explores his presence as an Aboriginal man within these worlds; as Houle adds, this act reminds the world that "we are still here" (as Aboriginal men) despite the history of genocide.[46]

As Lisa Tatonetti writes in her chapter in this volume, "'Tales of Burning Love,'" artistic interventions into stereotypical representations of Indigenous masculinities can challenge and redefine the boundaries or binaries that limit dynamic representations of gender. In this chapter, Tatonetti explores the affective power of female masculinities in Indigenous literature.[47] Tatonetti demonstrates that writers and artists use affective power to convey alternative expressions of gender and sexuality that are then experienced by the reader or viewer, thus offering them alternative understandings of Indigenous masculinity. During the performance series, the audience experienced Houle and Stimson's performances with their bodies and their senses. The embodied connection with the artistic intervention into heteronormative understandings of Indigenous gender and sexuality presented the audience members with the opportunity to confront those norms. In the same way that the affective responses of the characters discussed by Tatonetti require us to rethink binaries, so too does the work of performance artists. The power of Indigenous performance to provide us space to interrogate normative boundaries is important to the project of Indigenous survivance.[48]

As noted earlier, stereotypical representations of Indigenous peoples and the imposition of colonial values have attempted to render Aboriginal peoples invisible.[49] Specifically, colonial discourses of heteronormative masculinity have displaced models of Indigenous masculinity in favour of stereotypical representations. Histories of erasure have greatly influenced the identities of Indigenous men, but identities have also been recuperated through Indigenous interventions that make visible alternative histories and models of identity. The performances are an example of these interventions. Specifically, Stimson and Houle explored the use of storytelling and personal narrative to bring forward histories that have been ignored in order to identify their influence on Indigenous models of male identity. The artists also identified the resiliency of Indigenous peoples to that erasure, seen specifically in the resurrection of Buffalo Boy. Finally, an analysis of the performances demonstrates that the artists used their bodies and interactions with the spaces of the performances to destabilize taboos about Indigenous male bodies and to create an awareness of their messages in the audience.

Notes

1 In this chapter, I use both the terms "Aboriginal" and "Indigenous." While I understand that "Aboriginal" is contentious, as it is state-imposed, I use the term to refer to specific Canadian instances, as it is a term instituted by the Canadian state to refer to Indigenous peoples living in Canada. I also use "Aboriginal" when I refer to the work of authors who also used the term. In order to refer to a broader understanding of masculinities influenced by colonial understandings of gender and sexuality, I use the term "Indigenous."

2 Adrian Stimson in discussion with the author, Kingston, Ontario, 22 March 2012.

3 bell hooks, "Performance Practice as a Site of Opposition," in *Let's Get it On: The Politics of Black Performance,* ed. Catherine Ugwu (Seattle: Bay Press, 1995), 218–19; Lynne Bell and Lori Blondeau, "High Tech Storytellers, Unsettling Acts, Decolonizing Pedagogies," *INDIANacts: Aboriginal Performance Art,* 2002, accessed 12 August 2012, http://indianacts.gruntarchives.org/essay-high-tech-storytellers-bell-and-blondeau.html.

4 Carla Taunton, "Performing Resistance/Negotiating Sovereignty: Indigenous Women's Performance Art in Canada" (PhD diss., Queen's University, 2012), 3.

5 Mogwai, "Cody," in *Come on, Die Young,* Chemikal Underground (1992), YouTube, 6:33, http://www.sing365.com/music/lyric.nsf/Cody-lyrics-Mogwai/09245408D51E33B548256E6E0008D18B

6 Terrance Houle in discussion with the author, Kingston, Ontario, 22 March 2012..

7 Ibid.

8 Ryan Rice and Carla Taunton, "Buffalo Boy: Then and Now," *FUSE* 32, no. 2 (2009): 20.

9 Adrian Stimson, email message to the author, 2 May 2012.

10 Ibid.

11 Rice and Taunton, "Buffalo Boy," 1.

12 Adrian Stimson, "Artist Talk" (presented as part of Cultural Studies Speaks Series "Terrance Houle & Adrian Stimson Performance Series," Queen's University, Kingston, Ontario, 21 March 2012).

13 Wild Bill Cody was a late-nineteenth/early-twentieth-century figure who organized a travelling "Wild West Show" that relied on stereotypical representations of "cowboys and Indians" to entertain people living in North America and Europe. Members of the show included Sitting Bull, Annie Oakley, and Gabriel Dumont.

14 Alanis Obomsawin in Kathleen Buddle, "Anti-Hero Avengers and the Not-So-Lone Ranger," *Canadian Dimension* 41, no. 1 (2007): 48–50.

15 Ty P. Kāwika Tengan, *Native Men Remade: Gender and Nation in Contemporary Hawai'i* (Durham, NC: Duke University Press, 2008), 8.

16 Buddle, "Anti-Hero Avengers," 48–50.

17 Della Pollack, "Memory, Remembering and Histories of Change," in *The SAGE Handbook of Performance Studies*, ed. D. Soyini Madison and Judith Hamera (Thousand Oaks, CA: Sage Publications, 2006), 86.

18 Jessica Bradley, "Rebecca Belmore: Art and the Object of Performance," in *Rebecca Belmore: Fountain*, ed. Scott Watson and L.M. Bailey (Vancouver: Morris and Helen Belkin Art Gallery University of British Columbia, 2005), 42.

19 Adrian Stimson, "Buffalo Boy's Heart: On Buffalo Boy's 100 Years of Wearing His Heart on His Sleeve" (MA thesis, University of Saskatchewan, 2005), xi–xii.

20 Adrian Stimson in discussion with the author, Kingston, Ontario, 22 March 2012.

21 Michael Flood, Judith Kegan Gardiner, Bob Pease, and Keith Pringle, *International Encyclopedia of Men and Masculinities* (Oxon, UK: Routledge, 2007), 333.

22 R.W. Connell, "Globalization, Imperialism and Masculinities," in *Handbook of Men and Masculinities*, ed. Michael Kimmel, Jeff Hearn, and Robert W. Connell (Thousand Oaks, CA: SAGE Publications, 2004), 75.

23 Flood, Gardiner, Pease, and Pringle, *International Encyclopedia*, 335.

24 Tim Edwards, "Queering the Pitch?: Gay Masculinities," in *Handbook of Men and Masculinities*, ed. Michael Kimmell, Jeff Hearn, and R.W. Connell (Thousand Oaks, CA: SAGE Publications, 2004), 51, 86.

25 While a discussion of Two-Spirit identity is outside the scope of this paper, it is important to briefly define Two-Spirit identity, as Stimson explores the relationship between race, gender, and sexuality, and often discusses the loss of Two-Spirit identities in the face of colonialism. While I do not wish to label the complex identities that fall within or outside of the category of Two-Spirit, I do wish to provide a useful overview of the term in order to understand Stimson's investigations. Consequently, according to a recent anthology about Queer Indigenous studies, authors Qwo-Li Driskill, Chris Finley, Brian Joseph Gilley, and Scott Morgensen write that *Two-Spirit* "was proposed in Indigenous organizing in Canada and the United States to be inclusive of Indigenous people who identify as GLBTQ or through nationally specific terms from Indigenous languages." (3) In this connection, Driskill and hir co-authors write that when *Two-Spirit* and *queer* are linked, they invite a critique of colonial heteronormativity and, in turn, a decolonization of Indigenous knowledges of sexuality and gender. However, the authors hope to spur a conversation across queer Indigenous peoples and view *Two-Spirit* as an identity category that is contentious and a site "among many where the meanings of queer Indigenous critiques are debated." (3). In this same way, I too use *Two-Spirit* as an identity category, among many, that can be used to link communities in a conversation at the intersection of race, gender, and sexuality.

26 Rice and Taunton, "Buffalo Boy," 3.

27 Tengan, *Native Men Remade*, 3.

28 Ibid., 16.

29 Terrance Houle and Adrian Stimson in discussion with the author, Kingston, Ontario, 22 March 2012; Stimson, email message.

30 Stimson, email message.

31 The loincloth is Houle's powwow breechcloth that his mother made for him when he was a boy. In an interview with Houle (Kingston, Ontario 22 March 2012), he said that he started his art practice wearing his full Grass Dance regalia but saw that as influenced by the West. He started to explore how to get away from the Western culture that the Grass Dance, in part, corresponded to, and he chose to use only his loincloth. As is seen in his Kingston performance, he has moved beyond his loincloth to full nudity, exploring a full disconnection from clothing to investigate

the taboos of the nude male body as an expectation brought to Aboriginal communities by the West.

32 Tengan, *Native Men Remade*, 17–18.

33 Brigit Dåwes, *Native North American Theatre in a Global Age: Sites of Identity Construction and Transdifference* (Heidelberg, Germany: Universitätsverlag, 2006), 117–21.

34 Richard Hill, "Drag Racing (Dressing Up White) and the Canon Upside Down: Inversion in Contemporary Art and Visual Culture," in *The World Upside Down: Le Monde a Lenvers*, ed. Richard Hill (Banff: Banff Centre Press, 2011), 65.

35 Ibid., 65.

36 Terrance Houle, "Artist Talk" (presented as part of the Cultural Studies Speaks Series, "Terrance Houle & Adrian Stimson Performance Series," Queen's University, Kingston, Ontario, 21 March 2012).

37 Terrance Houle, in discussion with the author, Kingston, Ontario, 22 March 2012.

38 Marvin Carlson, *Performance: A Critical Introduction*, 2nd ed. (New York: Routledge, 2004), 167–9.

39 Diana Taylor, *The Archive and the Repertoire: Performing Cultural Memory in the Americas* (Durham, NC: Duke University Press, 2007), 15, 20, 29.

40 Elizabeth Archuleta, "Refiguring Indian Blood through Poetry, Photography, and Performance Art," *Studies in American Indian Literatures* 17, no. 4 (2005): 2.

41 Terrance Houle and Adrian Stimson, in discussion with the author, Kingston, Ontario, 22 March 2012.

42 "Terrance Houle: Visual Arts," *Indigenous Arts Network* (accessed 21 September 2011), http://indigenousartsnetwork.ca/artists/terrance_houle/interview/.

43 Whitney Light, "Terrance Houle," *Canadian Art* 26, no. 3 (2009): 162.

44 Terrance Houle, in discussion with the author, Kingston, Ontario, 22 March 2012.

45 Adrian Stimson, in discussion with the author, Kingston, Ontario, 22 March 2012.

46 Adrian Stimson and Terrance Houle, in discussion with the author, Kingston, Ontario, 22 March 2012.

47 See Tatonetti, "'Tales of Burning Love,'" 132–146 (in this volume).

48 Ibid.

49 Tengan, *Native Men Remade*, 8; Obomsawin in Buddle, "Anti-Hero Avengers," 48–50.

CHAPTER 7

"Tales of Burning Love": Female Masculinity in Contemporary Native Literature

Lisa Tatonetti

Judith Halberstam begins her landmark 1998 text, *Female Masculinity*, with the contention that her work is "part of a cultural onslaught on the privileged reservation of masculinity for men."[1] This claim resonates, albeit somewhat ironically, in Native American and Indigenous studies where theories about cultural challenges to mainstream power structures abound, and reservations, be they in the form of misgivings or mapped geographical locales, take centre stage. Speaking of dominant Eurowestern understandings of heteromasculinity, Halberstam notes the liminal nature of both the term and identity, pointing out "although we seem to have a difficult time defining masculinity, as a society we have little trouble recognizing it, and indeed spend massive amounts of time and money ratifying and supporting the versions of masculinity that we enjoy and trust."[2] Halberstam's analysis of female masculinities builds on Judith Butler's theories of sex and gender, which craft gender, and especially the behaviours that we use to mark certain gender identities, as performances rather than as naturalized aspects of identity. In terms of Eurowestern masculinity, such behaviours, as Brendan Hokowhitu explains, "were focused around the rational achievement of mind over body" and were tied to "power and strength."[3] While much early work in queer studies deconstructed sex/gender binaries by showing how these gendered behaviours are a form of cultural mimesis—a reproduction of a reproduction, with no original or essential identity to be had—little had been discussed about the parameters and consequences of female appropriations of behaviours, dress, and actions marked as specifically male. Thus, Halberstam broke new ground in her investigations of how dominant masculinity can be made legible when de-sutured from the male body, when understood as a mobile performance rather than as a biologically produced set of actions and reactions inherent to male-bodied people.

When I first began pondering the ways female characters deploy what might be deemed "masculine" behaviours and discourses in American Indian literatures, I returned to Halberstam. Upon rereading *Female Masculinity*, I found connections and disjunctions—moments in which the depictions of female masculinity in Native literatures both align with and exceed Halberstam's theory. Most relevant to Native studies is her recognition of the radical possibilities of non-white or what she calls "minority masculinities." These female masculinities, she suggests, not only "can undo the hierarchized relations between dominant and minority sexualities" but also "have the power to reorganize masculinity itself."[4] I see this contention as closely tied to Muscogee Creek/Cherokee scholar Craig Womack's by now oft-cited claim that "a queer Indian presence fundamentally challenges the American mythos about Indians.... Identifying an Indian as lesbian or gay makes the Native radically resistant to the popular tendency to make Indians artifacts of the past, since no one associates such terms with the warrior days when men were men and buffalo were scared."[5] I start this essay, then, by positing that looking closely at representations of female masculinities in Native literatures will show the truth of both Halberstam's and Womack's contentions. To riff off Womack, I suspicion there's something mighty queer happening in Indian Country.[6]

If Halberstam provides a jumping-off point for discussions of female masculinity, she does not offer the final word. Moreover, I contend that in the context of Indigenous literatures, re-seeing dominant ideologies of masculinity necessitates a recognition of what Halberstam's theory, as useful as it is, omits: female masculinities signify differently in First Nations and American Indian cultures. Halberstam argues that "the very existence of masculine women urges us to reconsider our most basic assumptions about the functions, forms, and representations of masculinity and forces us to ask why the bond between men and masculinity has remained relatively secure despite the continuous assaults made by feminists, gays, lesbians, and gender-queers on the naturalness of gender."[7] In Indigenous studies, such "basic assumptions" have always been under suspicion, have always been (un) grounded by the complexity of Native gender traditions, which fracture any idea of a monolithic masculine norm.

Historically, the existence of third and fourth gender traditions in Indigenous cultures is well documented. Such traditions are referenced in still-extant tribal traditions and oral histories as well as in letters, missionary accounts, and both early and more recent anthropological texts.[8] In terms of considering the function of female masculinity in Native literature, of particular interest to my project are the historical narratives of Indigenous women who held roles that would seem to exceed, resist, or subvert Western gender binaries. The rich array of ways Indigenous women inhabit and perform gender include well-known stories of warrior women in Plains nations like Woman Chief (Crow) or Brown Weasel Woman (Piegan), long-standing traditions of gender complementarity among the Haudenosaunee, and Beloved Women like Nancy Ward among the Cherokee. As Laguna Pueblo author Leslie Marmon Silko reminds us,

> In the old days, strong, sturdy women were most admired. One of my most vivid memories is of the crew of Laguna women, in their forties and fifties, who came to cover our house with adobe plaster. They handled ladders with great ease, and while two women ground the adobe mud on stones and added straw, another woman loaded the hod with mud and passed it up to the two women on ladders, who were smoothing the plaster on the wall with their hands. Since women owned the houses, they did the plastering.[9]

In each of these examples, Indigenous women hold or share power and take action in ways that challenge the legacies of female subordination inherent in heteropatriarchal gender binaries based on Eurowestern norms. While these Indigenous understandings would not have been understood as female masculinity in their times and cultural contexts, they provide a nuanced historical framework for reading contemporary representations of gender in Native literatures. Our knowledge of these precedents necessarily makes contemporary performances of female masculinity in Indigenous contexts signify differently. In fact, I suggest representations of female masculinity in Native literature can be read as the embodied trace of Two-Spirit histories in the way that, post-1962, a can of Campbell's tomato soup will always carry the trace of pop art.

When I began to look for representations of female masculinities in Native literature, I found such images widespread, which is unsurprising given the realities of class and culture in Indigenous communities where Native women often share or shoulder responsibilities of labour both in and outside of the house. As a result of these lived realities, representations of female masculinity abound in poetry, novels, and short stories, in fiction and creative non-fiction, in essay and film. They exist in the work of artists as diverse as Clint Alberta, Sherman Alexie, Beth Brant, Chrystos, Thirza Cuthand, Qwo-Li Driskill, Louise Erdrich, Janice Gould, Blake Hausman, Tomson Highway, Daniel Heath Justice, Carrie House, Winona LaDuke, M. Carmen Lane, Wilma Mankiller, Susan Power, Deborah Miranda, Cheryl Savageau, and Leslie Marmon Silko. (And I'm just getting started.) These images range from what I call "Big Moms," the strong female characters that abound in Indigenous literature (and real lives) who are most often not queer-identified, to overtly butch lesbians who embrace the performance of female masculinity as a central aspect of their lives.

My investigations of how and why these performances of female masculinity function as they do brought me back to Judith Butler and her considerations of the ways in which one comes to know self and gender in Eurowestern contexts. In "Melancholy Gender: Refused Identification," Butler reworks Freud's ideas of teleological sexual stages in which "the masculine and feminine are not dispositions...but accomplishments, ones that emerge in tandem with the achievement of heterosexuality."[10] (Note that even in Freud's theoretical model of progressive norms, the assumption of gender identity is a process.) In this configuration, "gender is achieved and stabilized through the accomplishment of heterosexual positioning and...threats to heterosexuality thus become threats to gender itself."[11] Butler explains that the moments in which one does not meet the accepted requirements of dominant gender performances—such as, for example, a female-bodied person enacting what are perceived to be "masculine" behaviours—create gender anxiety. This anxiety might, for example, "in a woman...induce a panic that she is losing her femininity; that she is not a woman, that she is no longer a proper woman; that, if she is not quite a man, she is like one and hence monstrous in some way."[12] While Butler is quick to point out that there are many ways to come to gender, I would suggest this classic Eurowestern configuration of identity formation is useful here because of its radical difference from the ways female masculinity is indexed in Native literature. As I'll demonstrate in this essay, rather than presenting female masculinity as a stage of stunted psychological growth, the stuff of gender anxiety and bodily horror, Anishinaabe writer Louise Erdrich, whose text I focus on here as an example for my claims, instead presents female masculinity as a type of affective power constructed in and through relationship.

Erdrich's earliest foray into explicit representations of queerness comes in her second novel, *The Beet Queen*. Published in 1986, *The Beet Queen* complicates gender expressions and expands Indigenous depictions of queer sexualities four years before Butler's *Gender Trouble* defines the concept of gender performativity, and four years, as well, before the term "Two-Spirit" was coined at the Third International Gathering of American Indian and First Nations Gays and Lesbians in Winnipeg.[13] Notably, all of the text's central characters—Mary and Karl Adare, a brother and sister abandoned by their mother; Celestine James, Mary's lifelong best friend; and Wallace Pfef, Karl's lover and surrogate father to Karl and Celestine's daughter, Dot (Wallacette) James—stretch conventional gender norms in some way. Julie Barak reads Mary, Celestine, and Dot as "manly-hearted women," a term anthropologists coined for American Indian women like Woman Chief or Brown Weasel Woman, who inhabited third gender roles by taking on the behaviours and occupations of men.[14] Tara Prince-Hughes maintains that "for [Erdrich's] characters, alternative genders are expressed by relatively stable identities marked by inclinations toward mediation, healing, community responsibility, and the work, dress, and behavior of the other sex."[15] These critics and others who have analyzed Erdrich agree she regularly eschews normative, Eurowestern binaries in her examinations of gender, sex, and desire.[16]

Gender roles, Erdrich shows repeatedly, are manifold, messy, and always contingent on the situated nature of relationship. This multiplicity is highlighted in her representations of female masculinity, which underline Halberstam's contention that "very often the unholy union of femaleness and masculinity can produce wildly unpredictable results."[17] In *The Beet Queen*, Erdrich's depiction of Celestine James's unruly masculinity revises the text's representations of *both* queerness and normative heterosexuality, showing the transformative possibilities of gender variance. As I noted in my thesis, I read this female masculinity as (1) specifically enmeshed in the power of affect, and (2) a type of affective power constructed in and through relationship. In their introduction to *The Affect Theory Reader*, Gregory J. Seigworth and Melissa Gregg build their definition of affect on Baruch Spinoza's famous pronouncement that "No one has yet determined what the body can do."[18] To understand the function of affect, they claim, we must recognize that "the capacity of the body is never defined by a body alone but is always aided and abetted by, and dovetails with, the field and context of its force-relations."[19] Affect is thus more than emotion: it is a *bodily* experience. However, unlike bodily drives like thirst or hunger, which are individual and, as Eve Kosofsky Sedgwick reminds us, "are more immediately tied to survival," the bodily experience of affect is necessarily *relational*.[20] In addition, to set up my claim that female masculinity involves affective power, it is helpful to understand how power is intimately tied to affect. "Power," Sedgwick explains, "is form of *relationality* that deals in…negotiations (including win-win negotiations) [and] the *exchange* of affect…. [In this way,] you can be relatively empowered or disempowered without annihilating someone else or being annihilated, or even castrating or being castrated."[21] In other words, power, like affect, necessitates community, necessitates interaction, and, importantly to my argument, implies a relationship that is not inherently antagonist. This is particularly evident in Indigenous contexts where, for example, in matriarchal or matrilineal communities, power historically operates outside the strictures of Eurowestern heteropatriarchy, resting instead on gender complementarity. Such is the generative, affective power of female masculinity in *The Beet Queen*, which is illustrated most prominently in the relationship between Celestine James and Karl Adare.

When Karl's abrupt departure from his lover Wallace brings him into Celestine's life, Karl and Celestine's subsequent liaisons are *based* on a series of gender performances that queer heteropatriarchal norms and expectations. From the novel's beginning, Karl is depicted as a character whose actions and behaviours have the potential to cause what Butler, as I've noted, terms "gender anxiety." Thus, Karl continually challenges gender proscriptions about male-bodied masculinity through his sometimes effeminate gender performance and his experience of a seemingly fluid bisexuality. Shortly after *The Beet Queen*'s 1932 opening, Karl hops a boxcar out of Argus and has his first sexual encounter with a man. While the narrator's early descriptions offer a tidy picture in which Karl's male femininity aligns his desire for men in a seemingly neat depiction of Western homosexuality, Karl's affective response to Celestine's female masculinity alters this homonormative binary. Thus the reader, having been schooled to read Karl as gay, might, like Karl himself, think, "I don't believe this happened," in response to Karl's abrupt erotic encounter with Celestine.[22] Such, I argue, is the transformational power of affect, which Seigworth and Gregg explain is "cast forward by its open-ended in-between-ness."[23] They further maintain that "affect is integral to a body's perpetual *becoming* (always becoming otherwise, however subtly, than what it already is), pulled beyond its seeming surface-boundedness by way of its relation to, indeed its composition through, the forces of encounter."[24] In *The Beet Queen*, female masculinity drives or is perhaps driven by this affective process of becoming. Female masculinity is, then, as we'll see, a type of relational, interactive alterity that indexes the powerful and productive effects of gender nonconformity.

This idea of the affective power of female masculinity forms the basis of my suspicion that there's something queer in Indian country. I suggest that female masculinity is what Womack might call a "radically resistant" identity position that has been heretofore unexamined in Native studies. I turn to a close reading of Karl and Celestine's relationship to make this case. The pair's first encounter occurs when Karl visits the family butcher shop his sister Mary owns and that Mary and Celestine now run. After Karl enters the shop in search of his sister, he and Celestine dance around each other in a contest of wills before they succumb to an awkward passion that parodies the "love-at-first-sight" encounters so common to romance novels. Thus, rather than flattery, the first words Karl utters to Celestine are "You're not pretty."[25] Celestine, in response, subsequently "cut[s] him off" when Karl attempts a sputtered apology. She then answers his question about her name with an abrupt "Celestine...as if it's any of your business."[26] Despite their awkwardness, Karl's "eyes are burning holes" as he looks at her. In fact, according to Celestine, he correctly approximates the introductory script of heterocouplehood, acting, she tells us, just "the way men behave in the world of romance."[27] This script, based on Eurowestern gender configurations, defines masculinity as a physical and psychological power inherent in the male body. By contrast, in such narratives, female bodies and psyches are slight, weak, lesser than; women are acted upon, "swept off their feet," or "carried away."

From the start, Celestine resists this narrative of submission, claiming instead an affective power in her and Karl's initial interaction: "Even though he says I'm not pretty, perhaps in the dusk, I am impossible to resist."[28] Additionally, she perceives herself as "impressive...not to be taken lightly," while describing Karl, on the other hand, as subordinate: he is "slightly smaller" than her and "irritating."[29] Ultimately, Celestine's female masculinity (and Karl and Celestine's own affective responses to the circulation of masculine performance) frames their erotic encounter, which strays far from the Harlequin-inspired "tales of burning love" Celestine reads. She explains: "I lunge from his grip but he comes right with me. I lose my balance. He is fighting me for the upper hand, straining down with all his might, but I am more than equal to his weight-lifting arms and thrashing legs. I could throw him to the side, I know, but I grow curious."[30] Here, Celestine describes foreplay as a contest of strength, where physical agility and brute force meet in some negotiated, erotic centre of gravity. Her description of their lovemaking shows how female masculinity subverts dominant ideological markers that "wed masculinity to maleness and [subsequently wed that male-bodied masculinity] to power and domination."[31] While masculinity still carries the marked weight of power in this scene, as illustrated by Celestine's use of terms like "the upper hand" to describe her prowess in their erotic wrestling, those masculine attributes are tied to Celestine's *female* body. Speaking of this encounter, Louise Flavin argues that "the comic deflation of the traditional lovers' scene affirms the absence of romanticized love."[32] In such a reading, Karl and Celestine's performance of desire falls short of a Eurowestern heteronormative ideal invoked by the term "romantic love." I would suggest this "failure" pivots on interpreting Celestine's female masculinity as lack. In such a line of thought, the sex between Karl and Celestine is not "romantic" because Celestine exceeds gendered expectations of female bodily power. However, such expectations hinge on non-Native understandings of sex and gender. I argue Erdrich's depiction of female masculinity—as seen in Karl's affective response to Celestine's masculine power—requires us to rethink such uninterrogated binaries.

Here again, Halberstam offers a way to revise these limited and limiting equations. In her 2011 book, *The Queer Art of Failure*, failure is equated with "queer struggle," "the refusal of legibility, and an art of unbecoming.... The queer art of failure turns on the impossible, the improbable, the unlikely, and the unremarkable. It quietly loses, and in losing it imagines other goals for life, for love, for art, and for being."[33] Halberstam suggests we can find meaning and value in lack, in absence, in difference, in the also-rans. Celestine's female masculinity and her awkward love scenes with Karl situate them in this liminal space, showing, as Halberstam notes, that "failure loves company."[34] Thus, while there may not be *heteronormative* romantic love between Celestine and Karl, as defined by the Eurowestern standards of the romance novel, there is unquestioningly attraction based on what I read as the affective power of Celestine's female masculinity. Karl is drawn to Celestine like a magnet despite the fact that he "cannot figure the sum of [her]. As if [she is] too much for him to compass."[35] He is consistently surprised by the strength of his embodied response. To regain equilibrium, he attempts to define Celestine's masculinity in terms he recognizes; however, his verbal pronouncements fail to adequately describe the force of her affective power. Their first meeting offers a perfect example of this struggle as Karl stumbles through the courtship ritual of flirting, saying, "'Pretty's not everything.... You're built....' He stops trying to hide his confusion.... 'If you curled the ends at least,' he says, attempting to recover, 'if you cut your hair. Or maybe it's the apron.'"[36] Karl and Celestine's subsequent relationship is built upon such unconventional "failures." For example, their first sexual encounter at the butcher shop concludes when Karl attempts to sell Celestine utility shears from his sample case. As he "takes his scissors and cuts [a] penny into a spiral," Celestine thinks, "So…this is what happens after the burning kiss, when the music roars. Imagine."[37] Karl subsequently refuses to leave until Celestine buys a knife, whereupon he "snaps the case shut" and disappears.[38] Yet despite the myriad of ways in which their initial meeting fails to live up to the over-determined narratives of heterosexual romance novels, Celestine has no doubt of Karl's eventual return since, she explains, "There is something about me he has to follow."[39] Though that claim might initially seem unfounded given Karl's wordless disappearance after their hasty sex, in the end, Celestine correctly estimates her attraction: Karl not only (inadvertently) arrives at Celestine's house and once again has sex with her, he also fails to leave. Celestine explains: "When I tell him he must go, he suddenly hits the floor like a toppled statue."[40] And, as in their first encounter, their subsequent sexual liaisons fail, at least in Celestine's estimation, to meet normative standards of heterocouplehood: "It is uncomfortable. In the love magazines, when passion holds sway, men don't fall down and roll on the floor and lay there like dead. But Karl does that."[41] Yet the two are drawn together by a desire seemingly out of their control, a desire I read as *contingent* upon Celestine's oft-acknowledged masculinity, which engenders an odd, less-than-romantic partnership that remains queerly generative in all its failures.

Moreover, in *The Beet Queen*, Celestine's female masculinity is augmented rather than challenged by her relationship with Karl, which underlines the relational, active nature of the affective experience. For example, Celestine compares Karl's "polished fingernails" to her own hands, those "of a woman who has handled too many knives, deep-nicked and marked with lines, toughened from spice and brine, gouged, even missing a tip and nail."[42] And, much as in the first scenes I analyzed, the text repeatedly makes such comparisons in their sexual encounters, as well. Female masculinity thus becomes legible only through relationship. But in terms of my overall argument, it's important to note that Celestine is not merely more masculine by comparison with the oft-feminized Karl; she is, in fact, depicted as masculine from childhood and also as having been accepted as such. While she could be read as Halberstam's tomboy, a figure who has "an extended childhood period of female masculinity,"[43] reading Celestine's female masculinity from an Indigenous studies perspective enables us to see that she has Two-Spirit precursors as well. In such Indigenous histories, Evelyn Blackwood explains, "The female candidate for cross-gender status displayed an interest in the male role during childhood. A girl avoided learning female tasks. Instead, as in the case of the Cocopa warrhameh, she played with boys and made bows and arrows with which to hunt birds and rabbits. The Mohave hwame '[threw] away their dolls and metates, and [refused] to shred bark or perform other feminine tasks.'"[44]

Looking back to their adolescence, Mary describes Celestine in ways that suggest such male identifications. Celestine, Mary tells us, was "strong. Her arms were thick from wrestling with her brother Russell, and she…was bigger than the eighth-grade boys."[45] But where the gender deviance of the tomboy causes gender anxiety and thus is usually contained post-puberty when "the full force of gender conformity descends on a girl," Celestine cultivates her female masculinity.[46] For example, when Celestine quits school to work in her late teens, Mary explains that she "looked good, big and lean"; she wore "tailored suits instead of dresses and…a leather shoulderbag…. She was handsome like a man. Her voice was low and penetrating and she smoked Viceroys."[47] Though Celestine clearly fails to meet dominant expectations for female gender performance, in Mary's description that failure is not perceived as lack. Instead of gender anxiety, Celestine's experience echoes Indigenous histories of gender variance where "though in different tribes the socializing processes varied, girls achieved the cross-gender role in each instance through accepted cultural channels."[48] Thus Erdrich's productive representations of female masculinity subvert common Eurowestern depictions of female masculinity as anxiety-producing deficit, as the fear "that, if she is not quite a man, she is like one and hence monstrous in some way."[49] Instead, through Mary's eyes, Celestine's female masculinity is sultry promise, smoke and penetration. Yet interestingly, in what could be read as queer failure piled upon queer failure, we find that Celestine does not identify as lesbian. Through her relationship with Karl, Celestine subverts what Halberstam calls the "rigid insistence" of dominant cultural narratives that contend "some form or another of female masculinity indicates prelesbianism."[50] In contradiction to such insistence, Celestine's failure to live up to a feminine ideal of gender behaviour is at the very heart of Karl's erotic attraction to her. For Celestine, gender failure, which she experiences and, in fact, cultivates from childhood, is the path to affective power. As my reading of Karl and Celestine's relationship demonstrates, Erdrich thus writes female masculinity as the improbable and the impossible, as bodily excess, and as the antithesis to heteronormative "tales of burning love." Ultimately, *The Beet Queen* demonstrates how an eroticized female masculinity can inhabit the space of the vanished heterosexual ideal through the queer art of failure.

I want to conclude as I began, by suggesting a larger issue is at stake in the recognition that there's something queer in Indian Country. At the heart of that queerness is a disobedience to dominant gender norms that exists in the unruly bodies of Big Moms and butch dykes. Ultimately, the study of these unruly women has significant implications for the field. I propose that analyses of female masculinity in Indigenous literatures, of which this essay is an early and exploratory example, rest on three ideas of import to Native American and Indigenous studies:

- First, female masculinity has the potential to challenge dominant stereo-types about Indigenous masculinities. This work is radically important given that, as Brian Klopotek explains,

> For at least the last century, hypermasculinity has been one of the foremost attributes of the Indian world that whites have imagined. With squaws and princesses usually playing secondary roles, Indian tribes are populated predominantly by noble or ignoble savages, wise old chiefs, and cunning warriors. These imagined Indian nations comprise an impos-sibly masculine race. Because of such perpetually outlandish representations of Indian gender, masculinity has become a crucial arena for contesting unrealistic images of Indians.[51]

The very existence of female masculinity fractures these monolithic, ex-ternally imposed understandings of Indigenous masculinity. Recognizing Native masculinities as not only multiple but also mobile requires a paradigm shift. So, for example, analyses of the circulation of female masculinity in the early work of butch-identified writers like Chrystos and Janice Gould, who lived in and write about California during the 1960s and 1970s, would both dispute and revise the limited, hypermas-culine narratives still so prevalent in representations of Red-Power–era masculinity.

- Second, the field has much to gain through the deployment of affect theory, which offers a language to discuss the integrated considerations of body, emotion, and reciprocal relationship that are so central to Indigenous communities and literatures. To do so, we can follow the ground-breaking work by theorists like Tanana Athabascan scholar Dian Million. Merging these two fields of critical inquiry acknowledges the weight and value of embodied experiences, of "colonialism as it is *felt* by those who experience it."[52] As I demonstrated here, the articulation of female masculinity is necessarily affective, as it relies on relationship, the body, and, most often, on that which is felt but not named. This affective turn, which is so evident in *The Beet Queen*, can also be seen in feature films like *Johnny Greyeyes* and in the experimental cinema of Thirza Cuthand where, in both cases, female masculinity is both a site of survivance and an affective power that can be read as an ethic of care.[53]

- Third, and perhaps most importantly, I want to suggest that such affective, transformative power holds the trace of Two-Spirit histories, of gender traditions that exist before and beyond the halls of academe. Here, I stake a claim not for Native studies as an addition to queer studies, but instead, for Indigeneity as the point of departure.

Collectively, what I hope these three claims demonstrate is that the study of female masculinity in Indigenous literatures functions not as another settler colonial imposition on Native texts and lives, but instead as a space of generative understanding that makes legible the embodied, relational ties between present-day Indigenous literatures and ongoing traditions of gender variance. Thus I propose a study of female masculinity that, to return to Halberstam's words, challenges "the privileged reservation of masculinity for men"[54] from the psychic and physical locale of the reservation. In this way, we meet Halberstam's call for new masculinities by using affective methodologies that not only employ but also *stem from* Indigenous understandings of sexualities, genders, and the world.

Notes

1   Judith Halberstam, *Female Masculinity* (Durham, NC: Duke University Press, 1998), xii.

2   Ibid., 1.

3   Brendan Hokowhitu, "Taxonomies of Indigeneity: Indigenous Heterosexual Patriarchal Masculinities," in this volume.

4   Halberstam, *Female Masculinity*, 29.

5   Craig Womack, *Red on Red: Native American Literary Separatism* (Minneapolis: University of Minnesota Press, 1999), 280.

6   Craig Womack, "Suspicioning: Imagining a Debate between Those Who Get Confused, and Those Who Don't, When They Read Critical Responses to the Poems of Joy Harjo, or What's an Old-Timey Gay Boy Like Me to Do?," *GLQ: A Journal of Lesbian and Gay Studies* 16, no. 1–2 (2010): 133–45.

7   Halberstam, *Female Masculinity*, 45.

8   See, for example, Evelyn Blackwood, "Sexuality and Gender in Certain Native American Tribes: The Case of Cross-Gender Females," *Signs: Journal of Women in Culture and Society* 10, no. 1 (1984): 27–42; Alfred W. Bowers, "Hidatsa Social and Ceremonial Organization," *Smithsonian Institution Bureau of American Ethnology*

Bulletin 194 (Washington, DC: U.S. Government Printing Office, 1965); Charles Callender and Lee M. Kochems, "The North American Berdache," *Current Anthropology* 24, no. 2 (1983): 443–70; George Catlin, *Letters and Notes on the Manners, Customs, and Conditions of North American Indians* (New York: Dover Publications, 1844, 1973); George Deveraux, "Institutionalized Homosexuality of the Mohave Indians," *Human Biology* 9 (1937): 498–523; Brian Joseph Gilley, *Becoming Two-Spirit: Gay Identity and Social Acceptance in Indian Country* (Lincoln: University of Nebraska Press, 2006); Jean-Guy A. Goulet, "The 'Berdache'/'Two-Spirit': A Comparison of Anthropological and Native Constructions of Gendered Identities Among the Northern Athapaskans," *Journal of Royal Anthropological Institute* 2 (1996): 683–701; Maurice Kenny, "Tinselled Bucks: An Historical Study in Indian Homosexuality," *Gay Sunshine* 26–27 (1975–76): 16–17, 15; Sue-Ellen Jacobs, "Berdache: A Brief Review of Literature," *Colorado Anthropologist* 1, no. 1 (1968): 25–40; Sue-Ellen Jacobs, Wesley Thomas, and Sabine Lang, eds., *Two-Spirit People: Native American Gender Identity, Sexuality, and Spirituality* (Urbana: University of Illinois Press, 1997); Sabine Lang, *Men as Women: Women as Men* (Austin: University of Texas Press, 1998); Beatrice Medicine, "Changing Native American Roles in an Urban Context," in Jacobs, Thomas, and Lang, *Two-Spirit People*, 145–55; Beatrice Medicine, "'Warrior Women': Sex Role Alternatives for Plains Women," in *The Hidden Half: Studies of Plains Indian Women*, ed. Patricia Albers and Beatrice Medicine (Washington, DC: University Press of America, 1983), 267–80; Will Roscoe, *The Zuni Man-Woman* (Albuquerque: University of New Mexico Press, 1991); Will Roscoe, *Changing Ones: Third and Fourth Genders in Native North America* (New York: St. Martin's Griffin, 2000); Claude E. Schaeffer, "The Kutenai Female Berdache," *Ethnohistory* 12, no. 3 (1965): 193–236; Wesley Thomas, "Navajo Cultural Constructions of Gender and Sexuality," in Jacobs, Thomas, and Lang, *Two-Spirit People*, 156–73; Wesley Thomas and Sue-Ellen Jacobs, "'…And We Are Still Here': From Berdache to Two-Spirit People," *American Indian Culture and Research Journal* 23, no. 2 (1999): 91–107; Harriet Whitehead, "The Bow and the Burden Strap: A New Look at Institutionalized Homosexuality in Native North America," in *Sexual Meanings: The Cultural Construction of Gender and Sexuality*, ed. Sherry B. Ortner and Harriet Whitehead (New York: Cambridge University Press, 1981), 80–115; and Walter Williams, *The Spirit and the Flesh: Sexual Diversity in American Indian Culture* (Boston: Beacon Press, 1992). This list is by no means comprehensive, but the sheer abundance of material speaks to the ubiquity of complex gender roles in Indigenous communities.

9 Leslie Marmon Silko, *Yellow Woman and a Beauty of the Spirit: Essays on Native American Life Today* (New York: Simon & Schuster, 1996), 66.

10 Judith Butler, "Melancholy Gender: Refused Identification," *Psychoanalytic Dialogues: The International Journal of Relational Perspectives* 5, no. 2 (1995): 168.

11 Ibid.

12 Ibid.

13 Jacobs, Thomas, and Lang, introduction to *Two-Spirit People*, 6; Qwo-Li Driskill, Chris Finley, Brian Joseph Gilley, and Scott Lauria Morgensen, eds., introduction to *Queer Indigenous Studies: Critical Interventions in Theory, Politics, and Literature* (Tucson: University of Arizona Press, 2011), 10.

14 Julie Barak, "Blurs, Blends, Berdaches: Gender Mixing in the Novels of Louise Erdrich," *Studies in American Indian Literatures* 8, no. 3 (1996): 55.

15 Tara Prince-Hughes, "Worlds In and Out of Balance: Alternative Genders and Gayness in the *Almanac of the Dead* and *The Beet Queen*," *Literature and Homosexuality* (2000): 8.

16 For further essays on Erdrich and gender, see Sandra Baringer, "'Captive Woman?': The Rewriting of Pocahontas in Three Contemporary Native American Novels," *SAIL* 11, no. 3, (1999): 42–63; Victoria Brehm, "The Metamorphoses of an Ojibwe *Manido," American Literature* 68, no. 4 (1996): 677–706; Susan Perez Castillo, "The Construction of Gender and Ethnicity in the Texts of Louise Silko and Louise Erdrich," *The Yearbook of English Studies* 24 (1994): 228–36; Susan Perez Castillo, "Women Aging Into Power: Fictional Representations of Power and Authority in Louise Erdrich's Female Characters," *Studies in American Indian Literatures* 8, no. 4 (1996): 13–20; Daniel Cornell, "Woman Looking: Revis(ion)ing Pauline's Subject Position in Louise Erdrich's *Tracks," Studies in American Indian Literatures* 4, no. 1 (1992): 49–64; J. James Iovannone, "'Mix-Ups, Messes, Confinements, and Double-Dealings': Transgendered Performances in Three Novels by Louise Erdrich," *Studies in American Indian Literatures* 21, no.1 (2009): 38–68; Karah Stokes, "What about the Sweetheart? The 'Different Shape' of Anishinabe Two Sister Stories in Louise Erdrich's *Love Medicine* and *Tales of Burning Love," MELUS* 24, no. 2 (1999): 89–105; and Annette Van Dyke, "Of Vision Quests and Spiritual Guardians: Female Power in the Novels of Louise Erdrich," in *The Chippewa Landscape of Louise Erdrich,* ed. Allan Chavkin. (Tuscaloosa: University of Alabama Press, 1999), 130–43.

17 Halberstam, *Female Masculinity,* 29.

18 Gregory J. Seigworth and Melissa Gregg, eds., introduction to *The Affect Theory Reader* (Durham, NC: Duke University Press), 3.

19 Ibid.

20 Eve Kosofsky Sedgwick, *Touching Feeling: Affect, Pedagogy, and Performativity* (Durham, NC: Duke University Press, 2003), 20.

21 Eve Kosofsky Sedgwick, "Melanie Klein and the Difference Affect Makes," *South Atlantic Quarterly* 106, no. 3 (2007): 631–2, emphasis mine.

22 Louise Erdrich, *The Beet Queen* (New York: Bantam, 1986), 128.

23 Seigworth and Gregg, introduction to *The Affect Theory Reader,* 3.

24 Ibid.

25 Erdrich, *The Beet Queen,* 125.

26 Ibid., 126.

27 Ibid., 127.

28 Ibid., 126.

29 Ibid., 127.

30 Ibid., 128.

31 Halberstam, *Female Masculinity,* 2.

32 Louise Flavin, "Gender Construction Amid Family Dissolution in Louise Erdrich's *The Beet Queen," Studies in American Indian Literatures* 7, no. 2 (1995): 20.

33 Judith Halberstam, *The Queer Art of Failure* (Durham, NC: Duke University Press, 2011), 88.

34 Halberstam, *The Queer Art of Failure,* 121.

35 Erdrich, *The Beet Queen,* 132.

36 Ibid., 127.

37 Ibid., 130.

38 Ibid.

39 Ibid., 131.

40 Ibid., 134.

41 Ibid.

42 Ibid., 133.

43 Halberstam, *Female Masculinity*, 5.

44 Blackwood, "Sexuality and Gender," 30.

45 Erdrich, *The Beet Queen*, 37.

46 Halberstam, *Female Masculinity*, 6.

47 Erdrich, *The Beet Queen*, 67.

48 Blackwood, "Sexuality and Gender," 30.

49 Butler, "Melancholy Gender," 168.

50 Halberstam, *Female Masculinity*, 52.

51 Brian Klopotek, "'I Guess Your Warrior Look Doesn't Work Every Time': Challenging Indian Masculinity in the Cinema," in *Across the Great Divide: Cultures of Manhood in the American West*, ed. Matthew Basso, Laura McCall, and Dee Garceau (New York: Routledge, 2001), 251.

52 Dian Millon, "Felt Theory: An Indigenous Feminist Approach to Affect and History," *Wicazo Sa Review* 24, no. 2 (2009): 58.

53 *Johnny Greyeyes*, directed by Jorge Manuel Manzano, starring Gail Maurice, Columpa Bobb, and Jonathan Fisher (Wolfe Video, 2002). Independent films produced and directed by Thirza Cuthand include *Lessons in Baby Dyke Theory* (1995), *Bisexual Wannabe* (1997), *Untouchable* (1998), *Through the Looking Glass* (1999), *Helpless Maiden Makes an "I" Statement* (2000), *Anhedonia* (2001), *Love & Numbers* (2004), *Madness in Four Actions* (2007), *You Are a Lesbian Vampire* (2008), and *Homelands* (2010).

54 Halberstam, *Female Masculinity*, xii.

CHAPTER 8

Oshki Ishkode, New Fire

Niigaanwewidam James Sinclair

Naanabozho

This story is in the words of a grandmother's gift to her grandsons. It's here, in Naanabozho, who was sent to teach Anishinaabeg about life. It's about fathers, sons, and everyone in between. Like many journeys, it also begins with an ending.

In a place not far from here, there lived an old woman, Nokomis. Nokomis was a kind and hardworking woman, but she was very lonely, for all she ever wanted was a daughter she could teach, sing alongside, and collect medicines with. Every day before she began her work she would travel down to the water and lay asemaa, asking to be blessed. One summer morning she arrived at the shoreline to find a young woman there waiting for her. Upon seeing her, Nokomis burst into tears and thanked Gichi Manito for this great gift, vowing to care for and take responsibility for this young woman for the rest of her life. Every day the pair worked together, laughed, shared stories and songs, and grew to care for one another very much. Like a parent with a child, for years this bond grew, strengthened, and became unbreakable.

One day, while in the forest collecting medicines together, the young woman strayed far from Nokomis. Soon, when she tried finding her way back to the old woman, she realized that she was travelling in circles. The young woman didn't worry, for she knew the forest was a rich and beautiful place where nothing could hurt her. Even as day grew into night, she did not worry. The young woman walked all night, travelling deeper and deeper into the forest until she came to a rocky landscape with huge, old trees she barely recognized. Still unafraid, she lay down to sleep under a great tree, knowing light would soon come and she could find her way home.

As she entered the dream world, the young woman suddenly saw a beautiful mountain covered in moss and snow. She climbed up this mountain and, as she travelled, could feel it getting colder and colder. Arriving at the top, she felt a wind envelop her, embracing her ankles and circling her legs, rushing up her body and, finally, entering her. She felt warmth and peace and growth and a new spirit emerge in her body as the sunrise came over the horizon. She could see nothing but a beautiful plain in front of her, full of waves of colour and hue. She saw and felt, for the first time, love.

The young woman was awakened by Nokomis, who had been searching for her all night throughout the forest. The two women embraced and spent the rest of the new day collecting new medicines in a part of the forest they had never seen before. They returned home, laughing and joyous over their new discovery. The young woman was having such a good time she even forgot about the dream she had.

After they returned home, Nokomis noticed changes in the young woman. One of the many changes was that she was getting bigger and bigger. Nokomis knew that she was no longer a young lady but a full-grown woman, but this was more than these kinds of changes. She asked her daughter if anything had happened that night she spent in the forest. The woman responded by saying nothing she could remember. Every day Nokomis noticed more changes and asked her daughter again. Still, she could recall nothing.

The season changed into the fall, as it always did. One cool morning, Nokomis and her daughter awoke to a great crash. They had barely enough time to get out of the way of a stampede of animals rushing through their territory. From them they heard that a great storm was headed their way from the west, destroying everything in his path with wind and fire. Too old to move, Nokomis begged her daughter to leave, telling her she would be okay. Her daughter, of course, refused—for their bond was unbreakable. Nervously, they travelled to the water and laid asemaa, asking for protection from this new force. As they stood at the shoreline they could see treetops falling as the storm travelled closer and closer. Soon, smoke and the smell of broken wood enveloped the two women as they held one another close.

The storm came over top of the two women and covered them in a huge shadow. Nokomis looked up and saw that this was not a great storm at all but a giant, incredibly beautiful in his vastness and strength. She sat in awe of the beauty of this being and his great power—which seemed to be deeply out of control. The giant seemed to be experimenting with what he could and could not do. His face seemed surprised with all he could destroy and light on fire with arrows from his fingers. His eyes appeared both horrified and satisfied as he peered back at all of the animals and trees he had killed in his wake. His body sagged, engulfed in a swirling wind that floated like a river around his legs, picking up rocks and flinging them in all directions. And, above all, Nokomis could feel a great sadness in the air, a remarkable heaviness.

Nokomis turned back to her daughter to see if what she was seeing and feeling was the same—and saw that she had disappeared. Only a small pile of cinder and ash was left in her place. Nokomis cried out and fell, horrified at her loss, running her fingers through the black dust. In it she discovered a small child, a newborn, coughing and struggling to breathe. Shielding it from the giant above, she picked up the child and enveloped it in her arms. Turning to face the great storm of confusion and destruction above her, she vowed to protect this last piece of her daughter with every ounce of her life. It was then that she realized that the name of her grandson was Naanabozho.

Nokomis turned instead however to silence. The giant, the storm, the fire, had disappeared. Suddenly, it began to snow, slowly dropping flakes on Nokomis and the baby. Animals emerged from the forest. The sky returned to the way it had been before. The world breathed a sigh of relief, for what follows a storm is always change. Life.

The baby cried and broke the silence as Naanabozho came alive in the arms of Nokomis. The old woman took in the child, promising herself that she would do all she could to prepare this tiny being for all the world could be.

For many years Nokomis and Naanabozho lived together. He was a curious boy, always asking questions, always testing boundaries, always playing. She taught him about everything she knew; how to work, provide for himself, and think. She even taught him how to not do these things. Giving him everything she carried, his mind filled with experience and words.

As the years wore on and he became a man, Naanabozho discovered that he possessed great powers. He could create things, imagine, and dream. Some days, Naanabozho made the most beautiful things the world had ever seen. On others, Naanabozho would grow angry and frustrated, hurting himself and those around him. On those days, the old woman would soothe his tears, sing him to sleep, and tell him he was loved. As he developed, Nokomis watched and ensured that he used his powers to help and heal the beings of Creation. She remembered his father and how quickly things can go awry.

One day, however, Naanabozho asked the question she did not want to answer: *Where are my mother and father?*

Nokomis paused, remembering her promise. She wondered how much to tell him. She knew what was coming next.

Naanabozho continued, sensing her nervousness. The next words left his mouth before he could stop them.

Who am I?

The silence between the old woman and the young man was thick. The old woman pretended to work, mostly to delay her response. After a long time, Nokomis said, *I will tell you when you are ready. Now help me pick these medicines.*

Naanabozho knew not to provoke his grandmother, so he bent down to dig up his roots.

Naanabozho asked Nokomis about his mother and father every day. He asked that same question, again and again: *Who am I?*

And, every day, the old woman said she would tell him when he was ready.

One day, the answer came. Nokomis told him the story of how she had found him.

Naanabozho was blinded by hearing what his father had done. Building in anger, he pronounced: *I want to punish him.*

Leave him be. He knows his mistakes, Nokomis said.

No. I want to destroy him.

Nokomis was very worried, but knew that Naanabozho would have to learn for himself. *Do what you must, but your father is very powerful. He is a spirit, a manito.*

What does he look like?

He is very beautiful and very dangerous. He is a giant.

Where can I find him?

In the west.

How will I know when I have met him?

You will know. He will find you.

Nokomis knew just then that she had given Naanabozho everything she could give.

On the day her grandson was to depart, she prepared a bundle for him to carry. It had many parts, including a song that would help him find his way home.

Naanabozho thanked his grandmother, realizing that he would not see her again for a long time. Fighting back tears, he told Nokomis he would always think of her.

Journeying west, Naanabozho travelled all day and night. He walked across sand and earth, plains and hills, lakes and streams. One day, he found a rocky land with huge trees that was hard to travel over. He was exhausted. Lying down under a great tree, he was almost asleep when a voice startled him.

Naanabozho, the voice said, *be careful of your father. He cannot be destroyed.*

Startled, Naanabozho demanded to know whose voice was speaking to him.

You cannot win, the voice continued.

Who is that? Naanabozho said, looking around.

Look up.

It was Baapaase, the woodpecker, who sat in the tree above him.

Baapaase, Naanabozho said. *What do you know? You're just an old auntie. You can't help me.*

I do not know much, but I do know that nothing can injure your father.

I can.

Go ahead and try. For now, however, I am cold. Go gather some flint in a small bag of moss. Come back and use those stones and dry grass to make a fire for me.

Grumbling, Naanabozho did as he was told, having been taught by his grandmother to never disrespect an old woman. Finding flint, however, was very hard. The search took Naanabozho a long time, but finally he returned to the woodpecker.

Take that flint, said Baapaase, *and sharpen it. Give it your thoughts while you do this. That will help you light that fire.*

Naanabozho did exactly as Baapaase asked but he was so tired he could barely keep his eyes open. All he could think of was sleep. He placed the moss bag beside his head and decided to take a nap, soon falling asleep. Naanabozho slept so long that he and the bag became covered by growth and earth, indistinguishable from the world.

Until one day, Naanabozho awoke to the sound of thunderous steps on the earth. He looked up. Baapaase was gone. And, before he could rise, he found himself underneath the shadow of a giant. Standing above him was a huge being, more beautiful then he could have ever imagined. Naanabozho knew immediately who this was.

Boozhoo nibaabaa, said Naanabozho.

Boozhoo ningozhis, said the giant, lifting Naanabozho up.

The two men walked together and spoke. They were curious about each other, and had much to share. Naanabozho listened intently to the giant's stories and experiences, soon growing to admire his father's greatness. In return, Naanabozho told the giant all he had learned from his travels, even making up a few stories to try and sound impressive. The two men talked over a long time, almost leading Naanabozho to forget why he had come to find his father in the first place.

One day, Naanabozho remembered. *Nibaabaa*, Naanabozho said, *I have come to punish you. Because of what you did, I have never felt love from my mother. I do not know who I am. I hurt deeply. I want to share this pain with you.*

You cannot hurt me, ningozhis, his father responded. *I am too powerful. Even if you could, you cannot bring back your mother. Go back to your grandmother and leave me be.*

I am not scared of you, Naanabozho called, retreating to prepare for battle. *I will destroy you.*

Gaawin, I will destroy you.

The next morning these two powerful beings met again. All of Creation turned to watch, for news of their impending battle had travelled quickly.

The giant flung arrows filled with fiery tips at his son. Naanabozho ducked, throwing rocks and sticks back at the giant. Both men were strong and agile, and only a few weapons hit their mark, landing instead on the world around them. The earth soon grew scorched and damaged with holes and ash. Trees were unearthed and animals were killed as everyone around the battle scrambled to escape the destruction. The water departed, the wind left, and the sun and moon sunk away. Birds migrated to save themselves. No one could have imagined that these two men could create such devastation.

Soon enough, the world was seared and silent.

Left with nothing to fling, the two men drew their fists, blasting the air with their blows. When their hands grew raw, they kicked and scratched and bit—using whatever parts of their bodies they had left to strike with. They created deep lesions on each other, cuts that could only grow into scars. For a long time, the battle raged with no advantage.

By now, Naanabozho and his father had only words left. Naanabozho, in his youthful ignorance, had been unprepared for this—he never thought the battle would get this far. His stories were still young while his father carried powerful vessels full of mystery, wisdom, and trickery. The giant knew he had the advantage, so he cast these on Naanabozho, leaving him with gaping wounds that left him weak.

The battle had turned.

Naanabozho fell to the earth, accepting his death. And, as he watched his father prepare a final devastating blow, Naanabozho thought a final thought—of his mother. He thought of his love for her, how she had sacrificed her life for him, and how much she loved his grandmother. She had gifted him all of these things—and he missed her. Closing his eyes, he stretched his arms out into the broken and burnt world and felt peace, when all of a sudden his fingers grazed the moss bag.

Naanabozho's memory stirred. He had a chance.

Wrapping his fingers around a tiny piece of flint, he flung it at his father's head. It slashed through the air and wounded the manito severely. Blood flowed across the giant's face, dripping into his eyes as he fell. Naanabozho's father crashed to the ground, gasping for breath.

Standing above his father, Naanabozho looked into his father's eyes and saw that the giant was scared, for he had never been defeated before. For the first time, Naanabozho felt empathy and helped the giant sit up.

Ningozhis, whispered his father, *you are now my equal. You have great powers, maybe even better than I. Let us make peace.*

Naanabozho nodded as tears fell from his eyes.

His father pulled out a pipe. *Let us smoke*, he said, *and tomorrow you can return to the Anishinaabeg.*

Naanabozho looked around. New plants and trees had sprung where the drops of his father's blood had fallen. There was hardly a sign that the battle had ever even taken place.

Turning back to his father, he saw that the giant had suddenly become an old man. Wrinkles and scars had formed on his face and he was hunched, humble, and frail.

The two men created a fire together and smoked, telling stories of their hopes, dreams, and failures. They shared food, laughter, tears. Then, when they were both exhausted, they took turns protecting one another as they slept. The next day, father and son embraced, and Naanabozho promised to return. The old man told his son that he would wait by the fire until then.

Returning home, Naanabozho felt lost in the new earth, for it had changed. He walked with new eyes now, a new heart, and a new direction. It was then that he remembered his grandmother's song—and found his way home.

Every day thereafter Naanabozho remembered his promise, turning to look back where his father remained. Every time he peered to the west, he could see the old man, waiting by the fire, watching him proudly. When the two men's eyes met Naanabozho would be flooded with the stories they shared, the memory of the pipe they smoked together, and the love they carried for one another. And, if he closed his eyes and thought deeply, Naanabozho could still feel the fire's warmth—no matter how far away he travelled or how long it took for him to remember to look.

Nimishomis

My grandson is here. In dis snow, he is here.

At dat building wit dat neon pink sign promising dat drink I sit in my car and stare at dat hood quickly being covered by dis white blanked. I know I should get out, look for him, but I'm frozen. Stuck in myself.

My grandson is here. I know he is. And I don' know if he's comin home.

I take a deep bret from my cigarette and look over to where he used to sit, beside me, eatin dose black jujubes. He was so young den. I could protect him. Not anymore.

He got out dere last night. I pick him up and he came wit me, but he was still gone. Not like da oder dimes he lef. Seven mons dis dime, da longes he's been away. He send only one letter dis dime, in his first week. Oter dan dat I had not heard from him. When I showed up he refused to see me. I tried to send him letters, telling him I wasn' disappointed. Trouble is, I was lyin.

I shoulda jus said I loved him.

Las week I got a note, written on da back side of a page ripped outta a book:

Hi Grandpa, I get out Friday at 3 pm.

And, beside dat, a 49 song:

My sweetheart don't like me anymore...
Because I drink whisky,
Dats ok I got anoder one...
Way yah hay ya ho wa...

I never taught him dat one. He musta heard me sing dat outside in dat back yard sometime. I jus don't remember. You don't teach kids dose songs, dey jus hear em I guess. I didn' tink anyone was listenin at dat time, listenin to me or my buddies in our drunkness.

I held dat piece of paper in my jacket and looked at it every day. I wondered where dat little boy musta been hiding. I even looked one time for dat hidin spot.

Damn dose men, dose drinks. Damn dose songs.

Dis here hotel is dark, cold, damp. People, covered in dat snow, walkin around everywhere. Come and go, back and fort, drunk.

I have been where dey are before too.

Here. Wit her. And my son.

Right dare.

In dat alley. Where he was born.

It was snowy den doo. On dat night dat check come. I dressed up, even wore my nice jacket. Dat one de army gave me when I came back. I only wore it once. Dat night. I remember dat.

She was so sore. So crabby. *Too full,* she said, *tummy pain. Maybe it's dis baby,* she said, rubbin her belly. *I wanna stay home,* she said.

I told her it was probably dat heartburn. She got it all de time in dose days. Convinced her to come wit me.

We didn make it far from dat door when she said to go in dat alley. I remember it too well now. She fell and I stood over her. Dose bricks felt warm from dat bar too. I remember.

I rolled her and her huge belly onto a damp box and can still remember dat smell of piss. She cried and screamed. I got scared, swore at her for ruinin dis night so early.

I laughed at first, asked if she was faking. She start yellin at me to stop. Den I saw blood fallin. Outta her, poolin aroun her feet. It was here, in dose warm walls and damp boxes and garbage bags and piss smell, my son came.

I didn know what to do. She screamed as dat pain cut drough her body for a few seconds and I didn know how to help. I called for someone down dat alley but only dat silence spoke back.

I asked if she was cold. She laughed for de first dime since we came in dat alley. That made me feel better.

It's comin, she said.

Den, she lifted her skird and squatted, holdin dat wall. I knelt down to hold her up. Her nails scratched indo da brick around her. I stared out into dat darkness and called again for someone to help us. I saw someone look and den go runnin'.

She whimpered and called out for me, but I was right dere. I said someting den, I'm not sure what. She was silent. Not knowing what to do, I sang dat song she loved, da only song I could remember.

> *My sweetheart don' like me anymore...*
> *Cause I drink whisky,*
> *Dats ok I got 'noder one...*
> *Way yah hay ya ho wa...*

She sang wit me, in between de waves of pain. For a long time we be like dat.

And den it happen, dose hands and feet and head come, makin her a bloody mess. I reached down to hold dat head steady as it came out and she helped too. It happened so fast I got angry dat she couldn' slow down. I also got pissed off dat she did dis here. I was scared, to be honest.

I'm not proud of any of dis.

In dat alley and wit a final push, my son came. We caught it and wrapped it in my jacket. I held my boy close and he is silent. I felt warm tears comin down my cheeks as I held him and lied back against dat wall. She was silent too.

I looked at my boy and could see him struggling do breate in de bubbles of blood. I took my finger and licked it clean, wiping de inside of dat mouth until he cry. My boy is okay.

I looked at her body on dat cardboard bed and remember tinking dat she might be dead. Den she began to moan and I brought her our little boy. She cried and held him in my jacket blanket. Dat one I got from the army. Dat was my boy's now.

De tree of us laid in dat dark cold place wit da warm walls and da piss smell and we rest for I don know how long. When I see she and dat baby is ok I went and go get help.

Dey had already arrived. Police too.

Later dere were dese white walls, white coats, and white lights. And den a white man telling me dat she was gone. Dey come too late to save her, he says.

Den dat man said dat baby was not comin home wit me.

He is sick, he said, *you and your wife made him sick.*

Whaddya mean, I say, *he's not sick. He's good.*

Dat man tell it to me but I don listen. I screamed and fight dem but I was too drunk, too weak, too tired. Dey would not even let me see my son to say bye.

I woke up days later. In dis hotel. I found a home in dis place, dis bar, dis drink. For a long time I get real lost in here.

Until dat day my son showed up, wit my grandson.

He sounded like me, but more like her. He had her eyes, her beauty. He had her voice. He gave me dat baby to take care of. I did. I tried to do dat.

So now I got to find him.

I open up dat car door and step onto dat pavement. A whiff of urine welcomes me home. Miigwech.

I reach dat sticky door and enter a wall of noise. Dat sound is the same as it always been. It's a familiar feelin walkin in here. I'm surprised I remember. Was so drunk all dat time.

But now, wit dis clear head, I remember dat first time I came here, when I was de same age as my grandson. I found dis place de first time I was free from dat skool wit dose bars on dose windows. After dad told us we had do go do dere. After dose men took us on dat cart with mom crying while we rode away. After our hair left us. After cryin all dose nights when no one came but dat strap and I promise to not cry no more. I never did.

I remember too much. I can stop it now. It's a part of dis noise.

I remember da last dime I saw my sister. I didn even know she was sick till I went in dat white room. We had dat time together, alone, when she told me we had to go home. We have to escape, she said to me. She told me she could handle dose women in da block robes and would come get me. I shoulda went back. I never saw her again.

The night she died I escaped without dat father seeing me during night check. I walked during de night, hid during de day. I walked but I didn know where I was going. After so long I was hungry and cold and lost and scared. When dat farmer who found me I just told him I came from dat skool cause I wanted something to eat.

He send for dose men to take me back do dat skool. Dat father beat me real good dat night. He hit me harder den ever but I refuse to cry. I promised myself and I kept it.

It was easy to come from dat home to dis one. Dis place had much of dat same feelin. People who promise good dings but give you someting else. Dese places even smell da same. Like piss.

I need to find my grandson now, make these memories stop.

I search in dat sound and smell, making sure to not meet eyes with dose people for too long. Fights start dat way.

Asking de bartender I find him, sitting wit a woman I never seen before. She is kissin his ear. I say his name. He turns and is not surprised to see me, tells me to sit down.

It is den I see him as a little boy again. Like what my son musta looked like.

I wanted much more for my grandson den dis. When he was little, just after he came to me, I ran into dat man at the Friendship Centre who told me dere were dose ceremonies going outside of town.

A powwow, I asked.

No, a lodge, dat man said, *the Midewiwin.*

I didn know de difference at dat time.

I went alone dat time and for da first time found dat life. Dat dere was more to life den dis hotel. I found a place dat talked about how to handle dat skool, dis bar, all dose dings I had experienced. I found a home in dat lodge. I brought my grandson and I showed him. Dose songs. Dose dances. Dose people. Dat fire. I did not understand everyting but we went back dere, every day, for four days. Den I went back dat next year. It's like I knew dat place bud I wanted do know more. Still doday I go and don know everyting but I am learning and am getting better. I brought my grandson until he was old enough to decide if he want to. One day, he told me he didn wanna come.

I shoulda told him do.

I sit wit my grandson and dat woman. He talks wit me about noting really. I tell him I want him do come home wit me. He laughs, orders two more. I don wanna drink, I tell him. He orders anyways. Then, he looks right into my eyes and sings:

> *My sweetheart don' like me anymore...*

He is too loud. I can' get him do listen. Dat woman joins him. She knows the song too.

> *Cause I drink whisky,*

I hate dat smell in dis place. I don' wanna be here anymore.

> *Dats ok I god 'noder one...*

We have to go, my boy. We have to go.

> *Way yah hay ya ho wa...*

He wants do drink, do pardy, do be like me.

His grandfadder.

He asks for twenty dollars. I give it do him knowing he will use it do order more drinks.

Dat woman tells him he has do go outside.

He tells me to wait here so I sit here, wait for him.

I am empty. I have tried do give him everything I didn' give my son, dat one born in dat alley. I tried do give him something else, tell him dose stories he needs do hear. Dat he is more den dis. I tried do sing him dose songs he needs to know. But, like me, he chose someting else.

I failed you, my son. You gave me your boy, and I failed you.

Dose drinks arrive. I pull one of dem toward me. I smell it. It smells good. I wait. I stare into de noise. I wait for a long dime. I stare at dat drink even.

Den dat room clears. What's goin on, I wonder.

I pour dose drinks ondo dat carpet as I go, staining dat carpet. It's nothin new.

I will give it one more dry with my boy. I won dake no for an answer. I will wait no longer. He is going to come home wit me now. I will dake him do dat lodge and teach him dat he is more.

Outside, many people stare into dat alley where my boy was born. I hear sirens. I hear someone ask for help. I look and see, lying on a cardboard box, my grandson, on da ground, bleeding. Dere, where his father was born, he lies, in blood.

I go do him. I hold his head, like I held his father. I sing him dat song I have been trying do teach him. For de first time I hear him sing it wit me. Maybe he does know it, after all.

Nibaabaa

my father is here. it took me years to find him. i was only two miles away. i must have walked by him a hundred times. now i am here getting information from the agency. it was not easy. they were not helpful. mom said that child and family don't like to be reminded of their screw-ups. they said they did not have adoption records dating back to those days. not important enough. they thought I wouldn't care. they were wrong. they were told to take the kids away if the parents were drinking they told me. because my parents drank i was like this they said. like what i ask mom. special mom said. growing up french was never my idea. in elementary the kids used to call me a retard. make fun of my face. i hated school. too hard. too many thoughts. school was for normal kids teacher said. if i was normal i would be all right. i am different. maybe school was for white kids. not for kids who were indian on the outside french on the inside my mom used to say. she said you are very special. more than anyone else she said. i had gifts that no one understood. you are special mom said before she died. i am special. daddy daddy why did you leave me why. i wasn't surprised when they told me about my other parents. people think i am stupid. i always knew. i wonder why they didn't try to find me. that's the funny thing about being left. you don't care to know. i always found reasons not to call. i forgot about it until my son was born. six months ago. his mother left before i even got to the hospital. all she said on the phone was that she was leaving. *you should come* she said. *I have to go.* i didn't even know i was a dad. we worked together at that bar. i did dishes. she was just like me. i still don't even know her last name. i tried to look after him but he's normal. he cries so much. i want to hit him. he is almost white. like his mother. i want him to know about being an indian. i sing him the only indian song i know. 49 songs i learned from other indians from the bar. he needs to know more. i can't give him all i have. now is the time for him to meet his grandfather. before i go. i want him to know him. to see him. so i carry my baby son up the stairs and find the apartment door. i knock and this man answers. my father. in a ripped shirt. my mom once said that endings have a beginning. i don't know if this is true. but this is an ending for sure. he stares at me. i tell him who i am. *It has been so long* he says. he is surprised. i am too. i cry. i am here dad. he sits on the couch. i remember that look from the kids in school. i'm not retarded i tell him. he asks me how old i am. i tell him 24. he asks how i am. i am fine. i show him his grandson. he stares at the baby. i stare at my dad. he offers me instant coffee. he doesn't look at me. his hand is shaking as he pours. we talk and talk. he tells me about the weather. his job. my mother. his life. i tell him about my mom and my school and my life. i tell him the story of how I found him. i even tell him some made up stories that they are still alive. i ask him if he knows where my mother is. he is quiet for a long time. *She is gone* he says. i am angry. a woman comes out of the bedroom. she smells like alcohol. she asks who i am. my father says i am a friend. she asks what is wrong with my face. my father tells her to leave. the woman laughs and leaves the room. i offer my father to hold my son. his grandson. he walks away and chases after her. he does not want my son. he is not looking at me. i ask him why he is not proud to meet his grandson. he is silent. i want my son to learn things i cannot teach him. this old man is still not looking at me. i want you to teach my son i say. take care of him. i want him to teach me too. i slam my fist on the coffee table. that's what fathers do i say. *Calm down*, he says. i hate you i say. i hate that you're not happy to see me. i hate that my mother is dead. i hate that you do not want to look at me. i hate that you do not want to touch your grandson. he's normal i tell him. not like me. he's normal. *You're normal too, my son* he tells me. no. i'm not i say. i'm special. special. WHY DON'T YOU WANT TO LOOK AT ME i scream. *I'm sorry, so sorry* he says. i hate you, i say. *Put the baby down* he tells me. i do. then i hit him right in the face so he falls to the floor. my son cries on the couch. the woman comes out of the bedroom. she picks up my son. i am crying. i hate crying. *Go* my dad says. i leave my son there. he should be normal there. i will come to him again. i will come back after i wash dishes tonight. i don't want to hurt him. i always lose my temper like this. i'm not normal. i'm special. mom i miss you. so much. i need help. *Come back, my son*, he calls to me. i will see you again. take care of your grandson i say.

Ninghozis

There is a voice. It's my grandmother. I can hear it.

I've never heard her before, but it's her.

Here.

At least, I think so. Where is here? A mall? A building? I see nothing but fluorescent lights. Here's some glass doors. I'm standing on wet pavement, but my feet are not cold. There's nothing here but space. No wind, no life, nothing.

Except that voice. My grandmother.

I was in that bar only a moment ago.

Fucking jerk. How was I to know that he was the brother of the guy I ganked. How was I to know that asshole was connected. That fucker was gonna kill me. I was just defending myself. If I didn't make a stand the first week I would've been a toy the whole time. They set me up, got her to bring me outside.

I didn't mean it, I yelled when they were on me, *that fucker was packing aces. What did he expect?*

Shit happens, I heard one of them say. There were too many. *Any new fish with no partner should watch his back in the pen,* another said, *and not fuck around.*

I was only protecting myself, you fucks.

You stabbed my fucking brother, some guy screamed and lunged. *You stupid fuck.*

I danced away from the flashing metal but couldn't escape the fists. Then, blackness.

I remembered by grandfather, sitting inside the bar. *Please god let them not know he is there,* I remember thinking.

You're fucked if you do me, I yelled at them, hoping to distract.

Who cares. I heard someone laugh. *Who cares.*

I remember the cold pavement on my cheek. Hands on my head pulling me away. Everything was slippery. My eyes opened and closed now, I saw my breath once. By now there was only silence. I heard myself wheeze. It was coming.

I remember being lifted up to face the asshole whose brother I ganked. Punched until my eyes opened.

Funny, he was a boy, like fourteen. With real old eyes. Staring, he drove that metal into my stomach.

Pain, breath, silence. Whiteness.

Then, here.

I should've went home when I got out. I was ashamed. My grandfather made me promise to change. I couldn't. He thinks that lodge is for me. I had too many questions and not many answers. I just knew when I was there I wanted to go somewhere else, anywhere. Then, I was in there. Away. There I wanted to be home.

I enter the glass doors and peer in. It's a mall but with no stores. Just empty rooms.

My feet hit carpet but there is no comfort. It's like my feet are still on pavement.

The doors lock behind me. I am trapped, but this time it's different. This is a place of nothing but it's something. How weird.

I hear my grandmother's voice, louder now. Like on an intercom.

It's my grandfather's song. The one he was trying to teach me all the time. The one he sang to me, only a few minutes ago now. I never listened. It's even in words I don't know.

I walk past the empty rooms, to a light at the end of a hall of empty stores. The light grows bigger with every step. Are those people there?

The song grows louder now. Why do I understand it?

I reach a water fountain, so I drink. Kinda gross in a mall, but this one tastes okay.

I walk, toward this song, to a fire, rich and healthy, with smoke billowing into a hole in the ceiling.

This is some mall.

The song goes on. The rhythm repeats, with ends with beginnings that end and begin again. I feel my heart beating.

There are people sitting around that fire, beautiful people. No one is singing. They're just staring, lifeless, sort of dead but not. They're like zombies. I think I should be scared but this is a mall, not a ceremony.

Suddenly, a young girl grabs my hand and pulls me toward the fire.

What do I have to lose. I go.

She begins to dance around that fire, holding my hand, in a circle. She pulls my hand up and down, like she's asking me to join. I can't look any stupider, so I do, copying her.

I take my first step, and the people literally come to life. They rise. They are smiling. There is suddenly happiness here. Creepy.

I turn to the girl, dancing beside me. *Why am I here?* I ask her.

She does not answer.

I dance slowly at first, but the song's getting faster. I touch each toe to the ground two times, move faster, repeat the rhythm. It is so quick I can't keep up. I sweat. The fire is so damn hot. I am not keeping up.

The young girl holds my hand. I watch her, try to keep pace. I am suddenly not struggling, I am having fun. I laugh. There are people connected to her hand, in a long snake moving through that empty mall. We return to the fire and circle it. Circle it. Circle it.

The young girl holds my hand and we dance together, faster, together. My grandmother's voice sings and sings and sings.

I know this. I have always known this. I did not know that I knew this but I feel life here. This place of nothing is actually full. I see it now.

I call out. I'm answered by people with laughter. I call again. They answer, accept me, love me.

Tears well in my eyes. I dance and remember. No endings here, only the song. Always. Continuing. This is a good place.

The little girl grows older, taller, beautiful. She ages quickly, until she is my grandmother, dancing, teaching, loving me, showing me what I know. She has been with me all along. *Nokomis, I never knew you were with me, I never knew.*

I'm here.

And as she speaks the people fade into the smoke. The fire dies into a cinder until there are only red coals, steaming under the white fluorescent lights.

I don't want this to end, I say, gripping my grandmother's hand.

I know, she says, *but you have to go.*

I feel tears on my cheeks. I am tired now, cold. The fire is almost out. The only sound I can hear is the mall water fountain flowing in the distance.

Are you ready? my grandmother asks.

I don't know, I say, continuing to hold her hand.

Let's see. Where have you been? she asks, squeezing my fingers. *Tell me.*

I tell her the only story I know.

Of my life. How my grandfather raised me. How he never spoke about her but I knew he loved her so, so much. How my father dropped me off as a baby with him one afternoon. How I wish I knew my dad, even if he was sick. How no one knows who my mother is. How I hurt so many. How I was in jail. How the men in the alley behind the bar stabbed me.

I tell her of my journey to this place. I tell her this story.

When I finish, she releases my hand.

You're ready now.

I like being here, I answer. *I don't want to go.*

I look at the old woman. She sits back, points with her lips to somewhere behind me. I look.

There is a tall young man, standing by the cinders. He is holding a drum. He was the one playing, helping with the song of my grandmother. He was keeping the beat for her, for the people, me.

The fire is dying, the young man says.

I have no matches, I say, *no wood.*

We don't need any, he says, pointing at my hand.

I am holding a stone. The young man hands me old, dry carpet from the floor. I touch the carpet to the rock and a spark jumps from my hand, sitting on the fabric. The man fans the flame with his hands, spreading the flame onto the rubber and plastic. It catches and we add it to the coals as it leaps back into life.

The mall lights up with the fire and I see it's not empty at all; it's full of people and animals and life. It was the light that emptied out what I could see. They had been there the entire time. I am in wonder at this place.

I rise and turn back to look at the man.

Miigwech nibaa....

But he is gone.

I am alone, with the fire. Waiting.

I feel new breath, new life. I close my eyes. I have to go. Like my grandmother told me.

I remember her song.

Then, I leave this home, come to another.

I open my eyes. My grandfather is here, in the room with the white walls. Singing his song. Again.

I join him. I know it now. My grandmother's song. She sang it to me while I slept. It's my song, more then the words.

We finish.

I love you, nimishomis. I want to come home.

I love you too my grandson. Dat was quite a night.

I want to find my dad. I want to find nibaabaa.

Me too, he replies, lifting me out of the bed, holding me, loving me.

Me too.

III. LIVING INDIGENOUS MASCULINITIES AND INDIGENOUS MANHOOD

CHAPTER 9

Patriotic Games: Boundaries and Masculinity in New Zealand Sport

Phillip Borell

In his 2004 article, "Tackling Māori Masculinity: A Colonial Genealogy of Savagery and Sport," Brendan Hokowhitu provides a genealogy of Māori masculinity through the lens of sport in New Zealand.[1] The aim of this essay will be to follow on from this work and to provide further insight into current issues in rugby league such as patriotism, nationalism, and masculinity. By looking at the progression of Māori masculinity as a colonial construct, I will examine the development of a prescribed Māori masculinity through sport in New Zealand. Questions will be raised as to the influence of continuing patterns of colonization in New Zealand sport and to what extent these colonial patterns continue to determine Māori masculinities in contemporary sport.

Deploying Mignolo's theory of coloniality, as discussed by Maldonado-Torres,[2] this paper will seek to add to the genealogy of Māori masculinity by applying coloniality (an examination of the recurring patterns of colonization) to the construction of Māori masculinity through sport. Referencing Hokowhitu's work through the gaze of coloniality I will attempt to add to the understanding of Māori masculinity in sport. In concluding the paper, I question whether or not there is an option for de-coloniality in professional sport. By providing an overview of a current case of an "unpatriotic" decision made by rugby league player James Tamou, I argue that there is now a "decolonial" option for Māori athletes to reclaim their masculinity outside of the colonial boundaries established by the nation-state.

Constructions of Māori Masculinity

> In the nineteenth century Māori masculine physicality was, like the untamed countryside, something to be conquered and civilised; in the twentieth century it was something to be harnessed to provide manual labor for New Zealand's developing colonial nation; in the twenty-first century it has become a spectacle played out by the overachievement of tāne (Māori men) on the sports field.
>
> —Brendan Hokowhitu, "Tackling Māori Masculinity"[3]

This statement by Hokowhitu offers insight into the colonizer's construction of an "accepted" Māori masculinity. Although a brief reference to the genealogy of Māori masculinity, this is an illustration of the transition, over time, of Māori masculinity from savage to sportsman.

While there is insufficient space here to provide a broader history of Māori and colonization,[4] or an elaborate genealogical discussion on Māori masculinity,[5] it is safe to say that the first encounters of Europeans with Māori were not only assumptive in relation to savagery and gender, they were also emblematic in terms of what was to follow regarding the representation, construction, and imposed limitations of Māori masculinity. That is, the discourses of savagery that have surrounded Māori men in various forms since first contact remain today and resonate in numerous contemporary discourses. For instance, in 1642 Abel Tasman "discovered" New Zealand, although during his brief journey to the West Coast of the South Island of New Zealand, Tasman failed to set foot on land. While not having ventured closer than the bays of Tai Tapu (Golden Bay, South Island), Tasman and his crew engaged with Māori, lost some lives, and left with their interpretations of what Māori men were. "Savage," "rough," and "uncivilized" are terms that could be used to sum up the accounts of Māori from Tasman's journals.

Over a century later the next explorer to "rediscover" New Zealand was Captain James Cook, who in 1769 further contributed to the determining of who and what Māori were. While managing to make landfall and communicate with Māori, Cook's detailing of Māori, and in particular Māori men, was limited.[6] Cook did not venture further than one kilometre inland and, as a result, did not see any of the developed agriculture, horticulture, or permanent villages of Māori society. As stated by Andrew Vayda, "Maori warriors, in Cook's opinion, killed everyone indiscriminately—whether man, woman, or child—and they took no prisoners at all."[7]

The writings of these explorers and others that followed shaped Europeans' perception of Māori for many years to come. Māori were to become known as a race of warriors, savages, and heathens.[8] With a sense of mystery surrounding the unknown "Other," an understanding of Māori needed to be forged in a manner that elevated the Pākehā (i.e., foreigner, today used for "European New Zealander") into a position of superiority. Albert Memmi perhaps summarizes these concepts best when he states that "Just as the bourgeoisie proposes an image of the proletariat, the existence of the colonizer requires that an image of the colonized be suggested."[9] Memmi's statement suggests that a definition of the colonized is necessary for the positioning of the colonizer as superior. Such definitions also serve to reinforce movements to enforce "change" in the practices of the colonized. Sport in New Zealand would become one such way that colonial constructs of masculinity would be developed and enforced.

Relatively recently, a counter history has arisen that challenges the assumed savagery of Māori men. For example, while warfare can be said to have been endemic in pre-contact Māori society, it did not define Māori existence or masculinity. According to Walker, the dominant role of Māori adults, including men, was gardening and other activities related to sourcing food, including hunting, fishing, fruit and plant gathering, and trapping. When not involved in the provision of sustenance, all "adults in the vicinity were in loco parentis."[10] Essentially, pre-colonial Māori masculinity, while involving war sparodically, for the most part was shaped by the everyday: gardening, hunting, and parenting the children of the community.

It is important to note here that masculinity was/is very much a Western construct; Hokowhitu reminds us that masculinity is a historical construction and cannot simply be analyzed from a contemporary snapshot.[11] To Māori the traits that defined "masculinity" would have differed significantly from those of the European. Māori male masculinities were developed as a result of their ability to provide. Pre-contact society was determined by stability and survival. That is not to say that war did not play its role in the forming of Māori masculine identities. Demonstrations of skills and prowess in warfare were among a number of ways to determine one's masculinity. However, masculinities were also based on generosity and the stability provided to the iwi (tribe) through leadership.

This historical overview briefly describes the historical underpinnings of a dominant narrative surrounding Māori men, while demonstrating that a counter narrative is becoming increasingly productive in forming concepts that reside beyond discourses based on savagery. The next section builds upon this discussion by focusing on the importance of sport to formations of Māori masculinities.

Coloniality, Sport, and Masculinity

The continuation of prescribed Māori identities—in particular, masculine identities—has led to an "accepted" understanding of what a Māori should be. As a result of the many, yet similarly themed, accounts of Māori masculinities, contemporary Māori masculine identities have been, and continue to be, shaped by the recurring patterns of understanding that saw Māori initially defined as barbaric, savage, and violent. These recurring patterns of identifying Māori masculinities can be understood further by applying the theoretical lens of coloniality.

As has been discussed in other works, certain accepted ideas of Māori masculinity are often transferred into the sporting arena.[12] While it may seem that particular features of a Māori masculinity are being accepted by the mainstream, what is occurring is the assertion of limitations and boundaries upon Māori men to conform and perform within a certain domain.

The notion of "coloniality," or the "coloniality of power," was first introduced by Walter Mignolo in the mid-1990s. The concept has been drawn upon further by Nelson Maldonado-Torres in his seminal piece, "On the Coloniality of Being."[13] This chapter will draw from this particular paper by Maldonado-Torres to examine the impact of colonization on Māori masculine identities.

As Maldonado-Torres states, "coloniality is different from colonialism."[14] Coloniality reflects recurring patterns of power that have become established over time as a result of colonization. Such patterns define culture, labour, inter-subjective relations, knowledge,[15] and, for the purposes of this chapter, masculinities and identities. Coloniality can be seen as a contemporary, lived continuation of colonization, or more directly it can be argued that "coloniality survives colonialism."[16]

One area where coloniality, and particularly the coloniality of labour, knowledge, and power, continues to be visible is within the field of sport. Post-contact, the Māori male was reduced to being childlike (i.e., unformed), unable to remove himself from the passion and physicality of warfare. Māori men were channelled into sports and manual labour as a means of taming their savage tendencies. Sport in New Zealand became somewhat of a vehicle of interaction, assimilation, and social promotion.

It can be seen that Māori masculinities, from the colonizer's perspective, were based on European ideals of masculinity and served to position the colonizer above the colonized. This can also be related to Frantz Fanon's chapter "The Fact of Blackness," where Fanon relates a personal perspective of events akin to what has happened in the forming of Māori masculine identities, noting that the white man "had woven me out of a thousand details, anecdotes, stories."[17] Fanon speaks of a situation where his identity was prescribed to him. Similarly, Māori masculine identities have been prescribed. Fanon also states that he was "expected to behave like a black man—or at least like a nigger."[18] Again, there is an implied expectation of what the identity of the "other," in the case of New Zealand Māori, should be.

In New Zealand, masculinity was promoted through education and sport. The accepted masculinities of the empire were introduced as a means of making civilized men of Māori. These elements of a Victorian masculinity became imbibed into what would come to be seen as a "traditional" Māori masculinity. This Māori hypermasculinity would initially be imposed, and maintained, via sporting pursuits. Through the English public school education model, cricket, in New Zealand, became an avenue of imposing "gentlemanly" qualities upon Māori males. The behaviours, patience, and disciplines of sports such as cricket were deemed perfect for civilizing the savage. Cricket allowed the colonizer to maintain dominance over the sport, and those participating, while demanding Māori embrace and accept qualities deemed "normal" by Pākehā. Cricket had previously been used, successfully, in other countries such as India and the Caribbean; even in the Pacific Island nations, cricket proved to be a successful civilizing tool.

According to Ryan, during the late nineteenth century, cricket secured an enthusiastic following among Pacific cultures.[19] But while cricket was securing an "enthusiastic following" in the Pacific nations, it failed to take a foothold in New Zealand with the Māori population. Reasons for this are most likely related to the fact that New Zealand cricket "remained for a long time a largely urban and predominantly middle class game."[20] Those Māori who did play cricket at the highest levels were almost certainly of "well-to-do status" with "the six identifiably Māori first-class cricketers who appeared prior to 1920…all well-educated and from relatively privileged backgrounds untypical of the majority Māori experience."[21]

Although cricket had not had the comprehensive civilizing effect on Māori as had been hoped, rugby union became a most effective tool for colonization. Maguire and Tuck argue that sport is one of the most significant arenas by which nations become, as they put it, "real."[22] The implication here is that national identities are, at times, determined through sports. Rugby union became immensely influential in helping to shape New Zealand national identity, as well as being the dominant influence on the nation's sporting identity.

In the late nineteenth century, rugby union was deemed the perfect culmination of "muscular Christianity and cultural imperialism in which the cooperation, discipline and healthful aspects of sport would supposedly enhance the civilising process and create common ground between coloniser and colonised."[23] This concept of a "common ground" would allow Pākehā to maintain a sense of power and control over Māori in rugby while appearing to be supportive of Māori upward mobility through sport. By imposing muscular Christianity and cultural imperialism as a means of forming an acceptable colonial society, Pākehā were establishing an understanding among Māori that to succeed one must adhere to those things deemed normal by the superior social group. These are colonial boundaries.

As Hokowhitu states, "The mentality of 'normalisation,' inherent in the fabric of European society at that time, meant that the colonists perceived themselves as superior and normal and consequently discounted Māori and tikanga Māori (Māori culture) as inferior and abnormal."[24] While this remained typical, rugby union would be used to align Māori with the more acceptable masculine virtues of morality, discipline, and teamwork as opposed to their "backward" traditions. Ryan notes the effect of rugby union and the perceived salvation it provided to Māori with regard to transforming the warrior tendencies believed to be fundamental to the Māori paradigm of thought. He talks of how "Bishop Bennett used to say that rugby saved his race, for it sublimated the warlike passions that had been glowing since the Māori wars of the 1860s and had turned to a peaceful, if occasionally hectic, pursuit of the warrior ambitions nurtured by a proud race in hundreds of years of isolation."[25] Comments like this fostered the majority understanding of Māori men as warriors and added to an accepted discourse surrounding Māori masculinities.[26]

Sports, and in particular rugby union, were becoming a means of social control; sports were emerging as a method for imposing and patrolling boundaries in a manner disguised as opportunity. The success of this medium of social control can be seen in that there were Māori, such as Bishop Bennett, who were acknowledging the normalizing processes of rugby union as something that had saved their communities. Ideas such as this allowed for the continuation of the justification of colonial dominance and regulation over knowledge, power, and labour. According to Ryan, "It was only to be expected that a warrior race such as the Māori should excel at...rugby football. War was a supreme recreation of the Māori...they carried this expertise into the complex skills of handling and kicking a rugby ball. The tribal warfare with its...savagery in the attack was transferred to the storming of the goal-line. The missionaries did much to end the bloodshed between the tribes...in more modern times the game of rugby football provides some kind of outlet."[27]

As Geoff Watson argues, schools like Te Aute were lauded for their civilizing influence over Māori. Such schools, modelled on the English public school system, were attributed with the success of Māori involvement in rugby union, as opposed to Māori agency. As a result, common stereotypes of Māori athletes today are heavily influenced by a sense of natural ability rather than an ability to learn and develop alongside the sport itself; such stereotypes work to maintain the boundaries established early in New Zealand sport by separating success and individuality from players.

Ryan acknowledges the various views of Māori sporting ability by stating that "it was also widely perceived, and is still in some quarters, that Māori sporting prowess was somehow genetic, derived not from application and mental resolve, but embodying a natural ease and athleticism that was not far removed from the supposedly primitive, animalistic world of the pre-European period."[28] Such a statement outlines the widely misconstrued view that Māori, rather than developing a sporting ability through determination and the acquiring of knowledge and skill, were/are predisposed to sporting talent via an innate savage tendency that harboured violent and athletic capabilities. Again, such sentiments reinforce the idea of control. Māori excellence in sport could not be due to agency and intelligence, as that would threaten Pākehā superiority.

The view that sport can serve as a mechanism for assimilation also indicates a sense of the socio-political control, within a sporting context, of maintaining control, or power, over "potential" Māori success. Such socio-political control can be argued to create subconscious boundaries and regulations that limit the extent to which Māori can achieve success. These boundaries could be seen to have continued from the early phases of integration via sports up to contemporary situations where power dynamics are challenged by athletes who wish to determine their own sporting identities beyond the confines of such colonial boundaries.

Hokowhitu writes about constructed Māori masculinities designed to "limit, homogenize, and reproduce an acceptable and imagined Māori masculinity."[29] It is this construction of a Māori masculinity that I believe has defined the boundaries and limits to which Māori can achieve, in a number of given fields, and the extent to which Māori men can determine their own masculinities and sporting identities.

In his PhD thesis, "The Browning of the All Blacks: Pacific People, Rugby and the Cultural Politics of Identity in New Zealand," Andrew Grainger discusses the impact of the colonial gaze in terms of defining and controlling the Other.[30] Grainger's examination of the Other involved the Polynesian rugby player, but we can equally apply his thoughts to the situation of Māori: "What is perhaps most relevant to our understanding of the Polynesian body is the operation of [colonization or] colonialism, the practices by which bodies are brought under colonial control, and the forms of inscription through which such power relations are established. The colonized body has been governed and controlled through various physical and discursive disciplinary strategies and the native body 'bears the imprint of the colonial gaze, its myths and its lies.'"[31]

As I have argued in this section, rugby union has had a profound effect on the post-colonial formations of Māori masculinity. It must be highlighted at this stage, however, that the example of James Tamou to follow in the succeeding section derives from a completely different sport to rugby union— that of rugby league. It should also be stated that rugby league has remained relatively sidelined in terms of its impact on shaping national identity, and similarly the research that has focused on Māori men and sport has typically focused on rugby union because of its prominence within the New Zealand psyche.[32] One area where rugby league has, however, contributed to national identities is in the recurring patterns of negative stereotype.

Although rugby league had its origins in rugby union, its development as its own sport in its own right and as an alternative sport to rugby union followed a schism in 1895 between unions in northern and southern England. The southern unions wished to maintain an amateur stance, whereas the working-class unions in the north wished to either compensate players for time taken off work to play the sport, or play on a Sunday (the one day off at the time). What resulted was a class-based split between the Southern Union and the Northern Union. The Northern Union (which would become known as the Rugby League) would become synonymous with the working class, while the Southern Union (and its rugby union) became synonymous with amateurism, the public school system in Britain, and, hence, the British aristocracy and upper-classes. As a result of this continued connection to the working class, rugby league is often seen as the poor cousin to rugby union and also carries stereotyped connotations of drunkenness, excessive violence, sexism, and a number of other hypermasculine traits that correlate with some of the predominant stereotypes attributed to Māori.

Although it is important for the reader to comprehend the differences between rugby and rugby league, particularly in relation to their historical development, this should not detract from the broader point, which is the imbrication of Māori masculinity with sport more generally, but in particular with the hypermasculine sports of both rugby and rugby league. Moreover, as the section to follow outlines the predominance of Māori masculinity within rugby and rugby league and the importance of sport to New Zealand national identity, it suggests not only the complicity of dominant forms of Māori masculine representation with New Zealand's nation-state but also the complexity of represenation that occurs in the spaces between gender and national borders.

James Tamou, Unpatriotic Decisions, and an Option for De-coloniality

> I've opened something up.... The New Zealand boys who might have been here since they were young might have been too scared, or too concerned about the media and hype about it, to play for NSW or Queensland. So I hope some boys might be looking at me and say, "Well, if he did it, that's what I want to do." I hope I might've started something there.
>
> —James Tamou, in Webster, "James Tamou Hopes His Experience Will Lead to More New Zealand Born Players Joining Origin Ranks"[33]

Recently, the influence of nationalism, identity, Indigeneity, and allegiance on the sporting landscape has become increasingly prominent. In April 2012, Māori rugby league player James Tamou made the conscious decision to represent Australia against his country of birth, New Zealand. Born in Palmerston North (a central North Island town), Tamou moved to Australia at the age of fourteen. His decision to represent Australia and the state of New South Wales sparked major media interest and saw significant backlash from the New Zealand public, in particular those involved with New Zealand rugby league. Prior to pledging his allegiance to Australia, Tamou had represented New Zealand Māori in rugby league and was considered to be on the fringe of a national call up to the New Zealand Kiwis team.[34]

Tamou's decision brought about questions of national identity and patriotism in professional sport. Although athletes representing countries other than those of their birth is not a new phenomenon in international professional sports, this particular case drew stern criticisms from both the New Zealand and Australian public and media. Two high-profile New Zealand

Rugby League (NZRL) representatives, both Māori, voiced their opinions in the media. The then current New Zealand Kiwis captain Benji Marshall and Kiwis High-Performance manager Tony Kemp were both vocal in their disapproval of Tamou's allegiance to Australia. As written by journalists Glenn Jackson and Chris Barclay, "While maintaining Tamou was entitled to his choice, it was clear Marshall felt uncomfortable about it.... 'Just listen to him talk and listen to his accent and tell me he's Australian,' Marshall said.... But hey, if that's where his heart is and that's where he wants to play, we don't want him to play for us. If he doesn't want to be part of our New Zealand team, good luck to him."[35] This statement made by Marshall was backed by a number of vocal New Zealand rugby league fans and was also echoed by Tony Kemp, who labelled the decision as a joke,[36] saying that Tamou was "confused...[and] this whole thing is ridiculous, it would be embarrassing for the game to see James Tamou running out in NSW and Australian jumpers."[37]

What becomes interesting here is that these comments were made by Māori males—men whose masculinity and sporting abilities have taken them to the pinnacle of rugby league representation and achievement in New Zealand and internationally. However, their identities are firmly rooted in a sense of New Zealand nationalism. The comments signal the coloniality of knowledge, power, and labour in New Zealand, unintentional by-products perhaps of the continuing colonial influence of the nation-state in the shaping of Māori male identity. At the very least, the remarks provide an insight into the effect colonization has had on the inability for Māori men to determine their own identities beyond national borders. The assumption is that James Tamou, as an athlete indigenous to Aotearoa-New Zealand, would, or should, play for the nation to which he is indigenous. However, this can be seen as an extension of the colonial narrative that is designed to link nationalism and patriotism with identity. Is it possible that Tamou's actions are intentionally or inadvertantly subversive to imbrication of Māori masculinity within New Zealand's dominant discourses of nationhood? Given the responses of high-profile rugby league aficionados like Kemp and Marshall, the answer would be yes. This further raises a broader question of the possibilities of the subversion of dominant masculinity in institutions such as sport, more commonly associated with the reproduction of dominant discourses.

Hokowhitu has discussed the ability of athletes to counter dominant narratives of race and to, in turn, disrupt racial or colonial narratives that have been accepted as the norm. He uses the examples of "Mohamed Ali's politicized irreverence and alignment with Islam"[38] and Indigenous Australian

rugby league player turned professional boxer "Anthony Mundine's politicized swaggering and alignment with the struggles of his people"[39] to
highlight how athletes have, in the past, transcended beyond established
racial or colonial narratives using sport as an apparatus. In representing
Australia, whether intentionally or not, Tamou is no different in terms of
disrupting the links between nationalism, Indigeneity, and sport. His ability
as an athlete has afforded him the luxury of representing either Australia or
New Zealand. By aligning with Australia, he has managed to resist dominant discourses of Māori masculinity and identity and the accepted ideas
surrounding nationalism and patriotism.

The concept of donor countries providing athletes to elite sporting
competitions can be seen around the world. It occurs prominently in soccer/
football, basketball and baseball.[40] This generally has the effect of improving
the calibre of the competition in the host nation while boosting the profile of
the particular sport in the donor nation. Yet Māori athletes have it somewhat
different in that they are representatives of both a country and a culture.
I call this phenomenon "donor culture."[41] Through the lens of coloniality,
athletes who find success in a foreign competition, or representing a foreign
country, are seen as having turned their back on their "country." In the case
with Tamou, however, there was never a question in his mind of having
turned his back on his culture. Tamou recently stated: "I'm playing on the
other side but I'll never forget where I'm from or where my family is from.
I'll always be a Māori."[42]

Representing Australia and New South Wales makes Tamou no less
Māori. His decision to represent a country other than New Zealand allows
him to define his own Māori masculinity. In his own words, "I'm comfortable now about where I am and I think that ship has sailed and I couldn't be
happier."[43] This can be seen as an indicator that he is in control of his own
labour and identity.

If coloniality is a form of control over knowledge, labour, and power via
the state, players such as Tamou are implementing a form of de-coloniality
through deciding for themselves to whom they wish to provide their labour. By determining their own masculinities, Māori athletes are now in
a position to go against recurring patterns of colonization in terms of self-
determination. It is possible that any future Māori athletes that may follow
Tamou's lead are participating in the reappropriations of dominant colonial
constructions of nationhood.

Initial criticisms of Tamou's decision to play State of Origin and to
represent Australia were based on the financial benefit players receive for

representing their (Australian) state. State of Origin players can earn up to $30,000 in representative bonuses, whereas by representing New Zealand players earn as little as $3,000.[44] While this may deter some athletes from representing New Zealand, professional athletes, like other professionals, should have the right to seek the highest-paying contract or salary. Unlike in the business world, atheletes face criticism in terms of loyalty and patriotism when they decide to move club or play for another country. As with any other professional, however, the option to take control of one's own "labour" should not be influenced by patriotism or the nation-state. This effectively demonstrates where enforced boundaries regarding patriotism, or nationalism, continue to render athletes "powerless" and subservient to the will of the nation-state.

The de-colonial turn, as Maldonado-Torres describes, involves interventions at the level of power, knowledge, and being through varied actions of decolonization.[45] The act of taking control of one's own labour skills in order to seek out the highest reward in terms of contracts, could, thus, be seen as an act of decolonization. That is, by removing the influence of the nation-state in determining one's identity, that person or athlete can be the very intervention necessary to curb the influences and implications of coloniality in defining masculine identities.

Maldonado-Torres states, "The de-colonial turn is about making visible the invisible and about analysing the mechanisms that produce such invisibility or distorted visibility in light of the large stock of ideas that must necessarily include the critical reflections of the invisible people themselves."[46] By representing Australia, and also New South Wales, and causing such controversy in the media, James Tamou has indeed made the invisible visible. In terms of a de-colonial option, Tamou has emerged as a prototype for the re-determining of Māori masculine identity. If coloniality refers to the recurring patterns of power as a result of colonization, then Tamou has become the "intervention" that Maldonado-Torres speaks of. Tamou has provided an opportunity to seek a form of self-determination previously unaccepted by the nation-state. His decision to represent another country, while maintaining his identity as Māori, removes the state's influence in determining, or continuing to determine, the identity of the Māori male. This can also be related back to the arguments of Maguire and Tuck wherein sport appears to be one of the last bastions of power for a subsiding nation-state. As the opening quote to this section by Tamou suggests, Tamou's actions signal the potential for a new era in the reclaiming of Māori masculinities in rugby league, and indeed professional sport in general.

Conclusion

Given the confluence of dominant forms of Māori masculinity in the formation of New Zealand's national identity, there remains a tacit understanding that Māori men will fall in line with more accepted forms of New Zealand masculinities; for Māori to define their own masculinity is considered betrayal. Māori must deal with established boundaries as a result of recurring patterns of colonization. While there may be certain leniencies with regard to the inner sanctum or perimeters of these boundaries, for Māori men to push through, or escape, the limits of these boundaries, they must challenge the mainstream acceptance of their role in the reproduction of the national narrative.

Sport in New Zealand has been used to maintain colonial influence. Hokowhitu's analysis can be used to demonstrate that the genealogy of Māori masculinity has developed out of savagery and into sport. By applying coloniality it can also be seen that, in this movement, colonial boundaries have been established as a means of maintaining control of knowledge, power, labour, and masculine identity. Such boundaries, until now, have proved to be the ultimate obstacle in seeking some sense of control over Māori masculinities. Sport has been an effective tool for the maintenance of colonial boundaries of power, knowledge, labour, and masculinity. By emphasizing the qualities deemed masculine in Western society, sports were used to further develop the "accepted" construct of Māori masculinity. Through his "unpatriotic" actions, James Tamou has provided an option for de-coloniality, a means for transitioning beyond the imposed colonial boundaries. This could potentially be, or lead into, a new phase in the genealogy of Māori masculinities in sport.

Ngā mihi tino nui ki a Brendan Hokowhitu mō tōna tautoko i te tuhinga o te wāhanga nei. Kia ora ra e hoa. "Ehara taku toa i te toa takitahi, engari he te toa takitini."

Notes

1   Brendan Hokowhitu, "Tackling Māori Masculinity: A Colonial Genealogy of Savagery and Sport," *The Contemporary Pacific* 16, no. 2 (2004): 259–84.

2   Nelson Maldonado-Torres, "On the Coloniality of Being: Contributions to the Development of a Concept," *Cultural Studies* 21, no. 2 (2007): 240–70.

3   Hokowhitu, "Tackling Māori Masculinity." 259.

4   For further reading on Māori history, see Maria Bargh, *Resistance: An Indigenous Response to Neoliberalism* (Wellington, New Zealand: Huia, 2007); Hugh Kawharu, ed., *Conflict and Compromise: Essays on the Māori since Colonisation* (Wellington, New Zealand: A.H. & A.W. Reed, 1975); and Ranginui Walker, *Ka Whawhai Tonu Matou: Stuggle Without End,* rev. ed. (Auckland, New Zealand: Peguin, 2004).

5   For further reading on Māori masculinity, see Mike Donaldson and Richard Howson, "Men, Migration and Hegemonic Masculinity," in *Migrant Men: Critical Studies of Masculinties and the Migration Experience,* ed. Mike Donaldson, Raymond Hibbins, Richard Howson, and Bob Pease (New York: Routledge, 2009); Brendan Hokowhitu, "Tackling Māori Masculinity"; Brendan Hokowhitu, "The Death of Koro Paka: 'Traditional' Māori Patriarchy," *Special Issues, Pacific Masculinities, The Contemporary Pacific* 20, no. 1 (2009): 115–41; Brendan Hokowhitu, "Producing Elite Indigenous Masculinities," *Settler Colonial Studies* 2, no. 2 (2012): 23–48; and Walker, *Ka Whawhai Tonu Matou.*

6   Cook did not encounter Māori women to any great extent. For the most, part Cook's interaction with Māori was with warriors, fishermen, and other men or boys.

7   Andrew P. Vayda, "Maori Prisoners and Slaves in the Nineteenth Century," *Ethnohistory* 8, no. 2 (1961): 144.

8   Harry C. Evison, *Te Wai Pounamu: The Greenstone Island* (Wellington, New Zealand: Aoraki Press), 21.

9   Albert Memmi, *The Colonizer and the Colonized* (Boston: Beacon Press, 1991), 123.

10 Walker, *Ka Whawhai Tonu Matou,* 63.

11 Hokowhitu, "Tackling Māori Masculinity," 264.

12 Hokowhitu, "Tackling Māori Masculinity"; Brendan Hokowhitu, "Authenicating Māori Physicality: Translations of 'Games' and 'Pastimes' by early Travellers and Missionaries to New Zealand," *International Journal of the History of Sport* 25, (2008): 1355–73; Brendan Hokowhitu, "Māori Rugby and Subversion: Creativity, Domestiction, Oppression and Decolonization," *International Journal of the History of Sport* 26, no. 16 (2009): 2314–34; C. Obel, "Researching Rugby in New Zealand: Reflections on Writing the Self and the Research Problem," *Sociology of Sport Journal* 21, no. 4 (2004): 418–34; G. Ryan, "The Paradox of Māori Rugby 1870–1914," in *Tackling Māori Myths: Rugby and New Zealand Society 1854–2004,* ed. G. Ryan (Dunedin, New Zealand: University of Otago Press, 2005).

13 Maldonado-Torres, "On the Coloniality of Being."

14 Ibid., 243.

15 Ibid.

16 Ibid.

17 Frantz Fanon, *Black Skin, White Masks* (New York: Grove Press, 1967), 111.

18 Ibid., 114.

19 G. Ryan, "Few and Far Between: Māori and Pacific Contributions to New Zealand Cricket," *Sport in Society* 10, no. 1 (2007): 75.

20 Ibid.

21 Ibid., 76.

22 J. Maguire and J. Tuck, "Making Sense of Global Patriot Games: Rugby Players' Perceptions of National Identity Politics," *Football Studies* 2, no. 1 (1999): 30.

23 Ryan, "The Paradox of Māori Rugby," 89.

24 Hokowhitu, "Tackling Māori Masculinity," 264.

25 Ryan, "The Paradox of Māori Rugby," 89.

26 Of note here is that the dominant discourses ignore other historical narratives of peaceful, passive resistance and spiritual-based resistance of several Māori prophet groups in the mid to late 1800s. For further reading on Māori prophet movements and passive resistance, see M. Derby, *The Prophet and the Policeman: The Story of Rua Kenana and John Cullen* (Auckland, New Zealand: Craig Potton Publishing, 2009); J. Frood, *Parihaka: Peace, Protest and Power* (Auckland, New Zealand: Elizabethan Promotions, 2002); T.M. Hohaia, *Parihaka: The Art of Passive Resistance* (Wellington, New Zealand: Victoria University Press, 2001); E. Stokes, *Pai Marire and the niu at Kuranui* (Hamilton, New Zealand: Centre for Māori Studies and Research, University of Waikato, 1980).

27 Ryan, "The Paradox of Māori Rugby," 89.

28 G. Ryan, "Few and Far Between: Māori and Pacific Contributions to New Zealand Cricket," *Sport in Society* 10, no. 1 (2007): 80.

29 Hokowhitu, "Tackling Māori Masculinity," 262.

30 Andrew Grainger, "The Browning of the All Blacks: Pacific Peoples, Rugby and the Cultural Politics of Identity in New Zealand" (PhD diss., University of Maryland, 2008).

31 Ibid., 192.

32 Phillip Borell, "He iti hoki te mokoroa: Māori Contributions to the Sport of Rugby League" (MA thesis, University of Canterbury, 2012), 67.

33 A. Webster, "James Tamou Hopes His Experience Will Lead to More New Zealand Born Players Joining Origin Ranks," *The Daily Telegraph*, 28 June 2012, http://www.dailytelegraph.com.au/sport/nrl/james-tamou-hopes-his-experience-will-lead-to-more-new-zealand-born-players-joining-origin-ranks/story-e6frexv9-1226410512562?nk=f5b3c10dda544437d913bc0ce8437df2.

34 The New Zealand Kiwis are the national men's rugby league representative team.

35 G. Jackson and C. Barclay, "Benji Marshall Slams Tamou Allegiance Switch," *Sydney Morning Herald*, 16 April 2012.

36 Ibid.

37 P. Badel, "New Zealand Hierarchy Label Blues Poaching of James Tamou as an 'Embarrassment,'" *Sunday Mail*, 15 April 2012.

38 Hokowhitu, "Māori Rugby and Subversion," 2339.

39 Ibid.

40 J. Maguire and R. Pearton, "Global Sport and the Migration Patterns of France '98 World Cup Finals Players: Some Preliminary Observations," *Soccer and Society* 1, no. 1 (2000): 175–89; Y. Takahashi and J. Horne, "Moving with the Bat and the Ball: Preliminary Reflections on the Migration of Japanese Baseball Labour," *International Review for the Sociology of Sport* 41 no. 7 (2006): 79–88.

41 Borell, "He iti hoki te mokoroa," 91.

42 M. Chammas, "James Tamou Has No Regrets about Snubbing NZ," *Sydney Morning Herald*, 4 July 2014.

43 Ibid.
44 Jackson and Barclay, "Benji Marshall Slams Tamou Allegiance Switch."
45 Maldonado-Torres, "On the Coloniality of Being," 262.
46 Ibid.

CHAPTER 10

Social Spaces of Maleness: The Role of Street Gangs in Practising Indigenous Masculinities

Robert Henry

Over the years, I have spoken with many different Indigenous communities and their members on the issues of Indigenous street gangs. I have listened to how they have come to express their concerns and fears that many of the young males in their communities are losing their traditional values and places in the communities. Many of these people have also expressed the concern that their "young people are not acting like Indians anymore. They are acting like gangsters. Don't they know who they are?" These comments kept coming back to me as I began work on my PhD research looking into the lives of Indigenous ex–gang members and how they have constructed their identities in and around different street gangs. These discussions led me to rethink the way that I have come to understand how gangs create spaces for some young Indigenous males to express their maleness. To unpack how street gangs have become spaces for some Indigenous males to participate in social activities of masculinity, I will focus on the framework presented in Robert Connell and James Messerschmidt's "Hegemonic Masculinity: Rethinking the Concept,"[1] and I will support their work with specific conversations that I have had with Indigenous men and youth who have left or are exiting the street gang lifestyle.

Connell and Messerschmidt explain that because masculinity embodies many different ideas and conjures up different positions of authority, it needs to be unpacked at what they construct as the global, regional, and local levels.[2] The embodiment of gender then needs to concentrate on how the male body is used in our everyday lives in order to navigate through our social practices.[3] With a focus on the body and its impact as a social space, one can then come to terms with how particular male bodies are predetermined to be associated with specific activities and behaviours based on their relationships to the larger social construct of a local, regional, and global politics of gender. Social spaces are a central concern particularly when looking into the issue of Indigenous male street gangs because of how local and regional constructions of colonized Indigenous bodies are socially constructed in Canadian urban centres and are easily moved to the margins and seen as lawless.[4]

This chapter is organized into three sections in order to deconstruct the impact that street gangs have on the practising of gender for Indigenous male youth. Following Connell and Messerschmidt's model, I will attempt to peel back the layers of how gangs have become spaces for some Indigenous males to participate in violent and hypermasculine notions of masculinity.[5] This analysis will draw from a critical anti-oppressive discourse about spaces of Indigenous masculinity to understand how social stratification maintains these marginalized spaces.[6]

The first section will focus on the Western global construction of masculinity. This section looks at the construction of how a real "man" has been constructed through Western patriarchal societies, and how being a man is connected to being tough, independent, and powerful. Western patriarchal societies have constructed men to participate in what Jackson Katz has termed the "tough guise."[7] This "tough guise" is one that many men are caught up in, trying to maintain their images of masculinity.

The second section focuses on what Connell and Messerschmidt describe as the regional, where the idea of masculinity is "constructed at the level of the culture or the nation-state."[8] Here is a description of how men of colour have been constructed to fit the role of criminal in Western societies, where much of the research on masculinity and crime has focused. Special attention will also be paid to the role that colonialism has played and continues to play in constructing Indigenous men as deviant and lawless.

The third section will look at the role street gangs play at a local level, where the gang becomes the social space in which some Indigenous males can participate in violent and hypermasculine constructions of masculinity, which they have learned through their personal experiences. The term "gang" and the issues that surround its definition will be addressed to understand how it has changed over time to fit particular political agendas. Research by Mark Totten will be focused upon because of its close connection to Indigenous gangs in Canada, particularly how he has constructed hypermasculinities and its relation to street-gang involvement.[9]

Global Perspectives of Masculinity

Masculinity, particularly in Western-patriarchal-capitalist society, has been constructed as the opposite of what it means to be feminine. Thus to be a man is to not have or participate in what has been constructed as feminine traits or activities. This division between men and women is most often presented through universal or natural terms supported with biological or scientific explanations of ability. French philosopher Pierre Bourdieu explains: "The division of the sexes appears to be 'in the order of things,' as people sometimes say to refer to what is normal, natural, to the point of being inevitable: it is present both—in the objectified state—in things (in the house, for example, every part of which is 'sexed'), in the whole social world, and—in the embodied state—in the habitus of the agents, functioning as systems of schemes of perception, thought and action."[10]

Through genetics and common-sense rhetoric throughout Western *history*, society has assumed that there are specific roles for men and women to hold based solely on sexist assumptions of ability, while at the same time maintaining the dominance of the male body because of its ability to perform specific tasks. Patriarchy then explains the power difference between men and women as something that has always been a part of human existences. In his seminal work, Allan Johnson explains that patriarchy is mired in essentialism, where men and women have always been seen as different and that Western sciences such as biology and genetics have come to support these differences.[11] Throughout "Why Patriarchy?" Johnson challenges the essentialist position of patriarchy because it "can't account for the enormous variability we find *among* women and *among* men, or for the similarities between men and women in similar situations."[12] Johnson states that patriarchy is not so much men controlling women, but rather men controlling men through fear of not living up to the ideal of a real man, where the use and threat of violence are called upon to control behaviours. But what is it to be a real man? Who is the ideal man, and how do these images and symbols of masculinity hedge society to construct who or what it is to be a "man"?

In the documentary *Tough Guise*, director Jackson Katz asked young adolescent men about the characteristics of what it means to be a real man. The answers that he received followed much of what Johnson discussed in another documentary five years earlier.[13] The young men described that being a man was about not showing any of what society has constructed as feminine or homosexual attributes. Men are not "pussies," "bitches," "fags," or "emotional"; real men, according to these youths, are tough, independent, and powerful. Therefore, because boys are taught at a young age to hide who they are in order to be what society tells them to be, many men grow up using what Katz describes as a "tough guise." This is a social guise that predominantly heterosexual males wear for the purpose of gaining the privileges granted to heterosexual males for being a "real man." From this Western global perspective of masculinity, being a man then is about being tough, independent, and powerful.

This construction of masculinity shapes the perceptions of young boys to seek out opportunities and ways to adhere to their standards of maleness. The reality is that only a select few young males are able to actively engage in what society sees as positive masculine behaviours, and will be viewed as "boys being boys," without being constructed as deviant.[14] For example, school-ground bullying is not addressed as bullying by many (although this is beginning to change with recent high-profile cases of suicides and bullying), but rather as boys roughhousing. Mental, physical, emotional, and spiritual hazing of individuals into different organizations, specifically sports teams, is not seen as destructive, but as team-building, even if violence is the centre of the initiation. It is through these formulations that males are given litmus tests to prove their maleness by carrying out violent acts and learning to live with them, with the realization that afterwards they will be a part of the group and will have the opportunity to participate in the same acts in the future by hazing the new "recruits."[15] Some young males, though, are unable to participate in social activities designed to prove one's maleness because of their racial and class identities. Once they do, marginalized males are often labelled as deviant, and are feared for their participation in these activities.

So why is it that when some youth enact socially constructed activities of what it means to be a man, their behaviour is considered criminal in nature? Why do some youth see crime as rites of passage to manhood in some communities? What has led these constructions of masculinity to be seen as "positive," or as "boys being boys," for some youths and not others?[16] The difficulty with this is that the world is not constructed on differences of gender alone. Race and class must also intersect to move the discussion of masculinity from the global to the regional.

The Regional: Crime and the Rites of Passage to Manhood

Labelling has a definite link to the construction of masculinity, particularly with men of colour who, even at the young ages of three and four, have already internalized the construction that white is good and black is bad.[17] Socialization processes influence children to understand that they are to be good or bad based on their skin colour. Notions of good and bad are encouraged in school settings, where teachers and school administration treat youth differently based on their race and class status.[18] For example, zero-tolerance policies for fighting and other aggressive behaviours are enacted primarily on those bodies society has constructed as deviant and not on the actual acts being committed.[19] As found throughout the narratives of ex–gang members, many were pushed out of the school setting by both teachers and students. "Dave," for example, says,[20]

> I had some learning disabilities and nobody, nobody could uh diagnose me kinda thing, so rather than deal with it they put me in a desk beside the principal's office and basically checked up on me every couple hours to make sure I was still sitting there. But other than that really I think they just passed me so they didn't have to deal with me. I didn't have no identity; I was an Indian um, took a lot of discrimination, racism from everybody, including teachers and one day I just had enough of it and I just started fighting.

Another individual, "Desmond," says,

> I was portrayed as the dumbest person around, you know. Like people wouldn't admit that to me because they knew, you know like I got the street smarts. Some people didn't understand why I was the way I was, but in the school yard, it just, like even the teachers disliked the way I was acting.... Sometimes they would just send me to the principal's office where I would just flip out and get suspended. Like, at one point, you know, they suspended me for a long period of time where I was just like there was no point in going back to school either way. So teachers would scream at me. One teacher slammed me against a wall, but that was about it.

The majority of the men in my PhD research discussed similar narratives where they found the need to fight and act aggressively towards others because it was the only way that they could get respect and protect themselves from the overt and covert racism that they felt in classrooms and on school grounds. When asked if the other students who were non-Aboriginal were suspended, the majority of participants could not remember. They could remember only that, when they came back to school (if they actually did return to the same school), the non-Aboriginal student would be there, and their attitude toward them would have changed such that they were shown respect on the school ground.

As individuals age, connections to other institutions and masculinity begin to shift. Indigenous peoples, nationally and globally, are often incarcerated at greater rates (in relation to their population size) than any other ethnic group.[21] The statistics regarding Canadian Indigenous males who are incarcerated are staggering. Just over 23.1 percent of all federal inmates are Indigenous, while only 4 percent of the total Canadian population is Indigenous.[22] In Saskatchewan, where the provincial Indigenous population is approximately 17 percent, approximately 80 percent of those housed in provincial justice facilities are Indigenous.[23] The provincial incarceration numbers are also followed closely by the youth who are part of the child welfare system,[24] where approximately 75 to 80 percent of youth are of Indigenous ancestry.[25] These statistics help to strengthen social perceptions of fear toward Indigenous peoples with the construction that the majority of them are criminals. This results in an increased connection for Indigenous male youth to see older males being removed from their community and incarcerated. This results in youth creating connections between the justice system as a legitimate right of passage to manhood.

In 2001, Emma Ogilvie and Allan Van Zyl discussed the role that incarceration played for some Indigenous males as a way to enter into specific rites of passage to manhood in northern Australia.[26] The authors found that the Indigenous youth in the northern communities saw that to become a "real" man they needed to be involved in the criminal justice system. Therefore, incarceration and where one was incarcerated became the litmus test of masculinity for young men and was privileged over traditional masculinity rites. The traditional values of the community were still seen; however, incarceration played a larger role in the construction of the rites of passage to manhood in the community.

The themes found within Ogilvie and Van Zyl's work resonates closely to statements made by individuals in my research. For example, "Bones" says, "By the time I was twelve years old, all my older cousins and all the older crew that I was hanging out with were already doing time, so to me, that's where I wanted to be. So I was excited. I was happy that yeah, man, I finally made it to juvy, you know what I mean. I knew my family were there, and all my cousins were gonna be there, so to me it was like, like a reunion kinda thing going there, you know what I mean?" Bones continues by explaining the way people felt at these "reunions" in the criminal justice centres:

> Everybody's happy to see each other and we looked after each other in there as well and you know, like uh, so it was no big thing

going to juvy 'cause you know you're always gonna have family there, you're always gonna have somebody there that you know and uh, that's the way it was like. It seemed like a routine, like a tradition at that time I guess, to put it. You went to juvy and then straight into adult and I just followed everybody. Like, in my own way, I was a leader 'cause I was the youngest. The youngest one all the time, but I was always the one that had, that was doing things to make things happen for, for our whatever we were, our crew. And so I went in and out. I went in and out of institutions all over Saskatchewan, different juvenile facilities and by the time I turned 18, they were already in the adult system. So, the next step now was to go to adult and that's what everybody strived for, you know, that's what everybody waited for.

With high rates of incarceration many youth know of or have family members who have been incarcerated in their lifetimes. Therefore, male youth begin to view the criminal justice system as something to not be feared, but rather as a way to construct a street identity and perform acts of hypermasculinity, to prove their image of a "real man"—tough, independent, and powerful.[27] The street gang becomes the social conduit for some young males to participate in acts of masculinity, and in particular violent acts of masculinity as they support and encourage violence to gain power and respect.

The Gang: A Space for Practising Indigenous Masculinity

One of the most pressing issues regarding street gangs is the lack of an agreed-upon definition to inform research, justice officials, and policy development.[28] The definitional issue has impacted research on gangs since Frederic Thrasher began to look into the culture of street gangs in the early part of the twentieth century. Thrasher's original gang research focused on 1,313 gangs in Chicago where he defined such a group as "an interstitial group originally formed spontaneously, and then integrated through conflict. It is characterized by the following types of behaviour: meeting face to face, milling, movement through space as a unit, conflict, and planning. The result of this collective behaviour is the development of tradition, unreflective internal structure, *esprit de corps*, solidarity, morale, group awareness, and attachment to local territory."[29]

The definition and notions of street gangs have changed from this early definition, where today the focus is on the criminality of specific groups.[30] Thus, the definition of street gangs has moved from a cohesive group of individuals who identify with the group and see the group as a piece of their identity, to that of criminal groups and organizations.[31] This transformation has had detrimental effects on ethnic youth where the "gang" label is used to create a moral panic and a fear of specific ethnic male youth.[32]

Definitions used by policy-makers today tend to focus specifically on criminality and organizational structure as the defining characteristics between street gangs and youth groups.[33] The problem with this is that such definitions do not address what is to be considered street gang crime, violent youth crime, or deviant crime, and assumes that street gangs are all structured as corporate organizations.[34] However, because street gangs have become synonymous with racialized youth and low socio-economic status, law enforcement officials, media, and the general public rely on racial and class constructions of who is to be a criminal for their rationalization of who is and who is not a gang member.[35] Thus, Indigenous youth groups more readily identified as a "gang" than other groups of youth, even if the Indigenous groups act and behave in the same manner as other groups.[36]

Hypermasculinities and the Gang

Mark Totten is considered one of Canada's leading researchers of street gangs. He has conducted research on street gangs and their members from across Canada for over fifteen years with particular interest in Indigenous street gangs.[37] Totten has often discussed the role of violence in constructing masculinity in the gang, and that through gang involvement, hypermasculinities are formed in order to encapsulate the image of the hegemonic male. He explains that many of the Indigenous males that participate in gang activities were sexually abused when they were children, and it is because of this that they are uncertain of their sexual orientation.[38] Totten proposes that this confusion then leads to heightened levels of violence toward women and children as gang members reassert their power as men.[39] The hypermasculine activities surrounding violence are seen as a way to reaffirm power taken from them at a young age. Totten also states that the loss of "traditional means of achieving masculinity (such as supporting families through hunting and trapping) is compensated for by a hyper-masculine exertion of power and control over women and children."[40] The loss of traditional masculine rites of passage can thus be seen as responsible for some of the abuse found in Indigenous communities. The gang then becomes the space in which Indigenous males can reassert their "global manhood" of power and control, lost through this cultural assimilation.

There are difficulties with Totten's construction of hypermasculinities though. One is that the number of youth in his studies who identified as being sexually assaulted was under 10 percent of the total youth that he studied, and therefore hypermasculinities found in the gang cannot be attributed to this construction of sexual identity confusion, although in some cases it may.[41] A second issue that becomes apparent by only focusing on the sexual exploitation of individuals is that it places the violent masculine behaviours, and blame, solely on the individuals. Thus, the social constructions of deviant bodies become ignored and we lose an opportunity to understand how Indigenous males generate social practice in their communities, through the use of the street-gang identity. This is not to say that some men who have been sexually exploited when they were younger use the gang as a way to escape this exploitation through hypermasculine acts; rather, this pathway needs to be explored in more detail to explain these (re)actions.

Because identity is a social and cultural construct, how we act, or wish to be perceived, is dependent on the social situations that are available to us throughout our daily lives. Messerschmidt maintains that we are all actively participating in, or resisting, particular socially constructed notions of gender, and that depending on the social situation and agents, we will act in accordance with what we have been constructed or taught to believe as to how our gender should act in that situation.[42] These social situations and agents also help to construct multiple ways of being a man, and in particular, the gang becomes a space for marginalized males to participate in hyperviolent constructions of masculinity.

These hyperviolent constructions of masculinity are magnified through colonization processes on Indigenous bodies. Colonization is a process of violence that was used to dehumanize Indigenous peoples in the attempt to control resources.[43] As a result, cultures of terror and fear were used to influence and inform policies to control Indigenous bodies, where "Indigenous" was synonymous with "savage" and "barbaric."[44] As Mohawk scholar Taiaiake Alfred asserts, "Raging violence is always more of a reaction to the internal and external hypocrisy of colonial relations than to injustices in economic or political forms."[45]

Historically, Alfred contends, "warriors" would protect communities from harm. Alfred's insight into the Indigenous "warrior," where protection of the community was the primary goal of warriors, resonates with how some Indigenous street gangs attempted to portray themselves and their members.[46] For example, Indigenous street gangs use traditional warrior symbolism in their tattoos, and early street gang codes were framed on the protection of the community. Over time, the gang lost this sense of community protection and began to focus only on the necessities of the gang itself. However, the gang continues to be seen as the vessel in which Indigenous male rites of passage can occur through the construction of the new "urban warrior."

To understand the connection of the "warrior" image to street gangs, I had asked the participants to explain the term "urban warrior," through the eyes of the gang and for recruitment purposes. The older gang members, or those that joined in the early part of 2000 in Saskatchewan, talked about a "code of ethics" that was followed by particular Indigenous gangs. Bones explains: "Yeah, that's the same way with us, 'cause children, man if there's children around, you know, you don't hit women, you don't uh, you don't hit children, and you always respect the elders. See, that's the way it was for us, too, over here in Saskatchewan. We respected the culture and anything that had to do with it and if a brother wanted to drop his colours and go that way, like go through the cultural way, we respected that and we let him go without giving minutes or nothing like that." Bones also explained that there was a shift that happened with these values, and that violence began to take over all aspects of controlling the gang: "I think what it basically was when the needles came in. That's when a lot of the values and everything that the gangs had. Our gang had at that time, started going to shit and started going down. Nobody was listening; nobody was following. All they were worried about was getting high and things like that and yeah, they didn't care about all that." Drugs and the profits through drug sales became the sole focus of the street gangs. These "ethical values" became secondary as the street gangs began to use youth as drug mules, and sell their "dope" in their own communities to women, children, and Elders. With the expansion of drug money, violence also escalated and was used to protect specific community territories.

In his study of youth and gangs, Robert Garot examined how youth in an American urban centre navigated their gang identity between the school and the street.[47] What he found was that the street gang was a way for young marginalized males to participate in violent hypermasculine activities, not to prove their heterosexuality, but rather to save what they call "face" in their community: "The most powerful challenge another can make is to one's *face*—how one sees oneself in relation to community. Especially when one's identity is vulnerable, one may be prone to defend it physically. In an ecology where everyone's identity is vulnerable because of the marginalization and alienation...not fighting to defend identity may pose a great risk.... Indeed if we feel we have been 'deprived of our rightful place in the world,' it is hard for most of us not to consider fighting to regain it."[48] Face, or the tough guise, becomes that symbol in which identity has been shaped and must be protected at all costs within the gang. This face is more often than not attributed to respect and how to retain respect in various situations and contexts.[49] Jacobs and Wright describe street conflicts as a place where "respect is all about toughness, and toughness flows from the ability to inspire fear."[50]

In my interviews with ex–gang members, the notion of toughness for fear was something that many of the individuals stated was needed to keep their respect in their community as well as in the gang. In one particular interview, "Dale" described how respect was gained through violence and fear between gang members: "Well, over the years, as I look back on it, you know, they only fuckin' did things for me out of fear. Like you know, they feared me, so they did pretty much whatever I wanted. A lot of them were like false friendships and that you know…they only pretended to be my friends out of, you know…. That's how I gained a lot of respect on the street and in the correctional too, was like violence, fighting." If individuals did not protect their "face" on the streets, they lost their status as a man because they were seen as weak. Fighting was also used as a way to move up in one's own gang, as described by "Baldhead": "Eventually I got up to the point and I had respect like throughout the whole crew. We had different disputes and we would fight like fist fighting for different positions in the gang. If a captain's spot came up and somebody wanted it, we'd have to fight for it. And that's just the way…that's what I got used to over those years." Therefore, those who were the most violent and not afraid to stand up for themselves are the ones who survived and not only gained economic opportunities but also became the role models for younger Indigenous men in the community.

Conclusion

The issues of masculinity and identity, and how they are associated with Indigenous gangs, have not been focused on in great detail within gang research, other than how they relate to violent acts of aggression. Authors who look at masculinity within ethnic street gangs focus on violence and the need to save "face."[51] By examining Johnson's and Katz's work on patriarchy and its role in constructing maleness and masculinity from a global perspective, one is able to decipher that the use of fear and violence is not only associated with gangs, but is rather constructed through processes of socialization to control "men" in order to maintain patriarchal control of Western social institutions.[52] Thus, in order to save face, a man must act like a man—but only through actions and behaviours related to those that society expects based on race and class. This in turn allows individuals to regain power stripped from them by others with whom they come into contact. For young men involved in street gangs, these actions and behaviours are associated with multiple acts of physical violence and/or hyperviolence and are determined by the reaction necessary to retain one's position in the street-gang hierarchy.[53] This is congruent with the idea of being a "man" in general Western society—that one controls others in a manner that exerts power over an individual.[54] However, because society has created the image of those not from the white middle class as having lesser values, violence is associated more readily with those who are not seen to fit into this social construction.[55]

Indigenous males are constructed in popular discourses and media as predictably more violent toward themselves and others, with higher incidences of suicide, violent suicide, and victimization.[56] Because of this they are more easily identified as criminals or participating in acts of criminal behaviour, and it is through this criminalization that Indigenous youth find themselves part of the child welfare or criminal justice systems.[57] These spaces that were designed to supress specific acts actually provide environments that generate gang growth.

The intersections of violence, gangs, and masculinity are complex and are compounded when race and class are added into the conversation. The impacts of colonization on Indigenous bodies need also to be understood outside of critical race theories because they do not address the impacts of colonization, but rather associate the impacts of racism the same for all non-white bodies in Western nations.[58] Social positions in Canada are deeply invested in colonization and, as such, Indigenous peoples continue to be marginalized and expected to fit particular deviant spaces. The portrayal and colonial construction of Indigenous gangs continue to support the colonial images of the savage, where Indigenous gangs are portrayed through media as violent, unpredictable, and unorganized.[59] Young Indigenous men then take to the streets as a way to practise masculinity because the street gangs are seen as the sites for specific rites of passage to occur for Indigenous youth. While Indigenous gangs create a space for some young men to initiate into "manhood," these street gangs actually limit and reinforce colonial constructs of the "savage" because of its continued reinforcement of respect through violence.

Notes

1 Robert W. Connell and James Messerschmidt, "Hegemonic Masculinity: Rethinking the Concept," *Gender and Society* 19, no. 6 (2005): 829–59.

2 Ibid.

3 Elizabeth Comack, *Out There, In Here: Masculinity, Violence and Prisoning* (Winnipeg: Fernwood Publishing, 2008), 23; James Messerschmidt, *Flesh and Blood: Adolescent Gender Diversity and Violence* (Lanham, MD: Rowman and Littlefield, 2004).

4 Sherene H. Razack, *Race, Space and the Law: Unmapping a White Settler Society* (Toronto: Between the Lines, 2002).

5 Connell and Messerschmidt, "Hegemonic Masculinity."

6 Ozlem Sensoy and Robin DiAngelo, *Is Everyone Really Equal? An Introduction to Key Concepts in Justice and Education* (New York: Teachers College Press, 2012).

7 *Violence, Media, and the Crisis in Masculinity* (documentary), directed by Jackson Katz (Media Education Foundation, 2002).

8 Connell and Messerschmidt, "Hegemonic Masculinity," 849.

9 Mark Totten, "Aboriginal Youth and Violent Gang Involvement in Canada: Quality Prevention Strategies," *IPC Review* 3 (2009): 135–56; Mark Totten, *Nasty, Brutish and Short: The Lives of Gang Members in Canada* (Toronto: James Lorimer & Company, 2012).

10 Pierre Bourdieu, *Masculine Domination* (Stanford, CA: Stanford University Press, 2001), 8.

11 Allan Johnson, *The Gender Knot: Unravelling Our Patriarchal Legacy* (Philadelphia: Temple University Press, 1997).

12 Ibid., 25

13 Katz, *Violence, Media, and the Crisis in Masculinity.*

14 Lisa Marie Cacho, *Social Death: Racialized Rightlessness and the Criminalization of the Unprotected* (New York, NY: NYU Press, 2012).

15 Allan Johnson, *The Gender Knot.*

16 The difficulty here is that "positive" is not really that positive, as to prove one's position of masculinity, they must also exert power over a social group. This primarily puts people of colour, women, those in poverty, or those from the LGBT community at greater risk to be assaulted. This is an area of research that needs to be explored in greater detail to fully understand the consequences and connections of masculinities to power and control through patriarchal notions of oppression.

17 *A Girl Like Me*, directed by Kiri Davis (Reel Works Teen Filmmaking, 2005).

18 Cathy Van Ingen and Joanie Halas, "Claiming Space: Aboriginal Students Within School Landscapes," *Children's Geographies* 4, no. 3 (2006): 379–98.

19 Mathew Fletcher, *American Indian Education: Counternarratives in Racism, Struggle, and the Law* (New York: Routledge, 2008).

20 The narratives that are shared are from my current research PhD study that focuses on using photovoice methods to understand how Indigenous street gangs shape notions of masculinity and identity. The names were pseudonyms chosen by the men themselves.

21 Office of the Correctional Investigator Canada, *Annual Report of the Office of the Correctional Investigator, 2013-14* (Ottawa: Government of Canada, 2014); Barbara Perry, "Impacts of Disparate Policing in Indian Country," *Policing & Society* 19, no. 3 (2009): 263-281.

22 Office of the Correctional Investigator Canada, *Annual Report of the Office of the Correctional Investigator, 2011–12* (Ottawa: Government of Canada, 2012).

23 Office of the Correctional Investigator Canada, *Spirit Matters: Aboriginal People and the Corrections and Conditional Release Act* (Ottawa: Government of Canada, 2012).

24 As the study has progressed, some of the men have discussed the impacts of residential schools and how they have impacted their parents' ability to parent them. None of the men in the current study expressed that they actively sought out the street gang as a way to create or repair damaged relationships caused by residential schools. These observations challenge some of the assumed connections between residential schools and street gangs. That being said, residential schooling has impacted the men's identities, even if they did not attend, as they have been affected by intergenerational trauma caused by the schools. However, by locating this solely on the residential school experience, we miss the opportunity to see how continued policies, such as the child welfare system, continue to create instability within families. From my speaking with the participants of this study, the child welfare system has had a greater effect on the men seeking connections with other youth, as they begin to bond through their movement in and out of the system. Over time these relationships became the foundation for the men to engage with other individuals who have experienced the removal from family, and the instability of place.

25 Saskatchewan Child Welfare Review Panel, *For the Good of Our Children and Youth: A New Vision, a New Direction* (Regina: Children's Advocate Office, 2010).

26 Emma Ogilvie and Allan Van Zyl, "Young Indigenous Males: Custody and the Rites of Passage," *Trends and Issues in Crime and Criminal Justice* 204 (2001): 1–6.

27 Robert Henry, "Through an Indigenous Lens: Indigenous Male Ex-Gang Members Ex-posed" (PhD dissertation, University of Saskatchewan, forthcoming).

28 Finn-Aage Esbensen, L. Thomas Winfree Jr., Ni He, and Terrance J. Taylor, "Youth Gangs and Definitional Issues: When is a Gang a Gang, and Why Does it Matter?" *Crime & Delinquency* 47, no. 1 (2001): 105–30; Jana Grekul and Patti LaBoucane-Benson, "An Investigation into the Formation and Recruitment of Aboriginal Gangs in Western Canada" (Ottawa: Public Safety Canada, 2006); Jana Grekul and Patti LaBoucane-Benson, "Aboriginal Gangs and their (Dis)placement: Contextualizing Recruitment, Membership, and Status," *Canadian Journal of Criminology and Criminal Justice* 50, no. 1 (2008): 59–82; Malcolm Klein and Cheryl Maxson, *Street Gang Patterns and Policies* (New York: Oxford University Press, 2006); Rob White, "Disputed Definitions and Fluid Identities: The Limitations of Social Profiling in Relation to Ethnic Youth Gangs," *Youth Justice* 8, no. 2 (2008): 149–61; Jane Wood and Emma Alleyne, "Street gang theory and research: Where are we now and where do we go from here?" *Aggression and Violent Behavior* 15, no. 2 (2009): 100–11.

29 Frederic Thrasher, *The Gang: A Study of 1313 Gangs in Chicago* (Chicago: University of Chicago Press, 1927), 46, original emphasis.

30 Klein and Maxson, *Street Gang Patterns and Policies*.

31 Ibid.; Walter Miller, "Gangs, Groups, and Serious Youth Crime," in *Critical Issues in Juvenile Delinquency*, ed. D. Shichor and D.H. Kelly (Lexington, MA: Heath, 1980), 115–38; James Short, *Gangs and Adolescent Violence* (Boulder, CO: University of Colorado, 1996); Wood and Alleyne, "Street gang theory and research."

32 Beth Bjerregaard, "Antigang Legislation and its Potential Impacts: The Promises and the Pitfalls," *Criminal Justice Policy Review* 14, no. 2 (2003): 171–92; Rob White, "Youth Gang Research in Australia," in *Studying Youth Gangs*, ed. J. Short and L. Hughes (Walnut Creek, CA: AltaMira Press, 2006).

33 Martin Bouchard, and Andrea Spindler. "Groups, Gangs, and Delinquency: Does Organization Matter?." *Journal of Criminal Justice* 38, no. 5 (2010): 921-933; Klein and Maxson, *Street Gang Patterns and Policies.*

34 Simon Hallsworth, *The Gang and Beyond: Interpreting Violent Street Worlds* (New York, NY: Palgrave MacMillan, 2013).

35 Ken Dowler, Thomas Fleming, and Stephen L. Muzzatti, "Constructing Crime: Media, Crime, and Popular Culture," *Canadian Journal of Criminology and Criminal Justice* 48, no. 6 (2006): 837–50; Joanne Minaker and Bryan Hogeveen, *Youth, Crime, and Society: Issues of Power and Justice* (Toronto: Pearson, 2009).

36 Robert Henry, "Not Just Another Thug: Implications of Defining Youth Gangs in a Prairie City" (MA thesis, University of Saskatchewan, 2009).

37 Totten, *Nasty, Brutish and Short.*

38 Totten, "Aboriginal Youth and Violent Gang Involvement in Canada."

39 Ibid.; Totten, *Nasty, Brutish and Short.*

40 Harry Blagg, *Crisis Intervention in Aboriginal Family Violence: Summary Report* (Commonwealth of Australia: Crime Research Centre, University of Western Australia, 2000); Totten, "Aboriginal Youth and Violent Gang Involvement in Canada," 142.

41 Totten, "Aboriginal Youth and Violent Gang Involvement in Canada"; Totten, *Nasty, Brutish and Short.*

42 James Messerschmidt, *Flesh and Blood.*

43 Sunera Thobani, *Exalted Subjects: Studies in the Making of Race and Nation in Canada* (Toronto: University of Toronto Press, 2007).

44 Michael Taussig, "Culture of Terror – Space of Death: Roger Casement's Putumayo Report and the Explanation of Torture," In *Violence in War and Peace: An Anthology*, edited by, Nancy Scheper-Hughes and Philippe Bourgois, 39-52. Malden: Blackwell Publishing, 2004.

45 Taiaiake Alfred, *Wasase: Indigenous Pathways of Action and Freedom* (Peterborough, ON: Broadview Press, 2005), 58.

46 Elizabeth Comack, Lawrence Deane, Larry Morrissette, and Jim Silver, *Indians Wear Red: Colonialism, Resistance, and Aboriginal Street Gangs* (Winnipeg, MB: Fernwood Press, 2013).

47 Robert Garot, *Who You Claim? Performing Gang Identity in School and on the Streets* (New York: New York University Press, 2010).

48 Ibid., 119.

49 Philippe Bourgois, *In Search of Respect: Selling Crack in El Barrio* (New York: Cambridge University Press, 1995); Garot, *Who You Claim?* Erving Goffman, *Interaction Ritual: Essays on Face to Face Behaviour* (New York: Patheon Books, 1967).

50 Bruce Jacobs and Richard Wright, *Street Justice: Retaliation in the Criminal Underworld* (New York: Cambridge University Press, 2006), 123.

51 Garot, *Who You Claim?*; Goffman, *Interaction Ritual*; Totten, *Nasty, Brutish and Short.*

52 Johnson, *The Gender Knot*; Katz, *Violence, Media, and the Crisis in Masculinity.*

53 Bourgois, *In Search of Respect*; Garot, *Who You Claim?*; Katz, *Violence, Media, and the Crisis in Masculinity*; Totten, *Nasty, Brutish and Short.*

54 Ann Bishop, *Becoming an Ally: Breaking the Cycle of Oppression* (Halifax, NS: Fernwood Press, 2002); Johnson, *The Gender Knot*; Katz, *Violence, Media and the Crisis in Masculinity.*

55 Alfred, *Wasase*; Brendan Hokowhitu, "Tackling Māori Masculinity: A Colonial Genealogy of Savagery and Sport," *The Contemporary Pacific* 16 (2004): 259–84; Brendan Hokowhitu, "The Death of the Koro Paka: Traditional Māori Patriarchy," *The Contemporary Pacific* 20, no. 1 (2008): 115–41.

56 Christopher Bagley, Michael Wood, and Heida Khumar, "Suicide and Careless Death in Young Males: Ecological Study of an Aboriginal Population in Canada," *Canadian Journal of Community Mental Health* 9, no. 1 (1990): 127–42; Laurence Kirmayer, "Suicide Among Canadian Aboriginal Peoples," *Transcultural Psychiatry Research Review* 31 (1994): 3–58; R. Niezen, "Suicide as a Way of Belonging: Causes and Consequences of Cluster Suicides in Aboriginal Communities," in *Healing Traditions: the Mental Health of Aboriginal Peoples in Canada*, ed. L.J. Kirmayer and G. Guthrie (Vancouver: UBC Press, 2009), 178–95.

57 Elizabeth Comack, *Racialized Policing: Aboriginal People's Encounters with Police* (Winnipeg, MB: Fernwood Publishing, 2012).

58 Bonita Lawrence and Enakshi Dua, "Decolonizing Antiracism," in *Racism, Colonialism, and Indigeneity in Canada: A Reader*, ed. M.J. Cannon and L. Sunseri (Don Mills, ON: Oxford University Press, 2011), 19–28.

59 Grekul and LaBoucane-Benson, "Aboriginal Gangs and their Displacement."

CHAPTER 11

Imprisonment and Indigenous Masculinity: Contesting Hegemonic Masculinity in a Toxic Environment

Allison Piché

As the chapter by Robert Henry in this volume indicates, it is impossible to discuss Indigenous male identity without also discussing the relationship Indigenous men have with the Canadian justice system. Likewise, one cannot have a comprehensive understanding of contemporary Indigenous masculinities in Canada or elsewhere without examining the gross overrepresentation of Indigenous men in correctional institutions. Within this examination, it is important that the voices of incarcerated Indigenous men are respected and considered as we think about approaches to combating their overrepresentation and challenging the more insidious articulations of masculinity that prevail in the prison context. This chapter examines the way in which specific representations of Indigenous masculinity are performed and perpetuated in Canadian correctional institutions and the ways in which arts- and education-based programming can work to problematize this process by working toward what James Messerschmidt terms "equality masculinities."[1]

I want to begin by highlighting the subjective framework from which I approach this topic. As a non-Indigenous scholar doing Indigenous studies research, and as a Euro-Canadian woman and volunteer-program facilitator within the Saskatchewan provincial correctional system, I find myself negotiating complicated positions and spaces. It is from these positions and the complicated theoretical relationship I have with them that I approach this topic. Robert Young states that "the difference is less a matter of geography [referring to working from the "Western perspective"] than where individuals locate themselves as speaking from, epistemologically, culturally, and politically, who they are speaking to, and how they define their own enunciative space."[2] I hope that by drawing attention to my own subjectivity, and in being self-reflexive, I will be able to share my perspective on the questions at hand, while engaging in ethical, respectful, and reciprocal community-based research.

In the past few years, I have worked at this research practice in my volunteer role as a program facilitator and researcher with the Inspired Minds: All Nations Creative Writing Program at the Saskatoon Correctional Centre (SCC). This program places student and faculty volunteers from the University of Saskatchewan as instructors of small creative writing courses in various living units at SCC. Together participants choose subject matter that interests them at the outset of each term and work with facilitators to explore these literary styles and techniques. It has been my experience that facilitators in the program seek to bridge differences between communities—incarcerated/free, Indigenous/non-Indigenous, university/prison—while at the same time trying to create both tangible and positive results for those involved in the education and creativity process. Our intention is to help build a healthy and supportive learning environment for participants to express themselves through their writing. Furthermore, we hope that the program can aid in re-engaging individuals in the learning process, helping them to become self-directed learners. The program's focus on the liberal arts is intended to aid in the development of critical thinking skills, allowing not only for the incorporation of various opinions and perspectives but also opening these existing perspectives to be challenged and transformed. In this chapter I draw from my experiences conducting research in such an environment.

Before turning to a discussion of the ways in which the prison classroom can create a transformative learning environment, and one that might aid in the process of recovering healthy Indigenous masculinities, it is first important to understand the history and contemporary reality of penitentiaries, colonial policy, and the ways in which these relate to studies of masculinity.

Masculinities in the Prison Context

While it is easy to construe that prisons (especially men's prisons) can be considered masculine spaces, articulations of masculinity are both complex and multiple within these spaces. As Elizabeth Comack explains, "Being kept in prison involves an experience in which men's identities and behavioural patterns are molded and remolded under conditions of confinement."[3]

Examining gender within the prison system requires examining a multitude of hegemonic and patriarchal structures that operate within these institutions—from the institutions themselves to the interactions and relations that develop between and within staff and inmates. I think it best to begin with examining the history of these institutions and their relationship with what were considered masculine ideals and values at a time when prisons began to replace more public forms of punishment and torture.

Mark E. Kann argues that "the dominant norms of manhood [in Early America] were central to the idea of the penitentiary as an institution of deterrence, punishment, and rehabilitation," and that "a man deprived of his liberty was less than a man."[4] In this way, prisons worked to emasculate the men they incarcerated. Loss of freedom was the punitive response to criminal acts, as power was removed from the individual and their care was placed in the hands of the state. Furthermore, these institutions also mandated a removal of individual and collective voice through the notion that solitary and silent reflection would help to facilitate conversion of the criminal into a law-abiding citizen.[5] Both the Auburn and Pennsylvania models were developed in the 1820s and were premised on forcing incarcerated men to remain silent for the duration of their sentence.[6] However, this goal of reform was limited to white convicts, as black males and other minority groups "were seen as outsiders who lacked the manly ability to discipline their passions and the manly freedom to govern, provision, and protect their families."[7] Penitentiaries became places to warehouse "incurable" men—those marginalized by American society as a result of race and socio-economic status.[8] Kann asserts that, at this time in America's history, a man's "worth was measured by his distance from dependency," and non-whites were viewed as inherently dependent on the state and were thus un-manly.[9]

For the most part, Canadian correctional institutions mirrored those south of the border. Kingston Penitentiary was built in 1835, and as Canada took shape over the course of the nineteenth century, so did our prison system. These first institutions followed the models used in the United States: "All were maximum security institutions, administered by a strict regime—productive labour during the day, solitary confinement during leisure time. A rule of silence was enforced at all times."[10] Though these rules have changed, the values eschewed at their inception continue to inform the operation of twenty-first-century institutions. Contemporary prisons still constitute a similar removal of power and voice, through loss of freedom, the continued use of solitary confinement, and the silencing of voices that challenge the status quo within correctional environments. The history of prisons in North

America is certainly more complex than this very brief overview; the areas highlighted are meant to draw attention to the fact that, from their outset, these institutions have been both gendered and racialized spaces.

At the same time that prisons in Canada were being constructed, policies of forced assimilation were enacted by the government on First Nations and Métis communities, impacting the gender balance and disrupting both men's and women's roles. In "Indigenous Masculinity: Carrying the Bones of Our Ancestors," Kim Anderson, Robert Alexander Innes, and John Swift describe the way in which the role of "protector" was taken from the men: "A few of the Elders talked about the dispossession of lands in the nineteenth century and how parceling Indigenous peoples onto reserves meant that they had little mobility or power, namely, of the management of their traditional territories. As Wil Campbell (Métis, Alberta) pointed out, 'How can he protect if he has nothing to protect?'"[11] This statement exemplifies the way in which gender roles were changed as a result of colonization and how the Canadian government—like the American—rendered the men dependent on the state, and—like prisoners—"un-manly." As Howard Adams describes in *Prison of Grass*, after being forced onto reserves, "all activities of the native community were completely under the control of colonizing officials, who made all the decisions affecting the daily operations of native people.... This grinding paternalism and prison-like authority persisted to this day."[12] This removal of control from Native communities had significant impacts on community life and livelihood. The reason these policies were so "successful" in their implementation was the belief of the wider populous that First Nations and Métis people were inferior. This lie became convincing as "perverted images were paraded before the public to help justify and legitimize the incarceration of the entire population of native people."[13]

In the twenty-first century, Corrections Canada does little more than warehouse offenders, a claim strengthened by a lack of funding directed toward programming and the resultant loss of services and programs. Even those programs still funded are unable to accommodate the needs of the current inmate population, and long waitlists negatively impact the ability of both federal and provincial corrections to provide treatment (medical, substance abuse, mental health) and support (educational, vocational) for those incarcerated.[14] As a result of their very structure and of the inadequate provision of services, these institutions perpetuate the cycle of violence for marginalized communities.

Racialized identities are also fostered by "correctional" institutions. In "Race, Gender, and Prison History," Angela Davis concludes her chapter by arguing that prisons perpetuate racism in American society: "The continued practice of throwing away entire populations depends upon the construction and perception—really the fixation—of those populations within the popular imagination as public enemies. It is precisely this relationship between racism and imprisonment that necessitates coalitional work between antiracist activists and prison activists; on the eve of the twenty-first century, these two movements are inseparable."[15] I believe that this sentiment holds true in the Canadian context as well. First, Canadian correctional institutions perpetuate racialized and stereotypical views of Aboriginal peoples, resulting in a negative public opinion and perception of Aboriginal people generally and of Aboriginal offenders more specifically. Second, the work of prison reformists and abolitionists cannot be effective without an understanding of the highly racialized nature of criminal justice in Canada.

Like African American and other minority group overrepresentation in prisons in the United States, Aboriginal overrepresentation in Canadian corrections must be understood within the history of colonialism in Canada. Deena Rymhs argues in *From the Iron House: Imprisonment in First Nations Writing* that "some critics place the residential school and the prison on a continuum with one another, in their containment of Aboriginal youth and in the similar type of cultural rupture they produce."[16] She acknowledges that the relationship between the rise in the number of incarcerated Aboriginal peoples and colonial policies—residential schooling, the '60s scoop,[17] the Indian Act[18]—as well as institutional and individual racism have resulted in and continue to impact these rates. High rates of substance abuse, family violence, and gang activity can also be linked to these policies and to the challenges faced by many First Nations, Métis, and Inuit youth in Canada today, and to current rates of incarceration.[19] Though overrepresentation of First Nations and Métis offenders is visible across Canadian institutions, these numbers are more pronounced in the Prairie provinces. In 2012, Saskatchewan had 1,621 inmates; of these, First Nations and Métis offenders made up 79 percent of those sentenced provincially and 67 percent of those sentenced federally.[20] In 2012, 78 percent of new admissions to provincial sentence were Aboriginal.[21] Not only are these rates inseparable from centuries of colonial policy but also the incarceration of so many First Nations and Métis men and women has profound effects on the ability of communities to engage in a process of recovery and decolonization.

Foucault highlights the link between colonization and incarceration, stating that "the prison is a natural consequence, no more than a higher degree, of the [social] hierarchy laid down step by step. The delinquent is an institutional product."[22] Under this framework our patriarchal social system has a substantial role to play in the overrepresentation of Aboriginal offenders. As explained in *Indians Wear Red*, "While colonialism manifests itself in a variety of ways, at its core is the complex poverty that shapes the lives of Aboriginal people and limits their true potential."[23] As a result, challenging and confronting colonial realities in Canada must occur in concert with confronting and challenging issues of complex poverty and toxic masculinities.

Understanding Masculinity

Raewyn Connell, in "Change Among the Gatekeepers: Men, Masculinities, and Gender Equality in the Global Arena," highlights a number of important ideas when discussing the impact of gender studies on men, stating that "in discussions of women's exclusion from power and decision making, men are implicitly present as the power holders," and further, that "the men who receive most of the benefits and the men who pay most of the costs are not the same individuals."[24] These ideas are important in examining the context of Indigenous masculinity in Canada and the way in which colonization has had varying levels of impact on the masculine experience. Of particular interest is her assertion that those (men) who receive the benefits and those who pay the cost are not the same people—this is especially true among marginalized peoples, in particular First Nations and Métis communities in Canada.

I am conscious that in engaging in a discussion of the ways in which hegemonic and other forms of masculinity are supported and contested within the correctional environment, I risk falling into the trap of what Connell and Messerschmidt call "usages that imply a fixed character type, or an assemblage of toxic traits."[25] I will endeavour not to essentialize masculinity as consisting merely of toxic or negative expressions by defining relevant terminology and its impact before delving into the ways in which these ideas and concepts impact relations among men in prison.

Multiple Masculinities

At the advent of the concept, hegemonic masculinity was best understood as the practice of "embody[ing] the current most honored way of being a man, it required all other men to position themselves in relation to it, and it ideologically legitimated the global subordination of women to men."[26] In its reformulation, Connell and Messerschmidt argue that hegemonic masculinity relies on the subordination of non-hegemonic masculinities and on the production of masculine ideals, though these might be impossible for boys and men to ever live up to or fully embody.[27] These ideas are central to the understanding of the way in which colonialism has impacted and continues to impact First Nations, Métis, and Inuit peoples in Canada, and the way representations of what Sam McKegney terms the "masculindian" become toxic to Indigenous men and communities.[28] Mike Donaldson (1993) further argues that "a fundamental element of hegemonic masculinity, then, is that women exist as potential sexual objects for men while men are negated as sexual objects for men."[29] This idea will be explored through an examination of how the gangster lifestyle and image have become attractive to First Nations and Métis men.

Hypermasculinity and toxic masculinity are other means of performing a specific kind of masculine identity. Hypermasculinity is often equated with negative traits and representation, as it relies on a specific enactment of the masculine—but it is important to note that this enactment can also be construed in positive ways. A person can be muscular, non-violent, *and* a feminist; violence and muscularity/build are not necessarily complementary categories. Connell and Messerschmidt point to the way in which there exists a "transnational business masculinity" wherein the elite engage in and articulate a form of hegemonic masculinity without embodying the kind of masculine ideal or "tough guise" Jackson Katz describes.[30] As such, I will use the terms "toxic masculinity" and "misguided masculinity" in referring to the "negative" hypermasculine traits enacted by some First Nations and Métis men in prison and on the street. Finally, Messerschmidt's concept of "equality masculinity" refers to "those that legitimate an egalitarian relationship between men and women, between masculinity and femininity, and among men."[31] It is toward this "equality masculinity" that we must strive—through enacting and promoting it at the local, regional, and national levels.

In prisons, the above articulations of masculinity are all the more tenuous and pronounced. As Kim Shayo Buchanan argues, "Many men's prisons are plagued by homophobia, high rates of physical violence, and an institutional culture that requires inmates to prove their masculinity by fighting."[32] Prisons are spaces where men have power over other men, a power that is embedded in the institutional structure and not merely at the individual level. Comack argues that we cannot lose sight of the relationship between the micro–interpersonal and macro–structure of prison itself; we must "acknowledge that *the act of imprisonment is itself a form of violence, one backed by the legitimated power of the state.*"[33]

In addition to grappling with hegemonic, toxic, and racialized definitions of manhood, Indigenous men must also negotiate to define themselves against colonized masculinities. In "Warriors, Healers, Lovers and Leaders,"

McKegney explores the way in which the imposition of patriarchal values and systems of governance disrupted Indigenous communities in that, through the Indian Act, "male power...ceased to flow from the dynamic relationship between the genders signified by twinship and complementarity, but rather had to be seized from the other half of gendered society, the women, and exercised to their exclusion."[34] Marginalized through colonial experiences and stripped of power and autonomy, male roles have been impacted as a result of these processes. McKegney argues that popular culture's toxic images of Indigenous masculinity "seek power through domination and violence rather than through communal responsibility and twinship with the feminine," and become appealing to Indigenous men "because they offer relief from the often untenable social conditions as well as a sense of masculine agency that colonization has rendered difficult for many Indigenous men to attain in other ways."[35]

The ubiquity of these combined hegemonic, racialized, hypermasculine, toxic, and colonized definitions of masculinity can be linked directly with the ways in which, for example, Aboriginal gangs choose to present themselves—by playing up and playing into the stereotypical media representations of Indigenous masculinity. Gang names alone highlight the way these forms of toxic masculinity are valued: Indian Posse, Saskatchewan/Manitoba Warriors, and Native Syndicate, for example. For youth in the Prairie provinces in particular, the "gang acts as, or promises to act as, a substitute family, filling the void left by family backgrounds marked by violence, substance abuse, and crime."[36] In their study of Aboriginal gangs, Jana Grekul and Patti LaBoucane-Benson highlight that for Aboriginal youth and families in the Prairies, "gangs are real, youth are being recruited into this lifestyle on the streets and in prisons, leaving school and family behind to take on the gangster identity."[37] There is a fluidity between the prison and the community in this setting, where this gangster image thrives. In their interviews with Elders across Canada, Anderson, Innes, and Swift note that a few of the Elders linked absent fathers to misguided masculinities which too often result in gang involvement.[38] Gangs can serve as a substitute community for men and women whose childhoods have been marked by violence.

The fluidity between community and the carceral is echoed in the book *Str8 Up and Gangs: The Untold Stories*, a compilation of true life stories of ex–gang members. Here John Siwak writes, "Around the time I was 11 years of age (1995), I was officially jumped into the gang.... Choosing this way, I decided that bein' scary and threatening gave me a sense of power. So with that, I vowed to be the biggest, baddest gangster I could be."[39] Another contributor, Marty Dustyhorn, writes, "When I was 15 years old, I wanted to join a gang. The reason for this was because all my cousins and brothers were 'down'.... I learned that I could not trust anybody and that fast money could be made if you were willing to hurt and manipulate people."[40] Siwak and Dustyhorn highlight the way in which one's gang and family are often synonymous. To reiterate the linkages previously made by Robert Henry in this volume, family and community violence is pervasive in the lives of Aboriginal gang members.

Toxic articulations of Indigenous masculinities can be one way to respond to the powerlessness experienced by some Indigenous men. Of note is the fact that gangs provide a sense of power—even though it might be misguided. This idea is articulated by Ronald Weitzer and Charis Kubrin in their analysis "Misogyny in Rap Music," where they state that "rap's messages have been incubated and resonate in communities where men have few opportunities for socioeconomic success and dignity and where respect is instead often earned by mistreating young women as well as other men."[41] A criminal lifestyle, often marked by violence and gang affiliation, provide a means for these men to attain "respect" and "power" by finding another group to marginalize. In their study of Aboriginal street gangs in Winnipeg, the authors of *Indians Wear Red* found that "in addition to violence, the men used the proceeds of crime to enhance their masculine capital through conspicuous consumption."[42] These men create victims in their need to assert power and control in negative and socially unacceptable ways, resulting in a reproduction of their own experiences for others. Similar findings come out of a 2006 study by the Canadian Centre for Justice Studies, which examined "Victimization and Offending among the Aboriginal Population in Canada." Though the authors do not refer to gang membership in the study, their findings are congruent with the argument that First Nations and Métis offenders often victimize other First Nations and Métis people and communities, as follows:

- In 2004, Aboriginal people experienced violent victimization at a rate of about three times greater than that of non-Aboriginal people.

- In 2004, violent incidents committed against Aboriginal people were most likely to occur in and around the victim's home (34 percent) compared to rates for non-Aboriginal victims (17 percent) and this difference can be partly explained by the fact that Aboriginal people are more likely to be victimized by someone they know.

- Aboriginal people experience much higher levels of spousal violence by current and ex-partners than their non-Aboriginal counterparts. This finding supports previous research suggesting that the prevalence of family violence is more extensive within Aboriginal communities.

• Aboriginal males had a rate of violent victimization that was almost three times higher than that of non-Aboriginal males.[43]

These findings are consistent with the autobiographical narratives in *Str8 Up and Gangs*, where First Nations and Métis ex–gang members focus on the harm done by Aboriginal gangs to their own people:

> "When you look at some of the gang names…it is Native people fighting and killing each other for their own land. I find it pretty sad to see this happening."
>
> —Phillip Charles Bear Morin[44]

> "In seeing the outcome of my actions over and over again, I began to see the negativity I was living and causing was killing my people."
>
> —John Siwak[45]

> "What are all the Indian brothers fighting one another for? Respect? Turf? Colours? What for? Because they can, I guess. Silly boys, when are you going to learn? Respect is earned, not taken. Fear is not respect."
>
> —Brendon Jimmy[46]

The victims of these crimes are often the families, friends, and communities of First Nations and Métis offenders and their removal to correctional facilities complicates the process of "recovering the masculine" through a return to gender-balanced family and community roles. The disruption of First Nations, Métis, and Inuit communities is perpetuated and compounded by the fact that so many fathers, brothers, and sons are behind bars.

One of the many remaining questions is how we can work to build and develop "equality masculinities" in the carceral space. The prison classroom is one means of combating both hegemonic and toxic masculinities in that it creates a space wherein participants can engage in discussions regarding power and privilege that could not be engaged in (in the same way) outside the classroom. In an institution where distrust is the norm, the classroom can become an environment where men feel comfortable sharing both their work and experiences with one another and where trust can be built and maintained. It is through the creative arts in particular—writing, in the case of our program—that many men have found an expressive outlet.

As part of my research project, I conducted interviews in the spring of 2013 with both participants of the program and key staff members who had been involved with the Inspired Minds program in some capacity. The following is an introduction to the creative writing program at Saskatoon Correctional Centre and some of my preliminary reflections on the possibilities for Indigenous men and masculinities within Inspired Minds.

Inspired Minds: All Nations Creative Writing

In July 2011, Professor Nancy Van Styvendale and I began to offer creative writing classes to two groups of inmates at Saskatoon Correctional Centre under the guidance of Diann Block, First Nations and Métis Cultural Coordinator. The mandate of Inspired Minds states,

> The workshops introduce students to basic literary terminology; develop their literacy through in- and out-of-class reading and discussion of literary texts; and enlarge their writing and editing skills. Students are given homework each week, and ample opportunity is given the following week to share and discuss this work with peers and instructors. Generally, workshops consist of sharing writing done over the week; introducing terminology and providing sample texts for discussion; guiding students through in-class writing exercises; and assigning homework for the following week's class.[47]

Participation occurs on a voluntary basis, all literacy levels are welcome, and inmates are provided with a certificate of completion, if they attend six of the eight sessions, signed by the Dean of the College of Arts and Science and the Vice Dean of Humanities and Fine Arts in the College of Arts and Science at the University of Saskatchewan. A main goal of the program is to provide programming to those with little access to other correctional programs, which often means working in higher security settings.

The program itself, as described above, focuses on literacy and creative writing skills development; however, other outcomes reflect the ability of arts and education programming to combat the valuing of toxic masculinity as well as the emasculation of imprisoned men. In this way, the program is able to subversively engage in a process of developing healthy Indigenous masculinities, with this being neither an outward intention nor one that is directly pursued by participants themselves. I say that it is not "directly pursued" because many of the men who choose to participate in the program do so initially out of boredom or an interest in improving their writing skills rather than engaging in transformative learning.

In March of 2013, I began interviewing inmates who had participated in the creative writing program and staff at Saskatoon Correctional Centre who had worked in units where the program was run. The purpose of these interviews was to gain qualitative data on individual experiences with the program and on its overall impact within the framework of corrections. Some of the earliest findings of this research shed light on the role that arts and education programming can play in "recovering the masculine" in the behaviour and attitude changes that come as an indirect result of participation.

Challenging Carceral Representations of Masculinity

As a creative writing program facilitated by University of Saskatchewan students and staff, the Inspired Minds program is in a unique position to provide an arts and education program that is able to operate within the confines of the prison system, while at the same time subverting these rigid and hegemonic power dynamics. For teachers coming from the broader community, the dynamic of the classroom reflects the fact that we are not employed by correctional services. This results in a more open and engaging environment where inmates are more likely to feel comfortable sharing their ideas, questions, and work than if a similar program was run and staffed by the Centre itself.

The program works to challenge both toxic articulations of masculinity and the emasculation of offenders vis-à-vis incarceration. Prison is understood as a place that removes individual agency and voice, and in many ways creative writing work is able to facilitate the return of this voice. In writing poetry, short fiction, autobiography, and exploring a host of other genres, participants have an opportunity to convey their stories and experiences and have these experiences heard and acknowledged. In her study on prison writings of Indigenous men, Rymhs argues that "the prison also produces authors who may not otherwise have been moved to write. More than a place of defeat and submission, the prison may be seen as a place of learning, where a nascent consciousness is born in the prisoner, often in defiant resistance to the institution containing him/her."[48] While Rymhs's study looks at well-known authors who have written while incarcerated and/or about their incarceration, I would also argue that even if the product of this process is not a published work, there is still a "nascent consciousness" developed and encouraged in the program participant.

The program participants are given authority and control over their work, something that is often removed through the reality of incarceration. Part of the creative writing process involves peer editing and feedback, which is often highlighted by participants as beneficial to their literary skill development and can also be beneficial to relationships with other participants.

At the same time that the above occurs, so too is there a breaking down of toxic masculine values and attitudes. The creative writing classroom becomes a space where individual posturing and assertion of power is not valued or responded to in the same way as within the general prison environment. It becomes a place where men engage in scholarly debate, discussion of controversial issues, and the sharing of thoughts and experiences through their writing without needing to play into structures of both hegemonic and toxic masculinity. Though this is true in the classroom environment, it is not necessarily true outside of it. One interviewee stated that, before the course was offered, he wrote as a means of venting frustrations: "Well you can say things on paper that you can't really tell people in here, because people, everyone has a big persona, like being a gangster and shit in here, you can't really tell people, you can't tell anyone really, the things that you feel. That's why I was doing it mostly." Distrust is rampant in the correctional environment, and this performance of persona, as evidenced above, has a direct impact on inmate relationships.

bell hooks explains, in *The Will to Change*, that the connection between masculinity and violence is linked to patriarchy, which she says accepts and values the expression of anger only in men.[49] The creative arts classroom combats this representation and valuing of violent masculinity by establishing an environment where the rules of the "Learning Contract" include, first and foremost, that participants will "respect themselves and their writing," and "respect other workshop participants and their writing."[50] Respect in the classroom context is a central tenet of the program; participants and facilitators do not need to use other means to attain respect—power in the classroom is shared.

In providing an environment where frustrations can be expressed through writing, the classes challenge the valuing of confrontational attitudes. Instead, classroom debate and discussion is encouraged and the students and instructor help to facilitate meaningful discussions about contemporary issues and literary work. One of the topics covered during debate is the Native American mascot controversy.[51] Teams were created a week in advance and different sides of the issue—either for or against the use of Native American mascots or imagery—were assigned to each group. Basic research material was provided and each team was to develop an argument in support of their assigned position. There was a substantial amount of classroom turnover the week of the debate and so what began as a debate turned into a scholarly discussion of the various positions.

Engaging in debate in this manner, where positions on an issue are assigned and do not necessarily reflect one's own beliefs, can help to remove personal feelings from the argument. Not all participants had the same position on the issue, but the group was able to discuss the pros and cons of each argument. This structure aids in the development of non-confrontational argument skills and demonstrates that there can be space for healthy disagreement without expressing an opinion or position in a visceral way.

While these are still preliminary reflections, it is important to highlight the way in which the "safe" space in the classroom can be temporal and fleeting. A number of interviewees described the way in which, following the conclusion of a course, interactions return to "normal"—a hegemonically masculine normal. Relationships with staff and with other inmates, which may have improved during the course, tended to revert to previous habits of interaction.

Conclusion

This chapter has explored the way in which articulations of masculinity manifest themselves in the prison environment and the way in which creative arts/education programming can work to combat them. However, I think that it is important to recognize that this process of recovery, particularly for incarcerated Indigenous men, is multi-layered, complex, and ongoing. In no way can creative writing and education programming in and of itself meet the diverse and changing needs of First Nations, Métis, and Inuit offenders. The process of developing healthy masculinities needs to be incorporated in other facets of correctional programming including (but not limited to) substance abuse treatment, violence prevention, parenting, and cultural and spiritual programs. Further, we need to rethink our standards for measuring program success; rather than relying on recidivism rates, we need to recognize that "less measurable returns, such as increased self confidence, healing, skills and understanding also make a difference to individuals and communities."[52] What also needs further examination is how to extend or expand the experience of the transformative classroom in a particularly toxic environment. Is it possible to achieve an equality masculinity within such a space? Part of the answer lies in building linkages with communities and community organizations in order to continue both the enactment of equality masculinities and the recovery of the masculine upon an offender's release from prison. These linkages are difficult to develop and maintain for a variety of reasons—funding, resources, community support, and the fact that we operate within a patriarchal social system—yet these elements are necessary if this process is to continue on the outside. Structural change also needs to occur at the policy and institutional levels so as to make maintaining these linkages easier.

Notes

1   James W. Messerschmidt, "Engendering Gendered Knowledge: Assessing the Academic Appropriation of Hegemonic Masculinity," *Men and Masculinities* 15, no. 1 (2012): 73.

2   Robert J.C. Young, *Postcolonialism: An Historical Introduction* (Malden, MA: Blackwell, 2001), 62.

3   Elizabeth Comack, *Out There/In Here: Masculinity, Violence and Prisoning* (Winnipeg: Fernwood Publishing, 2008), 111.

4   Mark E. Kann, "Gender and Prison History: Penitence for the Privileged: Manhood, Race and Penitentiaries in Early America," in *Gender and Prisons*, ed. Dana M. Britton (Burlington, VT: Ashgate Publishing Company, 2005), 9; Mark E. Kann, "Penitence for the Privileged: Manhood, Race, and Penitentiaries in Early America," in *Prison Masculinities*, ed. Don Sabo, Terry A. Kupers, and Willie London (Philadelphia: Temple University Press, 2001).

5   David J. Rothman, "Perfecting the Prison: United States, 1789–1865," in *The Oxford History of the Prison: The Practice of Punishment in Western Society* (New York: Oxford University Press, 1995), Chapter 4.

6   The Auburn system was developed at Auburn Prison in Auburn, New York; here inmates worked and ate together in silence during the day and returned to solitary confinement for the night. The Pennsylvania System (developed at Pittsburgh Penitentiary and Philadelphia Prison) kept inmates in solitary confinement for the duration of their stay; they worked, ate, and slept alone and in silence. *The Oxford History of the Prison*, 105–6.

7   Kann, "Penitence for the Privileged," 11.

8   Ibid., 13.

9   Ibid.

10 Correctional Service of Canada, "Penitentiaries in Canada," last modified 20 October 2014, http://www.csc-scc.gc.ca/about-us/006-1006-eng.shtml.

11 Kim Anderson, Robert Alexander Innes, and John Swift, "Indigenous Masculinities: Carrying the Bones of Our Ancestors," in *Canadian Men and Masculinities: Historical and Contemporary Perspectives*, ed. Christopher J. Greig and Wayne J. Martino (Toronto: Canadian Scholars' Press, 2012), 275.

12 Howard Adams, *Prison of Grass: Canada from a Native Point of View* (Saskatoon: Fifth House Publishers), 37.

13 Ibid., 38.

14 Howard Sapers, "Annual Report of the Office of the Correctional Investigator 2011–2012," *The Correctional Investigator Canada* (Ottawa: Office of the Correctional Investigator, 2012), 37–38.

15 Angela Y. David, "Race, Gender, and Prison History: From the Convict Lease System to the Supermax Prison," in *Prison Masculinities*, ed. Don Sabo, Terry A. Kupers, and Willie London (Philadelphia: Temple University Press, 2001), 44.

16 Deena Rymhs, *From the Iron House: Imprisonment in First Nations Writing* (Waterloo: Wilfrid Laurier University Press, 2008), 3.

17 The "'60s Scoop" refers to the period in the 1960s (but did not happen exclusively during this time) where First Nations children were taken from their families by the state and adopted into non–First Nations families. This policy resulted in significant cultural rupture and the abuse of many First Nations children at the hands of their Euro-Canadian adopted families.

18 The Indian Act (1876) is a Canadian statute which was enacted as a means of ensuring federal oversight of Indigenous populations in Canada. Historically, the goal of this document has been to assimilate First Nations peoples into Canadian society by providing the government with the power to define and control who is considered First Nations.

19 Jana Grekul and Patti LaBoucane-Benson, "Aboriginal Gangs and Their (Dis)placement: Contextualizing Recruitment, Membership, and Status," *Canadian Journal of Criminology and Criminal Justice* 50, no. 1 (2008): 59–82.

20 Saskatchewan, Ministry of Justice, "Average daily combined sentenced and remand count," http://www.justice.gov.sk.ca/Default.aspx?DN=e75de182-1c7a-4e60-8755-f186dd7b063c.

21 Ibid.

22 Michel Foucault, *Discipline and Punish: The Birth of the Prison* (New York: Pantheon Books, 1977), 301.

23 Elizabeth Comack, Lawrence Deane, Larry Morrissette, and Jim Silver, *Indians Wear Red: Colonialism, Resistance, and Aboriginal Street Gangs* (Winnipeg: Fernwood Publishing, 2013), 60.

24 Raewyn Connell, "Change Among the Gatekeepers: Men, Masculinities, and Gender Equality in the Global Arena," in *Men's Lives*, edited by Michael S. Kimmel and Michael A. Messner, 9th edition (Old Tappan, NJ: Pearson, 2012).

25 Raewyn Connell and James W. Messerschmidt, "Hegemonic Masculinity: Rethinking the Concept," *Gender & Society* 19, no. 6 (2005): 854.

26 Ibid., 832.

27 Ibid., 846.

28 Sam McKegney, "Warriors, Healers, Lovers and Leaders: Colonial Impositions of Indigenous Male Roles and Responsibilities," in *Canadian Perspectives on Men and Masculinities: An Interdisciplinary Reader*, ed. Jason A. Laker (Toronto: Oxford University Press, 2011), 255–6.

29 Mike Donaldson, "What is Hegemonic Masculinity?" *Theory and Society* 22 (1993): 645.

30 Connell and Messerschmidt, "Hegemonic Masculinity," 849.

31 Messerschmidt, "Engendering Gendered Knowledge," 73.

32 Kim Shayo Buchanan, "E-race-ing Gender: The Racial Construction of Prison Rape," in *Masculinities and the Law: A Multidimensional Approach*, ed. Frank Rudy Cooper and Ann C. McGinley (New York: New York University Press, 2012), 187.

33 Comack, *Out There/In Here*, 118, emphasis in original.

34 McKegney, "Warriors, Healers, Lovers and Leaders," 253.

35 Ibid., 259–260.

36 Grekul and LaBoucane-Benson, "Aboriginal Gangs and Their (Dis)placement," 68.

37 Ibid., 65–6.

38 Anderson, Innes, and Swift, "Carrying the Bones of our Ancestors," 279.

39 *Str8 Up and Gangs: The Untold Stories* (Saskatoon: Hear My Heart Books, 2012), 59.

40 Ibid., 19.

41 Ronald Weitzer and Charis Kubrin, "Misogyny in Rap Music: A Content Analysis of Prevalence and Meanings," in *Men's Lives*, 9th ed., ed. Michael S. Kimmel (London: Pearson, 2012), 505.

42 Comack, Deane, Morrissette, and Silver, *Indians Wear Red*, 21.

43 Andrea Taylor-Butts, Jodi-Anne Brzozowski, and Sara Johnson, "Victimization and Offending among the Aboriginal Population in Canada," *Juristat* 26, no. 3 (2006) (Statistics Canada catalogue no. 85-002).

44 *Str8 Up and Gangs*, 5.

45 Ibid., 59.

46 Ibid., 37.

47 Nancy Van Styvendale, "Inspired Minds: Overview of Principles, Activities, and Goals," unpublished manuscript, December 2013.

48 Rymhs, *From the Iron House*, 24.

49 bell hooks, *The Will to Change: Men, Masculinity, and Love* (New York: Atria Books, 2004), 7.

50 "Learning Contract" for Inspired Minds: All Nations Creative Writing Program (2011).

51 There is substantial debate and activism related to the use of images of Native peoples as mascots for sports teams.

52 Denise MacDonald, "'Getting on the BUS': Reflections on the First Cohort of a Transition to University Program," in *Moving Forward, Giving Back: Transformative Aboriginal Adult Education*, ed. Jim Silver (Winnipeg: Fernwood Publishing, 2013), 106.

CHAPTER 12

Diné Masculinities, Relationships, Colonization, and Regenerating an Egalitarian Way of Life

Lloyd L. Lee

In Diné (Navajo) philosophy, Sa'ah Naagháí Bik'eh Hózhóón (SNBH) is a foundational principle of the universe. It exemplifies values and beliefs and represents an animated and living journey. It is static dimension, active dimension, thought, speech, male, and female. SNBH is the central animating power of the universe, and as such, it produces a world described as hózhǫ́, the ideal environment of beauty, harmony, and happiness.[1] SNBH represents a combination of separate male and female concepts. The first concept, Sa'ah Naagháí, is defined as "indestructible and eternal being"; it is male and exhibits male-like qualities. The second concept, Bik'eh Hózhóón, is defined as "the director and cause of all that is good"; it is female and exhibits female-like qualities. The two do not operate alone and apart but are complements to and halves of each other.[2]

SNBH also represents a four-part planning and learning process central to the Diné way of learning and knowing. The process is comprehensive and includes Nitsáhákees (thinking), Nahat'á (planning), Iiná (living), and Siihasin (reflecting). It begins in the east following a circular path proceeding sunwise through all four cardinal directions. It also includes the four sacred mountains of the Diné people (Mount Blanca – east, Mount Taylor – south, San Francisco Peaks – west, and Mount Hesperus – north), the four sacred minerals associated with the four sacred mountains, the four parts of the day (dawn – white shell, day – turquoise, evening or sunset – abalone, night

– black jet), the four seasons of the year (spring, summer, fall, winter), and the lifespan of a human being (birth, adolescence, adulthood, and old age). Each provides and expounds on the meanings with the four-part planning and learning process. SNBH organizes a person's life. It sets a framework on how to live well and with beauty and happiness.

Following the SNBH paradigm, this chapter is organized into the four elements of thinking, planning, living, and reflecting. Nitsáhákees and Nahat'á set the stage by discussing the history and experiences of Diné masculinities; iiná represents the voices of contemporary Diné men who share their perspectives on relationships and the consequences of colonization, and siihasin discusses how Diné cultural teachings can be a factor in regenerating an egalitarian way of life between Diné men and women. I will share findings from my discussion and reflections with thirty Diné men on the impacts of colonization on male and female relationships, and I will also discuss how cultural teachings can help regenerate an egalitarian way of life between men and women.

Experiences of Diné Masculinities

Diné men learn how to be a hastiin (man) through a Diné way of life and from the creation scripture and journey narratives. All Indigenous peoples have creation narratives detailing their histories. These stories are the foundation of a people's identity and way of life. The stories of First Man, the twin protectors, and others exemplify for Diné men how to live and understand their responsibilities to their families and communities. The image of an ideal Diné man derives from these stories, but actual life experiences have proven that not all Diné men achieve this image.

The story of the twin protectors who searched for their father, the Sun, exemplifies to Diné men several core principles. For instance, the twins took responsibility for their actions. The twins protected the people from the monsters at the time. Though the twins were afraid to confront these horrible monsters, they were triumphant. The twins demonstrated independence with a strong sense of identity learned from their mother and extended family. The twins epitomized how a Diné man should live. A Diné man must be knowledgeable, smart, and unafraid of responsibility, and he must protect his family and people. The twins were one of the first Diné protectors. Diné protectors thought of their family and relatives first; they worked for the people and not themselves. The twins were strong and established a framework for Diné masculinities.

Diné men lived with their wives' families and made all possible efforts to ensure the survival of an extended family network. Most of the daily activities included finding and fetching water, collecting firewood, finding and hunting game, maintaining crops, teaching, and protecting their wives and extended family.[3] Most Diné men did not spend much time away from their extended family. At times, men visited their own biological parents, but for the majority of the time they lived with their wives' extended families. Men and women lived in an egalitarian and autonomous relationship. They integrated their work roles. Gender equity was a critical aspect of social life. Both male and female economic contributions were equally valued.

Diné men and women participated in the political system. Many of the heads or leaders of extended and clan families were men, although a significant number were women, too. Men in leadership positions lived ethical and respectful lives; they were examples for the rest of the natural community, which relied on these individuals to make good decisions.[4] If a leader did wrong, then the people let him know and if necessary removed him from the position. Leaders were supposed to follow the examples of the Diyin Dine'é (Holy People) and the twin protectors.

Diné men understood their role in life and in the extended and clan families. Not all of the men supported their families; some were selfish individuals who took advantage of people. Usually, these selfish men roamed by themselves.[5] Overall, most men made sure their families were prosperous and happy. They developed to be responsible, respectful, hospitable, knowledgeable, and healthy men. They advocated subsistence, self-sufficiency, respect, love, and humility.

Beginning in the seventeenth century and continuing until the nineteenth, Spanish and Mexican ways of life influenced Diné men. A significant cultural impact was the introduction of livestock, such as sheep, goats, and horses.[6] Diné men added the roles of sheepherder, horse caretaker, and horse rider. While the men continued to live a subsistence-based lifestyle during this era, warfare, sheepherding, and the horse affected how Diné men interacted with Diné women, with other Native peoples such as the Pueblos, Comanches, and Utes, and with Spanish and Mexican peoples. Warfare increased with the Pueblos, Comanches, Utes, Mexicans, and New Mexicans because of the need to protect and rescue family members.[7]

The horse allowed Diné men to frequently move away from the family for extended periods of time. Diné men adapted very well to using the horse for trading, protection, and travel.[8] The horse raised men's economic capacity, social status, ambition, and dependability. Those with horses ventured out to find food and to trade, and they interacted with more peoples. Diné masculinities became linked with how men maintained and cared for their horses.[9] Diné men showed responsibility in the care of their horses, which provided status within their communities. A Diné man with no horse or livestock in many cases had low status.[10] He needed to demonstrate to his future wife and her family that he was dependable and capable of providing for the family.[11]

Raising sheep also shaped Diné communities. Sheep furnished security; sheep raising was an integral part of one's identity as well as the community's, and influenced how Diné social groups were organized.[12] The ownership of sheep helped move people to cooperation and mutual interdependence with one another. Sheepherding was a main mechanism to teach the values of a Diné way of life. Sheepherding helped teach the principles of responsibility, respect, love, hospitality, knowledge, and health.

Diné men were hunters, farmers, teachers, storytellers, traders, shepherds, protectors, and healers; masculinities were based on a foundational image of spirituality, social ways, common living, and physical body. A Diné woman complemented a Diné man. Men lived the principles of iiná—to live well, to know the history of the people and the Diyin Dine'é, to live a path based on the philosophical concept of Sa'ah Naagháí Bik'eh Hózhóón, to use the four basic elements to survive, to know and practise K'é (family relations) and K'éí (clans), and to speak the Diné language. Diné boys went through a kinaaldá (puberty ceremony) to learn what it means to live as a young man. They learned stories, prayers, songs, and cultural knowledge. All of these attributes of Diné masculinities still exist, but they are not universal among all Diné men in the twenty-first century. Next, I will share several male perspectives on colonization and how it has impacted relationships between Diné men and women.

Contemporary Diné Male Perspectives on Relationships and Colonization

Between 2005 and 2008, I interviewed thirty Diné men. These men's ages ranged from eighteen to seventy. The majority of the men were bilingual speakers and quite a few followed only a traditional Diné spirituality. Each of the men willingly shared their thoughts on development, expression, colonization, and relationships. In this section, I will share some of the findings from my discussions with the men, using pseudonyms when quoting the men to protect their identities and families.

Demonstrating the importance of history, some of the men reflected on how colonialism has transformed Diné men and women. They noted that some Diné men do respect women, but some do not. According to several of the men I spoke with, the difference can be attributed to age and generation. For example, Scott talked about how it depends on age. He feels older Diné men are very respectful to women, but that younger men are losing their cultural identity, picking up a "new" culture, not knowing their relations, and displaying aggressive behaviour toward women.[13] He cited domestic abuse, drug use, and overall negativity on the reservation as evidence. Albert referred to drugs, alcohol, and a lack of discipline as reasons why some Diné men do not value Diné women.[14] John believes these men are not taught the proper way to treat women: "As a Diné, you are taught to be a good husband, father, son, et cetera,…in the sweat lodge during puberty. You are told that you are from a woman. You are reminded of your mothers, sisters, grandmothers, et cetera. In this way, Navajo men still respect Navajo women. However, today many Navajo 'men' who were not taught these ways degrade women, they use women for one thing only and leave. They learned to disrespect the sacred bonds of love, marriage, and et cetera."[15] Frank offered a similar perspective:

> Some men will respect the Navajo women, but there are those who don't—because of lack of understanding of the values of K'é and the clans. If we understand the values of a Diné woman, then the abuse can be lessened. But if we don't teach this to our children then when will this disrespect of Diné women stop? The woman is the home; she is the one that provides warmth, love and care. The woman is the child bearer and for that, she is to be revered. She brings life into the world. She brings love and warmth when everything seems bleak. She will restore the beauty in life. But an uneducated man about Diné women will do as he pleases.[16]

In the Diné creation scripture and journey narratives, Diné men and women worked together for iiná. Without both parties working together, living became stagnant and imbalanced. Both Diné men and women needed each other in order for life to continue.

Another issue that came up in terms of relationships between men and women was how they developed partnerships. Traditionally, uncles and grandmothers arranged marriages between men and women. When it was time for a son to marry, the families considered a mate from an "upstanding" family. Many times a dowry consisting of horses was required. Anthropologist Gladys A. Reichard described the arrangement:

The father of the boy takes the initiative rather than his mother's brother.... The matter is talked over in family council and in choosing a wife for a son the father's voice is final and may override that of the maternal uncle whereas the opinion of the girl's maternal uncle may take precedence over her father's or even over her own. Now let us suppose a girl is agreed upon, the proposal is made and accepted and the marriage takes place. Then it may be that the girl's family has also a son whom they will later marry to the sister of their son-in-law. Now in the first family there are a number of unmarried children and the second family may know of mates for them although not in the immediate family, nevertheless they will be clan members and mutual influence will be exerted to have them seek mates from the first family. And so it goes until we have an intricate network of clan and family alliances which is so complex that it defies any attempt to discover whether the affiliations are due primarily to desire for clan or family union or whether they are due merely to proximity of habitat.[17]

Marriages were arranged to ensure clan rules were followed properly and to determine which families were trustworthy.

In the twenty-first century, relationships between Diné men and women are complex. Many factors affect the communication and well-balanced nature necessary for companionship. Many young Diné choose whom they date and marry, and arranged marriages are no longer a common practice, though a few families continue to follow it.

Several of the men I spoke with believe problems in relationships have resulted from the loss of many cultural teachings, which is linked to the loss of arranged marriages. Frank, for example, said, "People don't care who they date, clan sisters/brothers and so forth. They are related to each other and they still go out. Sometimes, sad to say, but there are some guys/men out there who don't care about the essence and beauty of the female and they will abuse them, they will cheat and hit and sometimes even kill their girlfriends/wives over stupid little things."[18] Bruce concurred with Frank: "There is too much coming and going in relationships. There are hardly any Navajo couples that married whether it be traditional Navajo or not. There is a trail of broken homes, hurt children and loved ones following Navajo men and women that co-habit before they ever get married, especially children out of wedlock really breaks my heart."[19]

All of the men interviewed believe it is important for a Diné man to marry a Diné woman to maintain traditions, culture, and language. Steve framed what many of the men think of the idea of marrying and having a relationship with a Diné woman:

> Yes, it is important to have common values with the person you are marrying so that your chance of a successful marriage increases. I have heard that if you want to increase your chances of a successful marriage, marry someone with the same values (traditions, culture, language) and religion as you. Differences in values and religions cause a lot of problems in relationships, especially when deciding what values and religion the children are going to be raised with. Many marriages end in divorce because there are just too many problems that arise from the differences in values and religion. Therefore, common traditions, culture, and language are a big factor in deciding whom to marry. In Navajo, you are taught that marriage is for life, unlike American society, where divorce is very common.[20]

Cultural teachings and expectations regarding arranged marriages were clear and transparent for Diné families. Colonization impacted those cultural teachings and expectations. John believes American thought altered a traditional Diné perspective on what marriage should be and both Diné men and women follow too much of an American perspective on relationships.[21] He stated that Diné men and women needed to learn cultural ways: "Contemporary relationships between Navajo men and women are for the most part dictated by Western views of marriage or relationships. For example, Navajo women want to be romanced and showered with gifts as a token of love, et cetera. However, they do not fulfill the traditional roles of being a Navajo woman. Similarly, Navajo men spend too much time trying to please their women or to keep them happy and overlook the traditional teachings of being a Navajo male-in-law."[22]

John pointed to traditional roles of being a Navajo woman and a Navajo male-in-law, and referenced roles and responsibilities pertaining to a Diné way of life where rules in extended family networks were followed.[23] For instance, a Diné woman had specific duties and responsibilities in the home and in the fields. She had an arranged marriage. She took care of the children, herded sheep, planted corn, beans, squash, and other foods. She taught certain songs, stories, prayers, and other cultural teachings to both girls and boys in the extended family network. A Diné male-in-law always lived with his wife's extended family network. He helped his wife's extended family network and never talked to his mother-in-law. He offered his perspectives, but never disrespected the wife's extended family decisions. Overall, individuals in the Diné extended family network had specific duties and responsibilities, and followed certain rules.

Brian offered a counter perspective to John's: "I view contemporary relationships between Navajo men and Navajo women as optimistic. I believe in any working relationship, there is a lot of collaboration taking place. Each individual must respect each other's opinion no matter if it's negative or positive. There is no guarantee in any relationship; it depends on both parties, if they want to make it work."[24] With John and Brian offering different perspectives on relationships, the foundational issue both alluded to is the loss of Diné cultural ways.

In addition to social relations, language is key to cultural ways. Language in Diné communities is a cornerstone of Diné identity and way of life. Language is at the core of Diné being. More than half of the men I interviewed speak the Diné language. All of the men generally indicated that Diné language expresses what it truly means to be a Diné man. John said, "The Navajo language is important to the future of Diné society and it is important to understanding your role as a Diné man."[25] Michael definitely feels language establishes Diné masculinity, as he indicated that the English language cannot match Diné concepts of sexuality, spirit, work, and relations.[26] While many Diné men believe the Diné language is important to Diné masculinities, the reality in many Diné communities is that the language is shifting from Diné to English.

In terms of broader notions of culture, Diné men and women live a different lifestyle than that of their ancestors from 200 years ago, yet not all of the men think Diné masculinities and cultural ways have significantly changed. Paul felt no detrimental change had occurred because Diné peoples continue to speak the language, perform the healing ceremonies, herd sheep, grow corn, and think in Diné. He also believes speaking English has not changed Diné men directly; rather, English has enhanced Diné communities. Frank concurred, saying, "Speaking English and Navajo has made us powerful."[27] Ken also feels Diné masculinities have been impacted by speaking English and practising Christianity, but those markers do not change the fundamental meaning of Diné masculinities for him.[28]

Other men expressed that the dominant American way of life has indeed impacted and in many cases altered Diné masculinities. Peter explained his perspective:

The history between the U.S. and the Diné is not good most of the time. I think our people are still recovering from this horrible history. I think it can be difficult sometimes as a Diné man to keep our heads up in the face of the outside world and all the internal problems the Diné nation faces. I think it may be easy to escape from it all through alcohol or drugs, or adopting the ways of non-Natives to gain material wealth or prosperity. We have to adopt some of those ways but we also can't forget who we are or where we come from. Diné men today are different from our ancestors in terms of education, English language usage, and the pursuit of different careers. We today are different than the men that were born fifty years ago, with the nature of rapidly advancing technology and also in numbers of population and opportunities. I'm sure fifty years from now the life of the Diné man will also be very different.[29]

Peter and many of the other Diné men observed how Diné cultural ways have lessened and how this has impacted all spheres of Diné masculinities, including relationships.

John and several others expressed concern about the continuance of Diné cultural knowledge. John said, for example,

I return to an earlier statement that only by maintaining our language, cultural traditions (not the fry bread or the biil dress only) but all that defines our unique identity as Diné can we hope to give something to our children that they can be proud of. Otherwise, our children will become the same as everyone else, which was the goal of the founding fathers of America (one large melting pot). If we are to maintain our identity, sovereignty, our rights, then we need to do it and not talk about. I believe that only by being with a Navajo woman who respects and honours those values will it happen. Sure non-Navajos can do it too but they have to know the traditions, language, et cetera.[30]

In this passage, John alludes to the fact that Diné masculinities have been transformed and that this has impacted relationships between men and women overall. What becomes of Diné relationships among men and women is uncertain, but Diné communities in the past lived an egalitarian way of life. Men and women were equal partners who respected one another. In the twenty-first century, some Diné men do respect women while others do not and the impact colonization has had on all Diné communities is evident.

Egalitarian Diné Way of Life

Egalitarianism is defined as a belief in human equality, especially with respect to social, political, and economic affairs. Prior to colonization, Diné men and women lived an egalitarian way of life. For the past 200 years, however, Diné men and women have been infused with thoughts, ideologies, practices, and ways contrary to this thought and way of life. Diné men and women need to work together to ensure an equitable way of life.

One area to work on to regenerate an equitable way of life is the family. Many Diné families are single-parent homes, with the primary caregiver being the mother. Some Diné fathers are no longer in the home helping to take care of the children. Some are working away from home and return a few months out of the year. Other fathers are divorced from their wives and only see their children weekly or monthly. Some fathers do not see or visit their children on a regular basis; some fathers are dead, and some fathers are not allowed to see or visit their children.

In general, some Diné men will need to learn how to be responsible to their family and respectful toward Diné women, and learn how to communicate effectively with their wife, girlfriend, or partner. They can learn how to do this from their education, their upbringing, and by the Navajo Nation helping Diné families. A way the Navajo Nation can do this is to develop and sustain wellness centres around the reservation. These centres can teach individuals ways to communicate effectively between men and women, how to live and work well together, and how to solve problems together. Currently, the Navajo Nation has several wellness centres on the reservation, but they primarily focus on physical well-being and do not offer relationship workshops on a regular basis.

A second area to regenerate is in the political arena. Currently, only one woman is serving out of twenty-four delegates on the Navajo Nation Council. No woman has served as president of the Navajo Nation. Some Diné men and women will never vote for a Diné woman. It is through the understanding of the creation scripture and journey narratives and its teachings with regards to relations between men and women that both Diné men and women can benefit. If people still refuse to vote for a Diné woman because of the narratives or tradition, then half of the Diné population will never be given the opportunity to propose ideas, thoughts, and perspectives on how the Navajo Nation can sustain wellness and prosperity in the political arena. Diné cultural teachings do not exclude women.

A third area needing much attention is puberty ceremonies for boys. Currently, many Diné boys do not go through the ceremony. The male kinaadlá ceremony is primarily for the boy and male relatives. It is not as communal as the girl's ceremony, since the boy is isolated in the tacheii (sweat lodge) with other male relatives and friends to learn songs, prayers, and to get instruction on his role and responsibilities as a young man, father, and eventually grand-father. Many families do not have an older male relative who participated in the ceremony to initiate this process; in addition, many do not understand the significance of such a ceremony for boys. Those individuals who completed the ceremony have not come forth to maintain the ceremony; fortunately, a small number still continue the male puberty ceremony.

A fourth area to focus on is male role models. Diné communities have many challenges to overcome, including men dying young, beating up their wives, girlfriends, or partners, or abusing alcohol or drugs. Diné men need to know how to overcome these challenges and to have productive lives. While each man is not perfect in his decisions, Diné men can look at how male role models overcame their obstacles. Throughout history, Diné male role models have been a part of a community or family. For instance, the maternal uncle in many families was traditionally a pillar of stability. He is a person family members can go to for help. The Navajo government and Diné communities can create opportunities for male role models by providing the necessary building blocks to do so.

Family, politics, coming-of-age ceremonies, and role models are the beginning steps toward building an equitable way of life between Diné men and women. Both men and women will need to work together because the creation scripture and journey narratives prove how successful men and women are when they cooperate.

Conclusion

The thirty men interviewed recognized that colonization has altered Diné communities. History, education, family, language, lifestyle, and the concept of individuality have shaped Diné masculinities. Each of the thirty men talked about the degree of change to Diné masculinities.

Diné women are not dissimilar to men. Relationships between men and women show how American thought and way of life influence Diné attitudes and beliefs. In the past, families arranged marriages for sons and daughters. In the twenty-first century, many families do not arrange their children's marriages. Almost all Diné men and women date to find a companion. Most of the men I interviewed believe having a relationship with a Diné woman will help maintain a Diné way of life.

While original Diné thought continues, many principles are no longer known or practised. Diné masculinities will continue to change with each generation and ties to cultural teachings and philosophies might loosen or tighten. While cultural knowledge is taught to Diné children, American ideologies and perspectives continue to influence Diné thought. Nonetheless, commonalities exist between the traditional and present-day. The kinaaldá is still widely held for girls, and hopefully more boys will go through a puberty ceremony. Each of the thirty Diné men are living aspects of original values and principles based on the twin protectors, such as responsibility, respect, knowledge, health, wellness, courage, strength, hospitality, and perseverance.

Cultural teachings and philosophies can help regenerate egalitarian ways between Diné men and women. Four areas to start are the family, politics, puberty ceremonies, and role models. While the Navajo Nation cannot mandate any person or family to change the way they view life or the way they live, they can make a commitment to provide opportunities for Diné peoples to participate in a boy's puberty ceremony, to help solve problems for families, and to honour a Diné woman's contribution in the political arena. Diné men must work to make this equitable way of life a reality. They must apply responsibility to community and family with the idea of helping to sustain a well Navajo Nation. Diné men and women can regenerate what it means to be egalitarian; it starts with one man and one woman.

Notes

1   Gary Witherspoon, *Language and Art in the Navajo Universe* (Ann Arbor, MI: University of Michigan Press, 1977), 25.

2   Herbert John Benally, "Navajo Philosophy of Learning and Pedagogy," *Journal of Navajo Education* 12, no. 1 (1994), 24.

3   Lloyd L. Lee, *Diné Masculinities: Conceptualizations and Reflections* (North Charlestons, SC: Createspace Independent Publishing Platform, 2013), 30–1.

4   Ibid., 32.

5   Ibid.

6   Ibid.; LaVerne Harrell Clark, *They Sang for Horses: The Impact of the Horse on Navajo and Apache Folklore* (Boulder, CO: University Press of Colorado, 2001).

7   Lynn Robinson Bailey, *Indian Slave Trade in the Southwest: A Study of Slave-Taking and the Traffic in Indian Captives* (Gainesville, FL: Tower Publications, 1966); Frank McNitt, *Navajo Wars: Military Campaigns, Slave Raids, and Reprisals* (Albuquerque: University of New Mexico Press, 1972).

8   Clark, *They Sang for Horses.*

9   Ruth M. Underhill, *The Navajos* (Norman: University of Oklahoma Press, 1956).

10 Mrs. Nes-Bah, interview by Tom Ration, 27 August 1968, tape 144, side 1, transcript, American Indian Oral History Project Collection, Center for Southwest Research, Albuquerque, NM; Gladys A. Reichard, *Social Life of the Navajo Indians, with some Attention to Minor Ceremonies* (New York: Columbia University Press, 1928).

11 Anonymous, interview by Martin D. Topper, 12 December 1970, tape 757, side 1, American Indian Oral History Project Collection, Center for Southwest Research, Albuquerque, NM.

12 Peter Iverson, *Diné: A History of the Navajos* (Albuquerque: University of New Mexico Press, 2002), 23.

13 "Scott," interviewed by the author, 24 May 2008, Albuquerque, NM.

14 "Albert," interviewed by the author, June 2007, Tsaile, AZ.

15 "John," interviewed by the author, 20 August 2007, Albuquerque, NM.

16 "Frank," interviewed by the author, 30 August 2006, Phoenix, AZ.

17 Reichard, *Social Life of the Navajo Indians*, 69.

18 "Frank," interview.

19 "Bruce," interviewed by the author, 8 October 2007, Gallup, NM.

20 "Steve," interviewed by the author, 8 September 2006, Kayenta, AZ.

21 "John," interview.

22 Ibid.

23 Ibid.

24 "Brian," interviewed by the author, 10 February 2006, Fort Wingate, NM.

25 "John," interview.

26 "Michael," interviewed by the author, September 2007, Shiprock, NM.

27 "Frank," interview.

28 "Ken," interviewed by the author, January 2008, Fort Wingate, NM.

29 "Peter," interviewed by the author, August 2005, Albuquerque, NM.

30 "John," interview.

IV. CONVERSATIONS

CHAPTER 13

"The Face of Kū:" A Dialogue on Hawaiian Warriorhood

Ty P. Kāwika Tengan, with Thomas Ka'auwai Kaulukukui, Jr., and William Kahalepuna Richards, Jr.

In September 2012 I interviewed Kanaka 'Ōiwi (Native Hawaiian) community leaders Thomas Ka'auwai Kaulukukui, Jr. and William Kahalepuna Richards, Jr. on their participation as members of a community consultant group for a special exhibit *E Kū Ana Ka Paia* (The Walls Shall Stand) held in 2010 at the Bernice Pauahi Bishop Museum in Honolulu. This exhibit brought together the last three remaining carved wooden temple images of the deity Kū, who is most frequently (and reductively) referred to as the god of war. In actuality, Kū is a deity of male generative force and productivity, and including statecraft, governance, farming, fishing, and healing; even more broadly, Kū is seen as the masculine component of society that complements Hina, the feminine. Kaulukukui and Richards are both Vietnam veterans (Army paratrooper and Marine, respectively) and 'ōlohe (instructors and masters) of the Hawaiian martial art of lua. The edited sections below represent just a small component of their longer conversations that connected their experiences in the military to their understandings of Kū, Indigenous warriorhood, spirituality, and masculinity.

Interview with Thomas Ka'auwai Kaulukukui, Jr. on 24 September 2012 at the offices of the trustees of the Queen Lili'uokalani Trust (QLT) in downtown Honolulu. Born in 1945, he is a graduate of Kamehameha Schools (1963), Michigan State University (BS, 1967), and the William Richardson School of Law at the University of Hawai'i (JD, 1977). He was drafted into the Army in 1968 and served in Vietnam (1969 to 1970) as a platoon sergeant in 173rd Airborne

Brigade. He entered private practice in 1978 and was appointed a trial judge in 1988. In 1993 he relinquished his judgeship in order to serve the Hawaiian people on numerous boards and commissions, including his present position as chair of the QLT that serves orphan and destitute Hawaiian children.

Tengan: For you personally, what was the significance of the Kū exhibit?

Kaulukukui: I thought it was important to have those symbols of Kū returned, partly because I am interested in bringing what I think is more of a needed balance of the Kū [masculine] side of our history and our culture into what seems to be a current view of culture, which is in some ways dominated by the artistic and Hina [feminine] side.

Tengan: One of the issues that I recall from those community advisory group meetings was some of the concern about waking the Kū images up and animating them in some ways. Do you recall any of those discussions and your thoughts on that?

Kaulukukui: In my mind, I'm not really worried about that. From the little I knew about the power of, or the aspects of Kū, there are a lot of positive things about Kū which maybe we should awaken. Or, they should awaken us—that's the other way to put it. Maybe they would awaken in us some knowledge and interest in the aspects of Kū that we need in our own lives. I remember writing to somebody in an email, "And if the only aspect of Kū that is awakened is Kū the destroyer and Kū the god of war, I've seen that aspect before and I do not fear it."

Tengan: What is Kū? Who is he? What's he a symbol of in your mind?

Kaulukukui: Kū in terms of being the male energy or the masculine energy represents mainly *responsibility* to me. It's *kuleana* [responsibility]. That has been my training through my own parents and especially through my father. That responsibility is a number of concentric rings starting with self. The first is a responsibility for moral living, if you want to call it that. In terms of ethics, it's morality and having a good set of values. It is also a responsibility for physical health and strength. Because the male, just by virtue of physical build, has had the responsibility of protection, building, and carrying the heavy physical loads and all of those things which are important for a male role in society. So part of the kuleana, then, in the centre is to take care of your own physical being, and then whatever service you need to give to your family and your community. Then as the rings get broader, then the ambit of responsibility gets broader: family, community, people, nation, etc.

Now, what I think is important about that is that the foundations are spiritual. That if one has a belief that this kuleana comes down, not just because your elders or your father or somebody else told you that you have it, but that it is an inherent part of the DNA that nature put in you, then that responsibility stems from things which are much broader than are human beings. It comes from a foundation that's spiritual.

Tengan: That's great, because what I'm hearing in a lot of ways when you're talking about that sense of the spiritual is also about the mana [spiritual power and authority], right? Could you say a little bit about how you see mana?

Kaulukukui: Yes. In the simplest sense, I see mana as spiritual power but I think that spirit is expressed in a lot of ways. That spiritual power is expressed in our DNA, for example. It's expressed in nature. Mana to me is the source of spiritual power. Mana for me is competency that comes from practising the things we need to practise. Mana is reflected in our reputation, in our authority. So I think mana is not a concept that's outside of this; mana is a concept that permeates all of this.

Tengan: If you don't mind going back to some of the earlier comments about your experience in the war, how does one access and express that mana of Kū in that context?

Kaulukukui: A man realizes when he goes to war and faces battle that whatever he has to do in battle, the spirit he has to call up in order to do his job as a soldier, is inherent in him. That is a huge realization. As a matter of fact it's a frightening realization. Because you can do things in battle and be awarded medals for it. But if you did it the day after you got out of the Army and came home, you'd be in jail for murder. So you have this tremendous conflict between the Judeo-Christian ethic and the realization when you get into battle that it's in your DNA.

And so that's a very sobering realization: that any man who has to go to battle is going to find out that there are aspects of you—you can call them Kū aspects if you want to—that you didn't know you really had is actually in your DNA. And that's frightening because at some point you're going to be out of war. If you're going to come back to civilized society, you have to spend the rest of your life not awakening that Kū. So that's what I'm talking about when I say I have seen the face of Kū, I've seen it in me. Having had that personal experience I'm not really concerned that somebody who has the power is going to invoke a face of Kū that is going to be unfamiliar to me. And, therefore, many of our warriors, especially the young ones that come back from battle are in tremendous conflict. Because they have a sleeping Kū within them. The war god sleeps within them. And they're going to spend the rest of their life trying to make sure he doesn't wake up.

Tengan: Are there ways that you've been able to help some of these individuals to not wake that up or to manage it?

Kaulukukui: Yes, I've worked with veterans before. I think the most important thing is to recognize that rather than fight with that part of your nature, to recognize that it is part of your nature. First things first, you have to recognize who you are. Then, secondly, you have to recognize what is appropriate conduct in a civilized society and what was appropriate in war. Then you have to deal with the experience itself and try to translate the experience of battle into something that is positive, has made you stronger, so that you can move forward to carry your community responsibilities in the peacetime effort. Therefore, take those things which can be seen as a negative experience and look at the positive aspects for it that make you stronger and better to live a better life to carry your kuleana here. Then the other thing you have to do is to unburden yourself. You have to find a way to put down the burdens that you carry from battle so that you can move on to something else and do better. Then, lastly, you probably need to have some training and techniques; anger management, you know, "What do I do when, you know, when I hear the lion rattling the cage down there in the pit of my stomach?"

So it's a matter mainly of resolving these conflicts within yourself. The main thing I think is to find a way so that that battle experience can be cleansed first of all, put in its proper perspective, and used as a positive thing. That's why I have advocated, and am still trying to figure out how to do it, the cleansing ceremony as most Native people did, to help put aside that aspect of your life and to move on. I think that as long as we don't do that, we are going to continue to have problems with post-traumatic stress, etc. And I think that ceremony has to be done not by psychiatrists, but by warriors.

It's my feeling that we have in our DNA as a people, a special ability in the field of warriorhood. That's very interesting because I've spoken to a lot of Hawaiians who've been in the military and most of them were the top trainees. Billy Richards, who you talked to, he was one. So was I. And we have nothing in common other than that we are Hawaiian, or part-Hawaiian, and come from Hawai'i.

Tengan: What you said about Hawaiians excelling in the military is something I've heard over and over again.

Kaulukukui: I think there are a lot of aspects to it. I think it's in the DNA first of all. Secondly, I think it has to do with our upbringing. We are island people, we are isolated, we tend to be self-sufficient and in our DNA is the DNA of the risk-takers. There's a whole bunch of DNA of people who are not risk-takers: they're still in the Marquesas; they're still in Tahiti; they're still in Fiji. When the canoe left, our ancestors were the risk-takers. They came here and they made a life here. So in our DNA are the risk-takers.

Also, I think what motivates us is because we're a small part of the nation, and insignificant geographically in terms of size, we have always felt that we need to do our part. So we rise up and we do our part.

Maybe it's a tribal thing. Maybe we are more tribal than some people in different parts of the country because we are small. So when you get into the Marines or the Army, you have a tribe. A tribe with its own code, and we tend to be loyal and true and brave because we understand what it's like to be part of a tribe.

Tengan: Another thing I've heard too is the ways in which the military provides a kind of structure that Hawaiians really get, Hawaiian men in particular.

Kaulukukui: Yes. Some of them don't have that training, and we find, for instance in our lua [Hawaiian martial art] seminars, when they get structure, they love it. They love the clarity. You know, many of them, because their home life may not have the structure, love the clarity. It's very interesting to me because some of the fathers or the people that we deal with, they have not had that kind of structure. Some of them are really rough individuals. But when you impose the structure or expose them to it, they love it. You know, they're not babies—some of them are older. They get it and they say, "This feels right."

Tengan: Can you say more on the lua training?

Kaulukukui: I think for me, and for most who have had military training, the lua training is an affirmation of the fact that warriorhood, which we experience in the American military, is part of our DNA. In the law, there is this thing called relation-back doctrine, whereas something happens here but its effect relates back to something that happened before. So we have this experience in the American military and then we have this warriorhood experience. We understood it's something that we can do as a male human being. Then you go to lua training, and you realize, "Ah, it's a *Hawaiian* warrior thing." So your realization today that you are a Hawaiian warrior because it's part of your Hawaiian DNA, not just your male DNA as a matter of nature, relates *back* to the experience you have in the military because now you understand that you were *always* a Hawaiian warrior. My realization today is not that I am a Hawaiian warrior; the most powerful aspect of that training is that I have *always* been a Hawaiian warrior—my whole life. That my *people* are warriors. You know how powerful that is, that realization? That difference between realizing *today* that you are a Hawaiian warrior, and realizing that you have, for *generations*, been a Hawaiian warrior. *Tremendously* powerful.

So those of us veterans who go through the lua training, one of the realizations that we reach is, "You know why we're so good warriors in the American military and the Marines, in the paratroopers? Because I'm Hawaiian, and Hawaiians are warriors. That's why—I get it!" Right? That's a powerful realization. And that affects your whole life. Because now it's not a matter of, "I graduated today from the lua seminar, in October of 1993, and now I'm warrior." It's the realization someplace—whether you go through the ceremony or not—that that's who my people are; that's who I *am*. It's in my *DNA*, and therefore, I have kuleana, I have ikaika [strength], I have power that comes with it, and responsibility. The two things you got out of that is tremendous responsibility for leadership to express yourself in the right way and enormous mana, which is where the ability to express it comes from. And that's why what we have found is that it is life transforming. For me, for most of us, it transforms our lives. It's not like we didn't have leadership abilities before, or experiences before, it just transformed the way we look at ourselves, and the world. Enormously powerful.

Interview with William Kahalepuna Richards, Jr. on 21 September 2012 at the Honolulu offices of Partners in Development Foundation (PIDF), a non-profit organization that serves the Native Hawaiian community through social, environmental, and educational programs; he is director of communications there. A graduate of Kailua High School (1966), he entered the Marines in 1967 and, following completion of basic and infantry combat training, he was sent to the Republic of Vietnam where he was assigned to Kilo Company 3rd Battalion, 3rd Marine Regiment, 3rd Marine Division. After Vietnam, he stayed in California for about a year before returning to Hawai'i to eventually become part of the original crew of the Hōkūle'a voyaging canoe that helped to spark a revival in traditional voyaging across the Pacific and a renewal of older Oceanic relationships and identities. He has maintained his involvement in the voyaging family since then and has served as board member or director for numerous organizations that benefit Native Hawaiians, including the 'Aha Kāne Native Hawaiian Men's Foundation.

Tengan: One of the things I was struck by in the previous research I did on the Hale Mua [Native Hawaiian men's organization] was how many of the men were also in the military, and it got me interested in the connection with that formal warriorhood, and the kind that was emerging in Nā Koa [warrior organizations], the Pā Lua [lua schools], and the Hale Mua [men's house].

Richards: It's funny you use that word [*emerging*]; that's a term that Tommy [Kaulukukui] and I talk about. For the vets, people coming back from combat, we call them returning warriors and for those who are learning about warriorhood, we call them emerging warriors. Tommy and I, when we discuss things, our feeling is that whatever that warriorness is, it's innate in all Hawaiians. That's one of the things I always try to tell people. Like, our organization [PIDF], our values are the same ones we see on the wall [pointing to posters with these values], "pono" [goodness; morality], "aloha" [love; respect].[1] But to me, it's more than that. It's striving to be the best. But because we are a social service organization, we have a lot of Hina [feminine] values, yeah? But I think Kū [masculine] values are important too. We discuss it, Tommy and I, we talk about it, how back in our day, to do things Hawaiian, you either dance hula, you play music—you can paddle, or you can join the service. And for the most part, Hawaiians—not just Hawaiians, locals—they do *well* in the military. I went with four Hawaiians and one Nez Perce Indian who was living here, and we *all* excelled in boot camp. The drill instructors, they thought we were crazy! I remember one time we did a confidence course, like an obstacle course, and we climbed this tower three stories high. And I remember the drill instructor saying, "You Hawaiians better get down here, like, now!" And we were supposed to do this slide-for-life thing, and he said "now" so we all jumped [*laughter*]. And when we jumped, his eyes got really big and he's like, "No!" We got in, and all of us had taken some form of martial arts, so we broke into a roll, came up to attention, "Mission accomplished, aye, aye, sir!" And he was like, "Fucking Hawaiians" [*laughter*]. But it seems that Hawaiians and local people do really well in the service.

Tengan: I've heard that over and over again. Why do you think that is?

Richards: I think it's innate, it's just innate. You know?

Tengan: So, what particular qualities are innate?

Richards: For us, the things, like, when we do the obstacle course, it was *fun*. You know, if you look at your fellow recruits, it was like, it was *hard* for them, they saw it completely different. I mean, you're climbing under barbed wire, getting shot at, live fire, it was *fun*! It was like, yeah, no big deal. Even, we had this thing, after you go to boot camp, from boot camp, you go to ITR, Infantry Training Regiment, you go to BITS, Basically Infantry Training School, that's where you learn to use all the different weapons. And one of the things in BITS is, you get captured, they put you in a POW camp. So, the whole platoon gets captured. So we go to POW, me and two other Hawaiians, we get in there, they give us dry fish and rice. We never escaped; we just stayed! [*laughter*]. After potatoes and ham, and things like that, you know. Wow, rice and dry fish! We was grinding![2] And pretty soon, kind of like time out, and the guy says, "You guys are supposed to escape!" It was just fun, you know [*laughter*]. "Ok, ok, we'll bag [leave]." But I think it's just a different kind of outlook on how it went. The others that I saw it in who were not Hawaiians were American Indians, some of the Puerto Ricans; 'course you had your Southern boys, white Southerners, you know, they'd chew tobacco and do their stuff.

I don't want to make too lightly of this, because boot camp, combat training, the military, and war, is serious business. But I'd say we were able to *adapt* fairly well.

For the most part, the guys in my unit and the Hawaiians like that, they were well respected anywhere; they could hold their own. And most of us, we grew up in martial arts. Judo was something everybody took. When I was a kid, it was judo; around the '60s karate came in. When I was in high school, I started taking aikido. So when we got to boot camp, they give you like ten hours of hand-to-hand combat [training]. But our guys already were ma'a [accustomed] to it. In fact, our drill instructors would ask us to demonstrate. Which is different; again, I think the term "innate," it's just in there; it's just in there, waiting to come out. And I think sometimes that's the problem we have with kāne, is that there's a *warrior* in there fighting to come out but doesn't know what to do.

So it manifests itself in too many negative ways. The only warrior we had when I was in high school was a Primo[3] warrior. He emerges after a few beers.

So, joining Pāku'ialua [the first modern lua school] back when I did in '93 was good for me. There were a lot of things that were taught to us that started to make sense. Especially after travelling so much with *Hōkūle'a* and going to different island groups, where they challenge you, would be 300 Māoris or one Rarotongan. There was always this, there was a level, these *steps* to, aloha, you know—I'm not gonna aloha you, until I figure out what your intent is.

Tengan: I never heard it put that way, where there's steps to aloha.

Richards: When I went through my pani [graduation] with Pāku'ialua, that's one of the things I mentioned. As we travelled around and I saw that, I always felt like there was something *missing* with us. And now I understand what was missing, that we too had our own steps that needed to take place. And *intent* is important, you know. People's intentions, especially if they come visiting. Cause we're filled with aloha, we aloha so much—take my land, take my woman [*laughing*], take it all away. And it's kinda like, no matter where we went, everyplace else it wasn't that way. There's a point at which, yes [aloha is extended], but there's a lot of stuff happened prior to that, just to *determine* intent. So it filled a gap for me, lua did. It made me understand.

I think that going to Vietnam, it was feeling comfortable knowing that Kanaloa [Hawaiian god of the ocean] said OK, and Kū said OK, you know, on the beach that night; the threes that showed up when they needed to.[4] Graduating boot camp and BITS and Meritorious Mast with high honors, and then the threes show up and then meeting Marvin Monarco the Jicarilla Apache, and making it back without a scratch, these kinds of things.

Tengan: What did you think about yourself in relation to this other Apache Marine?

Richards: It's on that [DVD],[5] the story is about us. Monarco played a big part, and not only in my learning. Like I said, the Six [company commander] thought that, and he [Monarco] told me, "They think that if you're Native you can read their footprints," and he laughed. And he taught me as much as he could, but at the *same* time, he said—and we go back to innate—"It's in you," you know, "it's in there." And a lot of it *was*, you just figured it out.

And for some reason, not "some" reason, but, I don't think I'm suffering from any kind of form of PTSD. I don't know that, but I'm not a psychologist, so I can't tell you this stuff, yeah. I know when I was at the reunion, I was asked by a good friend of mine who was from Arkansas, he was in 81s, an FO, forward observer, with the 81-mm mortars, he tells me, "I gotta go to this, they're having a lecture on PTSD. You gotta come, you gotta come." So he drags me in. And I was listening, and the lady that was doing the presentation started talking about symptoms. Some obvious symptoms and not so obvious symptoms. And she was talking, and I went "hmmm" [*laughter*]. "Well, maybe." But I don't think I have it as bad as a lot of people. You know, I see some of my friends that are in pretty bad shape. There's one Samoan, he's from Hawai'i, he's never come home since coming back from Nam. I told him, "Brah, you should come home; you should go in the ocean and come home, just go in the ocean, you'll be fine."

Tengan: Is that what you did when you came back?

Richards: Yeah, well, OK. I come back, I'm training troops for combat, and after that I get sent to Marine barracks, San Diego. So, I was there, I became an E5; I was a sergeant under 2, sergeant and (only) seventeen months in the Corps. I got a small place in Mission Beach, right off the beach, an apartment. I started taking flying lessons, in my extra time. I'm doing this, I'm still in the Corps, and my cousin calls. My cousin's from Keaukaha. He had just gotten out of the Navy, where he served on a guided missile destroyer that was part of a carrier battle group. He got out of the Navy and he went home. But he wasn't ready to be home. He realized he wasn't ready to be home, so he moved to Inglewood California, in the L.A. area, where my uncle was living; my mom's brother, Uncle Clarence. After a while he calls me up, he goes, "You got room down there?" [I say,] "Ah, come!" So he came down to San Diego, to Mission Beach and he moves in with me. And I think it was the first week he go [says], "You surfing?" I go, "No." "You're not surfing? How come you're not surfing?" I say, "I dunno." And I hadn't made that transition yet back from Kū [who he called on during war] to Kanaloa [who he had grown up with on the ocean]. He says, "We go." So we went up the street, Mission Boulevard, went to the Dewey Weber

Surf Shop, and he bought two boards. One for him and one for me. And we paddled out, and that's where, I remember on the first wave, that's where everything, was kinda like the hā [breath] [exhales and says "haaa"]. I think that's one of the reasons why I'm OK. Is that my cousin came, put me back in the ocean, we connected with Kanaloa, and we surfed. We just surfed. I had my form of cleansing; my cleansing took place there. I have him to thank for it. When I think about PTSD and that decompression period, I think I have him to thank. There's that point out there when you go, "OK, Kū—pau [My time with you has come to an end]. Thank you for being with me for as long as you have. I'm going back to Kanaloa."

Afterword

In reflecting on the thoughts of Kaulukukui and Richards, I was struck by the notion that warriorhood is an "inherent" or "innate" quality that is "just in there" or "part of the DNA." The possibilities and limitations of this idea for Kanaka ʻŌiwi and other Indigenous men and women deserves further comment. Kim TallBear, associate professor of anthropology and Native American studies at the University of Texas at Austin and author of *Native American DNA: Tribal Belonging and the False Promise of Genetic Science* (University of Minnesota Press, 2013), notes that "indigenous people—when we invoke blood or DNA concepts—in talking about qualities or desires that we find in part constitutive of who we are, do not always mean literally that biology determines these qualities in a straightforward deterministic way."[6] Rather, she asserts that most Natives understand that "who we are as peoples is comprised of cultural and political (read sovereignty) factors, plus we are physical bodies descended from the bodies of our ancestors." The problem of genetically linking Indigenous warriorhood and U.S. soldiering is that it potentially ignores the "political economic conditions…[that] shape our high enlistment" and "den[ies] how profoundly U.S. colonization disrupted our ancestors' life ways and the degree to which it continues to oppressively structure our lives."[7] One should also examine the ways that militarization reconfigures traditional notions of the family, as Jennifer Nez Denetdale has done in Navajo country.[8]

With the foregoing caveats in mind, I would argue for a critical reading of the claims of inherent/innate warriorhood as assertions of Indigenous genealogical continuity and persistence in the face of U.S. settler colonialism (see also TallBear on "genetic memory" talk in the introduction to *Native American DNA*). In the present-day context of Native regeneration and struggles over cultural and political sovereignty, Indigenous service in the U.S. military can be seen as a contradictory thing. Hawai'i is home to the United States Pacific Command that has taken on an even greater significance following the Obama administration's move to "rebalance" to the Asia-Pacific region. Indeed, it is precisely the islands' military strategic value that led to the illegal overthrow and annexation and sustains a U.S. settler occupation of Hawai'i. Perhaps ironically, it is based on his experiences in the U.S. Army and his analysis of the international law of war that Dr. David Keanu Sai and his colleagues have articulated new strategies for de-occupation based on the core claim of state continuity—e.g., the Hawaiian Kingdom was never legally extinguished and so remains.[9] Similarly, I would argue that the interviews of Kaulukukui and Richards suggest that military experience potentially allows Native men and women to assert Indigenous genealogical (seen as both spiritual and political) continuity through their performance of warriorhood as soldiering. Clearly this is not an unproblematic articulation, as Tallbear and Denetdale remind us. However, it behooves scholars of Indigenous men and masculinities (as well as others) to pay critical attention to the words and experiences of the Indigenous veterans, and what their battles and traumas suggest for Native societies that are wrestling with the place of the military in their lands and waters. It might, as Kaulukukui suggests, "transform the way we look at ourselves, and the world." Similarly, the transition from war to peace in an ocean passage as described by Richards could help all of us ponder what it is we are "going back to" in our efforts to reconnect with land, water, culture, ancestors, and nation. As the past is literally "the time in front" (ka wā ma mua) in Hawaiian thought, projects of critical re-membering are also ones of finding new ways forward—i mua.

Notes

1   The glosses for these values comes from the "About" section of the PIDF website at http://www.pidf.org/about/overview.

2   In Hawai'i Creole English, also referred to as "pidgin," the phrase "We was grinding!" is like saying "We chowed down!"

3   Referring to the locally brewed Primo Beer.

4   Earlier in the interview, Richards explained that as a young man who grew up surfing and living next to the ocean, he had taken on the Hawaiian deity of Kanaloa

as his god. When he went to war, he made an explicit choice to take on Kū. While in Vietnam, signs that would appear in groups of three confirmed that Kū was watching over him.

5 Richards gave me a copy of a DVD entitled *Native American Veterans—Storytelling for Healing* (Administration for Native Americans, 2009) that he was a featured interviewee on.

6 Personal communication, 22 April 2015.

7 Ibid.

8 See Jennifer Nez Denetdale, "Securing Navajo National Boundaries: War, Patriotism, and the Diné Marriage Act of 2005," *Wicazo Sa Review* 24, no. 2 (Fall 2009): 131–148.

9 See http://www.hawaiiankingdom.org.

CHAPTER 14

Strong Men Stories: A Roundtable on Indigenous Masculinities

Sam McKegney, with Richard Van Camp, Warren Cariou, Gregory Scofield, and Daniel Heath Justice

Recorded on 1 February 2013 in the Indigenous Gender Class taught by Professor Niigaanwewidam James Sinclair, Centre for Creative Writing and Oral Culture, University of Manitoba, Winnipeg.

McKegney: Welcome everyone to "Strong Men Stories," a roundtable discussion with Richard Van Camp, Warren Cariou, Gregory Scofield, and Daniel Heath Justice. My name is Sam McKegney. I'm a Settler scholar of Indigenous literatures at Queen's University in Kingston, Ontario, and I'd like to begin by acknowledging the Peoples of the Anishinaabe and Métis nations on whose traditional lands the University of Manitoba rests and we're having this tremendous event today.

We hope this conversation is generative of further dialogue of value to those nations, and we offer it in the spirit of generating conversation. I'm honoured to be having this conversation in front of a class on Indigenous masculinities taught by Professor Niigaanwewidam Sinclair who's a public intellectual and scholar whose work inspires me and, I know, inspires many of those on this panel.

I would like to thank Warren Cariou and the Centre for Creative Writing and Oral Culture for facilitating and providing a wonderful space to conduct the conversation. I've entitled this event "Strong Men Stories" partially in homage to Bonita Lawrence and Kim Anderson's collection called *Strong Women Stories: Native Vision and Community Survival*.[1] I also want to honour with that title the power of the many depictions of masculinity, manhood, and gendered being in the literary art of the writers with whom I'll be speaking today.

Among the problems with critical discussions of Indigenous masculinities is that those conversations are all too often shadowed by absence: absence in the sense of the dearth of critical work available on the subject, whereas on Indigenous feminisms there are several key texts to which we can turn, from Paula Gunn Allen's work to Lee Maracle to Cheryl Suzack to others; absence in the sense of connection to traditional roles and responsibilities that have often been obfuscated by colonialism; and absence in the sense, at some times and in some places, of the lack of available male role models and mentors.

Part of the reason I began conducting interviews for *Masculindians: Conversations about Indigenous Manhood*[2]—which is a collection of interviews with Indigenous authors, activists, and Elders in which each of the authors involved in this roundtable is featured—is to begin to address the lack of critical attentiveness to Indigenous masculinities by attending to the thoughts and work of Indigenous thinkers. Another reason is to recognize that this deficit model is itself a simulation that obscures the work going on in story and in lived experience to foster empowered, culturally aware, and non-dominative models of Indigenous masculinity.

Which brings me to the four visionary literary artists with whom I'll be in conversation today, each of whose work grapples with issues that are crucial to generating masculine self-worth and fostering empowered, balanced, and mutually regenerative gender relations.

Richard Van Camp was raised in Fort Smith, Northwest Territories, and is the first published author from the Dogrib/Tlicho Nation. He's the author of a novel, *The Lesser Blessed*, which has recently been turned into a feature-length film, as well as multiple short-story collections, including *Angel Wing Splash Pattern, The Moon of Letting Go,* and *Godless but Loyal to Heaven.* He has written books for children and books for newborns, and with the Healthy Aboriginal Network, has authored and edited comics for Indigenous youth on topics like gang violence, sexual health, and suicide. He's also furiously dedicated as a mentor and advocate for young Indigenous writers.

Warren Cariou is a Métis writer and professor of English at University of Manitoba here in Winnipeg. Warren was born and raised in Meadow Lake, Saskatchewan, which features prominently in his memoir, *Lake of the Prairies: A Story of Belonging.* He's also author of *The Exalted Company of Roadside Martyrs: Two Novellas,* and writer/director of the film *Land of Oil and Water.* He has written numerous articles on the study of Indigenous literatures and holds a Canada Research Chair in Narrative Community and Indigenous Cultures.

Gregory Scofield is a poet, teacher, social worker, and youth worker whose maternal ancestry can be traced back five generations to the Red River Settlement and to Kinesota, Manitoba. He has published an autobiography, *Thunder Through My Veins: Memories of a Métis Childhood,* and several books of poetry, including *Native Canadiana: Songs from the Urban Rez, Sâkihtowin-Maskihkiy Êkwa Pêyak-Nikamowin: Love Medicine and One Song, I Knew Two Métis Women, Singing Home the Bones,* and *Louis: The Heretic Poems.*

Daniel Heath Justice is a Colorado-born Canadian citizen of the Cherokee Nation. He's the author of *Our Fire Survives the Storm: A Cherokee Literary History* and numerous critical essays in the field of Indigenous literary studies. With James Cox, he's the co-editor of *The Oxford Handbook of Indigenous American Literature.* He's also the author of the Indigenous epic fantasy novel *The Way of Thorn and Thunder: The Kynship Chronicles.* He is currently chair of First Nations Studies at the University of British Columbia.

So in an effort not to replicate the erroneous erasures of the deficit model in discussions of Indigenous masculinity, let us begin with strength. Where do we seek strength? In whom do you recognize it and how can it be shared?

Scofield: Whenever the word "strength" comes up in relation to me as a writer, me as a Métis person, me as a male person, I always mention that my strength was derived essentially from two women in my life, one of which was my mother and the other of which was my aunt.

I come from a generation—and there are many of us that are coming from this generation—where men were very much excluded. Men were not necessarily, at least in my experience, an ongoing, long-term part of my growing up. The men that were involved with my growing up were very adversary to the women that were raising me. A lot of the men that I had grown up with brought issues of violence, issues of poverty, issues of dominance, and it was really those two women in particular, my mom and my auntie, from whom I learned my strength as a man.

Cariou: Gregory and I both have Métis backgrounds, and are both born within a week of each other. And my own experience growing up was really different in a lot of ways, I think, from yours, especially because I was fortunate that my father was not only present in our family but he was a huge, almost larger-than-life presence. He was someone that a lot of people in the community looked up to, and we felt that we would gain a kind of acceptance in the community through him in a way.

He was an incredibly generous person and an amazing storyteller, and so he drew people to him. He was like a magnet that held together this gigantic family of fifteen siblings. So we'd have this huge extended family always circling around us, I think, in a lot of ways because they were very attracted by my father's storytelling abilities.

He was also a lawyer. That was his other role. People looked to him for advice, especially Aboriginal people from farther north in Saskatchewan. So for me, he provided a model for a kind of masculine engagement with the community that maybe some others didn't have in the same way. When I think of my own strength as a person, as a writer, as a storyteller, I'm always thinking of him first in a way.

Justice: My experience is similar in some ways with Gregory's. I learned about strength through my mom, and I've learned about men's strength from my dad as I've gotten older. My folks were together, they've been together my whole life, but my mom was always the disciplinarian. My mom was the force of nature and continues to be, and so she was the model of strength and power.

My dad is much quieter. My mom has the fiery temper, whereas my dad's temper is kind of the cold-ice temper that once in a while erupts. I'm very close with both of them, but it's only as I've gotten older that I've understood more of my dad's quiet strength. But my mom is the one who kept us going; it was my mom's jobs that kept the bills paid.

When I think of strength, I think of my mom crawling into the house because she had calcium heel spurs from working so hard and being on her feet so much, and just crying, crawling to the couch so she could heal up until the next day when she had to go out and work again. There was never any question that she was going to do it. So when I think of strength, I think of women. It's always been women in my life who've been the biggest intellectual influences and the biggest spiritual influences, and it's been the women in my life who have taught me the most about what kind of man I want to be and what kind of man I don't want to be.

Van Camp: I agree. Daniel nailed it for me. It's always been my mom that showed me what kind of man to be. I was really lucky because I ended up volunteering in my hometown of Fort Smith for about two years to drive the handi-bus, and I got to drive the Elders around in our community. I got to drive Irene Sanderson, Dora Torangeau, Seraphine Evans, and all these great matriarchs, and that was really—at about the age of twenty, twenty-one—where I was welcomed into my role as an Aboriginal man. They knew who my grandparents were, and they would take me to task on things. They would tell me stories and teachings and say, "Your best friends may be Cree or Dene, but you're Dogrib and your ways are different than our ways and you should really start to understand the difference about why you're not allowed to go into the sweat. Your grandfather will tell you why the Tlicho aren't supposed to go into the sweat."

That was really important to me, and I want to raise my hands with utmost respect to those dear aunties of mine, who took me under their wings. But it's always been my mom who has made me the strong man I am today. And my father, Jack, as well—he's always been there. He is a gentle man and doesn't have to raise his voice. I'm the oldest of four boys and when I'm home, he says, "I love it when you come home, Richard, because the wood's cut and everything's shovelled. Those brothers of yours don't listen to me anymore. They listen to you." He's joking when he says this, and there's a respect being passed on there as I'm the eldest and the bossiest. I know how to get my little brothers up and at it, but all roads lead to our parents. I love my parents very much. I'm very grateful.

McKegney: In our earlier interview, Gregory, you discussed getting in touch with your own masculinity as a process of getting in touch with your body, and feeling the places where you were physically strong. This you described eloquently as a "liberation through claiming." What do you and others on the panel see as the relationship between physical strength and strength of spirit, strength of conviction?

Scofield: I'm very much of a believer in the four aspects that we all carry: our mental beings, our spiritual beings, our physical beings, and our emotional beings. On one hand, I was very fortunate growing up with women. I was very fortunate growing up with storytellers, language keepers, bead workers, good cooks, and wonderful housekeepers. I was very fortunate growing up with nurturing women, engaging women, loving women, and women that basically channelled all of their attention and their focus and their love into me as a little boy.

So I was very fortunate growing up with an emotional sensibility. But one of the things that really suffered for me was a physical sensibility of how to carry my male body in this world. How do I carry my male self in this world, having grown up with women?

The roles that we're assigned and the societal expectations that are put on us growing up, in regard to being male and being masculine, have a lot to do with physical strength and the ability to fight your way through, whether that fight is a dead-end job, a bunch of kids that need to be fed, a car that needs to be fixed, or a roof that needs to be put on the house. There was something very physical about what the expectation was to be male.

That was one thing that my mom and my auntie were unable to help me with. They weren't able to guide me to what it was to be a physical male. So I started looking, literally, at the physical strength of my body and began lifting weights. I began working my body in a way that required strength, that required physical movement, and that required determination.

I grew up with men who were very physically violent. There was a lot of violence in my house, so in becoming physically strong, there was a real liberation in knowing that not only could I protect myself physically, but I could also therefore protect myself emotionally, mentally, and spiritually. That was my approach to strength.

McKegney: That kind of strength, on the one hand, is essential to a stable sense of selfhood in the protection of others; on the other hand, it creates the potential for acting outwards, and it brings me to something that Daniel said in our earlier interview regarding popular cultural representations of the male body. "What strikes me," you said, Daniel, "is that the male body is seen as capable of, and a source only, of violence and harm. If the male body isn't giving harm, it's taking pleasure. It's assaultive or extractive. One or the other; there's nothing else. So literature ought to give us alternatives."

I wonder if the panellists might reflect, firstly, on whether you agree with Daniel's assessment of popular cultural representations of the male body, and secondly, on what the alternatives might be that emerge in art, or in literature, that are protective strengths of physical masculinity.

Justice: I agree with myself [*laughter*]. I'm actually thinking of the writing of these amazing men on the panel in terms of alternative visions. If only these were the visions that were dominant: the vulnerability, the gentleness, the confusion, the uncertainty. All of those are also sources of strength; all of those are also powerful ways of revealing our humanity. Where vulnerability is not weakness; it is being open to the possibility of change and being open to the possibility of being transformed by love, by passion, by touch.

It's not about using somebody else's body for your own brief pleasure. It's about opening yourself up to somebody else's pleasure, and learning what becomes possible. I think the best Indigenous literature explores that, and that's what we need more of. It's not that these other visions aren't realities too; we know there are people who practise violence. But it doesn't have to be only that. The work here gives me hope for much better opportunities, and models of powerful men who are gentle men, who are loving men, who are generous men.

These are more of what we need, but they don't sell as well as men who are blowing things up, right? They don't sell as well as men who are demonstrating strength by how many people they can kill or wound or maim or assault.

Van Camp: A couple nights ago in Edmonton, we just finished having the most wonderful supper and I felt pregnant. At 8:30 p.m. I said, "Sweetie, I'm done; I just have to go lay down." I was thinking over and over in my mind: What have I done differently? Have I eaten anything new?

And then it hit me that this didn't belong to me. About 3:00 in the morning, I woke up and said, "It's my mom. Something's wrong with my mom." I couldn't call her at 3:00 in the morning—she was in Yellowknife, fast asleep—so I waited until 7:45 a.m. I called her and I said, "Mom, how are you?" She said, "Oh, I ate something bad at that conference. Maybe it was the cheese. I don't know. I've been walking around with a bowling ball inside my stomach." Wild, hey?

Another time my friend was showing off when I was about twenty. He had a new truck with those brand new anti-lock brakes. He was racing down the longest road in Fort Smith, but there's a dogleg turn and you're not supposed to hit it going anything more than 30 km/h—he was doing 110. I was grabbing for the seat belt, but the truck was so new that they hadn't put in the clasp yet. I was breaking my nails, digging underneath the bucket seat to try to find the other part.

It was a digital dashboard, so it was reading "90," "110," "120," "125," "127...." We were coming up to that turn, and so I yelled his full name—just like his mom does when she's mad at him. He started tapping on the brakes as I held onto the dashboard, and I said, "Take me home right now. How dare you do that to me? Look, your stupid truck isn't even ready, and they didn't even put the seat belts in. That's it. We're done." So he drove me home, and I slammed the door and went to bed. I had the worst feeling in the world.

The next morning, we got up and were having breakfast and my mom said, "Oh, I had the worst dream last night. I was 30,000 feet in the air in a big jumbo jet. We were going over the ocean with all these wonderful people, and all of a sudden the plane fell from the sky. Everyone was screaming. I had my seat belt, but I couldn't find the other side. Oh, it was a horror. I woke up so scared." My mom and I have always had that bond, and I give thanks. When she was fighting breast cancer, I was cold in the bones for a year; I just couldn't get warm. I think those sympathy pains that she and I share have made me a much better man, a much better human being, and a much better writer. I think that's why the young men in my stories are mostly protectors.

Scofield: As writers, as storytellers, and as poets, we bring a certain sensibility that I don't think has anything to do with masculinity. We bring the sensibility of the storyteller, the poet, and the writer. I think what's really important to understand in the context of this conversation is that many of the men in our communities— especially the generation that comes before us and the generation that comes before them—were emasculated by the church and through the process of colonization. The oppressed become the oppressors. The whole shift in our traditional communities is that the men started to take out their anger and their sadness and their lack of strength on the women to make themselves somehow feel strong.

Many of the people from our generation became broken people because of that. We didn't have the proper role modelling, and now there's this continuing shift within our communities—and when I say "our communities," I'm talking about all Aboriginal people in this country—where the men are literally being forced by the women to engage with that stuff. They're having to go back and question themselves and they're having to ask why they have behaved the way they have, why they have allowed things to happen the way they have.

The missing and murdered Aboriginal women in our country—the men have not been there to protect those women. They have not been there to look out for those women, whether in terms of the leadership or in terms of their own fathers, their own brothers, their own cousins. My belief is that Aboriginal men will only become strong again once our women become strong, because it was a reciprocal traditional relationship that had always existed between men and women, and there's a responsibility that goes with that.

Van Camp: That's true. When you go into the communities, who are the band managers, who are the chiefs, who are the teachers, who are the principals, who's involved with health, social science, early childhood? It's always the women. Always; so where are the men? A lot of times they're in the trades—fishing, mining, diving, heli-logging, et cetera. It's always the women, and will always be the women, who are the backbone, the marrow.

Cariou: I guess the question becomes, What's a viable model for men to model themselves after now? Should men model themselves after women? I think there's a good case to be made for that, in some ways. But are there ways we can look back at how our people did things four or five generations ago, before the twentieth century?

In my community there's a lot of violence and there's a lot of dysfunction, but there are a lot of really strong men who are not abusing their strength as well. I think there are examples. I remember my dad used to always talk about the voyageurs, the coureurs des bois, the Métis men who were so strong they could carry 200 pounds on their backs for 20 miles. There was maybe a bit of exaggeration there, but these were men whose physical strength was literally awesome.

Just the idea that their labour, what they did for a living, was something that they could be proud of—that they were providing for their families and building their communities—there's something there that I find really attractive. It's the notion that a man's physical labour or other labour is something he can be proud of.

Unfortunately, so often in our communities the men have to go away to work, and then that leaves a problem where the mothers are raising the kids without the men.

Scofield: One day we're going to be old men, and we're going to have young people sitting with us, listening to our stories, and maybe reading our books, and we'll become a part of their knowing. Those young people will go away and say, "I know the most amazing old man; he's a poet," or, "I know this amazing old man; he's such a good storyteller."

We're a part of that embodiment. We're those old men—we're the voyageurs that your dad had talked about. We're the new voyageurs. And that makes me very proud, because we're portaging that strength in a nurturing way that came from the women.

Because I didn't have male role models, I've had to model myself after the men that I most admire. I look at a man and I say, "Boy, I would have loved him for a dad," or, "Geez, I would have liked him for a brother." "Boy, that man is good with a baby; that baby just loves him. I want to be like that." There are sparks out there, but you have to be aware that they're sparkling, and that there's great power in little things—things which you can embody, which you can pull into yourself.

Van Camp: Here's a question I'd like to ask: I'd like to know when all of you, Sam included, first felt like a man? I'll start.

I used to work at a bush camp called *Sah Naji Kwe*—which means "Bear Healing Rock"—in Fort Rae, and we had about forty-eight kids out on the land.

Well, there was a torrential downpour. The rain was cold. One of the tents had burst, so all the sleeping bags were soaked, and my job as camp gopher was to run around and grab these little sleeping bags and get them dry. We had this big outside fire and it was always supposed to be going—that was the deal. Jennifer Naedzo, who was the unofficial camp boss, came running into the camp while I was trying to dry these sleeping bags. I had alder in the stoves and it was burning red-hot—you know, alder burns really hot.

Some of these sleeping bags were a little bit too close to the smoke, while I was trying to get all these little kids' sleeping bags dry. I had no sleep, trying to get all this done, and then Jennifer came running in and said, "That Centre Fire just went out." And I said, "What?" And she said, "The Centre Fire just went out. It's not supposed to go out." I said, "Well you go light it." And she said, "You're the man. You have to go light the fire."

I remember I felt like somebody woke up in my body and I said, "Yes, I'll be right back." I went running out there in the rain. I was using my hair, I was using everything I could, and I got that fire going again. *You're the man; you're supposed to make the fire....* It was a woman who led me into feeling like a man. I remember when I walked off that island, I was different. I knew my role: keep that fire going.

Justice: I can actually tell you the day: December 22, 2005. That night we thought my dad was going to die. He was in the ICU after having surgery that went badly. We're fortunate that he's with us today, but the doctor said then that he probably wouldn't survive the night. We needed to call family, and my mom was just not in a place to do it, so I had to be the one to call family and tell them. It was the hardest thing I'd ever done, especially when I had to call his older sister who was sick and couldn't come. I had to be the one to actually tell people that we weren't sure, but that Dad might not survive the night, and ask them to pray.

I had to call these people, and it was just gut-wrenching. But that was when I felt like I had grown up. I had taken up the task that no one else could do, and it was my responsibility. It was that moment of responsibility.... I still get a little choked up thinking about it, especially about my aunt, because she kept saying, "Oh no, oh...." I thought, "Oh God, I've killed her too." It was just awful. But I've never been the same after that. The time when I first really felt like I had taken up my duties as a man was when I took up the grieving duties, and stepped up as a potential herald of transition. Fortunately, he's a tough man and he made it. He's still around and he's still ornery.

Cariou: Sometimes I wonder if I've attained that yet. When I was growing up, I grew up among many physically powerful men like my uncles—my dad maybe not so much, though he was powerful in many other ways—but I always felt like I could not measure up. I felt like I would always be the wimpy kid who's sitting reading books when everybody else is out doing chores, fixing machines, cutting down trees, and things like that.

In my third or fourth year of university, through some intercession of my dad, this friend of his said, "Oh, I'll get you a summer job." I said, "That would be great to have a decent summer job," and he said, "Yeah, you're going to be on a concrete crew, so you're going to be pounding stakes into the ground all day and pouring concrete with a wheelbarrow." I could tell he'd chosen this for me as a kind of test, and I was just horrified.

But I really had no choice, so I reported for duty. That was a very tough summer in a way. I gained thirty pounds over that summer, and I remember always feeling like I was about to screw up. You'd carry wheelbarrows full of concrete—wet concrete—and dump it, and if you accidentally dumped the concrete before you got to the dumping place, you'd have to buy a case of beer for the crew. And I bought a lot of cases of beer.

But I remember I gradually got more physically strong, and I also sort of figured out how to do the job well enough that, by the end of the summer, the foreman came to me and said, "I'd hire you on if you were staying." I thought maybe he was just saying that, but I felt like—

Van Camp: Did you say, "Call my dad!"?

Cariou: That's right. So I went and told my dad that. And when I was actually telling my dad, that was the moment I thought, Okay, I've passed this test. Now I can go back to reading my books.

Van Camp: If I can say one thing: One of the things I love about you and your work, Warren, is your love of the land and your love for the land. That is a central theme in your work, whether it's your literature or your movie. I think you made your movie as a man and as a protector of the land, and as a keeper of that sacred land. It was an indictment.

You documented how many people will never in this lifetime, and possibly the next, be able to use their traplines, will never be able to use the land. You can't trust the fish. You documented that as a male protector. That was a role. I raise my hands to you for that. I never forgot it.

McKegney: Our eldest daughter came on the scene relatively early. I had just turned eighteen when she was born, although that certainly wasn't when I felt I had become a man. It took me a long time to grow into that role as a father. But I remember going away to university and being in the same city as my daughter's mother, Sherrie, who's a woman of tremendous strength and wisdom that she doesn't always see in herself, but everyone else recognizes. Sherrie and I weren't then a couple, but I was helping out with the parenting, of which, quite frankly, she was doing the lion's share while also going to university.

Spending that first year away from home, being with those two wonderful women, I realized that in that space I could find everything that I would ever want in the world. I also realized what those relationships required of me, and how I needed to honour them. So after moving away and still seeing myself as something of a kid—connected to the parents who would look after things if I couldn't—I remember calling my folks at the end of that first year and saying, "I'm not moving home this summer, I'm staying with Sherrie and Caiti," and the joy that was in their voices when they responded. So that's, I think, when I first felt like a man.

Scofield: This is a hard question for me to answer. I was just giving myself time while everybody was sharing their stories. To be honest, I have to say that I'm still very much growing into that role. I'm still finding my way. But the way I want to answer this question is that, the truth be told, I was born into it. I didn't have a monumental moment where I realized, "Hey, I'm a man." I've been protecting ever since I was a child.

I've spent my life protecting my mom, and I've spent my life protecting my aunts. I spent my life protecting whoever needed to be protected. Maybe not physically, because I wasn't able to, but in every other way I spent my life protecting them. I was always aware that strong men protect—that there was something innate about protecting that had to do with being a man.

So, if anything, I've realized that the more I deconstruct those things, the more I come into this sense of being male and being a man.

McKegney: Thank you all for the generosity of those responses, and Richard for that wonderful question. We will now take a ten-minute break and return with questions from the audience.

Our first question is from Dr. Niigaanwewidam Sinclair, professor of a course at the University of Manitoba on the study of Indigenous masculinities.

Sinclair: *Boozhoo* and welcome to my uncles and my brothers on this panel. I could listen to you all talk for a very long time. I'm really interested in popular images of Indigenous men and I'd like a quick foray through the panel as to Indigenous men that have been formative in your cultural world. It could be a figure within your community, or maybe a figure within pop media or pop culture.

I think about all of these different characters we've seen, and many of them are one-dimensional, simplistic representations that can reify certain stereotypes. But every once in a while, one comes along that's kind of interesting....

For me it was Chief Wahoo McDaniel, the professional wrestler. There were lots of problems with wrestling as a whole, but I remember that, when I was a kid, I would see professional wrestling at the Winnipeg Arena, and it was one of those few times when I saw what I was cheering for, because almost always the Indigenous wrestlers would be the "bad guys." They'd always be up to no good and sneaky.

I remember he would hold things in reverence—things like feathers. For me as a kid, growing up in a very assimilated environment, it was empowering to see that. There were certainly problems with that image, but it was also a source of empowerment for me. So I'm curious as to whether anyone else had experiences like that.

Scofield: In Maple Ridge when I was growing up, there were very few Aboriginal people, and there was a very well-known powwow dancer by the name of Ernie Philip that had lived in town, and I had gotten to be really good friends with his kids. I ended up going over to their house quite a bit, and then I'd end up going powwowing with them and got quite close with the family.

Ernie Philip was probably one of my first male Aboriginal role models. He was this grand champion, larger-than-life powwow dancer and had travelled all over the world, and he had been in movies alongside Chief Dan George, so I very much idolized him.

Justice: When I was growing up, not so much. I didn't want to be connected with that part of where I grew up, so I was looking elsewhere. But when I really started to embrace being Cherokee and taking up different images, I would say one of the ones that was hugely influential was Evan Adams as Thomas Builds-the-Fire in *Smoke Signals*. Victor didn't do it for me, but Thomas—God, he was cute. He was so cute. And he was smart and he was a storyteller and the world came alive. That was actually the first really significant popular image that really struck me.

Thomas was so different and so unique and so distinctive and so beautiful. He loved his grandmother and he was gentle, but he was the strongest figure in the film. That was a character that I still find so appealing on many levels. I also have a thing for nerdy guys, so that was part of it as well.

Cariou: In terms of pop culture, I actually can't think of an Indigenous male character who I saw, when I was growing up, that I thought was a positive model. I think in almost every instance, in Westerns or in other Hollywood representations, there were always things that I wouldn't actually want to be attached to.

So for me, the role models—certainly within my own family but also in the community—were often those lumberjack figures. There was a guy, the father of my friend, Stan Morin—Joe Morin—who was legendary for his strength. And growing up in a very racist community in which the Métis people and the Aboriginal people were subject to a lot of discrimination all the time, Joe Morin was someone who could walk anywhere in that town and be proud of who he was and no one was ever going to say anything bad about him because—not that he was ever violent, but—he was just so strong in his physical presence.

So I remember, as kids, we'd be proud because we knew him and we could tell people, "Hey we know Joe Morin." So that was an example. But from pop culture, I can't think of anything that I thought I wanted to identify with in any of those characters, to be honest.

Sinclair: One of my little hobby interests is discussing local heroes, the sort of celebrities within a local environment. And so when I say "pop," I'm thinking about the popular conceived locally as well.

Van Camp: My first Aboriginal role model was actually a bush cook named Dave King. Dave King was Dene. He could cook for thirty or 300—it didn't matter to him. He made fresh pies every day; he was a master baker. I've heard he has children, but when I was growing up I don't think he had any children of his own, because it was nothing for him to be picked up and then flown out on the land. He just loved being out there. And he loved my little brother, Roger. My little brother, Roger, was the apple of his eye, but Dave could never get Roger's name right. He called him Rodney. "Where's Rodney? I want to see Rodney." That's why, to this day, I call my brother's son Shaedon "Little Rodney"—just to honour Dave King.

Nothing fazed Dave King. He was always happy; he was always grateful and deeply respectful to be out on the land. He missed my dad when he wasn't working, so he'd show up at our house at 3:00 in the morning, often singing in our front yard, and we'd all have to get up because Dave wanted to visit. He'd get so lonely in town sometimes.

My dad would turn on ESPN on mute with subtitles and pretend to be listening to Dave, but he'd be watching ESPN. All of us would be trying to listen to Dave talking Dene, talking English. Then one day, you know that boxing promoter, Don King? Well, Dave was talking and saw Don King on TV and he said, "That's my brother. Our dad spent time in the States and spent time up in the North. We have the same nose." And we looked and they did have the same nose. To this day, when I see Don King, I say, "That's Dave King's brother."

I'll tell you a quick little story. One time there were whitecaps on Tsu Lake, and my dad was in charge of testing a new net. So my dad said, "Okay, let's go set the nets." It was really stormy. It was grey and it was cold, and he said, "Come on boys, we've got to go. We've got to go get these nets and see if they caught anything."

My dad was Dave's boss and Dave said to him, "I don't think this is a good day to go out on that boat." "Oh now, come on, we've got the best kicker; we've got the biggest boat; we've got lifejackets, extras, blankets, tarps—you name it." And Dave said, "It's going to rain." My dad said, "Oh no, we'll be right back." And he didn't listen.

So we all got in the boat and took off, and the second we went around the sound it was horrible. We got sliced by the wind. We started getting banged up against a huge rock island where the net was tied. My dad was trying to get the net and he was yelling at us, "Bail! Bail!" You know those little half Javex bottles? We were trying to bail with those, but half the boat was filling with water.

We started crying. We were crying and bailing. We were so scared. And all of a sudden we heard "brrrrrrrrrrrr," and we looked around and it was Dave King. He was so heavy—just him and that boat. He just came around, pulled up, and didn't say one word to my dad. He didn't have to. His beautiful brown hands grabbed the sides of the boat. He said, "Boys, get in the back." And we dove underneath the tarps.

There was a silver bowl full of fresh, hot bannock, just dripping with butter and jam, and—oh man—we just started French kissing it. It's so good that you start going down on it, you know what I mean? We were just tonguing that bannock, we were so happy. Instincts were kicking in, eh?

What happened was he tied a rope, he threw it to my dad, and Dad had to hold on with that boat of his sloshing pure water.

And Dave didn't say a single thing against my dad. He just went up and he kept cooking for all those students. So, Dave King was my first Aboriginal hero. Great man—I miss him.

McKegney: As our conversation draws to a close, it strikes me as surprising—particularly given the gentlemen sitting on this panel—that we've spoken very little about sex. In the interview that I had with Gregory earlier, he said, "People have oftentimes taken the spirit of out sex and sexuality, and if they haven't entirely taken the spirit out of sex, they've long since stopped looking to the ceremonies that accompany those things." As a final question, I wonder if each of you might comment on the factors that have influenced the alienation from spiritual sexual intimacy and on the pathways back to that kind of connection, particularly for men.

Scofield: The pathway back is for men to know their own bodies, to know the vulnerability that lives within their bodies, and to honour that vulnerability.

Cariou: I think there is some truth to the idea that things were different in our communities in earlier generations. Greg's book *Love Medicine* is an extraordinary example of an artist who's trying to go back, in a way, to the old stories, but making them very contemporary as well. I think Greg is showing us with that book how we need to return to the ways that some of our ancestors maybe thought, not only about physical intimacy between one person and another person, but also about connection in an intimate way to the land.

I was very fortunate to spend some time with Cree Elder Louis Bird, and to hear his stories of the Mushkegowuk Cree. As we spent more time with him, he would untangle different teachings and one of the teachings that came late in our discussion—when we had travelled a certain distance in our knowledge of the stories—involved untangling the meanings of sexual relationships that were in some of those stories.

I don't have time to go into detail about that, but the thing that I really took away from those amazing discussions was that he was very specific about the role of the man. The role of the man is to understand that giving pleasure is the primary thing, not receiving it. It was interesting because he felt, I think, that he didn't have to explain that to the women, but that the men needed that knowledge because they had forgotten it, or it had been forgotten somehow.

He saw this not just as an experience, or something that you're wanting to do, but as your actual role. This is a responsibility to give pleasure, and if you're not doing that you're not fulfilling your role as a man.

Van Camp: I wrote a little story called, "Why Ravens Smile to Little Old Ladies as They Walk By," and I had it published in *Angel Wing Splash Pattern*. I was deeply nervous about it. I was arguing with Kateri Akiwenzie-Damm, our dear friend and publisher of Kegedonce Press, saying, "I don't know about this." She said, "It's going in. Rene [Abrams] and I love it. It's got to go in."

You have to read the story. I don't want to give too much away, but when we went to press, that was the one story I was nervous about. I was at an event in Yellowknife and it just happened to be an erotica night. I got called up on the stage and they said, "Richard Van Camp, we ask you to read, 'Why Ravens Smile to Little Old Ladies as They Walk By.'" There were Elders in the audience, and my mom, so I said, "Well, I don't know about this." And someone said, "I double-Dogrib dare you!"

My little nipples just popped and I just about whipped off my own shirt. "What? You double-Dogrib dare me?" I went up there and I read this story and, man, everybody left with a perm. I mean, things just heated up—eggs dropped, fallopian tubes started clapping. It was phenomenal. It was a biblical moment. Anyways, as I was walking out of there, stunned at my own power and prowess and grace as a man, there was a little old Elder and she had her little kerchief on and her little nylon jacket and her flowered skirt and her little moccasin rubbers, and she pulled me aside and said, "That's my favourite story. Thank you so much for writing that story. I love that story."

That moment, I received what I consider the Pope's blessing to continue writing those beautiful, erotic stories. I've always gone against the medicine wheel because we don't talk about sexuality. When I say, "Where's sexuality in that medicine wheel?," people say, "It's emotional and physical and it's all of these things." Well guess what? We're not talking about it and because we're not talking about it, it is wounding us. Sex has become a weapon. So that's why I wrote the sexual health comic book, *Kiss Me Deadly*. You can download it for free anywhere in the world on the Internet [http://www.thehealthyaboriginal.net].

Scofield: There were five lines that almost broke the publication of *Love Medicine and One Song*:

> I heat the stones
> between your legs,
> my mouth,
> the lodge where you come
> to sweat.

When I wrote those lines I knew that something sacred had happened. I wrote those lines and I read them. And I said to myself, *I can't put that in a poem. I'm using the sweat lodge, I'm talking about the stones, I'm talking about those rounds, and I'm talking about it in that way. People will have a fit.*

I don't know how many tobacco offerings I did. I did a lot of praying. I asked the grannies and I asked the grandpas, "If I do this book, protect me and please let people take maskihkiy; please let people take the medicine from this book and the ceremony I am describing." Those five lines described a sexual act, but it was just as sacred as going into a sweat, and I wanted people to know that.

I was reading at an old bookstore in Montreal and these two Mohawk women had come to the reading that night and I'd gone out and smoked with them. One woman said, "My grandmother, she brought this book to the sweat. And in between rounds she was reading the book and she couldn't put it down. And she wanted us to tell you how proud she is of you and how beautiful this book is and how sacred this book is."

And I knew that I had done the medicine correctly. Anybody can do that sexual act, anybody can describe that act, anybody can make it ugly, anybody can make it dirty, but traditionally, that's a sacred thing—people coming together like that and honouring and respecting each other's bodies. That's a sacred thing.

Justice: Sexual shame was a weapon used against us. Sexual shame was never ours. That's something I always try to keep in mind: whatever shame we have around sexuality is one of those dubious gifts of colonialism that was intended to destroy us as individuals, as peoples, and destroy our links to one another, to the land, and to ourselves.

I grew up in a household where my folks were very sexual and were very open and there was no sense of sexual shame. But I inherited a lot of sexual shame from pop culture, and that's why it took me so long to come out. I think part of it is just to remember that that shame isn't ours; it does not belong to us.

Not only is sex sacred, but it's also fun. We also have to take up the idea of the pleasure principle, that to give pleasure is an enjoyable thing. The best sex of my life has been with a lot of laughter and a lot of giggling and smiling and all of the things that go into true intimacy.

Part of getting back to something different is to laugh more as you're loving and to have it be laughter about the joy of being with one another and the joy of sharing a moment of vulnerability, knowing you can trust this person or these people—whatever works for you.

I had the opportunity to look at some holdings at the Peabody Museum at Harvard, and one of the Cherokee items in the collection was a carved pipe of a copulating couple with the genitals towards the smoker. It was taken out of an old Cherokee site in the southeast. Somebody took a lot of time to create this pipe. It's a couple, and they look like they're having fun. To some people's eyes that's a dirty thing, but it is about beauty. It's a straight couple—so it's not necessarily my beauty—but it's a beautiful thing.

I think the more we can find beauty in ourselves and in one another the better—beauty of the *real* body, the body with all of its imperfections, with all of its scars, with all of its woundings. All of those things are beautiful. They're part of what makes us human, they're part of what makes us loveable. And if we can find ourselves loveable and extend that generosity to one another, I think we've done a great service to our People and the memory of our ancestors.

McKegney: Thank you so much to Niigaanwewidam and your Indigenous masculinities class for the attentiveness, respect, and thoughtful questions. And to Daniel, Gregory, Richard, and Warren, thank you for your creativity, your acts of brotherhood, and your beauty. It's been a pleasure to spend this time with all of you and I thank you.

Notes

1   Kim Anderson and Bonita Lawrence, *Strong Women Stories: Native Vision and Community Survival* (Toronto: Sumach, 2003).

2   Sam McKegney, *Masculindians: Conversations about Indigenous Manhood* (Winnipeg: University of Manitoba Press, 2014).

CHAPTER 15

A Conversation with Crazy Indians

Sasha Sky

The Crazy Indian Brotherhood was established in 2007 to help Indigenous men involved in gangs and the criminal system in Canada get the support to leave. It started with a grassroots approach from gang members who wanted a better life and who came together to create this change. This chapter offers a snippet of the conversation I had with members of a Crazy Indians local in May 2013 in a mid-sized Canadian city. As the reader will see, a theme throughout our discussion was the sense of "brotherhood" provided through this club. This is exemplified in that each man has to go through a process to determine that they are worthy of the cuts (similar to a jacket) that each man wears proudly. What does it take to make the "cut"? Each man has to be clean of drugs and alcohol, maintain healthy relationships with his partner and child(ren), and be working or upgrading his education and skills. Each member is also expected to participate in the community in a positive way.

In the interest of anonymity, I have labelled all responses as "participant" and distinguished between them using numbers. The participants came from both urban and reserve backgrounds and ranged from twenty-five to thirty years in age.

Sky: So to start: What does being a man mean to you, in your culture, where you came from?

Participant (P) 1: Being a man to me is respecting women, the life-givers. It also means taking care of your responsibilities, taking care of the young, whether or not you have children yourself. It also involves getting back to the culture, which a lot of us have lost. But there are a lot of teachings that help us to be that better man.

P 2: The meaning of a man to me goes back to the true meaning of being a true warrior. I think that as Aboriginal men we have to go back to our roots, go back to our original ways of thinking, back to our positive influence and positive surroundings. If we could do that, then we can become those providers, hunters, and warriors in the present moment.

P 3: Well back when I was involved in the crap, I only cared about myself. I didn't really care about my family. My point of view as a man back then was get the money and take care of me. Now that I'm a father, I see my role being a hunter-gatherer, to be that provider, be the warrior if I have to be.

P 4: Being a man to me is not getting involved in all the bullshit that society nowadays tells us we have to do. I was taught providing is more than just your household. As Native men, we have to start getting back to providing for all of us as a nation. And that involves doing all those things that our grandmothers and grandfathers left here for us to learn. Taking care of our elderly. Respecting our land, our culture. Right from animals and plants to our reserves where we live.

P 6: There's a lot that we have to, that we should be doing that we're not. You know, a lot of men are choosing to drink and do drugs and beat on their women. To me, that's the stuff that I'm trying to teach the younger ones to get out of. I work with youth and am more suited to working with boys because I have all those teachings to help guide them. I lived the gang life and I really didn't feel like a man doing that stuff. It was actually kind of scary at some points because you never knew if you were going to live or die or if you were going to go to jail. Now that I see a bigger picture I know what I have to be doing now as a man and that's taking care of not just my family, but my whole community and anybody that wants that help.

P 5: To me, it's about responsibility. You have to learn what your part is as a man and you have to carry out your responsibilities and let a woman do their responsibilities, what they're supposed to carry out. The way I look at it, within a household, the man is the one that watches the door and the woman is the one who runs the whole inside of the house. The man's responsibility is to make sure that he protects that doorway and keeps a safe home. It also teaches the man to be humble. You're supposed to work together, side by side. A woman has her responsibilities and a man has his responsibilities. It's a matter of talking to the old ones because they're the ones that are going to share that information with you so you can learn.

I also think as Indigenous males we have a warrior spirit in us. The warrior spirit is something that I try to acknowledge every day and I try to help other people find that within themselves as well.

Sky: So what did you learn about being a man? What were some of the teachings you learned either as a boy or later in life?

P 1: Throughout my life, I've learned a lot of different things but I've taken what felt right for me. I was shifted between foster homes so I was getting a piece of everything. I was getting how a man should treat a woman, because I was in homes where there was good men to their women. Or sometimes the woman overpowered the man. There was a lot of different ways that people were treating each other. But from all that I've really learned to just be humble to myself, to my family members, and being there for anyone who needs it. You know, if that means sitting down or even financially. Not abusing a woman is number one for me. That's the number one issue for me when I talk about learning what it is to be a man.

But definitely being a family man is number one, too, for me. And to always take care of them, of family comes first. And it's the same with this brotherhood—they're like family so they're a part of that now. They'll always come first before anything else.

P 2: I never had a dad for as long as I can remember. But it was through stories I heard that my dad had been around when I was younger. I was never taught how to be a man. I witnessed my mom's drunken boyfriends punch the shit out of her. I saw fights at a party. I accepted that life, the partying life and being surrounded by all that. Everything was interpretation that I took in growing up. Nobody said, "This is what a man is. You have to do this." You got those things in society, the labels that say this is a man's job or whatever. I've always done those. I think it comes back to being your true self, that's what a man is. Being honest, being humble, being willing to accept change and willing to follow the right path.

P 3: When I was a boy, my only example of a man was my father and I haven't seen him since I was eleven. But those first few years with him, he was an abusive drunk. My experience with men was seeing what he did and I tried not to be like him. Even through all the bad stuff that I've done throughout my life, I always treated women with respect.

It wasn't until I got older, until I became a man that I actually learned what it was to be a man. I learned that it's not always about being the tough guy. Sometimes you got to be the sensitive guy, the guy that feels. And growing up in the street, it was always "you got to be hard." You can't be crying and you can't be showing any emotion. You just be a fucking tough guy. It wasn't until after some tragedies in my life that's what woke me up. And having some friends, guys that I thought are hardcore guys, actually say to me: "It's ok to break down. It's okay to cry. Sometimes even the hardest rock will crack."

P 6: I was taught as a young boy that being a man meant you don't cry. I used to get hit when I would cry. You always have to be tough and you couldn't show any kind of emotion towards anyone. You always had to try to toughen up others by saying something mean to them.

I was also taught that we always had to be superior to women. So I started doing all the stuff that I seen growing up to my wife. We met when we were young, so I was always that guy. I'd see her crying and instead of showing her love and compassion I would tell her to "quit her fucking crying." I was abusive, too. As a man I've learned a lot of different things over the last eight years that I've been on my healing path. Now I know that we aren't superior to women and it's actually the other way around. I learned it's okay to take direction from a woman without questioning her or getting mad at her for it.

Culturally, I learned it's our job to keep that sacred fire. I take that very seriously. If someone offers me the tobacco and asks me to keep the fire [at a ceremony] other plans get postponed. My job is to go look after that fire so the Elders can do their job and help the people. Sitting by the fire is where I get a lot of my strength from when I'm feeling down. It gives you a sense of pride and belonging. It's a really uplifting feeling and it's a great thing to be a part of. We watch that fire and the woman takes care of the water. And together we can live in a good way as long as we uphold those responsibilities.

P 5: To me there's a big difference between what I thought was being a man when I was young to what I think being a man is now. I grew up in the same way, watching my father. I remember images of my father fighting at these parties and things like that. He would tell me not to cry. I remember you know, being at my auntie's funeral as a young man and have my dad tell me "don't cry." And I'd be like, eight years old. So I'd try my best to stop crying.

Back then I [thought] that being a man was being in control and not showing your feelings and not showing them anything. Being with my boys and robbing people when asked, fighting, or just being that person who had no fear. Then I was fortunate to spend time with an Elder and he would teach me sweatlodge, sundance, and took me to ceremonies. I really learned a lot from him. He taught me what being a man was about—it's learning that change. You got to look at who you used to be and you've got to look at who you are now. Being able to admit when you're wrong. You have to admit and you have to apologize for the things you've done to women. And I've still got that mentality today where I believe a man should cry to let that out. I think that's important. That's what my teacher always taught me but I'm at a spot right now where I'm struggling. I haven't cried in a long time and it doesn't want to come out.

Sky: So you all mentioned your fathers being teachers in some way, or not. Where else did you gain teachings?

P 1: I learned a lot from a lot of the foster homes that I was in. And while incarcerated there were a lot of people trying to help me change and trying to give me positive solutions. Trying to direct me and telling me take certain programs. And because I was in CAS [Children's Aid Society], I had a social worker that stuck very close to me and always wanted the better for me. She read my file throughout the years and she just really wanted to help me change. So I've been to a lot of facilities like treatment and camps, group homes—just met tons of people. And a lot of them were older people who always saw something in me. I find a lot of them have helped me. Even in school, the teachers. I'd say that I'd have to thank a lot of people out there for where I am today because they helped me develop my mind and change things.

P 2: I'll never want to take away from what my father—my dad taught me a lot. He just didn't have the right tools to teach me the way he wanted to teach me. The way that he taught me created all this anger and hate for everybody. I didn't care about nothing, my life, anything…. And I had all these people through my whole life saying, "This is what you need to do. This is what you need to do. This is what you need to do." How do they know? They didn't know.

My dad is still a drunk. But in a way he's a good man because he doesn't let those things that we let influence us, like money and power. All my life, I wanted to be that guy that everybody looks at and they say, "That's a man." My dad doesn't care about that shit. He has a strong heart. We all do. But our hearts are buried under pain. We need to heal and get back to where we were.

P 3: A lot of people showed me a lot of things but I learned what I wanted to. A lot of guys showed me some bad shit. A lot of guys showed me some good shit. I saw things on TV. I just chose what I thought was right for me. I never thought it was right to hit a woman. I never thought it was right to degrade a woman. But to be totally honest I did do it. I did degrade women from time to time.

I had my own moral compass growing up. Sometimes I went against it but I always felt like shit afterwards. I was really good for talking to women for money. I'd hook up with girls and have them get phones and cars for me and then just fuck off on them. Afterwards, I felt like shit, but I would do it again. When I had my first daughter, it was like *okay I'm doing this to women, she's going to be a woman and maybe I should stop.* My moral compass finally overrode my selfish needs. 'Cause really it was all about me—I didn't care.

P 6: On this subject, I can't really say that anyone taught me anything bad because everybody that I've known and got close to in my life has helped mould me into what I am today. Negative-wise, it was my friends who controlled my thoughts. I was more a follower than a leader. But on a positive side, my father taught me the importance of education and work. That's where I got my drive for work and school, from my father. Culturally, I had many teachers. But the most important man in my life—who took me out of the life and showed me how to be a man, was John.[1] He was the one that brought me to the sweatlodge, showed me the fire, that gave me that responsibility of the fire. He's taken me to sundance, he was there when I pierced for the first time. He was watching me when I had my first fast and my last. He was the man he could be. The cultural leader—or if you just needed someone to talk to, he was there to listen. If I just needed some advice or needed somebody to talk to he was the man for me.

P 5: I don't want to take away anything from my father. As messed up [as the] things I saw from him [were], my dad taught me a lot of things about being a man. Even with the womanizer he was, he always taught me to respect women. I remember every time I got into a disagreement with my mom, he'd always tell me, "You know, you listen to your mom. You don't talk back. That's your job as a male is to listen to your mom." If I got into disagreements with women he'd always be the one to tell me, "Don't get angry at women. Just let the woman say what she needs to say and then walk away. You're going to be angry so just walk away and cool off." And since I was a young age, he drilled me. He'd always tell me that when I grow up there's going to be somebody bigger, stronger, or tougher than me. And you're going to have to be ready for when you meet that guy. In life, you always have to be ready. He always told me that I have to have more experience. So I have to learn how to use that to my advantage and not hurt people.

My brother taught me a lot, too, about work ethic. He would drink all night; he'd drink until an hour before his shift. He'd get about an hour's sleep and then he'd work all day. So I used to watch that and I used to look up to that. When I got in the work force I would do the same thing. I mean, it wasn't the best, but it did teach me to go to work. A lot of my friends were partying with me and they didn't go to work. I was the one guy who'd leave the party and get an hour's sleep before work and they would get fired.

Then I went to the treatment centre and John, he taught me what being a man was. He always told me that he saw something inside of me and that he was there for me. I don't trust a lot of people so it's hard for me to let people in. But I let him in, and I would listen to what he'd say and he'd just teach me about being a man. He'd always teach me that when we get our life together we're going to help men and women. And these women are going to be hurt and these women are going to be struggling and they're going to be very beautiful women. He taught me that it's our responsibility to be there for them. To not look at them in a sexual way and not hit on them. We've got to be that man, we've got to help them. You've got to put all that other stuff aside, and he really used to talk to me about that—say to me, that's just what being a man is. And I try to just look at myself and be honest with myself every day. I always try to look at everything I do—*Am I living up to who I'm supposed to be?* I do that a lot.

P 3: I think what we should probably mention too is the influence of males now. And for me, and what I think everybody should have, is this club. My brothers right here, and my actual family-brothers are the largest male influence in my life. I model my life and the way that I live my life from them. They're my biggest teachers right now. When I think of [what] a man should be, [it's], *Well what would my brother do or what would their thoughts be?* Or I'll call them and say, "Hey, what do you think of this?" And I think if all men had that kind of support and that kind of brotherhood we might be a lot better off.

P 4: We've got to find that bridge or that thing that's going to bring "back then" and "today" together. And once we can find that thing to link those gaps we're going to be unstoppable like we were then. We were unstoppable then [before colonization] and they gave us those pains and hurts that slowed us down. And then they gave us alcohol, and that slowed us down even more. And then they gave us all these influences that make you sit and do nothing. It makes people not have that desire for that unity. To me, loyalty is the biggest influence in my life. I'm the most loyal person if you're loyal to me. But if you cross me, you lose that 100 percent. So if you can create a bond that you have this 100 percent loyalty, nothing can stop you. And that's how I see my family at home as a unit, my friends, and brothers here. Each different part of my life has to have that loyal bond. Without that, you lose a lot.

Sky: So I've heard from a couple of guys that being in a gang is like a family they didn't have, or there was that sense of loyalty there, like all this "good" stuff that it provided for them. What was the pull for you?

P 4: Security. To me, it was the security, the feeling that somebody was standing behind me. It was the feeling that I belonged to something. Because I grew up off reserve and I dealt with racism from people that hated me for being a Native American when at home I didn't even have an understanding that I was different. But I have all these people who hate me for it. So I began hating them. And I didn't belong with them. So then I moved to the reserve and they didn't like me because I didn't speak their way. So I became this violent person that people weren't friends with because of who I was inside. They were friends with me for what I could do for them. And now that I'm sober, I'm learning what those true friends are and I'm starting to get that security without being involved in all those things I had to be involved in.

P 3: I think that's kind of the allure of it. I mean, you grew up in a shit house, with shit parents, you've got a shit life. But you see these guys and they're always together. And you want that. Yeah there's bad stuff that goes with it—maybe you've got to go rob a guy—but when you look at it, the pros outweigh the cons. Yeah, I might go to jail, yeah, I might die, yeah, I might kill someone, but I'm going to have these guys that are going to have my back. And I think that's the whole allure of the gang life. And the money. If you're in the right kind of gang, you'll make lots of money. But most gangs really don't make much money. They just fuck around. Or they spend it as fast they get it. [There's also] the respect that comes with being in a gang. "Oh, his friends are these guys," you know? But what's inside, healing with spirituality and roots, we're losing that aspect of life.

P 6: Basically all that the gang provided for me was a sense of being, protection. Nobody would fuck with me because my friends were always there to help me out. There was a lot of bad shit that happened but I'm not going to completely discredit my gang life. Like I had a lot of good times. There's good people that are in those gangs, too. But when it came down to the money-making part, that's when shit got serious and people got hurt. Not things that I'm proud of, but there's pros and cons to it, I guess. They did take care of me. I was out in the big city all by myself. I didn't have my family and my friends that I have here. But these guys took me under their wing, gave me a house to live in and you know, put money in my pocket. I just had to do certain things to earn that so that's what I did.

But if it wasn't for my life, I wouldn't be good at my job right now. It's a main tool I use in my job as a child and youth worker (CYW) and addictions counsellor. Both things I have experience in, you know? Those tools really help me, especially with the boys. I can relate to them more than the guy who's just coming out of university who read a book about Indians, right? Or read a book about the streets. I was there you know, I've seen it. And I was a part of it, so that's where it benefitted me in my life today, in what I do for the youth and how I influence them. So that's why I say that I can't really look down on living that life, because if I didn't then I wouldn't be who I am today. Yeah, it was a little hard because I dropped out of school to go be a gang member. So I wasn't very good when I went [back]. But I just kept going and eventually I got it done. I ended up getting hired even before I even graduated, so I think I owe a lot of that to the experience that I had in life as well.

P 5: To me it was all about loyalty. Loyalty is a huge thing to me. Like the group of guys I grew up with, I knew that I could be at a bar and I could be fighting ten guys and there's only me and another guy, [and] I don't have a doubt in my mind that he's not going to be there to back me up. And I knew he thought the same thing about me. We were very tight like that. I just knew that I was protected around them. Those are things that we really didn't talk about, the way that we treated each other or the way that we acted. We just did them. So that's what it was for me, was that family and that loyalty. And I lost touch with guys that I was really close with when I quit drinking and I quit partying and things. But I still know that we're close. Like we haven't talked in a very long time but I still know that we have the memories of each other and those memories are never going to fade. You move on, but you're still there for each other. You just know that things are different now.

I have that same thing with this brotherhood right now because up until about twenty-five that's all I ever knew—was selling drugs or robbing people and drinking and partying and being a womanizer. I thought that was my life. So now I'm twenty-nine and I'm still fresh. Every day is a learning thing for me, and there's times when you think about going back to your old ways because you're hungry or certain things like that. That's where this brotherhood comes in, because I know that each one of these guys have come from where I come from. They're going to get me, not judge me or look at me a different way. They're just going to talk to me the way that I need them to talk to me.

That's something that bugs me a lot. Our people get judged all the time, you know? I dress the way I dress and I act the way I act because that's me, that's always going to be me. I'm trying to break that barrier of people judging. I think you should be able to be who you are, no matter work environment or whatever you're doing, you should be able to feel comfortable in the way you want to be.

P 3: I think that's a very good point. It's not that I'm not their friend anymore, I'm just not doing what they're doing. Even now, I struggle with alcohol. And I got these guys to help me. And it's great. It doesn't bother me that they do that because I need them to do that. I mean, this isn't a treatment group, but we're not going to let one of our brothers...fall off the wagon.

P 2: Same thing as someone else. Feeling that acceptance, that's what felt good, was having that stability of caring. Security.

Sky: So what made you guys leave?

P 1: For me, I think it was school and a job because I didn't have time for that. And getting older, I had to live on my own. I found an apartment, graduated, and had a job. Just working at a fast food place. It wasn't where I wanted to be but it was a job. It kept me busy and occupied. When my group of people wanted me to come out I said, "I can't, I got to work." You know they would razz me out, "You suck." But they would be happy for me too, you know? But a lot of my friends, some of them are doing something with their lives. And I think that was the best part of it. That we all grew up and accepted changes that we were going to make and supported one another in whatever it was we were going to do.

P 2: For me it was, I'd say, having my daughter. It changed me, my ways of thinking. It made me step back and really look at who I am. I seen the way that I was with all the women in my life. I had a lack of respect. I saw them as an object, that's all they were to me. But at the same time I'd protect them. But it comes down to the point of talking the talk and walking the walk. I'm going to change my life to cut out all those things that I want to tell my youth isn't good for them. And until I can do it, then I have no right to tell them what they shouldn't do.

P 3: Well, I'd like to say it was my kids. That was definitely part of it. But when I was doing all the drugs, the drinking, all the crime, and all that crap, one of the biggest things that changed me was a long prison sentence. Three and a half years. And the look on my mom's face when I got sentenced—like, to see my family that was there in the courtroom just break down and start crying when I was found guilty.

The last push for me was drugs. I had been up for like two weeks and I was hallucinating. I had all my curtains closed, I was just sitting in my basement, shuddering. And I came down from it after a couple of days and I just said, "Fuck it, no more. I'm not doing this again." And I just kind of snapped out of it. But I still wanted that sense of brotherhood; I still wanted to hang out with my boys. I still wanted to fuck all kinds of girls and do whatever I wanted. But I realized that I didn't want to do it like that anymore.

P 6: For me, my rock bottom was with addictions. In treatment, I heard a lot of people saying, "I'm doing this for my kids," but I didn't feel that way. I did it for myself because I didn't want to be that crackhead anymore that weighed ninety pounds.

The final push was my son's birthday. He didn't want to be with me because I wasn't very pleasant to be around. He wanted to be with my mom. So I called my mom to come get him. I went out with a friend. We were going to make some quick money. All we had to do was burn up a car and we get paid. Something went horribly wrong and I ended up getting blown up. I was burnt, I was hurt, and I was in the hospital for a few days. When I looked at myself in the mirror, it was just an ugly person. And I didn't want to do that anymore. It wasn't long after that I ended up in treatment where I met the Elders. They started seeing things in me—how kids interacted with me. An Elder was interviewing me about what I wanted to do. He was like, "I think you should work with kids." He went and signed me up for school and, next thing I knew, I was in a social work college course. That's where I started to change because I had people that believed in me.

Being a part of this brotherhood is keeping me grounded too. I don't like people beating around the bush about shit, you know? I like to be told straight up, and that's what I get from all of these guys in here. Compared to people I listened to before. Yeah, I'm grateful for everything that's happened.

P 5: My rock bottom wasn't one event; it was numerous events. I got sent to jail and there was a Native court worker. I don't know why, but she believed in me and she helped me. "I can get you a Gladue,"[2] she said. "If you write this report, I can get your record erased. It's a special protocol of diversion." I just spoke about the abuses as a kid, getting abused by an adult, the shitty life that I went through and the shitty things that I did. They ended up wiping my record clean. It was really eye-opening that I was supposed to do something.

So I tried to be good after that. It just wasn't working for me. I ended up having this really nice sports car and I crashed it right into a tree headfirst. I was blacked out drunk. I had one of my best friends in the seat beside me. But that's when I knew that I needed to make some changes in my life 'cause I was going down a really bad road. I almost killed my best friend. So I went to treatment a week after that.

Sky: The next question is, What do you think happened to Native men's identities throughout history?

P 6: It dates back to residential school and the sixties scoop—that's where our culture took a nosedive. The sexual, emotional, mental, physical abuse, all passed down to all these men, makes them feel weak. And the only way that they can make themselves strong is to try to dominate. That's how they help themselves feel like being a man again is trying to be dominant to people. Then you throw alcohol into that mix and you got yourself a war.

Over the last five years I've seen more men getting involved in things, so I've got hope that things are starting to make a comeback now. I just hope that this brotherhood here, that's part of our agenda, is to try to reach out and help. Maybe we can influence another man and that man can bring in another man and we can all grow together.

P 3: I think it's that whole loss of identity, right? I think we just kind of lost our way. And now we're trying to find it. But I think now we've kind of found it again, but we've just got to have more people come with us and get into it. We're getting to know it.

P 2: Yeah, it was never lost. We always had it. We're just uncovering it, cleaning all that shit off. And once we can see it for what it really is, we're going to become strong people. We're going to become who we were meant to be. With me, the influences came from everywhere, but it's the people in society telling me who I am. You need to tell the youth to stop criticizing [each other] for their negative things and giving them the scapegoat to blame it on. My dad is a violent person, so I'm violent person. But there's a reason he's a violent person, there's a reason for everything that we are.

Sky: What are some of the needs you see for boys or men in terms of healing? Where do we need to go?

P 1: I think we just need to keep on offering what we're doing here. Sharing. That's therapy in itself. I mean, we don't always sit down and talk like this. I think that's what needs to happen a little more. They have men's groups and I think the more that happens, the more that young men are going to start saying, "Well, I'm going to try that." If we get it so that it's widespread then these kids have no choice but to think that's the cool thing to do. That's where I see change happening.

P 3: Well, the needs are to build that foundation. To say, "It's okay to hang out with a group of friends but you don't have to go out and do bad things." Go do positive things. When I was a kid, me and my friends never said, "Hey man, let's go play a game of baseball." But I really believe that if someone had said, "Hey guys, let's go bowling," and we had the place to go bowling or had the money, we would have went. But there was never anywhere to go or never anywhere we wanted to go. Like, they had the Christian groups, but then you have to go in there and listen to them preaching about God. And most kids don't want to hear that. At least not right in their faces. If you were going to come and say, "Hey guys, we're going to take you bowling and then maybe we can talk. Not necessarily about God, we can just hang out and talk," I think that would have been a really good thing to have in my youth. But I really didn't have anything else to do, other than what I was doing. [So] for me, jail was nothing. I would go to jail, and there's all my buddies! It would be like a reunion.

P 2: I think we just need to tell each other that we can be more than all these labels that limit us. The negative influences around us—they're so impactful that we don't even see them anymore. Tell us we can be lawyers, we can be doctors; we can start saying those things and see what we can be. We just have to show the youth that it's positive. Youth look at positives as a negative in our communities. They want us to do that for them. We've been shipped and boarded everywhere, and that is what we expect.

P 6: From my experience, there's not one thing we can do. Like, we can't do the same thing for every situation. But just talking to that person in a way that's going to allow him to open up and clear some of that shit out of his heart that he's been dying to talk to somebody about. Gaining his trust by opening up to him, too.

Then you open that door for them so that they can start to open themselves up. As long as you plant that seed, I think it'll grow eventually. It may be ten years down the road, fifteen years down the road. But you know, the main thing is to just try and plant the seed and hope for the best for that young one.

P 2:   If you plant that seed in the proper environment where they don't have that negative influence and they have that nourishment and things that a plant needs to grow. They could pick up the phone and have that at any time. We need to create something that says "We're here beside you while you're doing it." You know what I'm saying? And not stop here because we can only go that far. But to take it that step further, push even further beyond that. Because many jobs say they can only do so much, but our youth need more than that.

P 5:   I think the biggest thing the young ones need is a support structure. We need to lead by example. If we say we're going to do something, then we've got to do it. They're watching us in everything that we do. If you don't have parents, you don't have a family, you're learning from your friends. That's how I learned. We need to find what attracts them in, what interests them. We need to create things that interest them. Like, a lot of our youth today are into hip hop, fighting, and different things. We need to create those programs to help to be there for them, open the doorway, and let them walk through it and say, "You know I can help with this." No matter how much pain I have and how numb I've got, I've still got a heart that can love. That's what I think is what the youth need—they just need to heal and we need to be there for them. There's a lot of pain that our people suffered through. There's a lot of pain that we have through our parents and residential school that we're still dealing with today. It was brought upon our generation, upon our youth's generation.

P 4:   You mentioned men, too, but most of us have our dedication to the youth. A man is old enough to make a choice if he wants to change on his own. There are a lot of people out there that are willing to help, but it's up to that man himself. But with a youth it's much easier to say, "Hey, come here," and bring them to you. And then they start to adapt to you, and you're showing them good things and they start to do that. So it's a lot easier to get a youth on your side than to get a grown man on your side.

P 2: But the young, it's not that you *can* be influenced, it's you *should* be influenced. Once it's a grown man, it's you *can* be influenced. But as a child or as a young teenager, you *should* have guidance and you *should* have these things.

Sky: Thanks, guys. This has been a really informative conversation.

Notes

1 Not his real name.
2 The participant is referring to a process involving sentencing that takes into account a person's Aboriginal background, which may include intergenerational effects of residential schooling, child welfare history, abuse, health issues, substance abuse, etc.

CHAPTER 16

"To Arrive Speaking": Voices from the Bidwewidam Indigenous Masculinities Project

Kim Anderson, John Swift, and Robert Alexander Innes

> We need to sound out an ecology that will nurture and sustain the Indigenous male spirit.
>
> Albert McLeod, Cree Elder[1]

Bidwewidam, an Anishinaabe word meaning "to arrive speaking," is a fitting title for the last chapter of this book, as it is the name of the Indigenous masculinities research project that led to this collection, and ultimately represents the intention of the book—to encourage dialogue about Indigenous men and masculinities. The concept of Bidwewidam came from Anishinaabe artist Rene Meshake, who, in the course of working with the Bidwewidam Indigenous Masculinities (BIM) project stated: "Picture yourself in the forest, and as you sit still, you hear voices becoming clearer and clearer as they come near to you. Bidwewidam describes the way Indigenous masculinities, identities, and mino-bimaadiziwin (the good life) come speaking as one voice."[2]

The intention of the BIM project was to develop a network of researchers, program, and policy workers and community members who could contribute to voicing and identifying needs and future directions for work in Indigenous masculinities. As researchers working in partnership with the Ontario Federation of Indigenous Friendship Centres (OFIFC) and the Native Youth Sexual Health Network (NYSHN), we spent three years gathering voices through interviews, focus groups, and now writing. These voices assisted us in beginning the process that Cree Elder Albert McLeod calls for: "to sound out an ecology that will nurture and sustain the Indigenous male spirit."

In this chapter, we will contribute to this exploration by sharing findings from focus groups we conducted across Canada with various communities of Indigenous men, women, queer/Two-Spirited peoples, and youth. These voices parallel many of the themes found in previous chapters, including identifying the impact of white heteropatriarchal, colonial, and hegemonic masculinities on Indigenous peoples; exploring issues of identity and representation; giving voice to the particular struggles of Indigenous men; and reclaiming culture-based masculine identities in all their expressions. Whereas there is no such thing as one voice, our findings demonstrate that there is a cohesiveness in the collective vision that emerges: Indigenous men and masculinities are embedded within a web of relations—human, animal, land, and spirit—that continue to define the many articulations of masculinities in Indigenous contexts. There is power in this recognition; a sacred returning that we hope will inspire. Ultimately, we take inspiration from the fact that Indigenous men came and were willing to speak about what Indigenous masculinity means to them, and that we can now share it here.

Bidwewidam Indigenous Masculinities Focus Groups

From 2011 to 2013, the BIM research team conducted focus groups with the following groups:

- Group #1: Indigenous youth at the National Association of Friendship Centres gathering (Whitehorse, Yukon).
- Group #2: Two-Spirited men (Winnipeg, Manitoba).
- Group #3: Indigenous fathers (Nanaimo, British Columbia).
- Group #4: Indigenous fathers (Edmonton, Alberta).
- Group #5: Kizhaay Anishinaaabe Niin (I am a Kind Man)[3] program workers (Toronto, Ontario).
- Group #6: "Crazy Indians" (former gang members, urban location).
- Group #7: Sto:lo grandmothers and women (interior British Columbia).
- Group #8: national "think tank" of stakeholders, including program and policy workers, researchers, community members, and activists (hosted in Orillia, Ontario).

These groups were chosen according to the research interests and networks of BIM leadership team members, and to address some of the diversity in thinking about Indigenous men and masculinities. With the exception of the national think tank (which was two days and more extensive in terms of exploration), we asked focus group participants to address the following questions: What does being a man mean in the Native culture(s) that you come from? What did you learn growing up? What does masculinity mean in your life now, and in the communities you are part of? Can you share anything you know or have learned about Native men's traditional roles and responsibilities? What do you think happened to Native men's identities and well-being throughout our histories? What are some of the needs you see for our boys and men in terms of achieving mino bimaadiziwin (the good life)? Where do we need to go next?

All of the data were coded and analyzed in NVivo software using grounded theory.[4]

Themes That Spoke

The most prominent themes that emerged from our data had to do with "roles and responsibilities," "culture," and "relationships," including those with family, children (fathering), women, community, and the land. These primary themes speak to the centrality of relationships and the belief that healthy men and masculinities are connected to the revitalization of Indigenous cultures The presence of negative behaviours, involving violence, sexism, and substance abuse were secondary themes that cut across participant responses. These behaviours were typically framed as the consequence of colonial practices and the dispossession of lands and cultures.

It is significant to note that whereas participants were asked only one question about the "traditional roles and responsibilities" of Indigenous men, this theme came up in response to a number of the other questions, demonstrating the connection between Indigenous identity and responsibility to family, community, and the greater web of relations. This corresponds to Anderson's work on Indigenous female identity, where she concluded that "Native women define themselves through responsibilities," and that "Native female identity is tied into the question 'What is it that you have to do?' and 'What is it that you are capable of doing?'"[5] Feminist theorists might not be surprised to find that Indigenous women define themselves vis-à-vis responsibility to family and community, but would the expectation be the same of men? Our findings indicate that in spite of invasive capitalistic and toxic masculinities that could position Indigenous men to be self-focused, responsibility to the collective, as well as to the natural and spirit world, is still prominent in expressions of Indigenous masculine consciousness. Whereas one might expect discussions around masculinities to grapple with concepts of *power*,[6] the discussions we had focused repeatedly on notions of *responsibility*. As one Inuit youth participant said, "Masculinity for me is about giving of oneself for others; masculinity doesn't only refer to identity—it refers to our actions" (Group #8).

Overall, the emergent themes consistently returned to the concept of Indigenous men *in relation;* Indigenous men and masculinities were framed in the context of relationships—to family, community, the natural and the spirit world, with negative behaviours associated with loss and dispossession from this web. Feelings of frustration, anger, powerlessness, shame, and grief expressed in some of the groups related to the inability to exercise and fulfill kinship roles and responsibilities to humans and non-humans as defined by the various Indigenous cultures of the participants.[7] The revitalization of Indigenous cultures was seen as a means to re-engage responsibilities and relations, which could then activate healing from invasive patriarchal or hegemonic masculinities and foster healthy Indigenous men and communities.

As a prologue to the themes, we begin with a discussion about the difficulties we encountered in addressing the subject and language of masculinities with focus group participants. This is significant in terms of analyzing the often incongruent relationship between Indigenous men and hegemonic masculinities.

Resistance: "To eliminate the masculinity out of it"

As has been shown in all the chapters in this book, the notion of Indigenous masculinities is difficult to define and describe. There are hundreds of Indigenous societies worldwide, all with their own particular traditional views of masculinities. They have all been affected by colonization, which means that Indigenous men in downtown Winnipeg, northern Yukon, southwest United States, or in Christchurch have succumbed to the hegemonic white patriarchal masculinity to varying degrees, accompanied by the dispossession of traditional masculinities. Our project and many chapters in this book focus on the experiences of Indigenous men living in Canada, but previous research from other parts of the world demonstrates common ground. For example, in 2008, Ty Tengan wrote, "One of the primary discursive formations I explore is that of the 'emasculation of the Hawaiian male,' whose loss of land, tradition, authenticity, culture, and power stems from the historical experience of colonialism and modernity."[8] Consequently, he suggests, "many indigenous Hawaiian men feel themselves to be disconnected, disempowered, and sometimes emasculated."[9]

On the whole, researchers investigating this area recognize that for a variety of complex and intersecting reasons, Indigenous masculinities cannot or perhaps should not be defined. As Sam McKegney has stated elsewhere, as we must "resist conceptualizations of Indigenous masculinity in the singular, so too must [we] resist the presumption that tribal-specific Indigenous masculinities remain stable and unchanging over time (or the valuation that they are deficient if they fail to do so)."[10] In addition, the current hegemonic nature in which the term "masculinity" is applied also adds another level of complexity.

It was not surprising, then, as we discovered early on in the research process, that it was difficult to find a language to talk about masculinities with focus group participants. Many participants struggled with the concept of "masculinity," equating it typically with hegemonic, patriarchal, or hyper-masculine identities that they were either trying to escape or did not see as relevant to describe their world views and traditional societies. Participants made comments such as "When you talk about masculinity—I don't think we had it—it's a white problem" (Group #3), or "Masculinity didn't really exist back then" (Group # 2). One participant equated hegemonic masculinities with an absence of Native culture, stating, "Well, there was no Native culture where I grew up, so being a man meant being strong and meant not sharing your feelings; it meant you were the boss; you were to be feared" (Group #5).

For many, "masculinity" signified stereotypical behaviours, as reflected in this comment from a participant in the youth group: "…the first thing I thought of is—masculinity was big muscles, being macho, the stereotype of being a macho man" (Group #1). Participants in the queer/Two-Spirited focus group (Group #2) offered similar stereotypical and male dominant images in response to what the word "masculinity" meant to them:

- Strong…physically strong.
- The head of the household.
- It's the top, like it's the leadership.
- Atlas holding the world up—every male that is masculine has to hold the world up, right?
- To be very stern, very…to be the top person.
- It means confidence.
- It means control.

These participants went on to talk about how ill suited these concepts were in terms of their own lives and often in the communities that they came from.

One participant reflected on the difference between men's roles in land-based communities and stereotypical masculine roles, addressing the difficulties associated with the language of "masculinity": "Some of the masculine roles aren't always masculine. In our culture, there was no such word. Masculinity: how do we really define that in words—it's a Western word. So being masculine. If you said *masculine* to us when this was in the bush, we'd be looking at you like, *what?*" (Group #2). In this quote, the participant alludes to a distinction between Western concepts of masculinity and those he associates with being "in the bush." Another participant made note of the gendered roles in the land-based culture that he grew up in, but struggled with the concept of masculinity—defining, rather, responsibilities for men as "leadership":[11] "On my reserve, the women and the men get separated on Equinox. The men go hunting and the women go gathering. For example, [women gather] berries and the medicine that's going to be needed for that day and the men are out there.... And [roles] were talked about, like my grandfather stood up and was saying, us men, we are providers. We [have] roles. We have to look after our children, roles and stuff like that. But it's kind of hard for me to put that in masculinity" (Group #2).

Authors in this book have also articulated the fault line between language of "the masculine" and men's practices in land-based cultures. In Chapter 9, Phillip Borell explains that men's roles in land-based Māori cultures, while often read by outsiders as hypermasculine and focused on warfare, "for the most part was shaped by the everyday: gardening, hunting and parenting the children of the community."[12] Lloyd Lee also talks about this among the Diné in Chapter 12, stating "Diné men lived with their wives' families and made all possible efforts to ensure the survival of an extended family network. Most of the daily activities included finding and fetching water, collecting firewood, finding and hunting game, maintaining crops, teaching, and protecting their wives and extended family."[13] As Kimberly Minor demonstrates with her essay on the Mandan (Chapter 5), even where there were hypermasculine roles related to warfare, there was a commitment to kinship inherent in Mandan war practices which was overlooked by outsiders.[14] What these authors are suggesting and what Allison Piché explicitly states in Chapter 11 is that in land-based societies, the notion of hypermasculinity was not as constrained as it is in current hegemonic masculinity environments. It is possible that this allowed Indigenous men the room to adopt or let go of the hypermasculine when the situation demanded it, and that asserting hypermasculine traits was not associated with negative male behaviour.

In referring to "masculinity" as "a Western word," participants from Group #2 also made the important point that language is key; we need to consider not only semantics in the English language but also how masculinity might be framed in Indigenous languages. Gendered concepts do not always translate well. How, then, might we discuss the concept of masculinities from inside Indigenous language thinking? Would this shift the discussion? This point was brought up at the national think tank (Group #8), when one participant commented, "My father spoke a genderless language" in reference to the gender-neutral pronouns in Cree. English-language approaches and thinking about "masculinities" thus continue to challenge us as researchers and participants in dialogue on this subject, and further research is needed to explore "masculinities" from Indigenous-language thinking.

Overall, our observation of this resistance to hegemonic masculinities is not to suggest that these roles were non-existent in the lives of participants. A number of participants identified the presence of patriarchal masculinities in their lives—speaking to men in their families and communities being the ones to "lay down the law, set the rules" (Group #3). Our subsection on "Relations Revisited" later in this chapter points out how male dominance, toxic masculinities, and violence have taken root in many Indigenous families and communities. What is interesting, however, is how many participants spoke about "masculinity" as a behaviour to recover from, as in the words of this participant from one of the fathers' groups: "I look at my community as just being my own family—something that I've found is to eliminate the masculinity out of it, and to use love and harmony and caring" (Group # 5). The themes we uncovered begin to articulate what *Indigenous* masculinities might mean to those working "to eliminate the 'masculinity' out of it."

Responsibilities and Relations

In Relation to Land

Men's relations with the land were central to the discussions on Indigenous masculinities and identities. One participant from British Columbia described the need for interaction with the land: "I see [the importance of] accessing the things that our people used to access all the time—like our foods and our medicines, even our means of travel. All of those things I think are very important because there is this feeling that you get when you're in a canoe.... I can't even tell you—you would only know if you are in a canoe doing an ocean travel and it's just, it's important. So I know that I need access to those things for me" (Group #3).

One of the Kizhaay Anishinaabe Niin workers talked about the craving for "traditional lifestyles" he sees among his Friendship Centre community. In response to this need, the Centre was planning on taking children out on snowshoes and teaching them how to set rabbit snares and traps. This worker remarked, "Some of the boys have never been on snowshoes!" and summed up their land-based program with "that's what I call a traditional value system." Another Kizhaay worker talked about a "cultural diversity" program in his Friendship Centre, stating "the program was very effective in utilizing our traditional men to teach young boys how to hunt, how to track, how to make calls, how to set fire, how to set up camp" (Group #5).

Participants in Groups # 4, #7, and #8 also talked about creating alternatives for boys who don't have access to older male relatives as land-based teachers. One participant from Group #4 reflected on it as a personal responsibility, pondering that it might be possible for him to connect some of the youth with one of his uncles. In terms of reconnecting Indigenous boys with land-based responsibilities, he pointed out "maybe that's a way to start," noting, "the thing is, I have to take care of it with myself." This participant indicated it would also be good to have support from the collective when he added, "Then again…I don't know of any men's groups that go out doing stuff like that." A participant from Group #8 provided an example of how such efforts don't have to be program based. He described how youth in his community had come to him, asking for instructions in hunting. To emphasize the need to learn proper protocols around respectful hunting, he asked these boys, "Do you want to learn how to kill or how to hunt?" He then asked hunters on his reserve to assist by bringing him their harvest so the boys could begin their hunting lessons by cleaning the animals. "We ended up with sixty-two deer!" he laughed.

The connection between hunting and traditional values was emphasized by one of the Group #4 participants, who stated: "Things like hunting and smudge and protocol—they're all together. You don't just go up there with a gun and shoot an animal. You pray before that; you prepare yourself before that, right? You don't find an animal—the animal finds you, if you're lucky enough and your prayers are answered. That's how it is, and you put that tobacco down. You're not only teaching the kids how to hunt; you're teaching them about their culture too." Teaching land-based men's skills was thus seen as an opportunity to build Indigenous youth identities in healthy ways that foster responsibility and relationships.

Hunting and fishing were also associated with responsibilities and identities around "providing" in the focus group discussions. In many cultures, men are cast in the role of "provider," and there were many references to this, notably from the focus group that we did with Sto:lo women (Group #7). These participants spoke of the long hours away from home that men in their community worked, particularly in the past. What is perhaps distinctly Indigenous about our findings is that most of the discourse around "providing" had to do with hunting and fishing, and how these practices reflect men's responsibilities to the collective. This cut across generations, as the comments came from youth as well as from older participants. As one youth from lower British Columbia commented, "Where I am from we're taught to fish at an early age, for our families and Elders" (Group #1). In the fathers group in Nanaimo, participants also talked about harvesting practices in terms of fulfilling responsibility to the extended family: "Families were always very close knit; you never [had] to worry about going to buy the bigger cost items like your meats, seafood. Anything like that—it was all harvested. With my family, I was the fisherman. My eldest brother was the hunter, so you know all the time me and my sons were the fishermen for the family. We provide all the needs for salmon, be it fresh or smoked. We had to do all of that—that was our job; that was passed down from generation [to generation]" (Group #3).

Fathers in the Edmonton focus group talked about the link between harvesting responsibilities and Indigenous masculine identity, noting the esteem that comes with this manner of providing: "I'm more than ready and equipped to take on that responsibility, you know, and I'm proud of that. I'm proud to be able to go knock down a moose and haul it out and provide for my family and drive around the community with my uncles and hand out meat. Makes me feel like a man. Makes me feel like a provider for my community and my people" (Group #4). This participant and others in his group discussed the challenges of trying to maintain traditional harvesting responsibilities with urbanization, but noted that many urban men continue to travel to home territories to hunt and fish. It is important to point out, however, that many Indigenous boys, youth, and men are dispossessed from their home communities and/or territories, and do no have access to the land for these opportunities. Even in cases where opportunities may exist, many Indigenous people have to contend with federal and provincial guidelines, enforcement agencies, continuing industrial expansion, and increased pollution, not to mention competition with sport hunters and fishers.

Some participants spoke of how criminalization affects their abilities to provide through harvesting. One of the Sto:lo women talked about her father's role of providing for the family through fishing, stating, "If he didn't fish, I don't know where we'd be today." She followed this with, "But the government deemed selling fish illegal.... We didn't because that was our provision of feeding us" (Group #7). Participants in the Edmonton focus group noted that criminal records can interfere with the ability to have a gun for hunting.

The participants' relationship to land and the stories they shared have a place within larger political conversations. In their paper "Warrior Societies in Contemporary Indigenous Communities," Alfred and Lowe suggest that "Canadians accept and celebrate indigenous movements for cultural restoration; indigenous spirituality is acknowledged as an aspect of the healing process, etc. Why is it that reconnecting to land and asserting nationhood, which are just as much a part of recovering from colonization, are criminalized by the state and disdained by the Settler population?"[15] The obvious answer is that land and nationhood assertions have political and economic implications. Alfred and Lowe point out how law is used as a critical mechanism in ensuring that the status quo of "disempowerment" remains intact. In terms of Indigenous masculine identities, it is significant to note that there is no room in the current political landscape for Indigenous men to participate in land-based practices in the ways their ancestors did; there is no room within this landscape for men to step into their roles as protectors of their families, lands, and way of life without confronting a colonial force that feels threatened and is sanctioned to use lethal force to ensure the "criminal" complies. These are important considerations as Indigenous communities move ahead with cultural resurgence work within their communities.

In closing this section, we note that while many of the participants spoke to the importance of their relationships with land, discussions focusing on the role and responsibility of men protecting the land were not as prevalent, which is an area that requires more attention. The voices we recorded, however, offer a rich beginning and so we present one final story from a participant in Group #4, as it captures the humour, the centrality of kinship, the significance of relations to the human, natural and spirit worlds, the connection to land, the land-based ceremonies, the passing on of traditional knowledge, and the sense of responsibilities that characterize the lives of many Indigenous men:

> Me and my brother were out hunting one time. We had this old Chevy—you could hear the thing rattling for two kilometres away [*laughing*]. Here we are, trying to hunt. We barely had any headlights, way out in the bush. So—*This guy must be crazy—he's gonna shoot something?* Everybody is probably running away. But we came to this lease road.... We went around this corner and a bull moose was standing there. We didn't even have to walk far.
>
> You've got to offer prayer or something. The animal will give itself up for your survival. First survival, we were taught, is to give back. When you kill that moose we take that bell and the tip of

the nose. So we poked a hole in that nose and [offered] tobacco and we put that in the tree. So it's just like you are given that—the old people say when you do that the moose will replace itself so they will always be around. And there was even a ceremony with that too—it's still out there. They have a blood soup ceremony where you eat soup and you have a pipe and smoke so we can have luck when we go hunting. So that we're not just sporting, we're not just hunting for sport. It's so that we can provide for our family and maybe some other family that doesn't have that means to have wild meat at their feasts—we can offer that. And when you do that, there's something in return. There's prayer involved that everybody benefits from.

There are those things we can share with young people. Yeah, if opportunity ever comes—go out there and reflect on things with these young people, yeah me too, I want to go out there.

In Relation to Family

Given that two of our focus groups were with Indigenous fathers, it is perhaps not surprising that fathering was a key theme in our data analysis. Participants in a number of the groups offered stories about their fathers, as well as stories about their own fathering practices. There was a lot of discussion among the Sto:lo women about how their fathers took care of them when they were children, generally enacting responsibilities around providing and caregiving. They talked mostly in loving ways of what these men provided. As one said, "It's really empowering listening to everyone talking about their husbands, their sons, their brothers, their dads, and I have also been really blessed" (Group #7). At the same time, the women acknowledged that they did not appreciate expectations that they were to serve their brothers and fathers when it came to domestic responsibilities, especially food preparation.

Some of the men told stories of missing fathers and learning from other men as a result. A participant from Group #3 talked about how there were "good and bad" messages he picked up from his uncles, as his father was largely absent due to addictions and incarceration. After noting that his uncles taught him the lessons of "you provide for your family you know you work your ass off, you know you're always there," he made reference to the toxic masculinities that he also learned: "My uncles took a really big part in teaching me what it was like to be a man—but you know—it was like a real man fucks a lot of women, has the whole trap line of women—a real man you know drinks, works, you know—there's a lot of good and bad sort of things all mixed up into it and it's real hard to figure out what it was" (Group #3). This participant's statement that "there's a lot of good and bad sort of things all mixed up into it" suggests that he had begun to challenge some of the "real man" activities he was taught.

Some participants in the Two-Spirited focus group (Group #2) talked about having trouble living up to expectations of hegemonic masculinities from their fathers or stepfathers. One noted, "When I'm with my father, I'm very…I'm a boy…I make it a point to be a little more masculine, so I don't embarrass him." Another said, "My stepfather was trying so hard to get me on the masculine side." Both of these participants mentioned that the women in their families did not impose the same expectations to perform masculinity. As one of them said, in some cases, the women made space for them: "My mother was just glad that I could help around, right? I'd rather do the women's work and then I just went off from there. And then I was given to my grandmother; that's all I know today is women's traditional medicines and stuff." This participant's experience is congruent with scholarship that Two-Spirited peoples were traditionally afforded a place to work with the gender group that was most suitable to them.[16]

Many participants talked about making a shift from the negative behaviours they witnessed in their fathers. A participant in Group #5 talked about "making a stand" in his twenties that involved taking on responsibility as a father, "regardless of how I seen it growing up." One Group #3 participant talked about being "keenly aware" of wanting to be close to his children even before having them. "I wanted to be able to show them affection—where I didn't get that from my father," he said. "I think in my father's time, you know, a man wouldn't cry." Several fathers talked about how it felt good to be nurturing to their children, even though these were not qualities associated with being "masculine" in the environments they grew up in:

> I feel proud that I am close to my son and he still comes to his father for that reassurance and I can sit there and bring him back up, take him, dust him off, give him a hug and tell him I love him. At thirty-four years old I can still do that for him…that's the closeness that I have been able to develop with my children and I'm proud to have that with them. It's not something that I had growing up, only in the last few years that I've seen that happen with me and my father. (Group #3)

> There are roles and ways that I act that I see maybe not as other people see as masculine—like showing love and affection to my

son and my daughter. I think that's pretty masculine—you know I don't care where I am, I don't let other people or a public image control that, I just do it. And I think they are teaching me that too, they are teaching me that, that's okay and that's what time requires, changing the poopy diapers and making the googly faces and stuff like that. (Group #3)

Perhaps because many of the men we spoke to were in fathers' groups, the commitment to working on their parenting and nurturing capacities came through. Nonetheless, their experiences suggest that there is a need for more supports for men who have a desire to be good fathers but are not sure what that entails. For some it could involve simply being given reassurances that there is nothing wrong with being affectionate with their children. However, for others, more in-depth and encompassing kinds of support networks are required.

In a number of groups, there were discussions about incorporating Indigenous culture into fathering practices. One participant talked about his father's experience of being dispossessed of his culture, and subsequently learning how to "be a man" by giving up addictive behaviours and adapting traditional roles around providing. This story offers a rich demonstration of the journey toward defining healthy Indigenous masculinities and then sharing those lessons through parenting:

My father grew up without a father—his mother went to residential schools and she told us that we were Spanish, because she went to Spanish[17] residential school. So part of his growing up was a cultural resurgence. [But] when he was hanging out on the rez, with his cousins, he was dressed as the Lone Ranger, and they said, "Sam, you can't be the Lone Ranger, because you're an Indian!"—and [with] all the politically charged nature of being an Indian, he started to cry. So, through his generation, he started this revitalization through the Friendship Centre movement, through the Seventh Fire prophecies. When he met my mother and started to become that role model of a man for me and my brothers growing up, he had to make decisions to put drugs and alcohol aside, and show us what it is to be a man.

So, very important in our family was going back to a traditional way of life, but through a contemporary model. So the idea of providers, my dad became a [tour-boat] operator. We're from a reserve that's a fishing reserve…so I was driving a twenty-eight-foot wooden boat when I was seven or eight. He was teaching me all these different things; we didn't have the childhood that other kids have, baseball, hockey, all that. My dad showed us how to use flare guns and how to set a hook. He was giving us skills and telling us how to be that provider. (Group #5)

Many of the participants talked about how important it is for boys to have positive role models in their fathers, or in other men in the case of absent fathers. As one of the Sto:lo women said, "It's hard for a single mother and even for a mother who hasn't been raised with a father…[one needs] male role models in your life to raise children—especially boys" (Group #7). The significance of role models and mentors will be discussed further in the next section.

In terms of responsibilities to family in general, "protecting" came up in Groups #1, #3, #5, #7, and #8. Men's responsibilities in terms of caring for and protecting women was raised a number of times among the Sto:lo women in their discussion of traditional ways. As one said, "It's the males' job to always protect and honour the female—and I believe that there's a teaching for that within our own community" (Group #7). Another participant in this group asserted that "patriarchal and paternalistic chaos" from colonization has interfered with men's responsibilities to "protect and care for the female."

Participants in several groups mentioned that men's abilities to protect have been damaged by colonization, and some talked about how resistance and recovery involve responsibilities around protection. With reference to family breakdown, one participant commented, "I feel like a need to protect against that somehow, somehow I need to fight [it]" (Group # 3). As with the discussions around providing, some participants brought up criminalization: "If someone is beating the hell out of your kid or your wife or your sister or your brother and you go when you protect them, right, that's a criminal act and you can get charged for that and thrown in jail, and I know there's a lot of us people who are in jail because of doing that, and that's just right to take care of your family like that. Instead of having some cop and judge who doesn't know the situation at all."

In this case, the participant gives voice to a sense of disempowerment: first by having to withstand the inordinate amount of violence experienced by Indigenous women and other kin, and then not being able to protect them because of the inevitable criminalization of Indigenous men who face the justice system. This disempowerment and disconnection from protecting responsibilities also came through in an embodied representation exercise with the youth group. During this exercise, one participant covered himself while lying on the ground, explaining, "When I think of masculinity, I think of protecting." When asked by the facilitator "What are you protecting right now?" his response was, "Myself—because that's all that I can protect right now" (Group #1).

Overall, comments in the focus groups demonstrated that the Indigenous men we talked to carry a profound sense of responsibility for their families: it is part of their identity. In cases where this has been fractured, participants acknowledged the pain and the need to find ways to reinstate these relationships and responsibilities. Our research also demonstrated that notions of "protecting" and "honouring" need to be explored further, as in some cases these terms can seem like mere platitudes. We frequently heard these terms but with little explanation as to what they mean in actual practice. Where they were specific, the men we interviewed associated protection with violence. It is possible that there are other ways men protect their families, but that our participants only mentioned protection against violence because it is considered masculine and therefore within the realm of their perceived masculine role that was under discussion.

In Relation to Community

In the section on land, we highlighted how some men take responsibility for community by sharing the meat and fish they harvest. Much of the remaining discussion around responsibility to community had to do with role modelling and mentoring.

In some cases, participants talked about how they had to look for mentors. One Sto:lo mother asked, "Who is the healthy man that can help me do the puberty rights teachings for my boys? Nobody in the family right now. I have to look outside my family to find other mentors. I would like to have teachings to give them, you see" (Group #7). Another Sto:lo woman pointed to the strength of including a broader sector of the community to raise children when she stated, "Each and every person has a different gift to offer… those are the people that you want to look at—to have them to teach your children in different gifts" (Group #7). A participant from Group #5 pointed out that in the past "everybody had traditional roles and kids [would] grow up seeing all these positive people in the community; they [would] want to be just like them." Similarly, another participant from Group #5 noted that children would witness these roles and envision their own: "Younger children growing up would say 'I wanna be a medicine man,' 'I wanna be the hunter,' 'I wanna be the fire carrier,' 'I wanna be the drummer.'"

One of the fathers talked about taking responsibility for finding other culture-based role models for his son, stating, "I know very little culturally. I know very little traditionally. As a father I have a responsibility to put those teachings in their path or put them in the path of teachers so they can get back what was taken" (Group #3). In the following quote, another father expresses how he tried to extend what he has learned to the greater community:

> When you talk about our community in [urban location], we're lacking positive role models for a lot of our youth to look up to. They find that who they are, who the role models are…[that they're] involved in gangs or [are] absentee fathers or [are using] alcohol and drugs. So on a personal level, within my own family, that's what I try to provide, and I do it for the betterment of my family, but I'm hoping that it's going out, that the glass is gotten overflowing with the way I'm living. So [if] other individuals in the community would like to come in and talk to me or look at me as a role model, that's very rewarding for me. (Group #5)

This participant went on to talk about how he tries to encourage other men through the Kizhaay program to be positive role models, to "take the first steps at living a violent-free life" (Group #5).

One participant talked about how his own path to finding traditional knowledge helped him understand how to be a "better man." Clan responsibilities were a big part of this knowledge and identity formation:

> When I became fourteen years of age I started to look for the cultural component that [my father] didn't have access to. So I started to learn from relationships—tobacco relationships rather than blood relationships. So finding traditional teachers and Elders and adopting them traditionally as uncles in order to learn…. For me, it was learning what Bear Clan meant—to have the morals of the clan and clan identity, to understand who I was. That's what being a man meant—being a good member of my clan as Bear Clan and holding up the values of that clan. Growing up, I learned how to provide, and what my responsibilities were as a man from my dad, but I needed to go out to the collective community to understand what those [cultural] things meant. (Group #5)

Another mentioned how working with Elders had encouraged him to take up healthier ways: "I learned totally different from what I've learned growing up. And I surround myself with good Elders now. So I've learned about being a man, and I'm starting to live by those Grandfather Teachings,[18] and it's just hard—the hardest thing—a lot harder than using anger and your fists" (Group #5).

One participant talked about the responsibility he now carries to pass on the culture-based knowledge that he had acquired, stating, "I was always told that one of these days you're going to be asked to pass this stuff [on]—you can't be sitting there listening all the time—you know, getting to that age when you're going to need to say something about these things" (Group #4).

In some of the groups there was discussion among the men about how to better relate to women in their communities. As one participant in Group #5 put it, "In teaching us to be better men, we need to honour our women." Some participants talked about relations with women that contrasted the male dominance of hegemonic masculinities:

> When it comes to assigning responsibilities, I will pass for my partner. And it comes from our teachings—from a female perspective, they establish the need—talking about clan mothers, who sat at the head, at the front of the clan system—they would establish what was needed in the community and the men were responsible for providing it. (Group #5)

> In the longhouse, the women have to sit back quietly and the men do all the speaking and everything. The women have to sit and be quiet but that's not it—because the women have the backbone—they tell their men what to do. (Group #7)

Finally, the need to repair these relations was raised by one participant who stated:

> I think the biggest thing I'm learning as a man and where I think things should go in the future for me is how we have mistreated our women in our culture. I grew up believing I'm supposed to dominate. My father was dominated by society and he was a powerless person so in turn he dominated who he could, which was the woman. [But] in the society that we come from it's actually the woman who holds the power, not the man. She represents the heartbeat of the earth. I think that's where we're wrong. (Group #5)

Relations Revisited

As mentioned in the introductory section, many of the participants expressed regret at the adoption of dysfunctional behaviours associated with hegemonic masculinities. The combination of violence and substance abuse was raised by a number of participants, with comments like, "It was okay to drink and fight, do whatever he wanted as a way of blowing off steam. So that's how I grew up. I adopted those things that my father adopted, so I used my fists" (Group #5). One participant in the youth group explained a drawing he did as part of the focus group exercise: "I [drew] a big, black eye and a bloody nose because I feel like a lot of times guys where we're from, I feel like that's how they're tough and strong. That's how they will try to prove it is to mess with them. It's also blank because I feel like a lot of guys try to hide what is really under there" (Group #1). Participants talked about substance abuse and violence as part of a trajectory of trauma and confusion, which sometimes they turned on themselves: "My dad drank and fell off the wagon, logged, fire fought, and whatever. He did drink and I believe, instead of taking his anger out on my mom or anything, he always took it out on himself and that's how he did it probably, through drinking, right?" (Group #7).

As pointed out in Robert Henry's chapter in this book (Chapter 10), Indigenous men can get trapped in expectations that they behave according to negative stereotypes. This was explained by one participant in Group #5: "I grew up in an urban area. Society basically told me, reminded me daily on the way to school who I was. So when I was growing up I kind of wouldn't let them down. I grew up and started using drugs and alcohol and playing right into their—what they expected of me" (Group #5).

What comes out of the interviews is a picture that shows how the vicious cycle of toxic Indigenous masculinity is externally imposed on Indigenous men and then internalized and passed on to other men, while at the same time being reinforced by society. Taiaiake Alfred argues that the colonization is a psychologically damaging process for Indigenous men, which often leads to acts of violence: "One factor is the psychological damage done to indigenous men, which often leads to social dysfunction, if not outright violence."[19] These manifestations of violence within the context of colonization are not unique to the men of Turtle Island (North America), as Ty Tengan's findings also speak to how violence in Hawaiian communities and homes has become "normal."[20]

Given the reality that colonization is an inherently violent ideology and practice, it is not surprising to see manifestations of violence erupt between people and between people and the land. However, once Indigenous men become aware that their behaviour is linked to colonization, even if they do not make the explicit link, they can then make the conscious decision to change. Many participants stressed that for them the key in recovering from toxic masculine behaviours was to revitalize Indigenous cultures, ceremonies, and lifeways. This has already been made apparent in the sections where we see men calling for rebuilding relations with the land and human relations. There were some participants who were closely connected to their cultural ways, and expressed how fortunate they knew they were. As one participant said: "I'm really proud of where I come from. I'm very fortunate to have what I have—it's not anything that's come out of the museum or anything like that—it's a way of life—it's how we conduct ourselves—that's the way we've grown up " (Group #3). Another participant in this group talked about accessing Indigenous culture:

> It took me a long time to realize that [our culture] is not gone, that just I was gone, my family was gone from it. You know, that whole idea that the culture is lost—not realizing that the culture is not lost—it's me, you know, it's my family that was lost from it; that it's always there.... Since I've come to that understanding that it doesn't matter how long it takes, it doesn't matter if it's my lifetime event that my children are going to have a better chance—not even my children—that the people that I see that were walking the same way that I was.... (Group #3)

This participant echoes the view of many Indigenous people who come to a realization that their culture has survived the onslaught of colonization, and by extension so have they. There is a recognition that, although their culture, like their families, is tattered from the colonial experience, they can still draw strength from it as a source to assist with recovery from historical trauma.

In some cases, revitalizing culture involved integrating values into daily practice, as with those who spoke about living according to the Seven Grandfather Teachings. Others gave the example of going in to schools to teach traditional drumming and singing to boys. Ceremonies are another way to provide identity formation, and there was particular mention of rites of passage. Men in the Vancouver Island focus group talked about the rigours of initiation into their Coast Salish longhouse:

> It's a real trial to go through [initiation]. Ours is the Spirit Dance. We achieve in four days what so many other First Nations have tried to achieve in the sweat lodge, if you are more familiar with that. The lack of food and water for the week of your initiation process is taking place—it's bringing on a delirium from the

absence of sustenance during the week alone. And during that time you get visions and that's when you really have a spiritual connection, and it's brought on by absence of water and food, you know if it's done properly you can really have an experience. (Group #3)

Sto:lo women noted that their rites of passage ceremonies offered a holistic development that is often missing:

If they build their big body, they are going to be strong, but they don't realize that that stage, they're moving into manhood, they also need to make their spirit strong and their mind strong. (Group #7)

My boys right away turn to protein shakes and muscles because that is what makes them a man, you see. Whereas, in our teachings and our puberty rites, teaches them to run, yes, run, breathe and when you are running, you're praying, you're thinking good thoughts, right. And you are also making your spirit strong by doing—all the teachings that go with that. (Group #7)

Sometimes these ceremonies didn't have to be big formal things, as explained by this participant: "When I put that first goose grease on my grandson's forehead a few months ago, that was an indication of a rite of passage, [of] that responsibility, that he's going to be a good hunter when he grows up" (Group #5). Other ceremonies that were raised included fasting, sun dances, vision quests, and being a fire keeper at or participating in sweat lodges.

Culturally appropriate rituals that acknowledge a boy's transition to manhood and celebrates a new stage in young males' lives, could be one ingredient that can act as a counter to the gang initiation ritual and set an entirely different trajectory for young males. The link between cultural persistence and revitalization as one remedy to colonization and to the toxic Indigenous masculinities was a very strong recurring theme throughout the interviews.

Overall, there was a general feeling that creating men's spaces was a good place to begin rebuilding relationships and responsibilities. A participant in Group #5 talked about the spin-off possibilities from creating spaces for men, as he has seen in his Kizhaay program:

You guys talked about softball teams and creating space and creating time for other men for engaging in healthy activities. So, for example, [in] my area [there are] three small towns; they're creating support groups outside of the Kizhaay groups now. So

instead of seeing the group once a week, some of the guys go
to three groups a week in three different cities; as well they are
hanging out on the weekends and doing things that are new.
Like they are going to ceremonies, they are going to powwows;
they are doing these things they never would have done. (Group
#5)

Participants appreciated the opportunity to dialogue, with a number remark-
ing that the focus group itself had been a positive experience. This can be a
beginning of building a community of men who are being and becoming
healthy by supporting other men. As one participant stated, "We need to
have those groups available, whether it be sharing circle or sweat lodge—
whatever that may be, that they know that they have a place to go" (Group
#5). In sounding out the Indigenous male ecology, our work with the focus
groups seemed like a good beginning: "I really think what you are doing is a
big plus. You need to have it heard or said—somewhere there's a small voice
way in the back that needs to be brought forward. You know what we've lost,
[what] we have to struggle back from to get where we were" (Group #3).

Conclusion

This chapter highlights some of the key discussion points we had in the
focus groups we conducted across Canada on Indigenous masculinities; it
also reflects many of the discussions presented in other chapters of this book.
Our chapter began with an acknowledgment that many of our focus group
participants had difficulty associating with concepts of "masculinity." Some
linked it to "white" culture; a notion that might otherwise be labelled as colonial masculinity, as described by Scott L. Morgensen in Chapter 2, which,
along with Leah Sneider's work in Chapter 3, provides important historical
context. In Chapter 1, Bob Antone provides a framework for core elements
in Haudenosaunee knowledge, making the distinction between Indigenous
and colonial worlds that exemplify very different versions of masculinities;
worlds that some of the focus group participants began to articulate. With
relation to women, Antone and others point to the "matrifocal" elements
within Indigenous cultures that continue to guard against wholehearted
adoption of patriarchal masculinities, or, as one participant said, the need
"to eliminate the masculinity out of it."

Identity formation was an underlying theme in many of the focus group
conversations, which ties into other works in this book on representation.
In particular, the chapters in section two demonstrate how Indigenous
artists have attempted to redefine themselves through non-hegemonic

masculinities, while acknowledging the struggles that continue to plague them. Niigaanwewidam James Sinclair's piece in Chapter 8 mirrors many of the issues raised by focus group participants: paying homage to a first grandmother, articulating struggles around fathering, violence and criminalization as experienced by Indigenous men, and expressing the need to go home to Indigenous cultures.

Several of the chapters in this book demonstrate how Indigenous men enact responsibilities through engagement with land, family, community, and culture, as we also discovered with our focus group participants. In Chapter 14, Sam McKegney quotes Cree/Métis poet and author Gregory Scofield, who responds to questions of manhood by stating, "I've been protecting ever since I was a child. I've spent my life protecting my mom, and I've spent my life protecting my aunts. I spent my life protecting whoever needed to be protected."[21] Responsibility comes up in Ty Tengan's discussion with Thomas Ka'auwai Kaulukukui, Jr. about men's roles as represented by the male deity Kū, in Chapter 13. Tengan writes that Kū represents "male generative force and productivity," which Kaulukukui further defines as responsibility to self, family, and nation.[22] Likewise, one of the "Crazy Indians" in Chapter 15 raises the notion that "as Native men, we have to start getting back to providing for all of us as a nation."[23] Responsibility, thus, is key in the discussions found in this book and in the dialogue we have engaged in with Indigenous men.

Collectively, our work in the focus groups and in this book represents an arrival at one point in "the speaking" that Indigenous masculinity studies can offer, perhaps providing what Leah Sneider sees in term of re-articulating a "focus instead on a set of values that have held strong and continue to guide and define Indigenous cultures in the face of ongoing colonization and neo-colonization."[24] But in our explorations of masculinities within Indigenous cultures, Brendan Hokowhitu reminds us to be wary of the "righteousness" that can arise with relation to what is perceived as pure Indigenous tradition, and what this means in terms of Indigenous masculinities.[25] The discussions we had with focus group participants showed how, indeed, Indigenous men live in environments of "both performing colonial heteropatriarchy and resisting it."[26] As Hokowhitu points out, there is merit in "strategic essentialism" and in embracing "an existentialism that effects responsibility."[27]

Moving forward, we see that more and more Indigenous men and those asserting masculine identities are now ready to speak. For at least thirty years, Indigenous women have been willing and able, mostly out of necessity for their own and their children's survival, to speak out and make others listen about the gendered and racialized violence they have experienced. Meanwhile, Indigenous men for the most part have kept silent about their experiences. Instead, their stories were told by others in a way that reinforced the negative perceptions of Indigenous men as victimizers. This book, along with Sam McKegney's *Masculindians: Conversations about Indigenous Manhood*,[28] demonstrates that Indigenous men have arrived and they have much to say about their identities and their struggles.

The ideas and challenges put forward in this book and further afield provide a sense of hope for not only the Indigenous people of today but also for future generations. As academic researchers, we are aware that our peoples have endured a world dominated by scholars who portray a much darker image, with forecasts such as, "The old [Indigenous] social structures are pulverized, the natives are 'atomized'—and colonist society cannot integrate them without destroying itself."[29] It is risky to speak of the unknown with certainty. What we do know, however, is that atoms cannot be destroyed in the truest sense of the word. Rather, there is a conversion of energy that takes place and it is this transformation that we may be witnessing now with our research project and this book. Rethinking our relationships with land, each other, and working together to challenge imperialism using cultural values, beliefs, and practices is hard work in this nascent field of Indigenous men and masculinities. But it is time to gather, and to listen.

The authors gratefully acknowledge the contributions of the "Bidwewidam Indigenous Masculinities Project" team: Wil Campbell, Sylvia Maracle, Magda Smolewski, Katherine Minich, Jessica Hill, Michael White, Jessica Danforth, Erin Konsmo, and Sasha Sky.

Notes

1 These words were offered at the Bidwewidam Indigenous Masculinities national think tank, Orillia, Ontario, 6 November 2013.

2 Rene Meshake quoted in Kim Anderson, *Bidwewidam: Indigenous Masculinities, Identites and Mino-Bimaadiziwin*. Toronto, ON: Ontario Federation of Indian Friendship Centres, 2013.

3 The Kizhaay Anishinaabe Niin program is an Ontario Federation of Indian Friendship Centres initiative that encourages and challenges men and boys to actively speak out against all forms of violence against women and to foster healthy relationships. The Kizhaay program currently has almost 100 facilitators who host community-based workshops and other activities aimed at building community engagement to end violence against women.

4   As Sasha Sky's chapter in this book is a transcript of Group #6, we have not included that material in our analysis here. We invite the reader to revisit Chapter 15 and consider how that group's discussions correspond to the findings presented in this paper.

5   Kim Anderson, *A Recognition of Being: Reconstructing Native Womanhood* (Toronto: Sumach/Canadian Scholars' Press, 2000), 229.

6   Michael Kaufman, "Men, Feminism, and Men's Contradictory Experiences of Power," in *Men and Power*, ed. Joseph A. Kuypers (Halifax: Fernwood Books, 1999), 59–83.

7   For a discussion on the importance and function of contemporary kinship to one community, see Robert Alexander Innes, *Elder Brother and the Law of the People: Contemporary Kinship and Cowessess First Nation* (Winnipeg: University of Manitoba Press, 2013).

8   Ty P. Tengan, *Native Men Remade: Gender and Nation in Contemporary Hawaii* (Durham. NC: Duke University Press, 2008), 8.

9   Ibid., 3.

10 Sam McKegney, "Warriors, Healers, Lovers, and Leaders: Colonial Impositions on Indigenous Male Roles and Responsibilities," in *Canadian Perspectives on Men and Masculinities: An Interdisciplinary Reader*, ed. Jason A. Laker (Toronto: Oxford University Press, 2012), 242–3.

11 This concept is also used by Lloyd Lee in Chapter 12 of this volume.

12 See Borell, "Patriotic Games," 169 (in this volume).

13 See Lee, "Diné Masculinities," 218 (in this volume).

14 See Minor, "Material Masculinity," 110 (in this volume).

15 Taiaiake Alfred and Lana Lowe, "Warrior Societies in Contemporary Indigenous Communities: A Background Paper Prepared for the Ipperwash Inquiry" (Toronto: Government of Ontario, 2005).

16 Kenneth Dollarhide, "Native American Spirituality: Understanding Gender as Sacred," *Transgender Tapestry* 115 (2008): 33–6; Brian Joseph Gilley, "Making Traditional Spaces: Cultural Compromise at Two-Spirit Gatherings in Oklahoma," *American Indian Culture and Research Journal* 28, no. 2 (2004): 81–95; Wesley Thomas, Sue-Ellen Jacobs, "'... And We re Still Here': From Berdache to Two-Spirit People," *American Indian Culture and Research Journal* 23, no. 2 (1999): 91–107.

17 The name of this residential school was St. Joseph's Residential School, which was referred to as "Spanish"—as it was located in the town of Spanish, Ontario. The name has nothing to do with the Spanish language or ethnicity.

18 This is a reference to the Seven Grandfather Teachings of the Anishnaabek, which encompass wisdom, love, respect, bravery, honesty, humility, and truth.

19 Alfred and Lowe, "Warrior Societies," 94.

20 Tengan, *Native Men Remade*, 149–50.

21 See McKegney, "Strong Men Stories," 258 (in this volume).

22 See Tengan, "'The Face of Kū,'" 231 (in this volume).

23 See Sky, "A Conversation with Crazy Indians," 269 (in this volume).

24 See Sneider, "Complementary Relationships," 75 (in this volume).

25 See Sneider, "Taxonomies of Indigeneity," 83 (in this volume).

26 Ibid., 84.

27 Ibid., 94, 95.

28 Sam McKegney, *Masculindians: Conversations about Indigenous Manhood* (Winnipeg: University of Manitoba Press, 2014).

29 Sartre in Albert Memmi, *The Colonizer and the Colonized* (Boston: Beacon Press, 1991), xxvii.

Acknowledgements

This book was initiated from partnerships and ideas created within a research project entitled "Indigenous Masculinities, Identities and Achieving Mino-Bimaadiziwin." We are grateful to the Social Sciences and Humanities Research Council (SSHRC) and the Ontario Federation of Indian Friendship Centres (OFIFC) for funding the original project from 2011 to 2014. Individuals who guided that project with us included Wil Campbell, Sylvia Maracle, Magda Smolewski, Katherine Minich, Jessica Hill, Michael White, Lance Logan-Key, Jessica Danforth, John Swift, and Sasha Sky. We are also grateful to the Native American Indigenous Studies Association (NAISA) for creating spaces of dialogue and interaction between Indigenous and allied scholars. The first discussions for this book came together after a series of panels on Indigenous masculinities at the NAISA 2012 conference.

Selected Bibliography

Abram, Susan. "Real Men: Masculinity, Spirituality, and Community in Late Eighteenth Century Cherokee Warfare." In *New Men: Manliness in Early America*. Edited by Thomas Foster. New York: New York University Press, 2011.

Anderson, Kim and Bonita Lawrence, eds. *Strong Women Stories: Native Vision and Community Survival.* Toronto: Sumach/Three O'Clock Press, 2003.

Anderson, Kim, Robert Alexander Innes, and John Swift. "Indigenous Masculinities: Carrying the Bones of Our Ancestors." In *Canadian Men and Masculinities: Historical and Contemporary Perspectives*. Edited by Christopher Greig and Wayne Martino. Toronto: Canadian Scholars' Press, 2012.

Andrew-Gee, Eric. "Aboriginal Men Murdered at Higher Rate than Aboriginal Women: The Death of 15-Year-Old Tina Fontaine Casts Spotlight on Homicide Epidemic Ravaging Indigenous Communities for Decades." *thestar.com*, 22 August 2014. http://www.thestar.com/news/gta/2014/08/22/aboriginal_men_murdered_at_higher_rate_than_aboriginal_women.html.

Bell, Betty. "Gender in Native America." In *A Companion to American Indian History*. Edited by Philip J. Deloria and Neal Salisbury. Malden, MA: Blackwell, 2002.

Berkhofer, Robert F. *The White Man's Indian: Images of the American Indian from Columbus to the Present*. New York: Vintage Books, 1978.

Beydoun, Khaled. "More Than Thugs: The Case of Richard Sherman and Other Men of Colour." *Aljazeera Online*, 29 January 2014. http://www.aljazeera.com/indepth/opinion/2014/01/more-than-thugsthe-case-richar-2014125134532950282.html.

Beynon, John. *Masculinities and Culture*. London: Open University Press, 2002.

Blackwood, Evelyn. "Sexuality and Gender in Certain Native American Tribes: The Case of Cross-gender Females." *Signs: Journal of Women in Culture and Society* 10, no. 1 (1984): 27–42.

Bourdieu, Pierre. *Masculine Domination*. Stanford, CA: Stanford University Press, 2001.

Butler, Judith. *Gender Trouble: Feminism and the Subversion of Identity*. London: Routledge, 1990.

———. "Melancholy Gender: Refused Identification." *Psychoanalytic Dialogues: The International Journal of Relational Perspectives* 5, no. 2 (1995): 165–180.

Canada. "Missing and Murdered Aboriginal Women: A National Operation Overview." Ottawa: Royal Canadian Mounted Police, 2014.

Canada. Office of the Correctional Investigator. *Aboriginal Inmates.* Ottawa: Government of Canada, Corrections Research Branch of the Department of Public Safety, 2008.

Canadian Press. "Alberta RCMP Shoot, Kill Man After Road Stop Altercation." *National Post Online,* 4 August 2013. http://news.nationalpost.com/2013/08/04/alberta-rcmp-shoot-kill-man-after-road-stop-altercation/.

Comack, Elizabeth. *Out There, In Here: Masculinity, Violence and Prisoning.* Winnipeg: Fernwood Publishing, 2008.

Connell, R. W. "Globalization, Imperialism and Masculinities." In *Handbook of Men and Masculinities.* Edited by Michael Kimmel, Jeff Hearn, and Robert W. Connell. Thousand Oaks, CA: SAGE Publications, 2004.

———. *Masculinities.* 2nd ed. Berkley: University of California Press, 2005.

Connell, R.W., and James W. Messerschmidt. "Hegemonic Masculinity: Rethinking the Concept." *Gender and Society* 19, no. 6 (2005): 829–59.

de Beauvoir, Simone. *The Second Sex.* Harmondsworth: Penguin, 1984.

Denetdale, Jennifer Nez. "Chairmen, Presidents, and Princesses: The Navajo Nation, Gender, and the Politics of Tradition." *Wicazo Sa Review* 21, no. 1 (2006): 9–28.

Donaldson, Mike, and Richard Howson. "Men, Migration and Hegemonic Masculinity." In *Migrant Men: Critical Studies of Masculinities and the Migration Experience.* Edited by Mike Donaldson, Richard Howson, Raymond Hibbins, and Bob Pease. New York: Routledge, 2009.

Driskill, Qwo-Li, Chris Finley, Brian Joseph Gilley, and Scott Lauria Morgensen, eds. *Queer Indigenous Studies: Critical Interventions in Theory, Politics, and Literature.* Tucson: University of Arizona Press, 2011.

Edwards, Tim. *Cultures of Masculinity.* New York: Routledge, 2006.

Fanon, Frantz. *Black Skin, White Masks.* New York: Grove Press, 1967.

Flood, Michael, Judith Kegan Gardiner, Bob Pease, and Keith Pringle. *International Encyclopedia of Men and Masculinities.* London: Routledge, 2007.

Grekul, Jana, and Patti LaBoucane-Benson. "Aboriginal Gangs and Their (Dis)placement: Contextualizing Recruitment, Membership, and Status." *Canadian Journal of Criminology and Criminal Justice* 50, no. 1 (2008): 59–82.

Gross, Lawrence. "Bimaadiziwin, or the 'Good Life,' as a Unifying Concept of Anishinaabe Religion." *American Indian Culture and Research Journal* 26, no. 1 (2002): 15–16.

Gutierrez, Ramón. *When Jesus Came, the Corn Mothers Went Away: Marriage, Sexuality, and Power in New Mexico, 1500–1846.* Stanford: Stanford University Press, 1991.

Halberstam, Judith. *Female Masculinity.* Durham, NC: Duke University Press, 1998.

Hokowhitu, Brendan. "Tackling Māori Masculinity: A Colonial Genealogy of Savagery and Sport." *The Contemporary Pacific* 16, no. 2 (2004): 259–283.

———. "Authenicating Māori Physicality: Translations of 'Games' and 'Pastimes' by early Travellers and Missionaries to New Zealand." *International Journal of the History of Sport* 25, (2008): 1355–1373.

———. "The Death of Koro Paka: 'Traditional' Māori Patriarchy." *Special Issues, Pacific Masculinities, The Contemporary Pacific* 20, no. 1 (2009): 115–141.

———. "Māori Rugby and Subversion: Creativity, Domestiction, Oppression and Decolonization," *International Journal of the History of Sport,* 26, no. 16 (2009): 2314–2344.

———. "Producing Elite Indigenous Masculinities." *Settler Colonial Studies* 2, no. 2 (2012): 23–48.

hooks, bell. *The Will to Change: Men, Masculinity, and Love.* New York: Atria Books, 2004.

Johnson, Allan. *The Gender Knot: Unravelling Our Patriarchal Legacy.* Philadelphia: Temple University Press, 1997.

Kivel, Paul. *Men's Work: How to Stop the Violence that Tears Our Lives Apart.* Center City, MN: Hazelden, 1998.

Lang, Sabine. *Men As Women, Women As Men: Changing Gender in Native American Cultures.* Austin: University of Texas Press, 1998.

LaRocque, Emma. "Métis and Feminist: Ethical Reflections on Feminism, Human Rights and Decolonization." In *Making Space for Indigenous Feminism.* Edited by Joyce Green. New York: Zed Books, 2007.

Lee, Lloyd. *Diné Masculinities: Conceptualizations and Realizations.* Createspace Publishing, 2013.

Maldonado-Torres, Nelson. "On the Coloniality of Being." *Cultural Studies* 21, no. 2 (2007): 240–270.

McGregor, Gaile. *The Noble Savage in the New World Garden: Notes toward a Syntactic of Place.* Toronto: University of Toronto Press, 1988.

McKegney, Sam. Interview with Taiaiake Alfred, "Indigenous Masculinity and Warriorism." 11 February 2011. http://taiaiake.posterous.com/81790039.

———. "Warriors, Healers, Lovers and Leaders: Colonial Impositions of Indigenous Male Roles and Responsibilities." In *Canadian Perspectives on Men and Masculinities: An Interdisciplinary Reader.* Edited by Jason A Laker. Toronto: Oxford University Press, 2011.

———. *Masculindians: Conversations about Indigenous Manhood.* Winnipeg: University of Manitoba Press, 2014.

Medicine, Beatrice. "'Warrior Women': Sex Role Alternatives for Plains Indian Women." In *Learning to Be an Anthropologist and Remaining "Native": Selected Writings.* Edited by Beatrice Medicine and Sue-Ellen Jacobs. Urbana: University of Illinois Press, 2001.

Messerschmidt, James. *Flesh and Blood: Adolescent Gender Diversity and Violence.* Mayland: Rowman and Littlefield, 2004.

———. "Engendering Gendered Knowledge: Assessing the Academic Appropriation of Hegemonic Masculinity." *Men and Masculinities* 15, no. 1 (2012): 56–76.

Morgensen, Scott Lauria. *Spaces Between Us: Queer Settler Colonialism and Indigenous Decolonization.* Minneapolis: University of Minnesota Press, 2011.

Mussell, W.J. "Warrior-Caregivers: Understanding the Challenges and Healing of First Nations Men." Ottawa: Aboriginal Healing Foundation, 2005.

Native Women's Association of Canada. *Voices of Our Sisters in Spirit: A Report to Families and Communities.* Ohsweken, ON; Saint-Lazare, PQ: Gibson Library Connections, 2008.

Native Women's Association of Canada. *Voices of Our Sisters in Spirit: A Report to Families and Communities,* 2nd ed. Ottawa: NWAC, March 2009. http://www.nwac.ca/sites/default/files/download/admin/NWAC_Voices of Our Sisters In SpiritII_March2009FINAL.pdf.

Pearce, Maryanne. "An Awkward Silence: Missing and Murdered Vulnerable Women and the Canadian Justice System." LLD diss., University of Ottawa, 2013.

Razack, Sherene H. *Race, Space and the Law: Unmapping a White Settler Society*. Toronto: Between the Lines Press, 2002.

———. "'It Happened More Than Once': Freezing Deaths in Saskatchewan." *Canadian Journal of Women and the Law* 26, no. 1 (2014): 51–80.

Rifkin, Mark. *When Did Indians Become Straight? Kinship, the History of Sexuality, and Native Sovereignty*. New York: Oxford University Press, 2010.

Smith, Andrea. *Conquest: Sexual Violence and American Indian Genocide*. Cambridge, MA: South End Press, 2005.

Str8 Up and Gangs: The Untold Stories. Saskatoon: Hear My Heart Books Inc., 2012.

Suzack, Cheryl, Shari M. Huhndorf, Jeanne Perreault, and Jean Barman, eds. *Indigenous Women and Feminism: Politics, Activism, Culture*. Vancouver: UBC Press, 2011.

Tengan, Ty P. Kāwika. *Native Men Remade: Gender and Nation in Contemporary Hawai'i*. Durham, NC: Duke University Press, 2008.

Thomas, Wesley. "Navajo Cultural Constructions of Gender and Sexuality." In *Two-Spirit People: Native American Gender Identity, Sexuality, and Spirituality*. Edited by Sue Ellen Jacobs, Wesley Thomas, and Sabine Lang. Chicago: University of Illinois Press, 1997.

Thomas, Wesley, and Sue-Ellen Jacobs. "'...And We Are Still Here': From *Berdache* to Two-Spirit People." *American Indian Culture and Research Journal* 23, no. 2 (1999): 91–107.

Troian, Martha. "An Independent Database Has Found Canada Lost Over 600 Missing and Murdered Aboriginal Men." *Vice News Online*, 20 May 2014. http://www.vice.com/en_ca/read/an-independent-database-has-concluded-canada-has-lost-over-600-missing-or-murdered-aboriginal-men.

Trudelle, Maureen Schwarz. *Fighting Colonialism with Hegemonic Culture: Native American Appropriation of Indian Stereotypes*. Albany: State University of New York Press, 2013.

Contributors

Kim Anderson (Cree/Métis) is an associate professor, teaching Indigenous studies at Wilfrid Laurier University, Brantford. She was the principal investigator on the SSHRC-funded Bidwewidam Indigenous Masculinities research project that led to this book. She is the author of *A Recognition of Being: Reconstructing Native Womanhood* (Canadian Scholars' Press, revised edition, 2015) and *Life Stages and Native Women: Memory, Teachings and Story Medicine* (University of Manitoba Press, 2011).

Robert Antone, PhD, Tayohahok member of the Turtle Clan, a citizen of the Oneida Nation of the Thames, Haudenosaunee, holds position on Onʌyota'aka Lotiyaneshu (Oneida Longhouse) Traditional Chiefs Council, and as executive director of Indigenous Healing Lodge – Kiikeewanniikaan, Muncey, Ontario. He is an associate professor in the First Nations Studies Program at Western University and an advocate of decolonization.

Phil Borell is of Ngāti Ranginui and Ngāti Tūwharetoa descent. His hapū (sub-tribe) is Pirirākau. Phil is currently lecturing in Aotahi: School of Māori and Indigenous Studies at the University of Canterbury, Christchurch, New Zealand. His research is centred predominantly around sport and Indigenous peoples, and his current works have given specific focus to Māori involvement in rugby leagues.

Warren Cariou (Métis) is a writer and professor of English at the University of Manitoba in Winnipeg. Warren was born and raised in Meadow Lake, Saskatchewan, which features prominently in his memoir *Lake of the Prairies: A Story of Belonging* (Anchor Canada, 2003). He is also author of *The Exalted Company of Roadside Martyrs: Two Novellas* (Coteau Books, 1999) and writer/director of the film *Land of Oil and Water* (2009). He has written numerous articles on the study of Indigenous literatures and holds a Canada Research Chair in Narrative, Community, and Indigenous Cultures.

Jessica Danforth is the founder and executive director of the Native Youth Sexual Health Network, a grassroots organization run for and by Indigenous youth that is dedicated to bodily, reproductive, gender, and sexual justice in the face of ongoing colonialism on Turtle Island. Danforth has spent more than half her life mobilizing individuals, families, and communities to reclaim their ancestral rights to self-determine decisions over their bodies and spaces. She has authored numerous articles, blogs, and monologues on activism and sexual health, and she is the editor of two books: *Sex Ed and Youth: Colonization, Sexuality and Communities of Colour* (Canadian Centre for Policy Alternatives, 2009) and *Feminism For Real: Deconstructing the Academic Industrial Complex of Feminism* (Canadian Centre for Policy Alternatives, 2011).

Daniel Heath Justice is a Colorado-born Canadian citizen of the Cherokee Nation. He holds the Canada Research Chair in Indigenous Literature and Expressive Culture at the University of British Columbia, on the unceded traditional territories of the Musqueam people. He is most recently co-editor with James H. Cox of the *Oxford Handbook of Indigenous American Literature*.

Robert Henry is a Métis from Prince Albert, Saskatchewan. Robert is currently in the Department of Native Studies at the University of Saskatchewan, where he has focused his PhD research on the usage of photovoice methods to understand relationships between Indigenous male youth and street gangs.

Brendan Hokowhitu, PhD, is both dean and professor in the Faculty of Native Studies at the University of Alberta.

Robert Alexander Innes is an assistant professor in the Department of Native Studies at the University of Saskatchewan and the author of *Elder Brother and the Law of the People: Contemporary Kinship and Cowessess First Nation* (University of Manitoba Press, 2013).

Lloyd L. Lee is an associate professor in the Native American Studies department at the University of New Mexico. He is a citizen of the Navajo Nation. He is Kiyaa'ánii (Towering House), born for Tł'ááshchí'í (Red Bottom). His maternal grandfather's clan is 'Áshįįhi (Salt) and his paternal grandfather's clan is Tábąąhá (Water's Edge). His research interests include Indigenous/Navajo identity, Indigenous/Navajo masculinities, Navajo transformative research, Indigenous/Navajo leadership development, Indigenous/Navajo philosophies, and Indigenous/Navajo community building. He is the director of the Institute for American Indian Research (IFAIR) at the University of New Mexico. He has published two books, *Diné Masculinities: Conceptualizations and Reflections* (North Charlestons, SC: Createspace Independent Publishing Platform, 2013) and *Diné Perspectives: Reclaiming and Revitalizing Navajo Thought* (Tucson, AZ: The University of Arizona Press, 2014).

Sam McKegney is a settler scholar of Indigenous literatures. He grew up in Anishinaabe territory on the Saugeen Peninsula along the shores of Lake Huron, and currently resides with his partner and their two daughters in traditional lands of the Haudenosaunee and Anishinaabe peoples, where he is an associate professor at Queen's University. He has published a collection of interviews entitled *Masculindians: Conversations about Indigenous Manhood* (University of Manitoba Press, 2014), a monograph called *Magic Weapons: Aboriginal Writers Remaking Community after Residential School* (University of Manitoba Press, 2007), and articles on such topics as environmental kinship, masculinity theory, prison writing, Indigenous governance, and Canadian hockey mythologies.

Kimberly Minor is a PhD candidate in Art History at the University of Oklahoma. She specializes in nineteenth-century Native American art and art of the American West. She received her MA from the University of Nebraska and BA from Wesleyan College.

Scott L. Morgensen is associate professor in the Department of Gender Studies at Queen's University. He is the author of *Spaces between Us: Queer Settler Colonialism and Indigenous Decolonization* (University of Minnesota Press, 2011). He is co-editor of *Queer Indigenous Studies: Critical Interventions in Theory, Politics, and Literature* (University of Arizona Press, 2011) and of "Karangatia: Calling Out Gender and Sexuality in Settler Societies," a special issue of the journal *Settler Colonial Studies* (2012).

Allison Piché is a sessional lecturer and recently completed her master's degree with the Department of Native Studies at the University of Saskatchewan. Her research examines the impact of culturally relevant arts and education programming in prison, focusing on Aboriginal overrepresentation in Canadian corrections. She co-facilitates the Inspired Minds: All Nations Creative Writing Program at the Saskatoon Correctional Centre and has taught creative writing to various groups of inmates through this initiative.

Gregory Scofield (Cree/Métis) is a poet, teacher, social worker, and youth worker whose maternal ancestry can be traced back five generations to the Red River Settlement and to Kinesota, Manitoba. He has published an autobiography, *Thunder Through My Veins: Memories of a Métis Childhood* (Harper Flamingo Press, 1999) and several books of poetry, including *Native Canadiana: Songs from the Urban Rez* (Polestar, 1996), *Love Medicine and One Song / Sâkihtowinmaskihkiy êkwa pêyaknikamowin* (Kegedonce Press, 2008), *Singing Home the Bones* (Polestar, 2005), and *Louis: The Heretic Poems* (Nightwood Editions, 2011).

Niigaanwewidam James Sinclair is Anishinaabe, originally from St. Peter's (Little Peguis) Indian Settlement near Selkirk, Manitoba. He is an international commentator on Indigenous issues for outlets like Al Jazeera, *The Guardian*, and national broadcasters like CTV, CBC, and *The Globe and Mail*, and co-editor of several books, including the award-winning *Manitowapow: Aboriginal Writings from the Land of Water* (Highwater Press, 2011), *Centering Anishinaabeg Studies: Understanding the World Through Stories* (Michigan State University Press, 2013), and *The Winter We Danced: Voices of the Past, the Future, and the Idle No More Movement* (Arbeiter Ring Press, 2014). Currently at the University of Manitoba, he teaches courses in Indigenous literatures, cultures, histories, and politics.

Sasha Sky is an Anishinaabe member from the community of Eagle Lake First Nation in northwestern Ontario. Trained as a couple and family therapist, it is her goal to create a space for Indigenous peoples to heal from the effects of colonization.

Leah Sneider is an assistant professor of English at Montgomery College, Maryland.

Erin Sutherland is a Métis PhD candidate and independent curator in the Department of Cultural Studies at Queen's University. Her research focuses on Indigenous performance art and curatorial methodologies. She co-curated the 2014 exhibition "Memory Keepers: Methodologies of Memory, Mapping and Gender" at Urban Shaman Aboriginal Contemporary Art Gallery in Winnipeg.

John Swift is Saulteaux and a member of Keeseekoose First Nation. He completed an MA in the Indigenous Governance Program at the University of Victoria and teaches in the First Nations Studies Department at Vancouver Island University.

Lisa Tatonetti is an associate professor of English at Kansas State University. She is the author of *The Queerness of Native American Literature* (University of Minnesota, 2014) and the co-editor of *Sovereign Erotics: A Collection of Two-Spirit Literature* (University of Arizona, 2011).

Ty P. Kāwika Tengan is an associate professor of Ethnic Studies and Anthropology at the University of Hawai'i at Mānoa. He is the author of *Native Men Remade: Gender and Nation in Contemporary Hawai'i* (Duke University Press, 2008) and is working on a manuscript on Native Hawaiian veterans.

Richard Van Camp was raised in Fort Smith, Northwest Territories, and is the first published author from the Tlicho Dene. He is a graduate of the En'owkin International School of Writing, the University of Victoria's BFA program, and UBC's MFA program in Creative Writing. He is the author of a novel, *The Lesser Blessed* (Douglas and McIntyre, 1996), which is now a movie with First Generation Films. He is the author of multiple short story collections including *Angel Wing Splash Pattern* (Kegedonce Press, 2002), *The Moon of Letting Go*, and *Godless but Loyal to Heaven* (Enfield and Wizenty, 2009 and 2012). He has written books for children, including *A Man Called Raven* and *What's the Most Beautiful Thing You Know about Horses?* (Children's Book Press, 1997 and 1998), illustrated by Cree artist George Littlechild, and books for newborns, including *Welcome Song for Baby* (Orca Book Publishers, 2007), *Nighty Night* (McKellar and Martin, 2011), and *Little You* (2013). And for the Healthy Aboriginal Network, he has authored two comics: *Path of the Warrior* (on gang prevention) and *Kiss Me Deadly* (on sexual health).

CPSIA information can be obtained
at www.ICGtesting.com
Printed in the USA
LVHW100854101222
734610LV00045B/850

9 780887 552274